Microsoft BizTalk 2010: Line of Business Systems Integration

A practical guide to integrating Line of Business systems with BizTalk Server 2010

Kent Weare

Richard Seroter

Sergei Moukhnitski

Thiago Almeida

Carl Darski

BIRMINGHAM - MUMBAI

Microsoft BizTalk 2010: Line of Business Systems Integration

First published: July 2011

Production Reference: 1080711

Published by Packt Publishing Ltd.
32 Lincoln Road
Olton
Birmingham, B27 6PA, UK.

ISBN 978-1-849681-90-2

www.packtpub.com

Cover Image by Mark Holland (MJH767@bham.ac.uk)

Credits

Authors
Kent Weare

Richard Seroter

Sergei Moukhnitski

Thiago Almeida

Carl Darski

Reviewers
Mick Badran

Stephen W. Thomas

Ben Cline

Acquisition Editor
Kerry George

Development Editor
Alina Lewis

Technical Editor
Ajay Shanker

Project Coordinator
Zainab Bagasrawala

Proofreader
Aaron Nash

Indexer
Monica Ajmera

Graphics
Geetanjali Sawant

Production Coordinator
Alwin Roy

Cover Work
Alwin Roy

Foreword

We know that it is rare in IT departments today that solutions do not have to integrate with other systems and even external entities. Systems just have to be connected to support the complex business processes and levels of automation that the business is demanding. Some of these systems are really at the core of the business. They can support operational functions like finance, human resources, and customer relationships. They can also be mission critical; if they stop for any length of time, the business would be significantly impacted.

We know that connecting systems is complicated and there are many choices, technologies, and products that play a role. Developers often build their own integration solutions and supporting infrastructure. The "last mile" of the integration problem is one of the hardest—how do you actually exchange data and messages between two systems—how do you hook them together?

The promise the industry at large has been looking at is the world of web services and service oriented architecture (SOA). We will never totally get to this world—there are too many systems, standards, and custom solutions that don't have "services" to call. But what if there was a solution and even a development framework that could on one end connect to these systems and on the other, expose the capabilities as "services". Let's call these "adapters". What if you could then hook these adapters into your integration platform and even into your own custom code? What if you could easily write your own "adapter"?

This book is all about how to take advantage of Microsoft's integration platform—BizTalk Server and how to use the various "adapters" that come with BizTalk Server to integrate with your line of business systems.

The Cloud is fast becoming an important part of this picture as well, to integrate with systems that live in the Cloud as well as to create processes and move data through the cloud. The book covers the cloud platforms being created to make this happen and practically how to do this today.

This book is a fantastic resource for the developer wanting to understand the techniques as well as the practical mechanics of connecting systems together.

Tony Meleg

Senior Technical Product Manager
Microsoft Corporation

About the Authors

Kent Weare, born in Regina, Saskatchewan, Canada, developed a love for Ice Hockey, Football and Technology. He attended the University of Regina where he obtained a Degree in Computer Science. After completing his undergrad degree, he spent time in India completing a Post Graduate diploma in Object Oriented Technology. He currently lives in Calgary, Alberta, Canada but remains a die-hard Saskatchewan Roughrider football fan.

Kent began his career at a small Internet startup before taking on a Junior roll with the Saskatchewan Government. Since then he has worked on projects for the Canadian Federal Government, a multi-national bank in the United States, Health Care projects in Eastern and Western Canada and has spent the last five years employed by a large Electricity Distribution company in Calgary. Kent's current responsibilities involve managing a Microsoft Solutions team that supports BizTalk, Exchange, Office Communication Server (OCS), and System Center.

During Kent's time at the Federal Government, he had an opportunity to participate in his first BizTalk project. Seven years later he is still "hooked" on BizTalk, having worked with every BizTalk version released since. In 2008, Kent was awarded his first Microsoft MVP award for BizTalk Server. He continues to be active in the BizTalk community and recently received his fourth consecutive MVP award. Kent maintains an active blog at `http://kentweare.blogspot.com` and may be seen presenting BizTalk related material at local and international user groups.

I would first off like to thank my parents (Keith and Joyce) for their unconditional love, support, and direction growing up. They are strong proponents of working hard, treating others with respect, and taught me the difference between right and wrong.

To my twin brother (Kurt), sister (Kim), and their families, thank you for your interest in the book and the encouragement to keep plugging away at it until it was completed.

Throughout my career many people have seen something in me that I haven't necessarily seen in myself. I am convinced that without this support, I would have never been in a position get into the MVP program or write this book. Special thanks to Les Phillips, Dave Patel, Ron Naidu, Vasu Iyengar, Lucie Duval, Neal Nishikawa, Darren Jeffrey, Brian Dempsey, and Alan Skiffington for giving me an opportunity and then giving me the tools to be successful. I would also like to thank my mentors Nipa Chakravarti and Karl Smith for their insight and challenging me to grow as a Leader.

Lastly, this book would not have been a reality without the support of my loving wife Melissa and daughter Brooke. Writing a book is a huge undertaking that consumed late nights, early mornings, and pretty much any spare time in-between. Thank you Melissa for your patience, support, and putting up with me sitting in front of the computer for hours on end while I worked on the book. Brooke, thank you for not hitting the blue (power) button too many times while I was writing. At times you really pushed the limits of Microsoft Word's auto-recovery feature.

Richard Seroter is a solutions architect for an industry-leading biotechnology company, a Microsoft MVP for BizTalk Server, and a Microsoft Connected Technology Advisor. He has spent the majority of his career consulting with customers as they planned and implemented their enterprise software solutions. Richard started his career working for two global IT consulting firms that gave him exposure to a diverse range of industries, technologies, and business challenges. Then, he joined Microsoft as a SOA/BPM technology specialist where his sole objective was to educate and collaborate with customers as they considered, designed, and architected BizTalk solutions. One of those customers liked Richard enough to bring him onboard full time as an architect after they committed to using BizTalk Server as their enterprise service bus. Once the BizTalk environment was successfully established, Richard transitioned into a solutions architect role where he now helps to identify enterprise best practices and apply good architectural principles to a wide set of IT initiatives.

Richard is the author of two books including *Applied Architecture Patterns on the Microsoft Platform* (Packt Publishing, 2010), which discusses where to use which part of Microsoft's platform technologies. He is also the author of *SOA Patterns for BizTalk Server 2009* (Packt Publishing, 2009), which takes a look at how to apply good SOA principles to a wide variety of BizTalk scenarios.

I'd like to thank Kent for bringing me onto this interesting project and allowing me to contribute some chapters. I have a sick passion for enterprise integration and Kent provided me a perfect outlet for more research into the topic.

Thanks to all of my co-workers who have inevitably influenced my thinking and made me a better architect and technologist. My manager, Nancy Lehrer, continues to be an exceptional mentor on my jagged path to superstardom. Finally, thanks to my family and my boys (Noah the human, Watson the dog) as they put up with late nights and absentmindedness.

Sergei Moukhnitski is a software architect with 15 years of experience developing software and systems. His area of professional interests is business process and integration technologies applied to ERP and CRM systems such as Microsoft Dynamics and SAP.

Thiago Almeida is a Senior Integrations Consultant for one of New Zealand's largest IT service providers. He has over eight years of experience working as a solutions architect and senior developer on projects for some of the country's largest companies.

Thiago has been awarded Most Valuable Professional in BizTalk from Microsoft in 2009 and 2010 to acknowledge his exceptional contributions to the BizTalk Server technical community. He runs the Auckland Connected Systems User Group, being a frequent speaker, and maintains a blog on BizTalk Server at `http://connectedthoughts.wordpress.com`

He is also a Microsoft Connected Technology Advisor and a Microsoft Virtual Technical Solution Professional in Integration, providing advanced technical input in BizTalk Server and associated integration technologies on client engagements with Microsoft.

I would like to thank my teammates for working on so many great projects and sharing real world BizTalk Server knowledge with me. I would also like to thank the Microsoft employees, fellow MVPs, and the co-authors for all the input and help. On a more personal note, I would like to thank my beautiful wife Karla for the encouragement and for putting up with the late nights and weekends spent working on this book. New Zealand's great scenery, beautiful beaches, and nice weather during such weekends are purposely not included in this acknowledgement.

Carl Darski is a software consultant who has diverse professional experience in sectors including telecommunications, oil and gas, power and mining. As an electrical engineer, Carl quickly recognized the growing importance of software integration technologies. He has assisted several clients in implementing BizTalk as an integration standard.

I would like to thank all my coworkers at Ideaca who have helped me both technically and professional over the past several years. A special thanks to Shane James whose BizTalk knowledge never ceases to amaze nor disappoint me.

About the Reviewers

Mick Badran has spent many years performing software integration from architect/design all the way through implementation. In the last 10 years, his expertise has been focused within the Microsoft Integration Stack covering products such as BizTalk, SharePoint, WCF, WF, and many related technologies.

Mick has been recognized by Microsoft as a MVP and performs engagements on behalf of Microsoft as a BizTalk Virtual Technology Specialist (V-TSP).

Mick's original passion was teaching Microsft technical classes sharing his knowledge. Over time, Mick still keeps this up while also carrying out Services engagements, working on medium and large projects.

Mick when not being part of the nerd herd enjoys martial arts, tennis, and being a life saver down at his local beach. Snorkling and diving also rate pretty highly on the list!

Stephen W. Thomas is an independent consultant specializing in BizTalk Server and other Microsoft Server technologies including Workflow and AppFabric. He has been working with BizTalk for over ten years. For the past seven years, Stephen has been recognized as a Microsoft Most Valuable Professional (MVP) in BizTalk Server.

Stephen has done consulting work for numerous clients including many in the Fortune 500. Stephen runs the BizTalk community site `http://www.BizTalkGurus.com`. The site offers a community forum, samples, various how-to videos, and Stephen's blog. Stephen has presented at several Microsoft TechEd events, multiple SOA Conferences, and various user groups. Stephen was a co-author of the book *Applied Architectural Patterns on the Microsoft Application Platform* by Packt Publishing.

Ben Cline currently works as a BizTalk architect at Paylocity. He is an active contributor and moderator on the MSDN forums and a member of the BizTalk MVP program. In addition to being a thought leader in the forums he maintains a blog on tips, tricks, and workarounds on BizTalk and other Microsoft technologies. In his spare time he enjoys finding and reporting bugs on pre-release versions of Microsoft products.

Ben actively consults on BizTalk development projects and works on administration and support projects for large international clients. He also frequently works on projects for Microsoft Learning.

I would like to thank my family for helping me squeeze a few more productive hours out of every day.

www.PacktPub.com

Support files, eBooks, discount offers and more

You might want to visit www.PacktPub.com for support files and downloads related to your book.

Did you know that Packt offers eBook versions of every book published, with PDF and ePub files available? You can upgrade to the eBook version at www.PacktPub.com and as a print book customer, you are entitled to a discount on the eBook copy. Get in touch with us at service@packtpub.com for more details.

At www.PacktPub.com, you can also read a collection of free technical articles, sign up for a range of free newsletters and receive exclusive discounts and offers on Packt books and eBooks.

http://PacktLib.PacktPub.com

Do you need instant solutions to your IT questions? PacktLib is Packt's online digital book library. Here, you can access, read and search across Packt's entire library of books.

Why Subscribe?

* Fully searchable across every book published by Packt
* Copy and paste, print and bookmark content
* On demand and accessible via web browser

Free Access for Packt account holders

If you have an account with Packt at www.PacktPub.com, you can use this to access PacktLib today and view nine entirely free books. Simply use your login credentials for immediate access.

Instant Updates on New Packt Books

Get notified! Find out when new books are published by following @PacktEnterprise on Twitter, or the *Packt Enterprise* Facebook page.

Table of Contents

Preface

Microsoft BizTalk is an integration server solution that allows businesses to connect disparate systems. In today's business climate of mergers and acquisitions, more and more enterprises are forced to exchange data across Line of Business systems using integration brokers like BizTalk Server 2010. What is often overlooked when integrating these systems is the pre-requisite knowledge that ERP and CRM systems demand in order to effectively integrate them. No longer is this knowledge locked up in the heads of expensive consultants. Gain an edge within your organization by developing valuable skills in the area of Line of Business integration from this book.

This book will show you how to integrate BizTalk with Line of Business systems using practical scenarios. Each chapter will take a Line of Business system, introduce some pre-requisite knowledge and demonstrate how you can integrate BizTalk with that Line of Business system, and then provide guidance based upon real world experience, taking your BizTalk knowledge further.

This book will enable you to master how to integrate BizTalk with Line of Business systems. The book starts by highlighting the technical foundation of WCF-LOB adapters and the common steps and important properties pertaining to popular WCF-LOB adapters. You will then move on to an overview of how to integrate with Microsoft SQL Server using the WCF based SQL Server adapter. The book then dives into topics such as integrating with Dynamics CRM, building BizTalk/SAP integrated solutions using IDOCs, the differences between IDOCs and RFCs/BAPIs, and WCF Integration through the Windows Azure AppFabric Service Bus amongst others.

What this book covers

Chapter 1, Consuming ASDK-based Adapters: Explore some of the inner workings of the WCF LOB SDK and WCF Custom Adapter.

Chapter 2, WCF-SQL Adapter: Learn how to retrieve and manipulate data using popular operations exposed by the WCF-SQL Adapter including Polling, Notifications, and Composite Operations.

Chapter 3, Integrating BizTalk Server and Microsoft Dynamics CRM: Discover different ways to integrate with Dynamics CRM 2011 and BizTalk Server including calling native Web Services and Proxy solutions. Also learn how to call a BizTalk exposed WCF Service via a CRM registered plug-in.

Chapter 4, WCF-SAP Adapter Sending and Receiving IDOCs: Understand how to install the WCF-SAP adapter's pre-requisite DLLs. Learn about extended, custom and out of the box IDOCs and how to send and receive them.

Chapter 5, WCF SAP Adapter RFCs and BAPIs: Distinguish the difference between SAP IDOCs, BAPIs and RFCs and when to use them.

Chapter 6, BizTalk Integration with Windows Azure AppFabric Service Bus: Discover Microsoft's AppFabric Service bus and learn how to build BizTalk solutions that complement Microsoft's Service bus in the Windows Azure Cloud.

Chapter 7, Integrating with SharePoint 2010: Build integrated SharePoint solutions using the Windows SharePoint Services Adapter and InfoPath.

Chapter 8, Integrating with SharePoint 2010 Web Services: Learn about manipulating SharePoint custom lists by consuming SharePoint's out of the box List Web Service.

Chapter 9, Microsoft Dynamics AX: Understand how to integrate with Microsoft Dynamics AX 2009 using the BizTalk adapter and .Net business connector.

Chapter 10, Integrating BizTalk Server and Salesforce.com: Discover how to establish bi-directional connectivity between SalesForce.com CRM and your on-premise services.

Who this book is for

If you are an experienced BizTalk developer who wants to integrate BizTalk with Line of Business systems using practical scenarios, then this book is for you. A solid understanding of BizTalk at an intermediate level is required. This book assumes developers are comfortable creating schemas, maps, orchestrations, ports, and messages in Visual Studio and configuring applications in the BizTalk Administration Console. However, experience in integrating with Line of Business systems is not necessarily required.

Conventions

In this book, you will find a number of styles of text that distinguish between different kinds of information. Here are some examples of these styles, and an explanation of their meaning.

Code words in text are shown as follows: "The `AfterReceiveRequest` operation can now validate the token through the helper function."

A block of code is set as follows:

```
private string serviceNamespace;
private string trustedTokenPolicyKey;
private string acsHostName;
private string trustedAudience;
```

Any command-line input or output is written as follows:

```
SAPCAR: processing archive RFC_25-20001765.SAR (version 2.01)
```

New terms and **important words** are shown in bold. Words that you see on the screen, in menus or dialog boxes for example, appear in the text like this: "Accept the license terms and click **Next**".

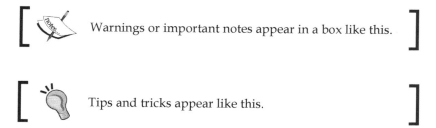

Warnings or important notes appear in a box like this.

Tips and tricks appear like this.

Reader feedback

Feedback from our readers is always welcome. Let us know what you think about this book—what you liked or may have disliked. Reader feedback is important for us to develop titles that you really get the most out of.

To send us general feedback, simply send an e-mail to feedback@packtpub.com, and mention the book title via the subject of your message.

If there is a book that you need and would like to see us publish, please send us a note in the **SUGGEST A TITLE** form on www.packtpub.com or e-mail suggest@packtpub.com.

If there is a topic that you have expertise in and you are interested in either writing or contributing to a book, see our author guide on www.packtpub.com/authors.

Customer support

Now that you are the proud owner of a Packt book, we have a number of things to help you to get the most from your purchase.

Downloading the example code

You can download the example code files for all Packt books you have purchased from your account at http://www.PacktPub.com. If you purchased this book elsewhere, you can visit http://www.PacktPub.com/support and register to have the files e-mailed directly to you.

Errata

Although we have taken every care to ensure the accuracy of our content, mistakes do happen. If you find a mistake in one of our books—maybe a mistake in the text or the code—we would be grateful if you would report this to us. By doing so, you can save other readers from frustration and help us improve subsequent versions of this book. If you find any errata, please report them by visiting http://www.packtpub.com/support, selecting your book, clicking on the **errata submission form** link, and entering the details of your errata. Once your errata are verified, your submission will be accepted and the errata will be uploaded on our website, or added to any list of existing errata, under the Errata section of that title. Any existing errata can be viewed by selecting your title from http://www.packtpub.com/support.

Piracy

Piracy of copyright material on the Internet is an ongoing problem across all media. At Packt, we take the protection of our copyright and licenses very seriously. If you come across any illegal copies of our works, in any form, on the Internet, please provide us with the location address or website name immediately so that we can pursue a remedy.

Please contact us at copyright@packtpub.com with a link to the suspected pirated material.

We appreciate your help in protecting our authors, and our ability to bring you valuable content.

Questions

You can contact us at questions@packtpub.com if you are having a problem with any aspect of the book, and we will do our best to address it.

1

Consuming ASDK-based Adapters

The **WCF LOB Adapter SDK (ASDK)** is a set of development tools and runtime components for execution and development of adapters for Line-of-Business Applications (**LOB**) such as SAP, Oracle, DBMS, and others. The biggest advantage offered by the ASDK-based adapters is that they can be consumed not only from BizTalk, but from any .NET WCF-compliant application using familiar WCF semantics coupled with rich configuration capabilities provided by WCF. If with the previous incarnations of BizTalk server developers had a choice between the ASDK-based adapters and the old COM-based LOB adapters, with the release of BizTalk Server 2010, and BizTalk Adapter Pack 2010 the only option developers would have is mastering the new technology — the old legacy LOB adapters, except the SQL Server adapter, have become history and can't be used with BizTalk 2010. In this chapter, we will cover the following topics:

- Understanding the ASDK-based adapter
- ASDK-based adapters vs. WCF services
- Installation of the BizTalk Adapter Pack 2010
- Using the ASDK development tools
- The WCF-Custom adapter and SOAP actions
- ASDK tools and features

The major goal is to make you familiar with common steps and techniques involved in building BizTalk applications using the ASDK-based adapters, so that in the subsequent chapters, we will be able to concentrate on the features specific to each particular adapter.

Understanding the ASDK-based adapter

If you read the product documentation, you will find that the ASDK-based adapters are built on top of the WCF Channel model and surface as custom WCF bindings. What this means is that WCF clients are able to communicate with ASDK-based adapters as if they were WCF services. Likely, the very first question you want to ask is whether the ASDK-based adapters are in fact WCF services just presented under the new fancy name. No, they are not! The use of the acronym WCF in the WCF LOB Adapter SDK is somewhat misleading; WCF forms the basis of the technology but the software does not revolve around web services. To understand how the adapters fit into the WCF infrastructure, let's recall some of the WCF fundamentals.

In order to establish communication process with clients, any WCF service must expose at least one endpoint. The WCF endpoints are based on three elements, known as the "A, B, and C" of the WCF. These three elements are:

- **A**ddress: It takes a form of the URI specifying the address where the service can be reached at.

- **B**inding: Bindings specify a communication protocol between the client and the service.

- **C**ontract: Contracts specify what operations are exposed by the service.

Communication between client and service is conducted through communication channels; one channel on the client side and its equivalent on the server side. On the server side, when you instantiate the `ServiceHost` class, it instantiates a channel listener, which in turn builds a communication channel for the service. On the client side, the proxy creates a channel factory, which is responsible for building the channel for the client. The channels consist of binding elements, each responsible for its own part of message processing to form a stack of binding elements.

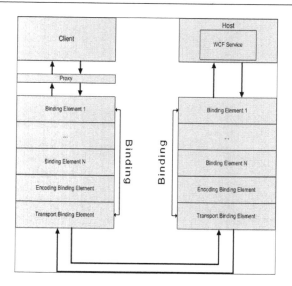

As you can notice in the previous diagram, the bottom layer in the communication channel is a transport layer, and that's exactly where the ASDK-based adapter fits within the channel stack.

The great thing about WCF is that it has been designed with extensibility in mind, which allows you to use custom transport bindings tailored to your specific needs. Much like the standard WCF transports, such as TCP, named pipes, HTTP, and MSMQ, the ASDK-based adapters are just a custom transport binding elements consumable from BizTalk applications using a standard WCF-custom adapter. As you can see in the following image, in the outbound scenario, the ASDK-based adapter instead of sending a message over the network like standard WCF transports, just communicates with the LOB system and then sends a response message to the client.

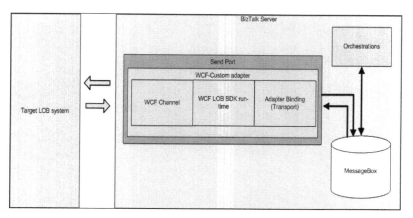

In the inbound scenario, ASDK-based adapter either monitors or listens for a notification from the target LOB system for particular events and generates a message containing event-specific data for the hosting application. We go into more details later in this and subsequent chapters.

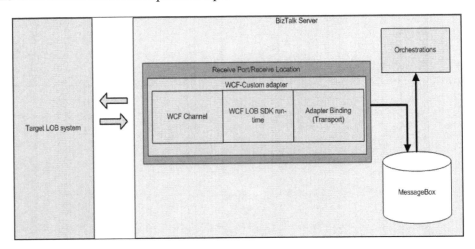

ASDK-based Adapters vs. WCF services

One of the frequently asked questions in relation to the new adapters is what is the reasoning behind introducing the ASDK technology? What's wrong with good old fashioned WCF-services that have been used for years to provide access to LOB applications and are perfectly consumable from virtually all applications? Why did Microsoft re-invent the wheel? Well, these are absolutely valid questions and here is the answer. There is nothing wrong with the WCF-services; they are as good as they have always been, but there is one big "but" — only if the LOB application is relatively static. Imagine the situation where your LOB application is evolving and you, as a developer, have to expose new metadata to the client applications? You either have to update existing contracts, or implement new ones with subsequent configuration steps applied to both the host and WCF-service. This has been a major pain for the development teams working on the LOB side.

Metadata is usually defined as data about data. This is a very broad definition; metadata in the WCF LOB Adapter SDK can be defined as the data types and the operations available in the target LOB system. For example, for SAP, it can be IDOCs and BAPIs or it can be stored procedures and data tables for the DBMS-based applications. It is up to the adapter designer to determine and expose the metadata for a particular LOB application.

In contrast, the ASDK-based adapters provide design time metadata discovery and resolution automatically, with no efforts from the development team to make new metadata (or functionality, according to our definition of the metadata) available for consumption. Details of this process are beyond the scope of this chapter, but if you are interested in diving deeper, the sample adapters provided with the WCF LOB Adapters SDK are at your disposal. Take a look at how the Contoso sample adapter located in the C:\Program Files\WCF LOB Adapter SDK\Documents\Samples directory implements the IMetadata*group of interfaces and the magic behind the automatic metadata discovery and resolution will become clear. Implementation of the IMetadata* interfaces does require substantial efforts from the adapter developers, but the end result is certainly worth it.

Now that you are familiar with the architectural foundations, let's proceed with installation of the adapters.

Installation

The installation procedure of the BizTalk Adapter Pack 2010 is not complicated, but as with everything BizTalk, requires accuracy and some patience. The very first thing to do is make sure your system meets the prerequisite requirements. You have to have the following components installed on your computer:

- Windows XP SP2, Windows Server 2003, Windows Server 2008, Windows Vista, or Windows 7
- Visual Studio 2010 for development purposes

- BizTalk Server 2010 with Windows Communication Foundation Adapter. The WCF adapter is not installed by default; you have to explicitly enable it upon installing BizTalk Server 2010.

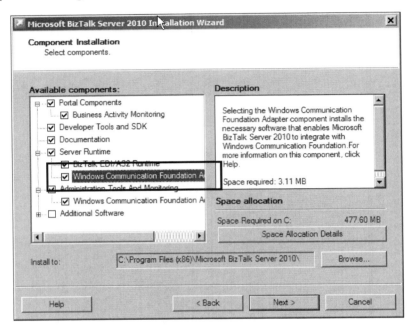

Once you've completed the verification, you can proceed with the installation, which essentially is a sequence of the following steps:

1. Installing WCF LOB Adapter SDK.
2. Installing BizTalk Adapter Pack 2010.
3. Installing additional client libraries to enable communication between adapters and their target LOB systems. The only adapter that doesn't require any additional components is the SQL adapter.

From the steps above, installation of the additional client libraries is the most time consuming and error prone process. We will explore this topic in detail in the chapter dedicated to the SAP adapter.

Even though installing the WCF LOB Adapter SDK and BizTalk Adapter Pack are straightforward procedures, there is a pitfall in a 64-bit environment. If your computer is running under a 32-bit operating system, you have to install only 32-bit versions of the WCF LOB Adapter SDK and BizTalk Adapter Pack. In a 64-bit environment, the picture is a bit more complicated. First you have to install 64-bit version of the WCF LOB Adapter SDK and 64-bit version of the BizTalk Adapter Pack 2010. Then, if you are using design time tools like Visual Studio and BizTalk Admin Console or 32-bit BizTalk host instances at the runtime, you will have to install 32-bit version of the BizTalk Adapter pack and the client libraries. This probably sounds counterintuitive, but if you take into account that Visual Studio and BizTalk Admin Console are 32-bit applications and therefore can interact only with 32-bit components, such requirement becomes clear. So, don't be surprised if the BizTalk setup program run in a 64-bit environment offers you to install both 32 and 64-bit versions of the BizTalk Adapter pack 2010. Now that we are familiar with the requirements, we can begin the installation of the ASDK Adapters.

Installing the WCF LOB Adapter SDK

The first step is to lay the foundation, that is install the WCF LOB Adapter SDK.

1. From the `\Setup\BT Setup` folder of the BizTalk installation DVD or ISO, launch `setup.exe`, then select **Install Microsoft BizTalk Adapters**.

2. Select **Step 1: Install Microsoft WCF LOB Adapter SDK**. Note that setup automatically installs the correct version; you don't have to explicitly choose between 32 and 64-bit.

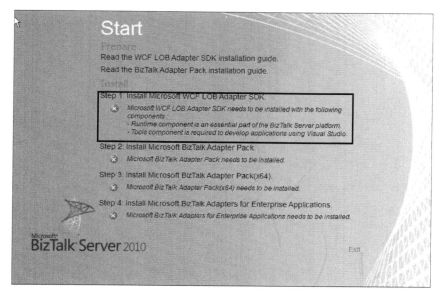

3. On the **Welcome** screen, click the **Next** button.

4. Accept the license terms and click **Next**.

5. On the **Installation Type** screen, click the **Custom** button. The **Custom Setup** screen will show up.

6. You always have to install the runtime components, despite whether you are planning to use the UI tools or not. If you are installing on the computer where you are planning to use the UI design-time components, such as **Add Adapter Service Reference plug-in** for Visual Studio, and **BizTalk Server Add-in** for BizTalk Administration Console, you have to enable the installation of the **Tools**, and the **BizTalk Server Add-in** components. For the walkthrough later in the chapter, you will also need the **Samples** provided with WCF LOB Adapter SDK.

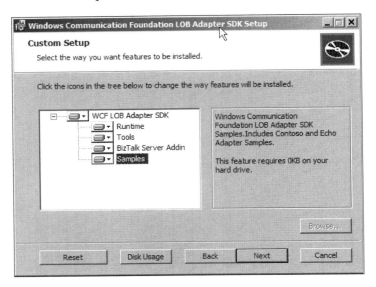

7. Click **Next**, then click **Install** to start installation.

8. When the installation completes, click the **Finish** button to close the WCF LOB Adapter SDK setup and return to the main adapter setup window.

Installing the BizTalk Adapter Pack 2010

We will now install the BizTalk Adapter Pack 2010. Note, that if you are in a 64-bit environment, the setup offers to install both 32 and 64-bit versions of the BizTalk Adapter Pack 2010.

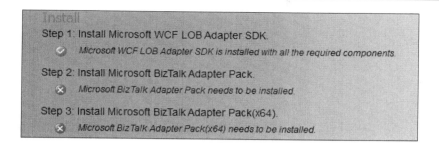

Here is the process to follow:

1. In the main adapter setup window, click the link to install the relevant version of the BizTalk Adapter Pack.

2. On the **Welcome** screen, click **Next**.

3. Accept the license terms and click **Next**.

4. On the **Choose Setup Type** screen, click the **Custom** button.

5. On the **Custom Setup** screen, select the adapters you want to use and click **Next**.

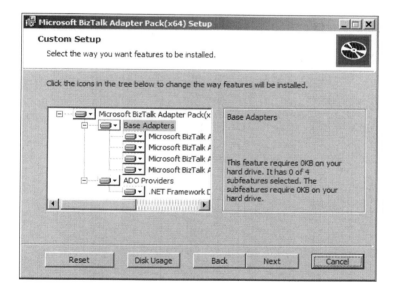

6. Click **Install** to begin installation.

7. When the installation completes, click **Finish** to finalize the procedure and close the setup window.

To complete the installation of the BizTalk Adapter Pack 2010, you have to install additional client components for all adapters except SQL. For the SAP adapter covered in this book, we will provide step-by-step guidance in chapter 4. If you are planning to use the SQL adapter only, no further steps are required and at this point, you have everything you need for using and developing with the SQL adapter.

Using the ASDK development tools

In this section, we will show you how to use the tools provided by the ASDK to enable BizTalk applications for consumption of the ASDK-based adapters. For this purpose, we will employ the Echo adapter, one of the two sample adapters supplied with the ASDK. This is a very simple adapter simulating operations to a fictitious LOB system, but at this point, we don't need anything complicated since the ASDK tools work in exactly the same fashion regardless of the adapter. So, simplicity of the Echo adapter is to our benefit—we will concentrate on the essence, leaving the complexity of the real-world adaptors to their respective chapters. As an additional bonus, the Echo adapter comes with full source code located in C:\Program Files\ WCF LOB Adapter SDK\Documents\Samples directory and an installation package. As of the moment of writing this book, the setup package for the Echo adapter was not updated for use with the Visual Studio 2010 and .NET 4.0; to make you life easier, we prepared setup for .NET 4.0 32/64 bit environments and put the packages in the ZIP file containing code samples for the book. If you didn't download the samples yet, please do it now.

Echo adapter

Let's start with a brief discussion of the functionality provided by the Echo adapter. Like its big brothers from the BizTalk Adapter Pack 2010, the Echo adapter supports two message exchange patterns.

- Inbound: In the inbound scenario, the Echo adapter, being a part of the receive port infrastructure, monitors a specified file folder for new files with TXT extension; once a new file arrives, the adapter sends a notification to the BizTalk application. The notification takes the form of an XML message conforming to the following XSD schema:

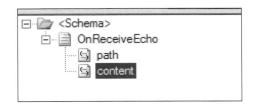

- The **path** element contains the name of the folder being monitored for new files; the **content** element, as its name suggests, holds the content of a new file. If you wish to map this operation to the functionality provided by the real world adapters from BizTalk Adapters Pack 2010, it resembles the notification operations supported by the SQL adapter. When configured for notification, the adapter notifies the client application that there are data in the database meeting the specified criteria. We will discuss these operations in detail in subsequent chapters.

- Outbound: In the outbound scenario, being a part of the send port infrastructure, the adapter echoes (or repeats) an incoming string a specified number of times then sends the response back to a caller. The XSD schema for request and response messages are shown in the following image:

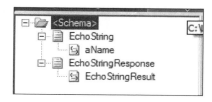

- The real world analogy for the **EchoString** operation is executing for example a select statement against a specified table by the SQL adapter and sending the result set back to a client.

To make its operations fully configurable, the Echo adapter exposes two binding properties:

- **Count**. This property specifies how many times incoming messages have to be echoed/repeated.

- **FileSystemWatcherFolder**. We will use this property to specify the folder to monitor for new `*.txt` files.

Since the Echo adapter is not automatically installed with the WCF LOB Adapter SDK, we will have to take care of it. The installation is straightforward and unlikely to cause difficulties.

Here are the steps:

1. Navigate to `C:\LOBIntegration\Chapter01\EchoAdapter\Setup32` directory and get familiar with the `readme.doc` file.

2. Launch `setup.exe` and follow the setup wizard. Accept the default values for all screens.

3. If you are working in a 64-bit environment, now navigate to `C:\LOBIntegration\Chapter01\EchoAdapter\Setup64` and repeat the procedure.

Now that you have installed the Echo adapter, we can proceed with building the BizTalk application consuming the Echo adapter. For your convenience, we provided a complete and ready to deploy application identical to what we are going to build. The application is located in the `C:\LOBIntegration\Chapter01\Walkthrough` directory; you can use it as a reference to be sure that you are on the right track building your own application.

Building the BizTalk application

Our BizTalk application will consist of a single orchestration acting in a pretty much "pass-through" mode. The orchestration will receive an inbound **OnReceiveEcho** message from the Echo adapter, construct an outbound **EchoString** message by mapping the **content** element of the inbound message to the **aName** element of the outbound message, and then submit it to the adapter for echoing. The response will be received by the orchestration and written to the **Application Event Log**. When we complete the walkthrough, the orchestration will resemble the following image:

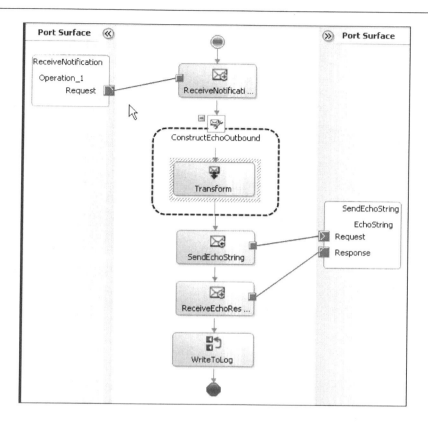

Here is the process to follow:

1. To get started, verify that the `c:\temp` folder exists on your computer. If not, please create it. If you recall, the adapter exposes the **FileSystemWatcherFolder** property to specify the folder to monitor for the files with `*.txt` extension. We will use the default value which is `c:\temp`.

2. Open Visual Studio and create a new BizTalk project with the settings shown in the following image. For the location, you can specify a folder of your choice.

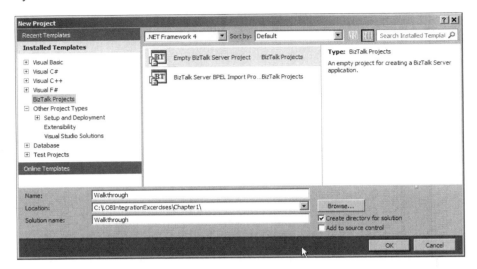

3. Now, the most important part. We need to generate the schemas representing the operations exposed by the adapter that you intend to use with the current application. The tool of choice for the task is the **Consume Adapter Service plug-in**, a metadata browser and artifacts generation tool, which you installed recently as a part of the ASDK. Besides XSD schemas, this plugin also generates a physical port binding file. This means that you can configure the port automatically by importing the binding file using the BizTalk Administration Console. The binding file typically contains physical port configuration settings including the connection string to the target LOB and the port SOAP actions based on the operations for which metadata were generated.

   ◦ To reach the Consume Adapter Service window, first right-click on the **EchoAdapterSample** project and choose **Add | Add Generated Items**.

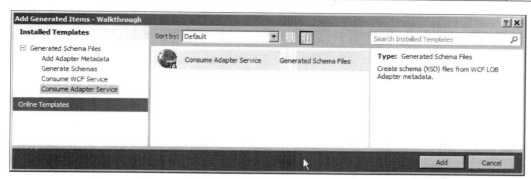

- ○ Once the **Add Generated Items** window appears, in the **Installed Templates** column, select **Consume Adapter Service** and click the **Add** button to open the **Consume Adapter Service Wizard** window.

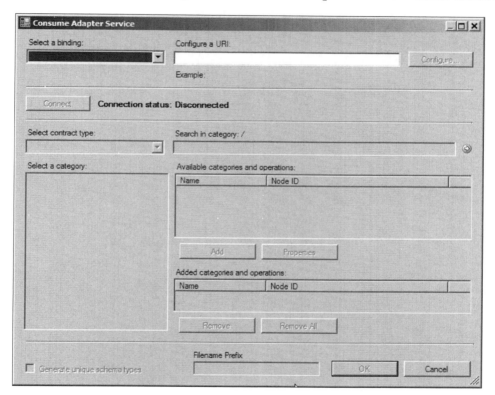

- The very first thing we need to do here is choose **echoAdapterBinding** from the **Select a binding:** drop down. If you don't see **echoAdapterBinding** in the drop down, make sure you installed the 32-bit version of the adapter.

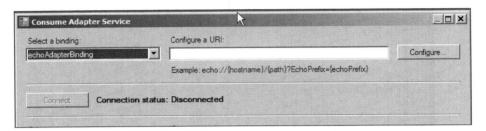

- Once the binding is set, click the **Configure** button to bring up the **Configure Adapter** dialog to configure the connection string and set credentials, URI, and binding properties.

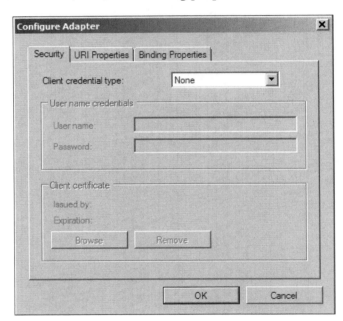

° The first step to generating the artifacts is establishing a connection to the target system. Most LOB systems require valid client credentials as part of the connection procedure and our Echo system is not an exception, though it is quite forgiving—after selecting **Username** for the **Client credential type** drop down, you can type in anything you like for the **User name** and **Password**, but please don't leave them blank.

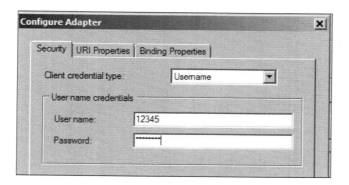

° Further, besides valid credentials, in order to establish a connection we have to provide additional parameters such as host name, port number, and other LOB application specific parameters—this is what the **URI Properties** tab is for. Switch to this tab and note the properties presented there. As with the user name and password, you can type in anything you like or accept the defaults.

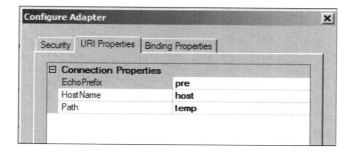

While the Echo Adapter requires only three elements to build the connection URI, the real-world adapters from the BizTalk Adapters Pack 2010 require more details in order to connect to their LOB systems. For comparison, the following image shows the properties required to establish a connection to SAP:

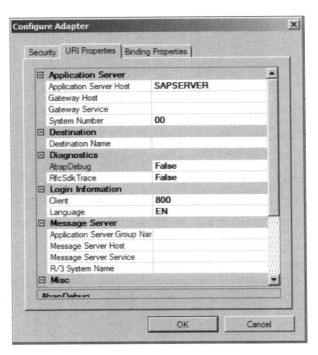

<ul>
<li>○ Finally, we need to configure the bindings exposed by the adapter by setting the properties presented on the Binding Properties tab. For our scenario, we can accept the default values for all properties.</li>
</ul>

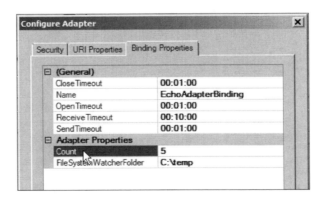

○ Now, click **OK** to close the Configure Adapter dialog and return to the **Consume Adapter Service** window. Note that the **Configure a URI** text box now contains a configured connection string, which is built from the URI properties tab values.

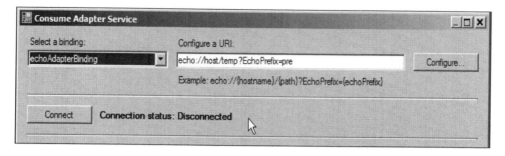

○ Provided the connection string we've built is correct, clicking the **Connect** button establishes an active connection to the Echo system. If the connection is accepted, we will see the category tree populated with outbound categories — the outbound contract type is what the Consume Adapter Service plugin chooses by default.

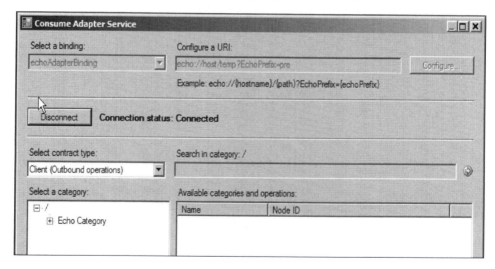

○ Next, we need to select the operations that we want to use in our application and add them to the list of desired operations. In the **Select a category tree** click the **Echo Category** node, then in the **Available categories and operations** panel, select **EchoString** and click the **Add** button. This action adds EchoString to the list of desired operations at the bottom of the screen. The last step is to help the **Consume Adapter Service add-in** to generate descriptive file names by setting the file name prefix at the bottom of the screen to **EchoOutbound**.

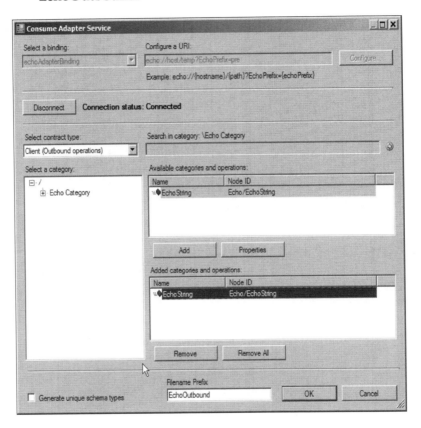

○ Finally, click **OK** to close the **Consume Adapter Service Wizard** window and return to Visual Studio, where we see two new files added to our BizTalk project. One file is the XSD schema for the EchoString operation, the other is an XML binding file. After deploying the application, you will import this file using the **BizTalk Admin Console** to create a physical **WCF-Custom** send port configured to perform the EchoString operation.

Unfortunately, one of the inconveniences we have to deal with is that the **Consume Adapter Service add-in** doesn't allow generating artifacts for different contract types in one run. To generate the schema and binding file for the inbound operation, we need to open the **Consume Adapter Service add-in** again and repeat the procedure. On the **Security** tab, specify the username and password, for the properties on the **URI Properties** and **Binding Properties** tabs, you can accept the default values.

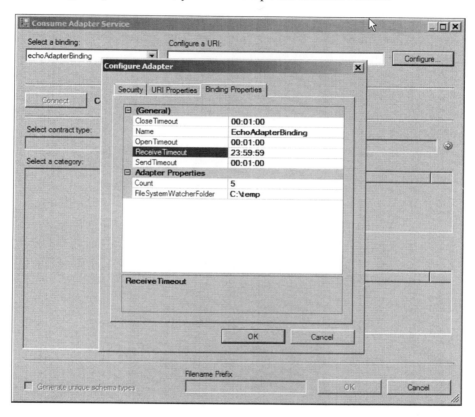

- ° Then, once you've established a successful connection, select **Service** in the **Select contract type** drop down, click **EchoCategory** in the **Select a category** panel, and add **OnReceiveEcho** to the list of desired operations. Set the **Filename Prefix** at the bottom of the screen to **EchoInbound**.

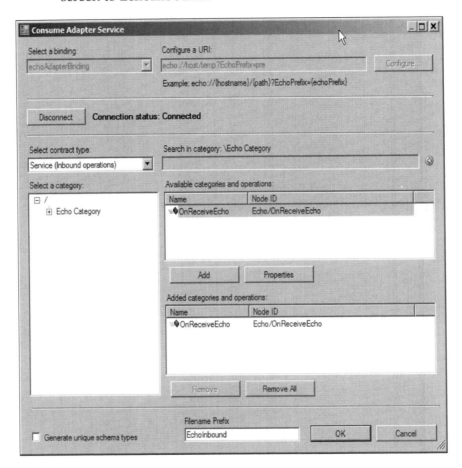

- ° Click **OK** to return to Visual Studio. Our Visual Studio solution with two new added files should now look like this:

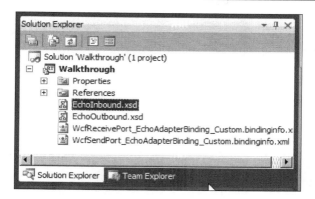

- Finally, to complete the schemas, double click the `EchoOutbound.xsd` file to open the schema editor and distinguish the **EchoStringResult** field. We will use this field in our orchestration.

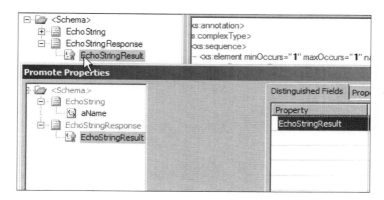

- Technically speaking, at this point, we have all bits and pieces required to build our BizTalk application. Before we proceed, let's make a few cosmetic changes.

- First, rename the `WcfSendPort_EchoAdapterBinding_Custom.bindinginfo.xml` to `SendPort.Bindinginfo.xml`. Similarly, rename the `WcfReceivePort_EchoAdapterBinding_Custom.bindinginfo.xml` to `ReceivePort.Bindinginfo.xml`.

- ° Next, we need to give more descriptive names for the receive port and receive location. Open the `ReceivePort.bindinginfo.xml` file, and change the **ReceivePort** and **ReceiveLocation Name** attributes as follows:

```
<DistributionListCollection />
<ReceivePortCollection>
  <ReceivePort Name="Echo ReceiveNotification" IsTwoWay="false" Bin
    <Description>ReceivePort for EchoAdapterBinding.</Description>
    <ReceiveLocations>
      <ReceiveLocation Name="EchoWcfCustom ReceiveNotification">
        <Description xsi:nil="true" />
```

- ° For the `SendPort.bindinginfo.xml` file, locate the **SendPort** node and change the **Name** attribute to **SendEchoString**.

```
<SendPortCollection>
  <SendPort Name="SendEchoString" IsStatic="true" IsTwoW
    <Description>SendPort for EchoAdapterBinding.</Descr
```

4. Now that we have prepared all the artifacts, we can proceed and build our sample application.

5. Add a BizTalk orchestration to the project and name it **ProcessEcho.**

6. Switch to the **OrchestrationView** and create three orchestration messages with the following values:

   ° Identifier: **msgReceiveNotification**, Message Type: **Walkthrough. EchoInbound**

   ° Identifier: **msgEchoStringRequest**, Type: **Walkthrough. EchoOutbound.EchoString**

   ° Identifier: **msgEchoStringResponse**, Type: **Walkthrough. EchoOutbound.EchoStringResponse**

7. To construct the outbound message, add a map to the project and name it.

8. **Inbound_To_Outbound**.

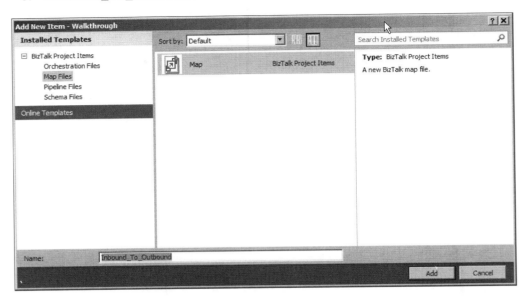

9. Specify **OnReceiveEcho** as the source message type, for the destination schema, specify **EchoOutbound**, and select **EchoString** as the root node. Once the source and destination schemas are set, connect the **content** and **aName** elements.

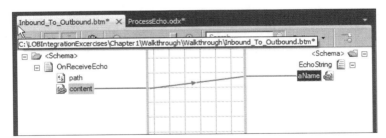

10. Next, we need to sketch the orchestration flow. From the toolbox, drag on the orchestration surface the shapes in the order and with the properties as follows:

    ○ Shape: **Receive**, Name: **ReceiveNotification**, Activate: True, Message: **msgReceiveNotification**

- ○ Shape: **Construct**, Name: **ConstructEchoOutbound**, Message Constructed: **msgEchoStringRequest**. Inside the Construct drag the Transform shape and configure it with the following values: Name: **Transform**, Input Messages: **msgReceiveNotification**, Map Name: **Inbound_To_Outbound**, Output Messages: **msgEchoStringRequest**

- ○ Shape: **Send**, Name: **SendEchoString**, Message: **msgEchoStringRequest**

- ○ Shape: **Receive**, Name: **ReceiveEchoResponse**, Message: **msgEchoStringResponse**

- ○ Shape: **Expression**, Name: **WriteToLog**

11. Configure the **WriteToLog** expression shape to execute the following code:

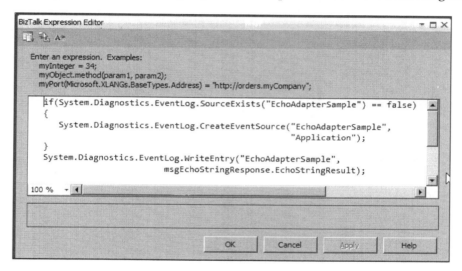

12. To enable the orchestration for receiving and sending messages, we need to add two logical orchestration ports. The first port will be a one-way port for receiving an initial inbound message; the second will be a Request-Response port for sending an outbound message to the adapter for processing and receiving a response. Right-click on the **Port Surface** and select **New Configured Port** to start the **Port Configuration Wizard**. Here are the settings for the first one-way port.

- ○ Name: **ReceiveInitialEcho**

     ○   Port Type: **Create New Port**, Port Type Name: **InitialEchoType**, Communication Pattern: **One-Way**, Access Restriction: **Internal**

     ○   Port Direction of Communication: **I will always be receiving messages on this port**, Port Binding: **Specify later**

13. Run the Wizard one more time to create a logical port for the outbound operation.

     ○   Name: **SendEchoString**

     ○   Port Type: **Create New Port**, Port Type Name: **SendEchoStringType**, Communication Pattern: **Request-Response**, Access Restriction: **Internal**

     ○   Port Direction of Communication: **I will always be sending request, and receiving response on this port**, Port Binding: **Specify later**

14. Join the logical ports with the relevant shapes. Connect **Request** of the **ReceiveNotification** receive port with the ReceiveNotification shape. For the **SendEchoString** send port, connect **Request** with the **SendEchoString** shape, and **Response** with the **ReceiveEchoResponse** shape. When you finish, the orchestration should match the following image:

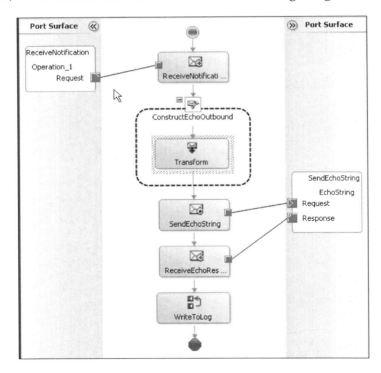

15. Build the application and address error messages, if any.

16. The last thing to do before we deploy the application is specify a strong name key for the application assembly, and provide the name for the BizTalk application. In the **Solution Explorer**, right-click on the project name and select **Properties**. From the **Project Properties** window, switch to the **Signing** tab to specify a strong name key file. You can either generate a new, or use any existing key file from your computer. Then, activate the **Deployment** tab and type **Chapter01_Walkthrough** for the application name.

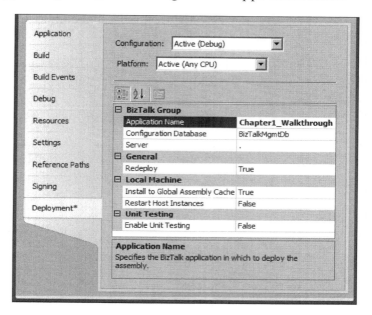

17. Almost there; we are finally at the deployment stage. Go to the BizTalk Admin Console and create a new application named **Chapter01_Walkthrough**. You have to create the application first; otherwise Visual Studio will deploy the solution in the default application in the group.

18. In the **Solution Explorer**, right-click on the solution name, select **Deploy**, and wait for the message confirming that the deployment succeeded.

19. To complete the deployment, we need to create the application physical ports. This is where the binding files, generated for us by the Consume Adapter Service plugin, come into play. Open the BizTalk Administration Console, expand the **Applications** node, right-click **Chapter01_ Walkthrough**, and select **Import | Bindings**. Navigate to the solution directory and import the binding file for the receive port. Then, repeat the procedure to import the bindings for the send port. Disregard a pop-up message informing you of the application name not matching and click **Yes**.

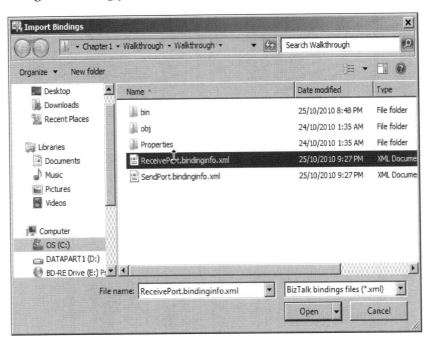

20. For security reasons, the **Consume Adapter Service** addin doesn't include the usernames and passwords when generating binding files. For the physical ports, we have to set them manually using the **WCF-Custom Transport Properties** window. Let's start with the send port. In BizTalk Administration Console, double-click the **SendEchoString** port, then click **Configure**, switch to the **Credentials** tab, and type in any username and password.

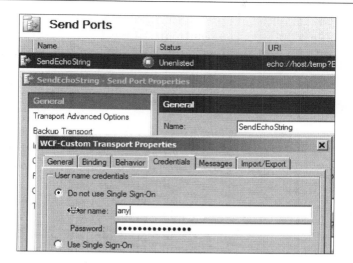

21. Specify the username and password for the receive location. In the BizTalk Admin Console, double-click the **EchoWcfCustom_ReceiveNotification** receive location and then click **Configure** to open the **WCF-Custom Transport Properties** window. As you can see, for the receive location, this window has a slightly different look. There is no **Credentials** tab; instead, you have to switch to the **Other** tab and specify the username and password there.

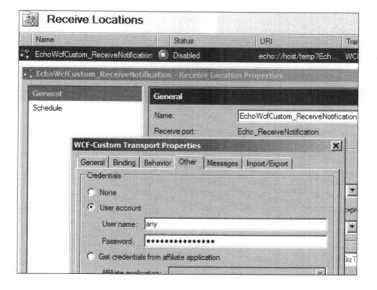

22. The last step before we start the application is to bind the orchestration. In the BizTalk Administration Console, double click **ProcessEcho** orchestration to open the **Orchestration Properties** window. Activate the **Bindings** tab and set the properties as shown in the following image:

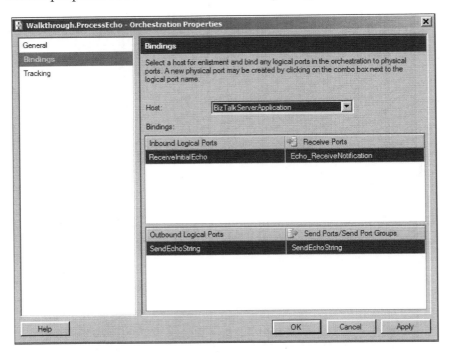

23. Click **OK** to close the **Orchestration Properties** window and then start the application.

If we submit a file to the c:\temp folder monitored by the adapter, we will get the following error message:

```
The adapter failed to transmit message going to send port
"SendEchoString" with URL " echo://host/temp?EchoPrefix=pre ".
It will be retransmitted after the retry interval specified for
this Send Port. Details:"Microsoft.ServiceModel.Channels.Common.
UnsupportedOperationException: Incorrect Action
<BtsActionMapping xmlns:xsi="http://www.w3.org/2001/XMLSchema-
instance" xmlns:xsd="http://www.w3.org/2001/XMLSchema">
  <Operation Name="EchoString" Action="Echo/EchoString" />
</BtsActionMapping>. Correct the specified Action, or refer to the
documentation on the allowed formats for the Actions. Note that
Actions are case-sensitive.
```

The problem is exactly what the error message is telling us—the SOAP action settings applied to the send port are not understood by the adapter. One of the most often asked questions on the MSDN forums is "I imported bindings with the SOAP action settings as generated by the Consume Adapter Service plug-in, so why are they nor understood by the adapter?". We will demystify the subject and shed some light on how the WCF-custom adapter processes the actions shortly, right after we finish the walkthrough. For now, to fix the problem and complete the application, go to the BizTalk Admin Console and do the following:

1. Double-click the `SendEchoString` send port. In the **Send Port Properties** windows click **Configure** to open the **WCF-Custom Transport** Properties window.

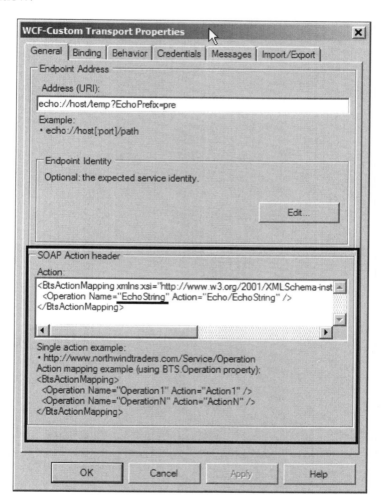

2. In the **Action** text box of the **SOAP Action Header** section, note the value of the **Name** attribute, which is **EchoString**. What you have to do is to make your orchestration logical send port name match the value of the **Name** attribute. The first option is to change the logical port name from Operation_1 to EchoString and then, of course, to re-deploy the application.

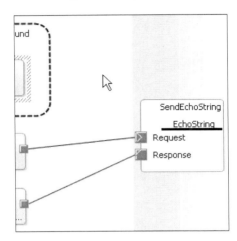

3. An alternative option, if you don't want to redeploy the application, is to set the **Name** attribute value to **Operation_1**, so that the content of the **Action** box looks as follows:

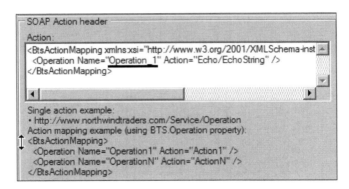

4. Although from a pure technical standpoint this is a perfectly valid solution, using such non-descriptive names is a questionable practice and should be avoided. We presented it here with the only purpose being to illustrate the concept. The best approach is not to leave the operation name with the default value Operation_1, but to give it a descriptive name upon designing the orchestration and then adjust the physical port action mapping.

So, let's do it right and just change the logical port operation name to EchoString. Once done, re-deploy the application. Now, you can create a file containing a single word "Echo", drop it to the `C:\temp` folder, and watch the event log for the echoed messages returned by the Echo adapter. Please don't forget, the file must have a TXT extension.

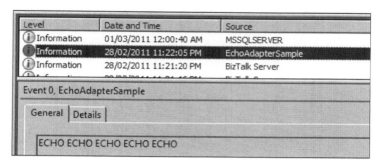

The WCF-Custom adapter and SOAP actions

Now, as promised, let's take a deeper look at the SOAP actions and how the WCF-Custom adapter deals with them. The idea behind the SOAP actions is quite simple. Essentially, the SOAP action is just a tag attached to the incoming WCF messages telling the adapter what operation it has to perform.

To illustrate the concept by a concrete example, let's refer to the source code provided with the Echo adapter. The point of our interest is the Execute method of the `Microsoft.ServiceModel.Channels.Common.IOutboundHandler` interface. This interface is one of the core interfaces that all ASDK-based adapters supporting outbound operations must implement. The Execute is called by the ASDK runtime to perform an outbound operation. Here is the implementation:

```
/// <summary>
/// Executes the request message on the target system and returns a response message.
/// If there isn't a response, this method should return null
/// </summary>
/// <param name="message">The Message to be executed</param>
/// <param name="timeout">The timeout for the operation</param>
/// <returns>the response message, null if there was no response</returns>
public Message Execute(Message message, TimeSpan timeout)
{
    OperationMetadata om =
        this.MetadataLookup.GetOperationDefinitionFromInputMessageAction(message.Head
    if (om == null)
    {
        throw new AdapterException("Invalid operation " + message.Headers.Action);
    }

    switch (message.Headers.Action)
    {
        case "Echo/EchoString":
            return CreateEchoStringResponseMessage(message);

        default: throw new AdapterException("Invalid Operation " + message.Headers.Ac
    }
}
```

The code is self-explanatory and as you can clearly see, is action-centric. If the action coming with the SOAP header is recognized, the adapter performs the requested operation, if not, then the adapter responds with "Invalid Operation" exception. Since the Echo adapter exposes only one operation, using actions may seem unnecessary, but imagine the situation when an adapter exposes multiple operations? In such cases, using the SOAP actions is quite a logical way to help the adapter to decide what operation to perform.

There are two different ways to associate a BizTalk message with the appropriate SOAP action (or to attach the appropriate processing tag as you wish). One is to configure physical send ports using so called Action Mappings. The other is to set the actions dynamically at runtime.

Action Mappings

You will use the Action Mappings in the majority of cases — this is the easiest way to configure physical ports since the Consume Adapter Service Wizard does most of the job. For each operation that you selected at the design time, the **Consume Adapter Service Wizard** will generate a corresponding **Operation** entry inside the **BtsActionMapping** wrapper and place the mapping into the physical port binding file it will generate. In the general form, the action mapping looks as follows:

```
<BtsActionMapping>
    <Operation Name ="Operation1" Action = "Action1" \>
    <Operation Name = "Operation2" Action = "Action2"\>
        ...
    <Operation Name = "OpertionN" Action = "ActionN"\>
</BtsActionMapping>
```

To process the actions mappings and attach the SOAP actions tags to incoming messages, the WCF-Custom adapter uses the following algorithm:

When the outbound message leaves an orchestration, the orchestration instance sets the **BTS.Operation** context property with the logical port operation name. Once the subscription mechanism pulls the message from the message box and hands it over to the physical port for processing, the WCF-Custom adapter tries to look up the actions map for the Operation with the Name matching the BTS.Operation property. If a match is found, then the adapter attaches the corresponding Action value to the message and sends it to the custom binding for execution. If a match was not found, then the WCF-Custom adapter treats the entire BtsActionMapping as one big action, so the custom binding will get the following action: `<BtsActionMapping><Operation Name="Operation 1" Action =......</ BtsActionMapping>` with quite a predictable consequence — "Invalid action" exception. So, the rule is clear: for each orchestration outbound operation, there must be an Operation entry in the corresponding physical port action mappings with the Name attribute value matching the orchestration operation name.

It is important to note that for the content-based routing scenarios, where you don't use orchestrations and rely solely on the functionality provided by the messaging engine, you don't have to write a custom pipeline component to set the BTS.Operation context property. Luckily, the WCF-custom adapter supports an alternative single action format.

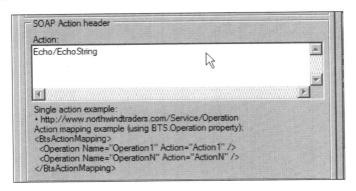

Essentially, this means that all messages arriving to the send port configured for the single action processing will be tagged with the same action regardless of the **BTS. Operation** context property. Since the Echo adapter supports only one operation, the single action approach is an alternative solution perfectly applicable to our sample application.

Setting SOAP actions dynamically

In the situations where you want to postpone the decision on what operation has to be performed until the runtime, you can use the **WCF.Action** context property. All you need to do is to add an **Expression** shape to your orchestration and configure the shape to execute the code similar to the presented below:

```
YourOutboundMessage(WCF.Action)="DesiredAction"
```

As you can see, the WCF-Custom adapter offers enough flexibility to address virtually any situation you may encounter. Once you understand the concept and available options, all it takes is accuracy and no longer than a couple of minutes to configure send ports.

ASDK tools and features

At this point, you essentially have all the necessary information to start building applications that rely on the ASDK-based adapters. Nonetheless, as with any serious technology, which the ASDK no doubt is, there are areas and features which can become the source of headaches or make your work less productive if used indiscriminately. And, as with any serious technology, there are tools to help you effectively resolve potential problems.

In this section, we will discuss the following topics, applicable to all ASDK-based adapters:

- Generating the schemas - helpful tips
- Dealing with timeouts
- Tracking and tracing

Generating the schemas

When you have finished the walkthrough, you will likely come to the conclusion that generating the schemas is probably the most important step to whether your experience with the adapters will be fast and smooth, or whether you will have to spend a considerable amount of time troubleshooting your application. If this was your verdict, you were absolutely right. Here, we would like to provide you with a few tips and suggestions, which may improve your productivity and help to avoid potential issues:

- If you are not happy with the names of the schema files generated by the **Consume Adapter Service** plugin, feel free to change them to your liking or to the naming conventions adopted by your organization.

- As you likely know, BizTalk schemas are compiled into .Net classes. You are free to change the name and the namespace of the .NET class to be generated. Just click the schema file in the Solution explorer and make a change in the **Properties** window. Doing so, you will make referencing the types defined in the XSD files easier and more visual.

- Feel free to distinguish or promote schema fields as needed. Nonetheless, be aware that if for whatever reason you need to re-regenerate the schemas, your promotions will be lost.

- In the vast majority of cases, you won't have a need to change the namespace and root node name for the schemas generated by the Consume Adapter Service plugin. As you know, these two elements constitute the document type, the cornerstone of the messaging engine subscription mechanism. If you still have a very compelling reason to change the type, the change has to be accompanied by a custom pipeline component. For the inbound scenarios, the pipeline component has to convert the document produced by the adapter to match your custom document type. Otherwise, the messaging engine will throw the infamous "subscription not found" exception. For the outbound scenarios, your custom pipeline component has to convert your custom document to match the type expected by the adapter that is the type generated for you by the Consume Adapter Service plugin. Otherwise the message will be rejected by the adapter.

- You have to be extra cautious if you are planning to use the ASDK adapters with more than one application in the same BizTalk group. If you generated the schemas for the same operation in different Visual Studio projects, you will end up with a situation where the same message type will be presented twice in the BizTalk management database. The consequence of this configuration is that the messaging engine will throw exceptions reporting its inability to resolve the message type or find a subscription because multiple schemas matched the message type.

- To avoid such a situation, we recommend putting the schemas generated by the **Consume Adapter Service add-in** into a separate Visual Studio BizTalk project which you will reference from your other Visual Studio BizTalk projects. Upon deployment, you will need to add assembly with the schemas to a separate BizTalk application named for example `YourOrganization. Common`, and then reference this application from the other BizTalk applications in the group.

- An alternative option is to to configure XMLReceive or XMLTransmit pipeline with fully qualified schema name set in the DocumentSpecNames property.

- Working with the **Consume Adapter Service Wizard**, you likely noticed the **Generate Unique Schema Types** checkbox at the bottom of the **Consume Adapter Service Wizard** and are wondering whether this might be a simpler solution to the problem we just discussed.

- Unfortunately, this checkbox deals with a fundamentally similar, but ultimately different issue. Consider the scenario where you want to generate a schema for the operation called for example **LOBOperationA**. The schema for **LOBOperationA** uses a parameter of complex type **CT1**. Assume you closed **the Consume Adapter Service Wizard**, and sometime later re-opened it to generate schema **for LOBOperationB**, which uses the same complex type **CT1**. After you generate the schema for the **LOBOperationB** and compile the project, you will get an error message reporting that the same type **CT1** is defined twice in different XSD files. To address such situation you can do the following:

  ○ Whenever possible, generate the schemas for all operations you are planning to use in a single run to the Consume Adapter Service addin. The addin is able to recognize the situation and place the definition of the shared types in a single, separate XSD file referenced by the main XSD files using the **Import** directive.

  ○ If your application is evolving and your only option is generating schemas across multiple runs, checking off the **Generate Unique Schema Types** solves the problem by generating unique namespaces for the complex types.

The best approach is to make only one run to the plugin and generate all schemas in one batch, but, as often happens, this solution is not always possible in real life projects. So, in many cases your best bet is to use the Generate Unique Schema Types checkbox. Even if the operation does not use share types, keeping this checkbox checked will do no harm.

Timeouts

If you've followed the walkthrough, you should have noticed the group of timeout-related binding properties available at the design time on the Binding Properties page of the Configure Adapter dialog.

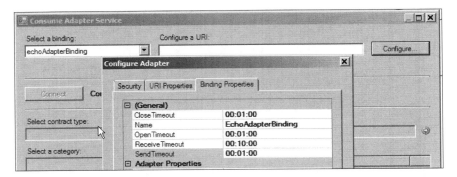

After you imported the binding file generated by the ASDK, these properties are accessible through the **Bindings** tab of the **WCF-Custom Transport** properties dialog.

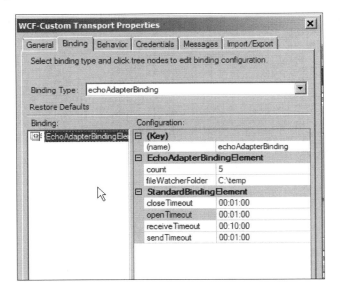

The purpose of each property and the default values as set by the ASDK are listed in the following table:

Property	Purpose
openTimeout	Open connection timeout. The default value is 1 minute.
closeTimeout	Close connection time out. The default value is 1 minute.
sendTimeout.	Outbound request-response timeout. This property specifies for how long the adapter waits for the response from the target LOB before throwing an exception. The default value is 1 minute.
receiveTimeout	Receive operation timeout. Essentially, this property specifies for how long adapter waits for an inbound message from the target LOB. Default value is 10 minutes.

When dealing with the timeout exceptions in the outbound scenarios, it may be tempting to solve the problem by simply increasing the sendTimeout value. However, your first line of defense should be communicating with the LOB application administrator to determine whether the problem can be resolved by optimizing performance on the LOB application side. Masking the problem by blindly increasing the sendTimeOut value is definitely not the best solution.

For the inbound operations, you have to set the receiveTimeout property to the value large enough to not interfere with your particular receive location configuration. If you are pulling your hair out trying to figure out why your adapter is behaving totally "unexplainably"—for example, polling the database at random with no apparent pattern intervals instead of using the dedicated configuration properties, the first thing to check is the receiveTimeout settings. In many cases, adjusting this property magically resolves even seemingly unrelated problems. We will return to this subject in subsequent chapters. The default value is 10 minutes; the maximum supported value is 24.20:31:23.6470000 (24 days).

Tracing and message logging

In the situations when your adapter is behaving not as expected, tracing and message logging are handy features provided by the ASDK to help you identify the root of the problem .They are especially useful in the inbound scenarios, where the ASDK adapters and their underlying LOBs may act as clients. In such scenarios, possible exceptions, for example the receive timeouts that we've just discussed, will not be propagated to your BizTalk application. At best, the exceptions may appear in the **Event Viewer** of your BizTalk computer, or not at all at worst, leaving you guessing in the dark.

Using the tracing and message logging capabilities, you can trace and log communication between BizTalk Server and ASDK adapters, within ASDK adapters, and also between ASDK adapters and their target LOB applications in the case of the SAP adapter. In a nutshell, to activate tracing, all you have to do is add tracing options to your application configuration file — Visual Studio for design-time tracing or BizTalk server for runtime. We have put the file names and their locations in the following table:

Application/Environment	Location
Visual Studio, 32-bit environment	`<installation drive>:\Program Files \ Microsoft Visual Studio 10.0\Common7\IDE\ devenv.exe.config`
Visual Studio, 64-bit environment	`<installation drive>:\Program Files (x86)\ Microsoft Visual Studio 10.0\Common7\IDE\ devenv.exe.config`
BizTalkServer, 32-bit environment	`<installation drive>:\Program Files\ Microsoft BizTalk Server 2010\BTSNTSvc.exe. config`
BizTalkServer, 64-bit environment	`<installation drive>:\Program Files (x86)\ Microsoft BizTalk Server 2010\BTSNTSvc.exe. config` for 32-bit host instances
	`<installation drive>:\Program Files (x86)\ Microsoft BizTalk Server 2010\BTSNTSvc64. exe.config` for 64-bit host instances

The product documentation offers ready-to-use configuration sections that you can copy-paste to the appropriate configuration file. Currently, it is available at `http:// msdn.microsoft.com/en-us/library/cc185440(BTS.10).aspx`. If the location changes, you can search using your favorite search engine by "WCF LOB SDK Diagnostic tracing".

Summary

In this chapter, we've laid a good foundation for discussing the features and functionality of the adapters from BizTalk Adapters Pack 2010. We have covered:

- Architectural fundamentals and the reasoning behind introducing a new WCF-based technology, the WCF LOB Adapter SDK (ASDK)
- The major steps involved in enabling BizTalk Applications for consumption of the ASDK-based adapters
- Some of the best practices to make your work more productive and trouble free

In the next chapter, we will introduce you to the WCF SQL Adapter, probably the most widely used adapter from the BizTalk Adapter Pack 2010.

2
WCF LOB SQL Adapter

The **WCF LOB SQL Adapter** is the adapter in the BizTalk Adapter Pack 2010 that offers connectivity to SQL Server databases. It is very common for BizTalk Server solutions to interact with SQL Server databases, making this one of BizTalk's most popular adapters. Like all adapters in the pack it is based on the Microsoft Windows Communication Foundation Line-of-Business Adapter SDK (ASDK). As described in Chapter 1 it can not only be consumed from BizTalk Server solutions, but also from any .NET-based application.

The WCF LOB SQL Adapter (further in the chapter we refer it as the ASDK SQL adapter or just the adapter) should be used as a replacement for the old SQL Adapter. The ASDK SQL adapter offers a variety of new features, improved performance, and supports all versions of SQL Server since SQL Server 2000. The old SQL Adapter relied upon the SQLXML features of SQL Server, whereas the new adapter follows the .NET Framework and communicates with SQL Server through ADO.NET.

 For a more in-depth discussion between the two adapters, refer to this blog post: `http://connectedthoughts.wordpress.com/2011/01/18/wcf-sql-versus-the-old-sql-adapter/`

In the first half of the chapter we will cover the following topics:

- Supported operations
- Consuming adapter at design time in Visual Studio
- Configuring physical ports with BizTalk Admin Console
- Consuming via WCF-Custom vs. WCF-SQL dedicated adapter

In the second part we will build a series of BizTalk applications to illustrate the most common integration scenarios you will likely encounter in your projects.

To get the most from this chapter you have to be familiar with the Consume Adapter Service wizard provided by the ASDK and with the major steps involved in enabling BizTalk applications for consuming the ASDK-based adapters. If you need to refresh your memory, or if you didn't install the BizTalk Adapter Pack 2010 yet, please refer to Chapter 1 where we covered these topics in detail.

Supported operations

The ASDK SQL adapter provides an extensive set of flexible and configurable operations covering virtually all needs a developer may encounter. Depending on where particular operation fits within the messaging subsystem of BizTalk Server, the operations are split into two groups—inbound and outbound.

Inbound operations

In the inbound scenarios the ASDK SQL adapter being a part of the receive port infrastructure queries data from SQL Server. The data is then submitted to the MessageBox for further processing.

The following inbound operations supported by the adapter and their description are listed in the following table:

Operation	Description
TypedPolling	TypedPolling is the most common inbound operation. The schema representing the result set generated by the polling statement is strongly typed, which is very convenient for message transformations using the BizTalk mapper. We will discuss this operation in detail in the Examples section.
Polling	Similar to the TypedPolling operation. The difference is the schema representing the resultset generated by the polling statement is weakly typed. Typically it is used in classic .NET scenarios and rarely by BizTalk Server applications.
Notification	The notification option allows the adapter to receive notifications about changes in the database. We will discuss this operation in the Examples sections.
XmlPolling	The ASDK SQL adapter provides XmlPolling to support existing stored procedures that return XML and for compatibility with the old SQL Adapter. For this operation the Consume Adapter Service wizard offers no support. The schemas for XmlPolling are generated either at runtime by using XMLSCHEMA argument of the FOR XML clause, or manually in Visual Studio.

Outbound operations

In the outbound scenarios the ASDK SQL adapter, being a part of the send port infrastructure, executes operations against database entities and communicates the response back to the caller.

The table below shows the outbound operations supported by the adapters:

Operation	Description
Strongly-Typed Procedures	Enables the BizTalk application to call strongly typed stored procedures. The response message generated by the adapter is strongly typed.
Procedures	Similar to calling Strongly-Typed procedures. The difference is the schema representing the resultset generated by the adapter is weakly typed.
Scalar Functions	Enables the BizTalk solution to call scalar functions and receive scalar value results back.
Table Valued Functions	Enables the BizTalk solution to call table-valued functions and receiving strongly-typed results back.
Tables	Enables the BizTalk solution to execute Select, Insert, Update, and Delete operations against SQL Server tables, and also enables table columns with of `varchar(max)`, `nvarchar(max)`, or `varbinary(max)` data types to be set through the VarText and VarBinary operation types.
Views	Enables the BizTalk solution to execute Select, Insert, Update, and Delete operations against SQL Server views, and also enables view columns of `varchar(max)`, `nvarchar(max)`, or `varbinary(max)` data types to be set through the VarText and VarBinary operation types.
Execute Non Query	Enables execution of any non-SELECT statements including DDL statements. For the INSERT, UPDATE, and DELETE statements the response message contains the number of affected rows. For other statements it is always -1.
Execute Reader	Enables execution of any SELECT statement against tables and views. You can execute multiple statements separated by a semicolon. The response message contains an array of DataSets.
Execute Scalar	Enables execution of any SELECT statement. Only the first column of the first row in the resultset is returned.
Composite Operation	Composite operation is a special type of operation supported by the adapter. It enables the BizTalk solution to combine in any order multiple Insert, Update, Delete, Procedure, and Strongly Typed-Procedure operations into a single operation executed within a single transaction.

We will show the most frequently used outbound operations in the Exercises part of the chapter.

Consuming ASDK SQL Adapter in Visual Studio

As you will remember from Chapter 1, generating the schemas and binding files for the operations you intend to use in your project is one of the major steps enabling consumption of the ASDK-based adapters in BizTalk applications. The tool of choice for this task is the Consume Adapter Service wizard, a design-time tool offered by ASDK. To call the wizard we have to right-click Visual Studio project, select **Add...**, and then **Add Generated Items....** In the **Add Generated Items** windows we need to select **Consume Adapter Service** and click **Add**. Once the **Consume Adapter Service** window shows up, the very first step is to specify the appropriate binding. The ASDK SQL adapter is represented by the sqlBinding—this is what you have to choose in the **Select a binding** drop down list before performing other operations in the Consume Adapter Service wizard.

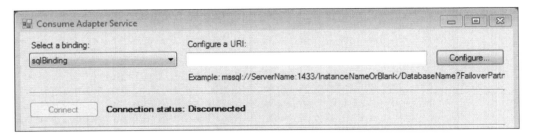

Then, after selecting the binding, we click the **Configure** button to open the Configure Adapter window to specify the database connectivity and binding properties.

Providing credentials

The **Security** tab of the Configure Adapter window allows us to specify credentials to access SQL Server. The ASDK SQL adapter supports only two modes—Windows authentication and SQL Server authentication, but the Client credential type drop down list offers four:

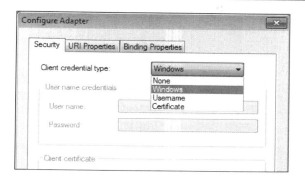

These options are common and intended to cover requirements of different ASDK-based adapters, so let us review the options with respect to the ASDK SQL Adapter:

- **None** – This option is the same as Windows.

- **Windows** – The adapter will use Windows authentication to connect to SQL Server.

- **Username** – The adapter will connect to SQL Server using credentials supplied in the User name and Password fields.

- **Certificate** – Even if the Certificate option is chosen, the adapter will ignore it and use Windows authentication. Users mapped to certificates are not supported, so this option does not apply to the ASDK SQL adapter.

Keep in mind that only the SQL Server objects that the user has permissions to will be shown on the Consume Adapter Service wizard. So please ensure when selecting Windows authentication mode, that the account Visual Studio is running under has the appropriate access to the database objects required for your project. The same applies to the user name specified for the SQL Server authentication.

Connecting to SQL Server URI properties

The URI Properties tab is where we specify the values for the properties necessary to build a connection string to the SQL Server.

For example, to connect to a database called AdventureWorksCh2 on the default instance of SQL Server called BT2010DEV-PC, running on the default port 1433 with no failover server we can specify the following:

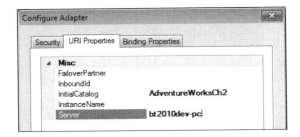

This will map to the following connection URI:

```
mssql://BT2010DEV-PC//AdventureWorksCh2?
```

 Instead of using the URI Properties tab, you can also type connection string into the URI textbox of the main Consume Adapter Service wizard window if this is more convenient for you.

In the general form the URI connection string to the SQL Server looks as follows:

mssql://[Server_Name[:Portno]]/[SQL_SERVER_Instance_Name]/[Database_Name]?FailoverPartner=[Partner_Server_Name]&InboundId=[Inbound_ID] where:

- Server name (Server_Name), port ([:Portno]), and instance name ([SQL_SERVER_Instance_Name]) determine the SQL Server instance to connect to and Database name ([Database_Name]) specifies the database. If you connect to the default instance of the SQL Server, you can leave the SQL_SERVER_Instance_Name part blank.

- The partner server name ([Partner_Server_Name]) is used if the SQL Server instance also has a failover partner to be used by the adapter if the primary server does not respond.

- The last part of the Connection URI to note is InboundID ([Inbound_ID]). It must be set when using TypedPolling operations to generate unique schemas and uniquely identify the corresponding receive location. If we generate schemas with an InboundID, then it is imperative that we also provide this same InboundID in the corresponding Receive Location configuration. If we do not, we will receive a runtime error indicating that BizTalk could not find the document specification by message type.

- Internally, the LOB SQL adapter uses a combination of the URI and binding properties to build a final ADO.NET connection string as explained in the following blog post:

  ```
  http://connectedthoughts.wordpress.com/2011/01/18/how-the-wcf-
  sql-adapter-builds-the-ado-net-connection-string/
  ```

Binding Properties

The **Binding Properties** tab is where we can configure runtime behaviour of the adapter:

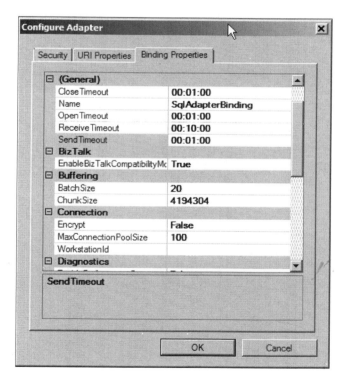

The properties presented on this tab are reflected in the binding file generated by the Consume Adapter Service wizard. For the outbound operations we can usually accept the default values since the defaults are adequate for the majority of the situations. In the situations where the default values are not satisfactory, we can always make adjustments on the physical ports using the BizTalk Admin Console.

For the Inbound operations the picture is a bit more complicated. Due to the nature of the Inbound operations, the Consume Adapter Service Wizard offers no default values and we have to provide configuration settings explicitly. We can do it either at the design time and then import the binding file to create configured receive locations, or we can provide the settings later using BizTalk Admin Console. The only exception is the **PolingStatement** property used to configure the **TypedPolling** inbound operation. This property directly impacts the schema that Consume Adapter Service wizard generates for the operation and therefore must be set at the development time. When we deploy the application, we must ensure that the PollingStatement property set on the receive location is the same as we used at the development time. If this sounds confusing, please read on. We provide detailed coverage of the TypedPolling operation and applicable configuration properties in the examples sections.

Generating schemas

Once we are done with the connectivity and binding settings, we click OK to close the Configure Adapter window and return to the main Consume Adapter Service window. At this point the **Configure a URI** text control contains a connection uri string built off the properties we specified on the **URI** tab of the Configure Adapter window.

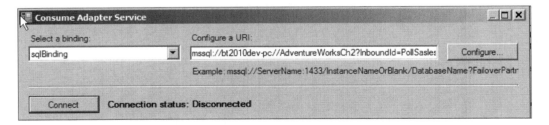

Now we click the **Connect** button; if connection is established successfully, the **Consume Adapter Service** wizard grants us access to the operations exposed by the adapter:

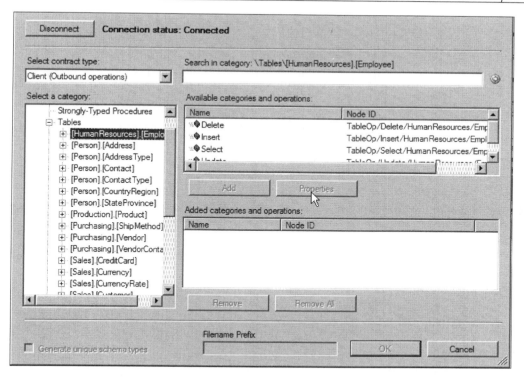

First, we need to select contract type in the **Select contract type** control. Then, in the **Available categories and operations** panel we can select desired operations and click **Add** to add the operations to the **Added categories and operations** list. Once we collected all desired operations, we can click **OK** to close the wizard. This action will return us to Visual Studio where we will see one or more xsd schemas and a binding file added to the project. If we need to generate the schemas for another contract type, we will have to make another trip to the Consume Adapter Service Wizard and repeat the procedure.

ASDK SQL Adapter in the BizTalk Administration Console

After we have deployed an application, and using the BizTalk Admin Console imported the binding files generated for us by the Consume Adapter Service Wizard, we may need to adjust adapter configuration for a particular environment.

Inbound operations

To access adapter properties for the inbound scenarios, we have to navigate to the appropriate receive location and double-click it to bring up the **Receive Location Properties** window. Then click **OK** to open the **WCF-Custom Transport Properties** multi tab dialog.

The **General** tab offers us the Address (URI) text control to set or modify connection string:

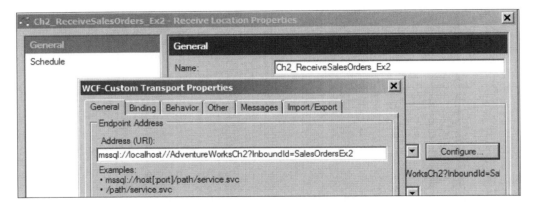

The **Bindings** tab, as its name suggests, is where we can get access to the binding properties:

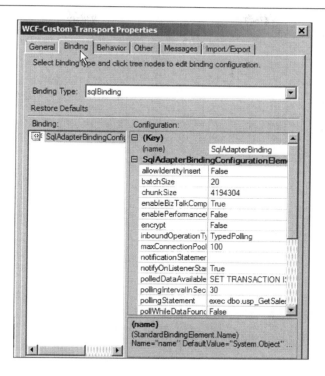

The tab named **Other** is used to specify credentials to access the target database:

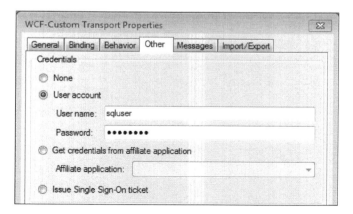

We can employ the following options to specify credentials:

- **None** – the adapter will use Windows authentication and the identity of the account Receive Handler host instance is running under

- **User account** – this option allows specifying user name and password to connect to the target database with SQL Server authentication mode
- **Get credentials from affiliate application** – allow specifying a Single Sign-On affiliate application to get the credentials from

In the majority of cases you won't need to deal with the configuration options provided by the **Behavior**, **Messages**, and **Import/Export** tabs. If it is still necessary, please refer to the WCF-Custom adapter documentation.

Outbound operations

The configuration procedure for the outbound scenarios is essentially the same as for the inbound. You have to locate the appropriate send port, double-click it to open the **Send Port Properties** window, and then click the **Configure** button to open the **WCF-Custom Transport Properties** window. The **General** tab provides you access to the URI connection string and also to the SOAP actions.

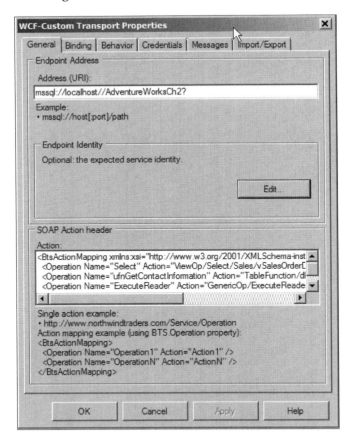

The **Credentials** tab as you can guess allows you to provide credentials to access the database:

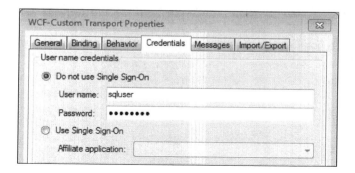

Available options are:

- **Do Not Use Single Sign On** – the adapter will connect to the database using Windows authentication and the Send Handler account identity if the User name and Password fields are blank. Otherwise the adapter will use SQL Server authentication with the credentials specified in the User name and Password controls.

- **Use Single Sign On** allows the selection of a Single Sign On affiliate application to provide the credentials.

As with the receive locations, the properties presented on the **General, Bindings, and Credentials** tabs cover the majority of configuration scenarios. For complex situations, please refer to the WCF-Custom adapter documentation.

WCF-SQL vs. WCF-Custom adapter

Besides WCF-Custom, the sqlBinding representing the ASDK SQL adapter can also be accessed through the dedicated WCF-SQL BizTalk adapter installed with the BizTalk Server 2010 Adapter Pack. The difference between these adapters is the WCF-SQL adapter offers a bit more intuitive UI tailored specifically for the sqlBinding. For example, by clicking **Configure** on the **General** tab of the dedicated WCF-SQL adapter we can populate a table to build a connection string, while with generic WCF-Custom we have to type in the entire string directly as you just have seen in the previous section.

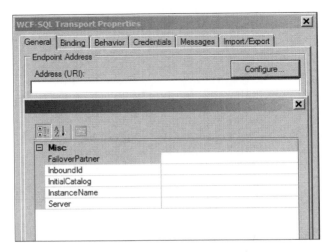

To create the WCF-SQL adapter we need to perform the following steps in the BizTalk Admin Console:

1. Right mouse click on **Adapters** and then select **New – Adapter**.

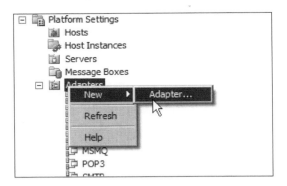

2. Click the **Adapter** drop-down list and select **WCF-SQL**. In the **Name** text box, type in **WCF-SQL** and click **OK** button:

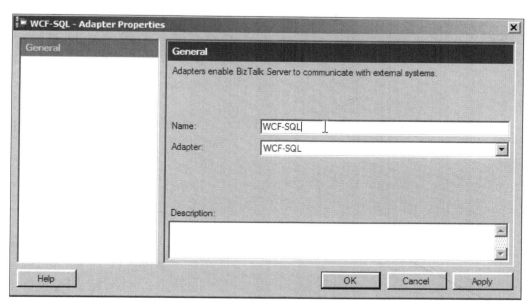

It is important to understand that no matter whether you use the WCF-Custom Adapter or WCF-SQL adapter you are not losing functionality. Using the WCF-SQL adapter simplifies the administration tasks that are involved in maintaining BizTalk environment. Since the WCF-Custom adapter can leverage many different bindings including Oracle, SQL, SAP, and bindings that allow us to connect to the cloud, it may be beneficial to explicitly create dedicated adapters to avoid confusion. The trade-off is that the binding files generated for you at the development time will be of no help, since they use the WCF-Custom adapter. The bottom line is that there is no right or wrong way; you can choose either depending on your personal style and preferences. In this chapter we rely on WCF-Custom; in the SAP chapter, we will use the dedicated WCF-SAP adapter so that you will be able to compare approaches. To finalize this discussion we want to provide you with a URL you may find useful if you choose to use the WCF-SQL adapter and therefore need to configure the SOAP actions manually. Following the links presented on the page located at http:// msdn.microsoft.com/en-US/library/dd788515(v=BTS.10).aspx, you will find the SOAP actions for the operations supported by the ASDK SQL adapter.

ASDK SQL adapter examples

In this section we will cover some of the frequently used operations provided by the ASDK SQL adapter. We prepared a few easy to follow examples that focus on the details of the adapter operations and not on building the entire BizTalk application itself or the details of the SQL Server objects used.

For these examples we have a scenario where sales order details are kept inside a few different tables in a SQL Server database. Scripts to generate database artifacts are provided with the sample code accompanying this chapter.

The three main tables used in the examples are SalesOrderHeader, SalesOrderStatus, and SalesOrderDetails.

The **SalesOrderHeader** table contains the base information about the order including when it is due, shipped, the Account number, CustomerID, SalesPersonID, and so on:

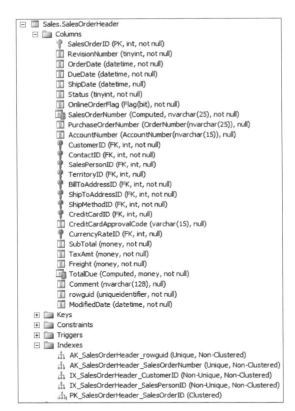

The **SalesOrderStatus** table tracks the status of the Order from a systems integration perspective. Since we do not want BizTalk to process orders multiple times, we need to manage the records that have been consumed. This table provides us the ability to mark records as being processed by specifying a GUID in the **ProcessingIndicator** field. When it is set to NULL it identifies that the rows need to be processed by BizTalk Server.

The **OrderStatus** column is used to identify different stages of the sales order processing, and SalesOrderID is the link to the tables actually holding sales order information:

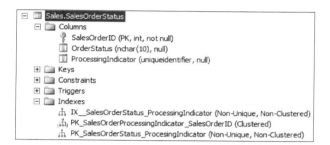

The **SalesOrderDetail** table provides us with some supplementary information about the order including the **UnitPrice**, **Discount**, **CarrierTracking Number**, and so on:

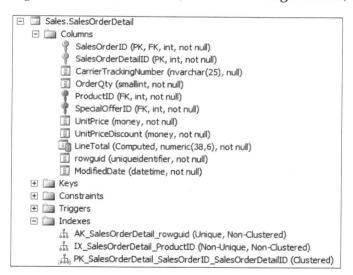

The best practices for the old SQL adapter still apply to the new ASDK SQL adapter when it comes to designing the receive side T-SQL code to avoid deadlocks. The main difference is the new adapter does not require FOR XML at the end of stored procedures, and the schemas it generates are easier to configure for debatching. The old SQL adapter best practices can be found online here: `http://msdn.microsoft.com/en-us/library/cc507804(BTS.10).aspx`

SQL Server deadlocks can occur or duplicate data retrieved if the T-SQL code being called by the adapter cannot be changed to follow best practices and there are multiple BizTalk Server host instances mapped to the host that runs the polling receive location. In these cases, clustering the host can be a way of ensuring that the solution is highly available while still avoiding deadlocks.

More information on clustering BizTalk hosts can be found here: `http://kentweare.blogspot.com/2009/04/clustering-biztalk-hosts.html`.

Another option is to set the appropriate to your scenario transaction isolation level. Follow this link `http://msdn.microsoft.com/en-us/library/dd788041(v=bts.10).aspx for details.`

Example 1—TypedPolling and debatching

This first example will demonstrate how the **TypedPolling** operation of the ASDK SQL adapter can be used to poll the database for sales orders that haven't yet been processed by the BizTalk Server.

The **TypedPolling** operation is the most frequent operation used when BizTalk Server solutions need to poll SQL Server for data. The schema for the polling results is strongly typed and can be easily used in maps or have its elements promoted for content-based routing.

We have created a stored procedure that returns the first 100 rows that have not yet been processed by BizTalk Server. We will describe the store procedure in more details later.

Since we already have a stored procedure, as provided in our database script for this example, our next step is to generate the typed schema representing the resultset generated by the procedure. In the Consume Adapter Service Wizard we set **sqlBinding** as the binding and click **Configure** to open the **Configure Adapter** window to specify the URI and Binding Properties. On the **URI Properties** tab we set the properties to connect to our sample **AdventureWorksCh2** database. Note, if your SQL server is local, you can specify "localhost" for the **Server** property:

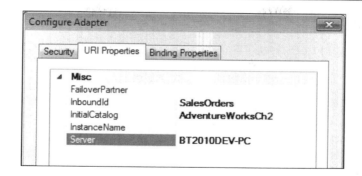

The value of **InboundId** is used by the adapter when building the namespace for the TypedPolling inbound operation schemas and also in the binding file that it generates containing the BizTalk port configuration that will be used later. This value ensures the connection URI is unique across multiple receive locations that poll from the same database. It is very important that we use the same **InboundId** when configuring our Receive Location as we used in the Consume Adapter Service wizard. Otherwise, we can expect a BizTalk runtime error.

The **Binding Properties** tab is where we set the adapter properties that support the typed polling operation. Here are some of the significant properties that we need to set:

1. The **inboundOperationType** needs to be set to for this scenario. Since we are interested in receiving a strongly typed result set from SQL Server, we need to populate this property with a value of **TypedPolling.**

2. The **PolledDataAvailableStatement** is used at runtime to check whether any data is available to be polled. If it returns a positive value in its first column then the **PollingStatement** statementis executed. The benefit approach to this is that we can provide a lightweight query to determine if data exists as opposed to a more complex polling query that may consume more resources when executing. In this example we configure the **PolledDataAvailableStatement** with a query that checks for sales orders not yet processed:

    ```
    SET TRANSACTION ISOLATION LEVEL READ COMMITTED
    SELECT COUNT(*) FROM Sales.SalesOrderStatus  WITH(UPDLOCK ROWLOCK
    READPAST)
    WHERE OrderStatus = 'Pending'AND ProcessingIndicator IS NULL
    ```
    update prevented ↓

    records that are locked are not returned

3. You may have noticed we are setting the isolation level at the beginning of the statement and providing SQL hints on the select query. This is to avoid deadlocks in multi-server environments.

4. The **PollingStatement** setting is the statement that will be executed every time the **PolledDataAvailableStatement** returns a positive value. The same **PollingStatement** used during development must be used when configuring receive location. This is required since the setting is used by the adapter at the runtime to create a message matching the schema generated by the Consume Adapter Service wizard. For the purpose of this example we are going to set our PollingStatement to a stored procedure that returns the first 100 sales orders that haven't yet been processed and marks them as processed:

```
exec dbo.usp_GetSalesOrdersToProcess
```

> You can also separate multiple T-SQL statements with a semi-colon. For example, if you have a stored procedure to get the sales orders and another to mark them as processed, the PollingStatement can be:
>
> ```
> exec dbo.usp_GetSalesOrdersToProcess; exec dbo.usp_
> UpdateSalesOrdersToProcess
> ```

Our stored procedure updates the ProcessingIndicator column with a new GUID value for the first 100 rows where the ProcessingIndicator is NULL. Then it returns the data in the SalesOrderHeader table that relate to those 100 rows. We have chosen to update the records that we want to process before selecting them. By using this approach, we can ensure that we are controlling the amount of records that we want to return to BizTalk per polling event. Here is the stored procedure:

```
CREATE PROCEDURE [dbo].[usp_GetSalesOrdersToProcess]
AS
SET nocounton
set xact_abort on
SET TRANSACTION ISOLATION LEVEL READ COMMITTED

declare @procIndicator uniqueidentifier
set @procIndicator =NEWID();


UPDATE Sales.SalesOrderStatus WITH (ROWLOCK)
SET ProcessingIndicator = @procIndicator,
    OrderStatus ='Processing'
FROM (
SELECT TOP 100 SalesOrderID
FROM  Sales.SalesOrderStatus WITH(UPDLOCK ROWLOCK READPAST)
```

```
WHERE ProcessingIndicator IS NULL AND OrderStatus ='Pending' ORDER
BY SalesOrderID)
AS t1
WHERE (Sales.SalesOrderStatus.SalesOrderID = t1.SalesOrderID)

SELECT TOP 100 soh.[SalesOrderID],[RevisionNumber]
,[OrderDate],[DueDate]
,[ShipDate],[Status]
,[SalesOrderNumber],[PurchaseOrderNumber]
,[AccountNumber],[CustomerID]
,[ContactID],[BillToAddressID]
,[ShipToAddressID],[ShipMethodID]
,[CreditCardApprovalCode],[SubTotal]
,[TaxAmt],[Freight]
,[TotalDue],[Comment]
FROM Sales.SalesOrderHeader soh WITH(UPDLOCKROWLOCKREADPAST)
    INNERJOIN Sales.SalesOrderStatus sos ON soh.SalesOrderID = sos.
SalesOrderID
WHERE sos.ProcessingIndicator = @procIndicator
```

5. The **PollingIntervalInSeconds** specifies how often BizTalk Server will run the SQL statement set on the **PolledDataAvailableStatement** property. The polling interval must be set carefully to both avoid unnecessary polling when the data doesn't change often but to also poll at a frequency high enough to pick up the changes on a timely basis. We set it to 60 seconds.

6. The last property to cover for our example is **PollWhileDataFound**. Our goal is to get batches of 100 sales orders from SQL Server. Setting a limit on the number of rows returned by the polling statement in conjunction with the **PollWhileDataFound** property (when set to true) is a good practice to ensure multiple smaller messages are created by the adapter. This technique is also important because more than one message can be processed in parallel by BizTalk Server instead of creating one large message. When set to true, the **PollWhileDataFound** property instructs the adapter to ignore the **PollingInterval** property and call the polling statement continuously. For our current example, we have set this property to **False** so that we can clearly understand BizTalk's polling behavior. If we processed all data continually it would reduce our visibility into BizTalk's polling cycles.

Here is the **Binding Properties** tab configured for our example:

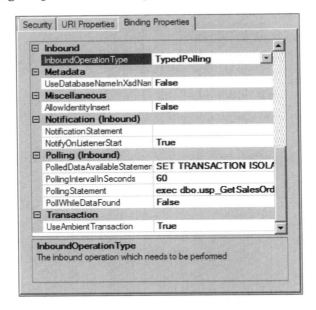

A property that deserves special attention in polling scenarios is **ReceiveTimeout**. This property indicates the amount of time that the adapter will wait for an inbound message. The Microsoft documentation recommends setting this property to the maximum allowed value of 24.20:31:23.6470000 (24 days). Setting a large value like this does not impact the performance of the adapter. We do need to ensure that this value exceeds our Polling interval to ensure that we have connectivity between our BizTalk Server(s) and SQL Server before reaching this timeout threshold.

For more information regarding ASDK SQL Adapter properties, please visit the following TechNet link: `http://technet.microsoft.com/en-us/library/dd787981(BTS.10).aspx`

After we have set the binding properties we need to connect to our SQL Server, select
Service (Inbound operations), select the root / category, and add the **TypedPolling**
operation:

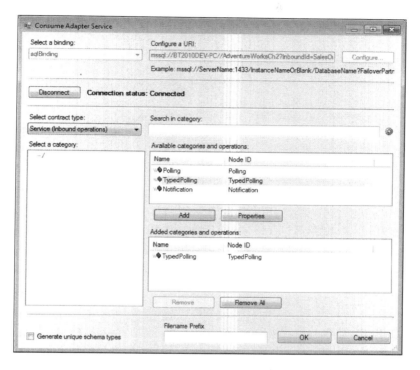

Once we have configured our Consume Adapter Service wizard as illustrated in the
preceding image, we can now click the **OK** button. The Consume Adapter Service
wizard then adds a schema to the BizTalk Server project (the schema is called
`TypedPolling.SalesOrders.xsd` in this example) and also creates a binding file
containing configuration details for the physical receive port and location.

The schema that will be used in our Typed Polling scenario includes an array of the result sets of the stored procedure. The schema is easy to configure if we want it further debatched by BizTalk Server. Our stored procedure was created to return 100 sales orders at the most with each poll. We can modify the schema created by the adapter so that the **XmlDisassembler** pipeline will split each of these repeating nodes into individual messages. The first step is to set the <Schema> node's **Envelope** property to Yes:

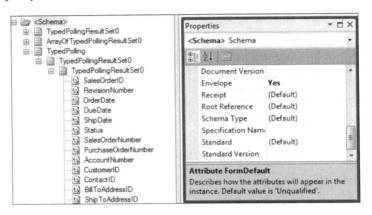

Then, set the **Body Xpath** value of the TypedPolling node to the first TypedPollingResultSet0. This will tell the XmlDisassembler that anything below this record should be disassembled into a separate message:

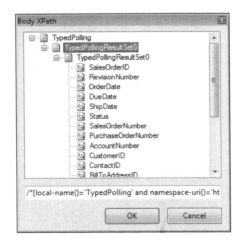

The previous two steps are all that need to be set during development for the TypedPolling schema to configure its messages to be debatched.

After deploying the solution, the binding file that was created by the Consume Adapter Service wizard can be imported into the BizTalk Administration Console to create the receive port and receive location with all the URI and binding settings we created during development. Included in the sample code is a sample binding file for the entire solution.

This receive location will then poll for sales orders that have not yet been processed, pass them to BizTalk Server as a batch, and each message containing the sales order information is debatched. The following XML shows one of the debatched messages:

```xml
<TypedPollingResultSet0 xmlns="http://schemas.microsoft.com/
Sql/2008/05/TypedPolling/SalesOrders">
<SalesOrderID>43669</SalesOrderID>
<RevisionNumber>10</RevisionNumber>
<OrderDate>2001-07-01T00:00:00Z</OrderDate>
<DueDate>2001-07-13T00:00:00Z</DueDate>
<ShipDate>2001-07-08T00:00:00Z</ShipDate>
<Status>5</Status>
<SalesOrderNumber>SO43669</SalesOrderNumber>
<PurchaseOrderNumber>PO14123169936</PurchaseOrderNumber>
<AccountNumber>10-4020-000578</AccountNumber>
<CustomerID>578</CustomerID>
<ContactID>295</ContactID>
<BillToAddressID>895</BillToAddressID>
<ShipToAddressID>895</ShipToAddressID>
<ShipMethodID>5</ShipMethodID>
<CreditCardApprovalCode>25877Vi80261</CreditCardApprovalCode>
<SubTotal>881.4687</SubTotal>
<TaxAmt>70.5175</TaxAmt>
<Freight>22.0367</Freight>
<TotalDue>974.0229</TotalDue>
</TypedPollingResultSet0>
```

This example demonstrated how the ASDK SQL Adapter and BizTalk Server's out of the box functionality can be used to poll and extract data from SQL Server.

Example 2—Select, Table Valued Function, and Execute Reader

This second example builds on the first but focuses on the outbound operations. We will extend the scenario by making subsequent calls to other sales order related tables to retrieve data that completes the message with all the required details about the sales order.

For this example we will query other SQL Server objects related to each debatched message from the first example to demonstrate some of the outbound adapter operations, and then build a final canonical message with all the sales order details.

The following database objects are used to enrich the sales order details:

- A SQL view called Sales.vSalesOrderDetailProduct that returns order line detail including product information. The ASDK SQL adapter supports querying SQL Server tables and views. The limitation with using this approach is we cannot join Views with other Views or Tables from an ASDK SQL adapter call. However, there is a resolution to this problem. The SQL Server View can be modified to accommodate any additional data requirements that we may have.

- A table-valued function ufnGetContactInformation that returns contact details. Table-valued functions work much like Stored Procedures, from a BizTalk perspective. We are able to provide a strongly typed request and receive a strongly typed response.

- A dynamic select statement that will be executed by using the ExecuteReader operation to retrieve extra customer details. The ExecuteReader operation is a very flexible operation since it does not have strongly typed result sets and developers do not require access to the table at design time. The challenge with this approach is it requires the BizTalk developer to deal with untyped response messages coming from SQL Server. This may require us to write custom XSLT if we want to parse, or transform these response messages.

To generate the schemas for the outbound operations used in this example, after establishing successful connection, we set **Client(Outbound operations)** in the **Select contract type** drop down list. In the **Select a category** panel we expanded the Views node, select vSalesOrderDetailView and added "Select" to the list of desired operations. Then, we added ufnGetContactInformation function located under the **Table Valued Functions** node. Lastly, we add **ExecuteReader** operation located under the "/" root node.

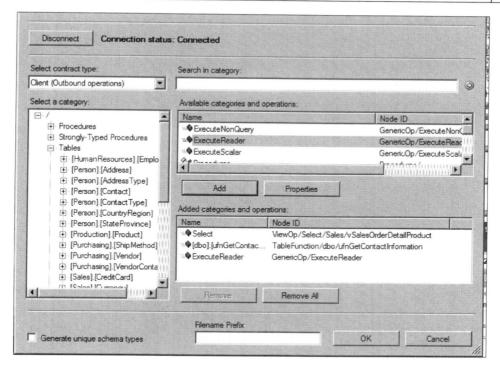

We can now click the **OK** button to close the wizard and generate the schemas.

First let's discuss the schema for the SELECT operation we want to execute on the vSalesOrderDetailProduct view. To build a SELECT statement, the ASDK SQL adapter requires us to specify desired columns separated by commas in the **Columns** element under the **Select** node. The **Query** element under the same node is where we specify the "WHERE" clause to filter out the result set of the SELECT statement.

The response part of the schema is strongly typed and contains all the columns from the vSalesOrderDetailProduct view. Note the columns are defined with the Min. Occurs. xsd property set to 0. It means the resulting response message from the adapter will contain only the columns listed in the **Columns** element:

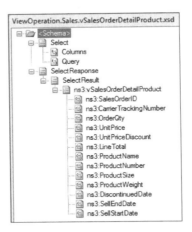

For the table-valued functions the Consume Adapter Service wizard generates a schema that allows us to provide values for the function parameters — note the **ContactId** element under the **ufnGetContactInformation** node. The response part of the schema is strongly typed and contains the definition of the table returned by the ufnGetContactInformation function:

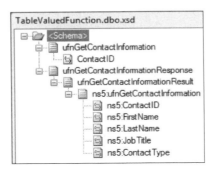

To perform the **ExecuteReader** operation, we need to specify a SELECT statement in the **Query** element under the **ExecuteReader** node. The response generated by the adapter for this operation is an array of the DataSet nodes. Each DataSet node in the schema has two <Any> elements, the first will have a schema of the DataSet, and the second will be an ADO.NET diffgram of the data itself:

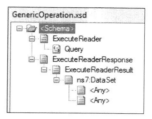

Now that we have the schemas for the outbound operations, we can create a single map to generate all three request messages at once from the incoming sales order header message. To generate a multi-destination map we double clicked the Transform shape, specified **Transform.SalesOrder_to_LookupRequests** name for a New Map, and then specified the request and three response messages:

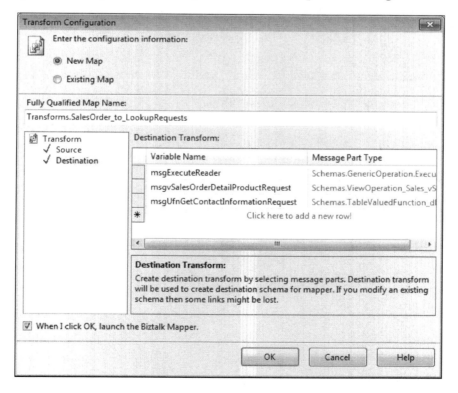

Once we clicked **OK** the Map designer showed up containing our three schemas packed in one destination schema.

The following image shows the fully configured map used in our sample application:

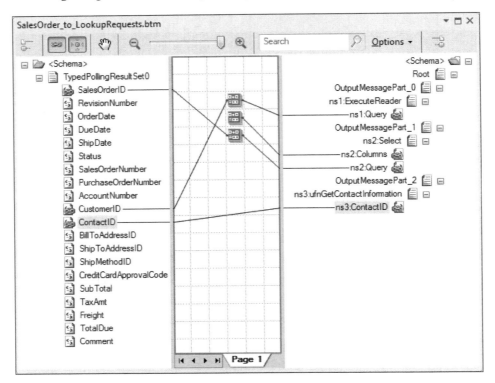

To set the **Query** property of the **ExecuteReader** request message, we use a string concatenate functoid to build a select statement made up of multiple table joins to return address information for a customer. We then link the CustomerID element from the source message to finalize the statement with the WHERE clause:

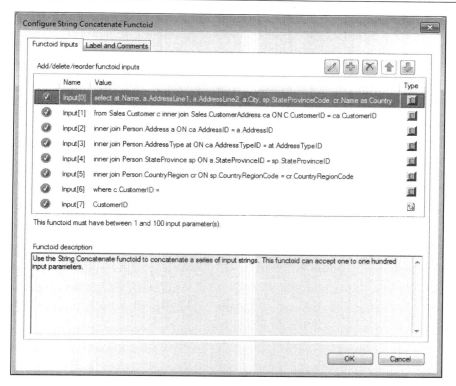

For the select statement we want to run against the vSalesOrderDetailsProduct view, we need to specify the required columns and a WHERE clause. A string concatenate functoid is used to set the Columns element to *. This will tell the adapter that all columns from the view should be selected. Another string concatenate functoid is used to populate the Query element. We use the SalesOrderID element from the input schema to build the WHERE clause **where SalesOrderID =SalesOrderID**.

Lastly, we need to specify the input parameter for the ufnGetContactInformation table valued function. This function has only one parameter: ContactID. So we drag the ContactID from the source schema to the ContactID element of the destination schema.

A nice feature of BizTalk is the ability to reuse logical ports within an orchestration. This allows us to bind our logical port to a single physical port in the BizTalk Administration Console, for all three lookups. This reduces the amount of send ports that we have to create and maintain. We can also use a parallel shape in the orchestration to execute all three operations at the same time.

To represent a complete sales order, we have a schema named SalesOrder.xsd. After the parallel shape finishes and all three operations have been run against SQL Server, we can then map their responses and the original sales order header data to the final SalesOrder message:

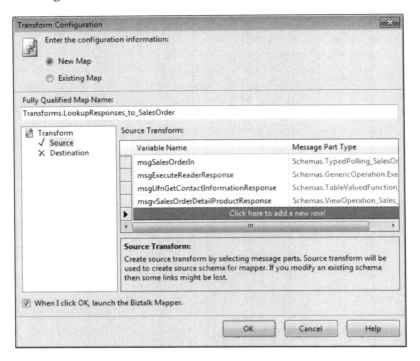

This is what the LookupResponses_to_SalesOrder map looks like:

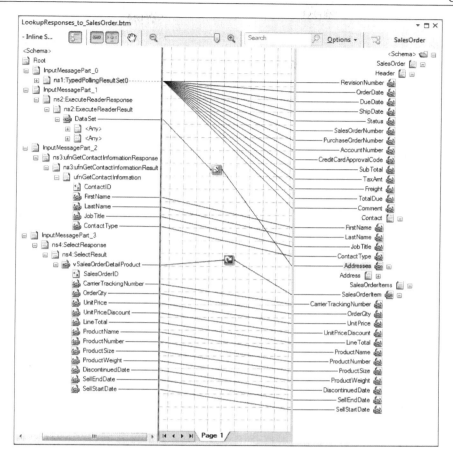

As you can see, the preceding map is pretty straightforward with the exception of the ExecuteReaderResponse node. As we previously discussed, the Execute Reader operation has a tradeoff. The tradeoff is that our result set will be untyped, which means we need to perform some custom work to transform this message into a strongly typed message. To achieve this we need to write some XSLT and use an Inline XSLT Call Template scripting functoid to map the diffgram contents:

```
<xsl:templatename="AddressTemplate">
  <xsl:paramname="param1" />
    <xsl:iftest="count(//NewTable) > 0">
      <xsl:elementname="Addresses">
        <xsl:for-eachselect="//NewTable">
          <xsl:elementname="Address">
            <xsl:iftest="Name">
              <xsl:elementname="Name">
                <xsl:value-ofselect="Name"/>
```

```
          </xsl:element>
        </xsl:if>
        <xsl:if test="AddressLine1">
          <xsl:element name="AddressLine1">
          <xsl:value-ofselect="AddressLine1"/>
          </xsl:element>
        </xsl:if>
        <xsl:if test="AddressLine2">
          <xsl:element name="AddressLine2">
            <xsl:value-ofselect="AddressLine2"/>
          </xsl:element>
        </xsl:if>
        <xsl:if test="City">
          <xsl:element name="City">
            <xsl:value-ofselect="City"/>
          </xsl:element>
        </xsl:if>
        <xsl:if test="StateProvinceCode">
          <xsl:element name="StateProvinceCode">
            <xsl:value-ofselect="StateProvinceCode"/>
          </xsl:element>
        </xsl:if>
        <xsl:if test="Country">
          <xsl:element name="Country">
            <xsl:value-ofselect="Country"/>
          </xsl:element>
        </xsl:if>
      </xsl:element>
    </xsl:for-each>
  </xsl:element>
  </xsl:if>
</xsl:template>
```

That is it for the development phase of the example. The final orchestration with the two maps and all three outbound operations executed in parallel looks like this:

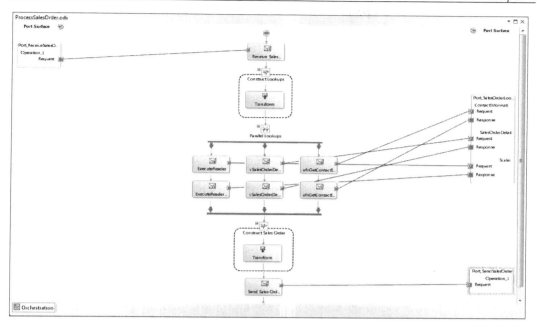

Now that the development of the solution is done we can deploy it and import the binding file that is available in the `BindingFiles` folder that is part of this chapter's source code. This binding file creates a send port, which is shared by the three operations with the same binding properties as the ones we set when creating the schemas. The important part to review is the SOAP Action header property on the General tab of the WCF-Custom adapter:

```
<BtsActionMappingxmlns:xsi=http://www.w3.org/2001/XMLSchema-
instancexmlns:xsd="http://www.w3.org/2001/XMLSchema">
<OperationName="Select"
Action="ViewOp/Select/Sales/vSalesOrderDetailProduct" />
<OperationName="ufnGetContactInformation"
Action="TableFunction/dbo/ufnGetContactInformation" />
<OperationName="ExecuteReader"
Action="GenericOp/ExecuteReader" />
</BtsActionMapping>
```

This provides a mapping between the operations and the SOAP actions. Please refer back to Chapter 1 for detailed information pertaining to how SOAP actions and operations work together.

When we enable our solution, after a few seconds we will have new messages containing sales order data. Here is an example of a processed sales order:

```xml
<ns0:SalesOrder xmlns:ns0=http://Schemas.SalesOrder xmlns:xsi="http://
www.w3.org/2001/XMLSchema-instance">
<Header>
<RevisionNumber>28</RevisionNumber>
<OrderDate>2001-07-01T00:00:00Z</OrderDate>
<DueDate>2001-07-13T00:00:00Z</DueDate>
<ShipDate>2001-07-08T00:00:00Z</ShipDate>
<Status>5</Status>
<SalesOrderNumber>SO43660</SalesOrderNumber>
<PurchaseOrderNumber>PO18850127500</PurchaseOrderNumber>
<AccountNumber>10-4020-000117</AccountNumber>
<CreditCardApprovalCode>115213Vi29411</CreditCardApprovalCode>
<SubTotal>1553.1035</SubTotal>
<TaxAmt>124.2483</TaxAmt>
<Freight>38.8276</Freight>
<TotalDue>1716.1794</TotalDue>
<Contact>
<FirstName>Takiko</FirstName>
<LastName>Collins</LastName>
<JobTitle>Purchasing Manager</JobTitle>
<ContactType>Store Contact</ContactType>
<Addresses>
<Address>
<Name>Main Office</Name>
<AddressLine1>6055 Shawnee Industrial Way</AddressLine1>
<City>Suwanee</City>
<StateProvinceCode>GA </StateProvinceCode>
<Country>United States</Country>
</Address>
</Addresses>
</Contact>
</Header>
<Items>
<Item>
<CarrierTrackingNumber>6431-4D57-83</CarrierTrackingNumber>
<OrderQty>1</OrderQty>
<UnitPrice>419.4589</UnitPrice>
<UnitPriceDiscount>0.0000</UnitPriceDiscount>
<LineTotal>419.458900</LineTotal>
<ProductName>Road-650 Red, 44</ProductName>
```

```
<ProductNumber>BK-R50R-44</ProductNumber>
<ProductSize>44</ProductSize>
<ProductWeight>18.77</ProductWeight>
<SellEndDate>2003-06-30T00:00:00Z</SellEndDate>
<SellStartDate>2001-07-01T00:00:00Z</SellStartDate>
</Item>
<Item>
<CarrierTrackingNumber>6431-4D57-83</CarrierTrackingNumber>
<OrderQty>1</OrderQty>
<UnitPrice>874.7940</UnitPrice>
<UnitPriceDiscount>0.0000</UnitPriceDiscount>
<LineTotal>874.794000</LineTotal>
<ProductName>Road-450 Red, 52</ProductName>
<ProductNumber>BK-R68R-52</ProductNumber>
<ProductSize>52</ProductSize>
<ProductWeight>17.42</ProductWeight>
<SellEndDate>2002-06-30T00:00:00Z</SellEndDate>
<SellStartDate>2001-07-01T00:00:00Z</SellStartDate>
</Item>
</Items>
</ns0:SalesOrder>
```

Example 3–Query notification and multiple result sets

In this example we will introduce two advanced features of the ASDK SQL Adapter. We will use query notifications to replace the typed polling used in previous examples to retrieve sales orders that haven't yet been processed. We will also use multiple result sets to retrieve information from the sales order and replace the lookup operations created in Example 2.

Although polling inbound operations are very common, the polling principle itself requires some consideration. Polling frequently when there is no data to be returned is a waste of systems resources. Polling infrequently when there is data to be returned means the solution is not as efficient as it could be. Careful consideration of the polling interval and polling statement can mitigate these constraints but notification is an alternate and often better option.

The ASDK SQL adapter help information has a great section on the differences between notification and polling and may be found in the following article:

`http://msdn.microsoft.com/en-us/library/`
`dd788096(BTS.10).aspx`

ADO.NET provides the ASDK SQL adapter with a notification option: query notifications. Query notifications are built on top of SQL Server Service Broker queues and raise events into BizTalk Server whenever the results of a SQL Server query changes. The adapter encapsulates this feature, using the ADO.NET SqlDependency notification object to receive the notification information when a query result changes.

We can configure the notification properties in the Configure Adapter window and the **Binding** properties tab. The two available properties are **NotificationStatement** and **NotifyOnListenerStart**. These settings have no impact on the SQL Schemas that we will generate in the Consume Adapter Service wizard and will be discussed in greater detail when we configure our Receive Location.

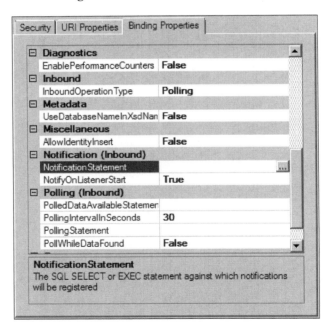

Once the Connection URI has been entered, we need to click **Connect** and ensure **Service (Inbound operations)** is selected as the contract type since Query Notification is an inbound operation. Next, we select the **Notification** operation and click the **OK** button.

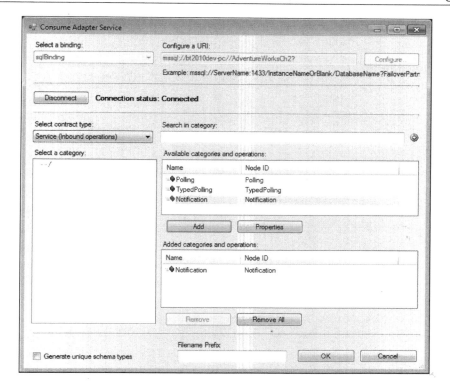

The schema created for the Notification operation is universal and serves to simply tell your BizTalk Server solution that there is data for it to process:

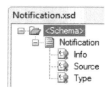

The elements of the schema relate to information received by ADO.NET about the query change contains:

- **Info** – This one element holds a value of the System.Data.SqlClient. SqlNotificationInfo enumeration providing additional information about notification received by the adapter.

- **Source** – This will contain a value of the System.Data.SqlClient. SqlNotificationSource enumeration indicating the source of the notification received by the adapter.

- **Type** – This will contain a value of the System.Data.SqlClient. SqlNotificationType enumeration. Most of the time this will be a change, indicating that there was a change on the data of the notification query.

  Please refer to the MSDN for the detailed information on these enumerations.

When the **NotifyOnListenerStart** binding option, in our Receive Location, is set to true, a notification message with hardcoded values of Info = ListenerStarted, Source = SqlBinding, and Type = Startup is generated by the adapter.

Our orchestration will filter out the unwanted notification messages, retrieve any sales orders to be processed, and then debatch the sales orders. Note how we have distinguished all three elements of the notification schema. This is because we will use them in a **Decide** shape in this orchestration. Here is the beginning of the orchestration, including the expression we use to filter out only insert, update, or listener started notifications:

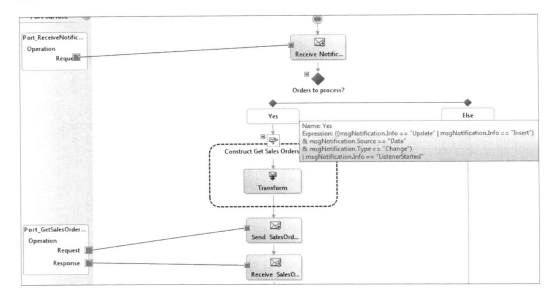

If the notification matches our decide shape criteria, the orchestration executes a stored procedure called **usp_GetSalesOrdersToProcess** that retrieves the list of sales orders to be processed. Before debatching, via an Xpath statement within a Message Assignment shape, the orchestration first checks if there is actual data to be processed by counting the number of sales orders returned by the stored procedure. This is important since a raised notification does not always mean there are sales orders to be processed because we have **NotifiyOnListenerStart** set to True. Here is the part of the orchestration that debatches the orders into individual messages:

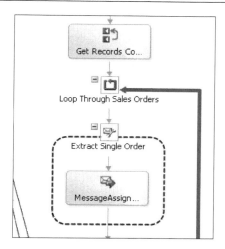

We provide the response message msgGetSalesOrdersToProcessResp to the xpath method available in orchestration expression shape. This xpath expression will count the number of nodes returned by the stored procedure. Here is the full expression used to determine if we have sales orders that need to be processed:

```
recCount = System.Convert.ToInt32(xpath(msgGetSalesOrdersToProcess
Resp, "count(/*[local-name()='usp_GetSalesOrdersToProcessResponse'
and namespace-uri()='http://schemas.microsoft.com/Sql/2008/05/
TypedProcedures/dbo']/*[local-name()='StoredProcedureResultSet0'
and namespace-uri()='http://schemas.microsoft.com/Sql/2008/05/
TypedProcedures/dbo']/*[local-name()='StoredProcedureResultSet0'
and namespace-uri()='http://schemas.microsoft.com/Sql/2008/05/
ProceduresResultSets/dbo/usp_GetSalesOrdersToProcess'])"));
```

Use the **Instance XPath** property of the element you would like to evaluate in the BizTalk schema editor to find out the correct xpath to use. The property is described in the following page:

```
http://msdn.microsoft.com/en-us/library/
ee253960(BTS.10).aspx
```

Now we have query notifications replacing typed polling. The development implementation is more complex but the main advantages of the changes made to the solution are as follows:

- Once the process indicator has been set, our outstanding Sales Orders will be processed immediately

- There are fewer calls to the database since we are not polling anymore, keeping system resource utilization to a minimum

The next improvement we will make to the solution is related to how we enrich the sales order information before sending out the final sales order message. A great feature of the ASDK SQL Adapter is that it can handle multiple resultsets. We have created a stored procedure called usp_GetSalesOrderDetails that takes in the sales order ID and performs three distinct select statements, one for each of the three lookups of Example2—the function call, the select statement, and the view call. Here is the stored procedure:

```
CREATE PROCEDURE [dbo].[usp_GetSalesOrderDetails]
@SalesOrderId [int]
AS
SET no count on
setxact_aborton
SET TRANSACTION ISOLATION LEVEL READ COMMITTED

DECLARE @ContactId int

SELECT * FROM Sales.vSalesOrderDetailProduct
WHERE SalesOrderID = @SalesOrderId

SELECT
at.Name, a.AddressLine1
, a.AddressLine2, a.City
, sp.StateProvinceCode, cr.Name as Country
FROM
Sales.SalesOrderHeader soh
inner join Sales.Customer c on soh.CustomerID = c.CustomerID
inner join Sales.CustomerAddress ca ON C.CustomerID = ca.CustomerID
inner join Person.Address a ON ca.AddressID = a.AddressID
inner join Person.AddressType at ON ca.AddressTypeID =
at.AddressTypeID
inner join Person.StateProvince sp ON a.StateProvinceID =
sp.StateProvinceID
innerjoin Person.CountryRegion cr ON sp.CountryRegionCode =
cr.CountryRegionCode
WHERE soh.SalesOrderID = @SalesOrderId

SELECT @ContactId = ContactId FROM Sales.SalesOrderHeader
WHERE SalesOrderID = @SalesOrderId
SELECT * FROM dbo.ufnGetContactInformation(@ContactId)
```

The ASDK SQL adapter will handle the generation of a schema that conforms to all three result sets. Here is what the stored procedure schema looks like after it is selected in the Consume Adapter Service wizard as the Strongly-Typed Procedures outbound operation. Note how it has SalesOrderId as an input under the usp_GetSalesOrderDetails node, and returns all three strongly typed results:

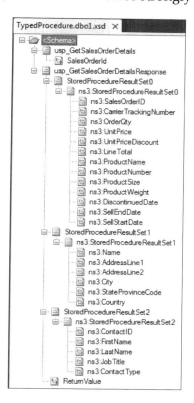

By creating this stored procedure and using the multiple result sets feature we see the following advantages:

- Only one connection is made to the database to extract all the sales order details

- Only one schema is created for all three results, making it easier to use in maps

Once we have enriched our sales order information, we are going to write our SQL Response from SQL Server to disk so that we can see an XML document containing three different result sets.

The next step in the process is to update our SalesOrderTable with the status "Processed" for the processed orders. To accomplish this, we have a very simple map:

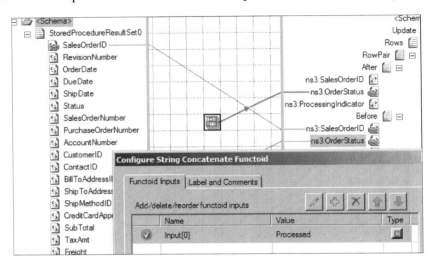

The final step in our orchestration is to write the result of our SalesOrderStatus table update to a file folder via the FILE adapter:

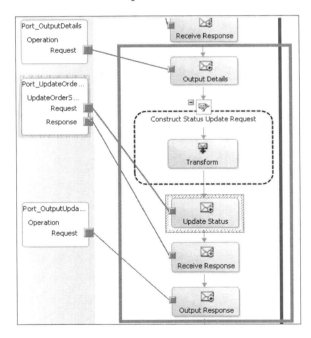

After the solution has been deployed, we need to configure our SQL Notification Receive Location. The sqlBinding settings is used to configure query notifications are:

1. **InboundOperationType** must be set to **Notification.**

2. **NotificationStatement**: This is where we set the SQL statement that the adapter will monitor for changes. When the results of the statement change, the adapter raises a notification. In this example we will configure it with a query very similar to the **PolledDataAvailableStatement** that was used for typed polling in Example 1. For the notification query we use a select statement that checks for sales orders not yet processed:

```
SELECT SalesOrderID FROM Sales.SalesOrderStatus
WHERE ProcessingIndicator  IS NULL and OrderStatus ='Pending'
```

3. The **NotifiyOnListenerStart** property generates a notification whenever a receive location is enabled. This ensures that BizTalk will retrieve any updated data from SQL Server while the Receive Location was disabled. In our solution we want to process any outstanding sales order as soon as possible so we will leave it set to **True**.

Here is what the Binding Properties tab looks like for our Notification Receive Location after it has been configured as discussed above:

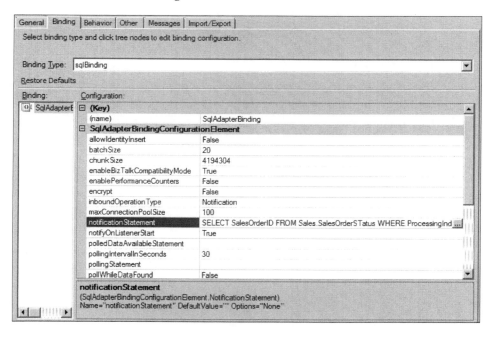

Example 4 – Composite Operations

The last operation that we are going to discuss in this chapter is the Composite Operation. The purpose of a Composite Operation is to be able to execute multiple database actions in the context of a single unit of work, or transaction. Even though we are calling multiple actions we expect all actions to either succeed or fail as a group. The idea is that if we need to insert/update multiple tables, we want all inserts/updates to succeed otherwise we want to rollback the action so that our tables remain in sync.

Once again we find ourselves in the Consume Adapter Service wizard. There are two tables of particular interest to us: **SpecialOffer** and **SpecialOfferProduct**. The SpecialOfferProduct table links Special Offers and Products together. We want to perform Insert operations against both of these tables.

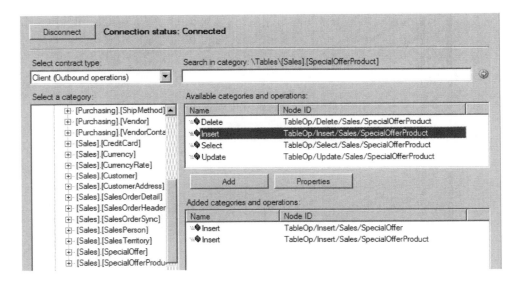

Once the wizard has been completed, we will discover two schemas of interest to us that model our Database tables: SpecialOffer.xsd and SpecialOfferProduct.xsd:

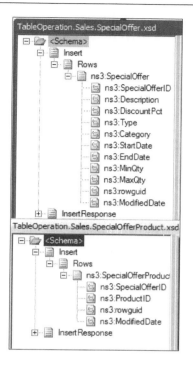

In order to build a Composite Operation, we need to have a single schema that contains multiple root nodes. Under the first root node, we add all the operation execution request schemas, and under the other we add all the operation response schemas. The only naming convention rule for the root nodes is that the operations response root node has to be the same as the operations root node and suffixed with 'Response'. For this example we have created a schema called **CompositeSchema. xsd**, and created two root nodes: **Request** and **RequestResponse**.

Once we have the root nodes we use the Import property of BizTalk Server schemas to import the two update schemas into the composite one:

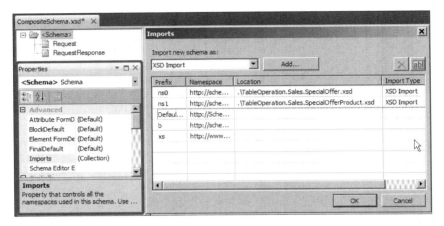

With our schemas imported, we need to ensure that all parent nodes have the correct Data Structure Type specified. As you can see in the following image, we have two **Insert** nodes underneath the **Request** root node. Within each of these Insert nodes we provide the Data Structure type for our **SpecialOffer** request and **SpecialOfferProduct** request. Similarly, we do the same for **RequestResponse** nodes:

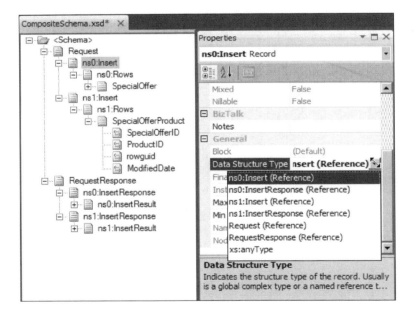

Here is our map that will demonstrate taking data from a single request and splitting the data across our multiple request nodes in our composite schema. When this is run through BizTalk, we will insert data into both our **SpecialOffer** and **SpecialOfferProduct** tables as a single transaction:

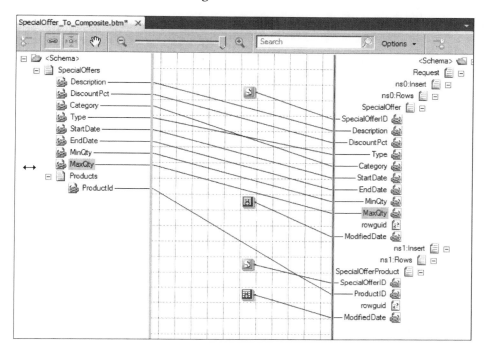

On the solicit response send port that we created for the composite operation we need to use a special Action name called **CompositeOperation**:

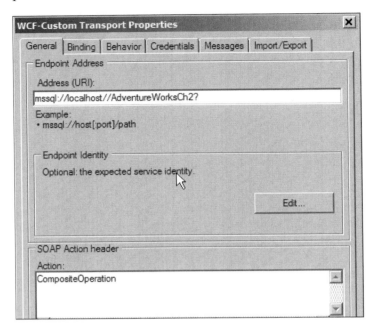

Another adapter property to be aware of is on the **Binding** tab and is called **useAmbientTransaction,** which should be set to **True.** In conjunction with providing CompositeOperation in our SOAP Action header, this property instructs the adapter that multiple operations will be executed and these operations have to be executed as a single transaction.

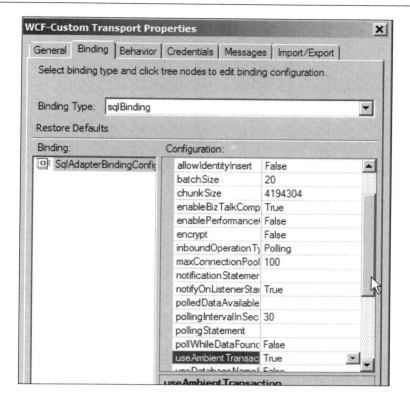

By using a composite operation against the two table updates we have the following benefits:

- The same transaction is used for both operations. This means if there is an exception both are rolled back. This is important for our solution since we want both updates to be executed together, and if one of them fails both get rolled back.

- The same database connection is used. The adapter will use the same connection from the connection pool for all the update, insert and delete statements in the composite operation, minimizing the risk of running out of connections in the pool.

Now with our composite schema in place and our map to transform our incoming request to the composite message, we can build out the rest of our solution:

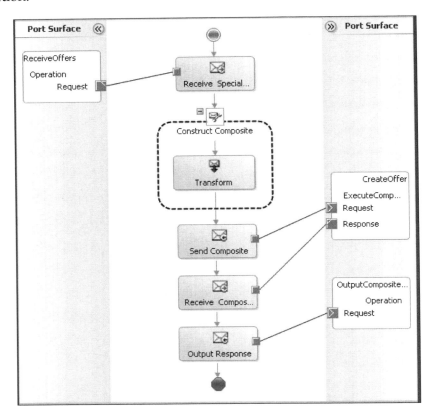

With our application deployed we can initialize this process by copying the ...\ `Chapter02\Example4\SpecialOffer.xml` file and pasting it into the `Chapter02\ Example4\FileDrop` folder.

If we examine our SpecialOffer and SpecialOfferProduct tables we will discover that we have the SpecialOfferID of 182 (will likely be different on your system since the first scripting functoid in the Special_Offer_To_Composite map generates a random number for SpecialOfferID) in both of these tables with a similar timestamp. These records were written to this database as a single transaction. As expected, there were no issues when we ran this composite operation so there is no data being passed back in the SQL Server response.

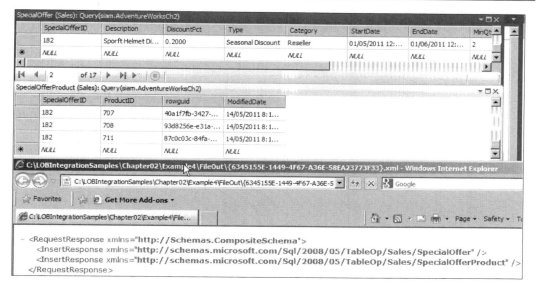

Summary

In this chapter we learned how to integrate SQL Server and BizTalk Server 2010 using the ASDK SQL adapter.

BizTalk Server solutions often integrate to SQL Server, and the best practices and examples in this chapter should help a BizTalk developer when building integrated solutions.

In the next chapter, we'll take a look at integrating BizTalk Server and Microsoft Dynamics CRM.

3
Integrating BizTalk Server and Microsoft Dynamics CRM

Microsoft Dynamics CRM 2011 is the latest and greatest relationship management software from Microsoft. This release of the product introduced a wide range of improvements to the user interface, a new WCF programming model, role-based forms, data analysis dashboards, tight integration with SharePoint 2010, Windows Azure integration, and much more. Dynamics CRM 2011 should be considered by anyone evaluating small or large CRM projects. But how do we make Dynamics CRM an integrated part of our enterprise landscape? This chapter focuses on that question.

In this chapter, we will cover:

- What is Microsoft Dynamics CRM and what problems does it solve?
- Why you should integrate Dynamics CRM with BizTalk Server
- How BizTalk Server makes requests to Dynamics CRM
- How Dynamics CRM sends data to BizTalk Server

What is Microsoft Dynamics CRM?

Customer relationship management is a critical part of virtually every business. Dynamics CRM 2011 offers a solution for the three traditional areas of CRM: sales, marketing, and customer service.

For customers interested in managing a sales team, Dynamics CRM 2011 has a strong set of features. This includes organizing teams into territories, defining price lists, managing opportunities, maintaining organization structures, tracking sales pipelines, enabling mobile access, and much more.

If you are using Dynamics CRM 2011 for marketing efforts, then you have the ability to import data from multiple sources, plan campaigns and set up target lists, create mass communications, track responses to campaigns, share leads with the sales team, and analyze the success of a marketing program.

Dynamics CRM 2011 also serves as a powerful hub for customer service scenarios. Features include rich account management, case routing and management, a built-in knowledge base, scheduling of call center resources, scripted Q&A workflows called Dialogs, contract management, and more.

Besides these three areas, Microsoft pitches Dynamics CRM as a general purpose application platform called xRM, where the "X" stands for any sort of relationship management. Dynamics CRM has a robust underlying framework for screen design, security roles, data auditing, entity definition, workflow, and mobility, among others. Instead of building these foundational aspects into every application, we can build our data-driven applications within Dynamics CRM.

Microsoft has made a big move into the cloud with this release of Dynamics CRM 2011. For the first time in company history, a product was released online (Dynamics CRM Online) prior to on-premises software. The hosted version of the application runs an identical codebase to the on-premises version meaning that code built to support a local instance will work just fine in the cloud. In addition to the big play in CRM hosting, Microsoft has also baked Windows Azure integration into Dynamics CRM 2011. Specifically, we now have the ability to configure a call-out to an Azure AppFabric Service Bus endpoint. To do this, the downstream service must implement a specific WCF interface and within CRM, the Azure AppFabric plugin is configured to call that downstream service through the Azure AppFabric Service Bus relay service. For BizTalk Server to accommodate this pattern, we would want to build a proxy service that implements the required Dynamics CRM 2011 interface and forwards requests into a BizTalk Server endpoint. This chapter will not demonstrate this scenario, however, as the focus will be on integrating with an on-premises instance only.

Why Integrate Dynamics CRM and BizTalk Server?

There are numerous reasons to tie these two technologies together. Recall that BizTalk Server is an enterprise integration bus that connects disparate applications. There can be a natural inclination to hoard data within a particular application, but if we embrace real-time message exchange, we can actually have a more agile enterprise.

Consider a scenario when a customer's full "contact history" resides in multiple systems. The Dynamics CRM 2011 contact center may only serve a specific audience, and other systems within the company hold additional details about the company's customers. One design choice could be to bulk load that information into Dynamics CRM 2011 on a scheduled interval. However, it may be more effective to call out to a BizTalk Server service that aggregates data across systems and returns a composite view of a customer's history with a company.

In a similar manner, think about how information is shared between systems. A public website for a company may include a registration page where visitors sign up for more information and deeper access to content. That registration event is relevant to multiple systems within the company. We could send that initial registration message to BizTalk Server and then broadcast that message to the multiple systems that want to know about that customer. A marketing application may want to respond with a personalized email welcoming that person to the website. The sales team may decide to follow up with that person if they expressed interest in purchasing products. Our Dynamics CRM 2011 customer service center could choose to automatically add the registration event so that it is ready whenever that customer calls in. In this case, BizTalk Server acts as a central router of data and invokes the exposed Dynamics CRM services to create customers and transactions.

In the remainder of this chapter, we will look at how we look up data residing in Dynamics CRM, how we push new data into Dynamics CRM, and how we push data out of Dynamics CRM.

Communicating from BizTalk Server to Dynamics CRM

The way that you send requests from BizTalk Server to Dynamics CRM 2011 has changed significantly in this release. In the previous versions of Dynamics CRM, a BizTalk "send" adapter was available for communicating with the platform. Dynamics CRM 2011 no longer ships with an adapter and developers are encouraged to use the WCF endpoints exposed by the product.

Dynamics CRM has both a WCF REST and SOAP endpoint. The REST endpoint can only be used within the CRM application itself. For instance, you can build what is called a **web resource** that is embedded in a Dynamics CRM page. This resource could be a Microsoft Silverlight or HTML page that looks up data from three different Dynamics CRM entities and aggregates them on the page. This web resource can communicate with the Dynamics CRM REST API, which is friendly to JavaScript clients. Unfortunately, you cannot use the REST endpoint from outside of the Dynamics CRM environment, but because BizTalk cannot communicate with REST services, this has little impact on the BizTalk integration story.

The Dynamics CRM SOAP API, unlike its ASMX web service predecessor, is static and operates with a generic `Entity` data structure. Instead of having a dynamic WSDL that exposes typed definitions for all of the standard and custom entities in the system, the Dynamics CRM 2011 SOAP API has a set of operations (for example, Create, Retrieve) that function with a single object type. The `Entity` object has a property identifying which concrete object it represents (for example, Account or Contract), and a name/value pair collection that represents the columns and values in the object it represents. For instance, an Entity may have a `LogicalName` set to "Account" and columns for "telephone1", "emailaddress", and "websiteurl."

In essence, this means that we have two choices when interacting with Dynamics CRM 2011 from BizTalk Server. Our first option is to directly consume and invoke the untyped SOAP API. Doing this involves creating maps from a canonical schema to the type-less `Entity` schema. In the case of doing a Retrieve operation, we may also have to map the type-less Entity message back to a structured message for more processing. Below, we will walk through an example of this.

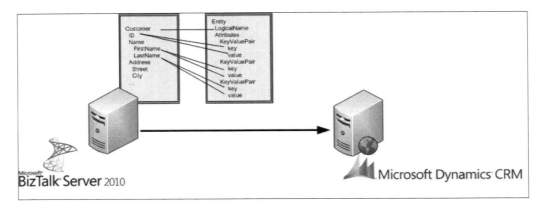

The second option involves creating a typed proxy service for BizTalk Server to invoke. Dynamics CRM has a feature-rich Solution Development Kit (SDK) that allows us to create typed objects and send them to the Dynamics CRM SOAP endpoint. This proxy service will then expose a typed interface to BizTalk that operates as desired with a strongly typed schema. An upcoming exercise demonstrates this scenario.

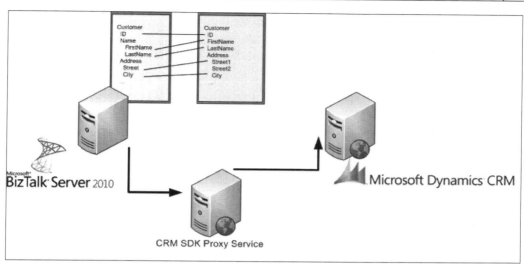

Which choice is best? For simple solutions, it may be fine to interact directly with the Dynamics CRM 2011 SOAP API. If you are updating a couple fields on an entity, or retrieving a pair of data values, the messiness of the untyped schema is worth the straightforward solution. However, if you are making large scale changes to entities, or getting back an entire entity and publishing to the BizTalk bus for more subscribers to receive, then working strictly with a typed proxy service is the best route. However, we will look at both scenarios below, and you can make that choice for yourself.

Integrating Directly with the Dynamics CRM 2011 SOAP API

In the following series of steps, we will look at how to consume the native Dynamics CRM SOAP interface in BizTalk Server. We will first look at how to query Dynamics CRM to return an Entity. After that, we will see the steps for creating a new Entity in Dynamics CRM.

Querying Dynamics CRM from BizTalk Server

In this scenario, BizTalk Server will request details about a specific Dynamics CRM "contact" record and send the result of that inquiry to another system.

Building the BizTalk components

In this first set of steps, we define the canonical BizTalk schema, add the Dynamics CRM schemas, create a mapping between the formats, and build an orchestration that ties all the pieces together:

1. Go to the code package for this book and navigate to `C:\LOBIntegration\` `Chapter3-DynamicsCrm` and open the Visual Studio 2010 solution file named `Chapter3-DynamicsCrm.sln`.

2. In Visual Studio 2010, create a new BizTalk project named **Chapter3-DynamicsCRM.AccountInt**. This project will hold all the BizTalk artifacts for this solution. Right-click the project, choose **Properties**, and set the strong name key, and the deployment application to **Chapter3**.

3. Right-click the BizTalk project and choose to add a new item. Select the (XML) schema item type and name the schema `Customer_XML.xsd`.

4. This schema reflects our organization's internal definition of a customer. The result of our query to Dynamics CRM should be mapped to this structure. Our customers are defined by an identifier, name, set of addresses, set of phone numbers, and an email address. The following image reflects the structure of the schema:

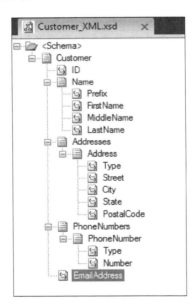

5. Add a reference to the Dynamics CRM SOAP endpoint in order to generate the artifacts that we need to consume the service. The WCF SOAP endpoint for a Dynamics CRM 2011 instance takes the form of: `http://<server name>/<instance name>/XRMServices/2011/Organization.svc`

6. Right-click the BizTalk project and choose **Add** and then **Add Generated Items**. Select **Consume WCF Service**. On the **Metadata source** page of the BizTalk WCF Service Consuming Wizard, choose the source of the metadata to be the **Metadata Exchange (MEX) endpoint**. On the **Metadata Endpoint** page of the wizard, enter the URL of your Dynamics CRM SOAP endpoint. After clicking the **Get** button next to the **Metadata Address (URL)**, move to the next page of the wizard and click **Import**.

7. The wizard adds a host of files to the BizTalk project. This includes two binding files, an orchestration (that includes message and orchestration port definitions), and seven schemas that represent the data types used by this service.

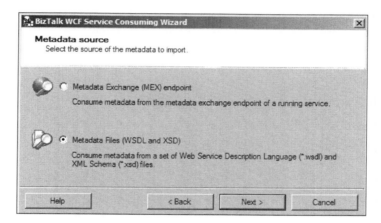

8. Unfortunately, the schemas generated for this endpoint are not considered valid. They do not have the proper links between each other and an error is shown when you open one. You could either manually correct each schema, or, better yet, leverage the valid BizTalk schemas included in the Dynamics CRM SDK that can be downloaded from the Microsoft website.

9. Delete the seven XSD schemas added by the service reference.

10. Right click the BizTalk project and choose **Add** then **Existing Item**. Navigate to where you have unpacked the Dynamics CRM SDK package and find the `sdk\schemas\crmbiztalkintegration` folder and choose the seven "organizationservice" schemas and click **Add**.

11. Unfortunately, the orchestration that was generated by the Dynamics CRM service reference will now contain errors due to small changes in the type names of the new schemas compared to the generated ones. So why go through the effort of adding the service reference at all if we are just going to replace all the schemas and end up with a broken orchestration? One benefit of still adding the service reference is acquiring the binding files. The Dynamics CRM endpoint has specific configurations that do not exactly match the standard BizTalk WCF bindings. These binding files make it simpler to get our Dynamics CRM send port correct the first time. Note that in real life, it is best to build a single project that contains the Dynamics CRM schemas and reference it in future projects.

12. Exclude the generated orchestration from the BizTalk project and build the project to confirm that the added schemas are valid.

13. Right-click the BizTalk project and choose to add a new item. Select the **Map** type and name it `Customer_To_CrmContactQuery.btm` and click **Add**.

14. For the source schema, select the `Chapter3-DynamicsCRM.AccountInt.Customer_XML` message type. This map takes in the `Customer` message type which initially only contains a value in the `ID` field. When a response is received from Dynamics CRM, we will populate the rest of the `Customer` message's nodes.

15. For the destination schema, select the `Chapter3-DynamicsCRM.AccountInt.organizationservice_schemas_microsoft_com_xrm_2011_contracts_services` message type. When prompted, select `Retrieve` as the root node. Our map now looks like the following image:

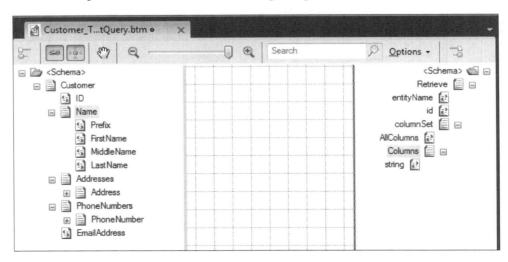

16 The `Retrieve` schema for Dynamics CRM is untyped, as mentioned earlier. Provide the name of the entity being queried (`entityName`), the unique ID of the target record (`id`), and either a list of which specific attributes we want (`Columns`) or request every attribute of the record (`AllColumns`).

17. We could hard-code the `entityName` value by setting the value attribute of the node from the **Properties** window of the BizTalk Mapper, but those settings can be difficult to locate later on. One way to visually indicate a default node value is through a functoid. From the Visual Studio 2010 toolbox, open the **Advanced Functoids** tab and drag a **Value Mapping** functoid to the mapping grid. Open the functoid by double-clicking it and set the value of the first parameter to `true` (so that it always applies) and set the **Result** value to `contact` (which is the formal name of the Dynamics CRM entity). Finally, drag the output of the functoid to the `entityName` node in the destination schema.

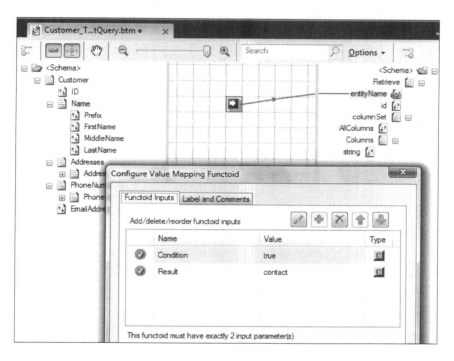

18. As mentioned above, the only field in the source schema that initially contains a value is the ID field. Map that source field to the id field in the destination. Note that because the destination field id has a pattern attached to it that looks for a GUID format, set the **Value** property of the source node to a valid GUID so that the map can be tested successfully. Do not worry about introducing side effects at runtime as any **Value** set on a source schema node is ignored outside of Visual Studio 2010. However, be aware that setting the **Value** property of a destination schema node **does** result in that value being pushed to the mapped message at runtime.

19. There are 146 fields in the Dynamics CRM contact object, so choosing to return all columns may be excessive. If you do want to retrieve all columns, simply set the destination schema's AllColumns node to true. However, in this case, we will only request specific columns. To generate the repeating elements under the Columns node, write some custom XSLT. From the Visual Studio 2010 toolbox, under **Advanced Functoids**, drag the **Scripting** functoid to the mapping grid.

20. Double-click the functoid and switch to the **Script Functoid Configuration** tab. Choose the **Inline XSLT** option since there is no source schema input to this custom XSLT and the objective is to emit a set of XML elements. Enter the following XML to retrieve just the desired columns. Notice the explicit namespace declaration to properly "type" the string and prevent errors during service invocation:

```
<string xmlns="http://schemas.microsoft.com/2003/10/
Serialization/Arrays">salutation</string>
<string xmlns="http://schemas.microsoft.com/2003/10/
Serialization/Arrays">firstname</string>
<string xmlns="http://schemas.microsoft.com/2003/10/
Serialization/Arrays">middlename</string>
<string xmlns="http://schemas.microsoft.com/2003/10/
Serialization/Arrays">lastname</string>
<string xmlns="http://schemas.microsoft.com/2003/10/
Serialization/Arrays">address1_addresstypecode</string>
<string xmlns="http://schemas.microsoft.com/2003/10/
Serialization/Arrays">address1_line1</string>
<string xmlns="http://schemas.microsoft.com/2003/10/
Serialization/Arrays">address1_city</string>
<string xmlns="http://schemas.microsoft.com/2003/10/
Serialization/Arrays">address1_stateorprovince</string>
<string xmlns="http://schemas.microsoft.com/2003/10/
Serialization/Arrays">address1_postalcode</string>
<string xmlns="http://schemas.microsoft.com/2003/10/
Serialization/Arrays">telephone1</string>
```

```
<string xmlns="http://schemas.microsoft.com/2003/10/
Serialization/Arrays">emailaddress1</string>
```

21. Save and close the map.

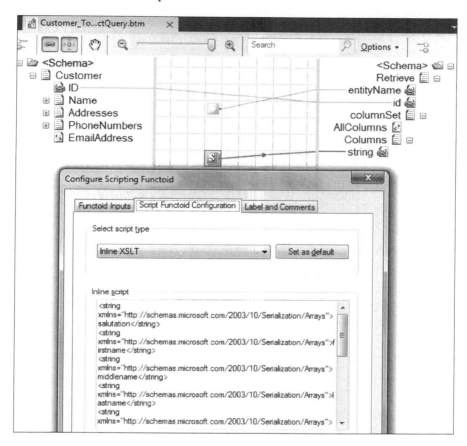

22. Right-click the BizTalk project and add a new item. Select the **Map** type, set the name to `CrmContact_To_Customer.btm`.

23. For the source schema, select the `Chapter3-DynamicsCRM.AccountInt.organizationservice_schemas_microsoft_com_xrm_2011_contracts_services` type and choose `RetrieveResponse` as the root.

24. For the destination schema, select the `Chapter3-DynamicsCRM.`
    `AccountIntCustomer_XML` message type. The resulting map will look like
    this:

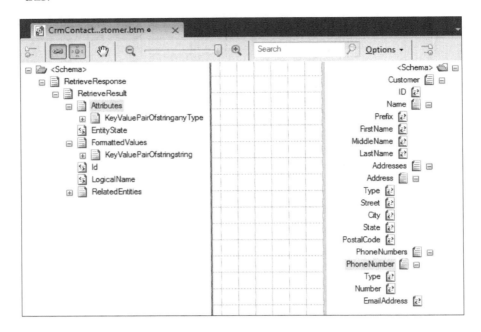

25. The message coming back from Dynamics CRM (which is the source of
    this map) contains an array of fields and values for the returned entity.
    The `Attributes` node contains all of the entity values. When there is an
    option set, or list of values, involved (e.g. `addresstypecode`) the Attributes
    value would be "1" while the `FormattedValues` node, which contains
    friendlier representations for option set values, would have an entry for
    `addresstypecode` where the value would be "Default Value".

26. To map the repeating `KeyValuePairOfstringanyType` to the structured
    destination fields, we can either build one long custom XSLT block,
    individual XSLT blocks for each section, or try and use other functoids (for
    example, **Logical** functoids with **Value Mapping**) to match the repeating
    source nodes to the destination node. In this example, build individual blocks
    of XSLT necessary to populate the entire destination schema.

27. Drag a Scripting functoid to the mapping surface and set it to use **Inline
    XSLT**. This functoid connects to the destination `ID` node and has no link from
    a source field. The XSLT for this functoid looks for the `value` node associated
    with the `key` node that holds the `contactid` value.

```
<ID>
<xsl:value-of select="//*[local-name()='KeyValuePairOfstringanyTy
pe'][*[local-name()='key']='contactid']/*[local-name()='value']"/>
</ID>
```

28. Next, drag another Scripting functoid to the mapping surface and set it to also use **Inline XSLT**. Connect it to the Name destination node. Much like the previous functoid, it will find the value nodes corresponding to the key nodes for each element under the Name. Highlighted here are the portions of the XSLT that retrieve the requested values.

```
<Name>
<Prefix>
<xsl:value-of select="//*[local-name()='KeyValuePairOfstr
inganyType'][*[local-name()='key']='salutation']/*[local-
name()='value']"/>
</Prefix>
<FirstName>
<xsl:value-of select="//*[local-name()='KeyValuePairOfstringanyTy
pe'][*[local-name()='key']='firstname']/*[local-name()='value']"/>
</FirstName>
<MiddleName>
<xsl:value-of select="//*[local-name()='KeyValuePairOfstr
inganyType'][*[local-name()='key']='middlename']/*[local-
name()='value']"/>
</MiddleName>
<LastName>
<xsl:value-of select="//*[local-name()='KeyValuePairOfstringanyTy
pe'][*[local-name()='key']='lastname']/*[local-name()='value']"/>
</LastName>
</Name>
```

29. Add another Scripting functoid that uses **Inline XSLT** and connects to the destination node named Addresses:

```
<Addresses>
<Address>
<Type>
<xsl:value-of select="//*[local-name()='KeyValuePairOfstringstri
ng'][*[local-name()='key']='address1_addresstypecode']/*[local-
name()='value']"/>
</Type>
<Street>
<xsl:value-of select="//*[local-name()='KeyValuePairOfstrin
ganyType'][*[local-name()='key']='address1_line1']/*[local-
name()='value']"/>
</Street>
```

```
<City>
<xsl:value-of select="//*[local-name()='KeyValuePairOfstri
nganyType'][*[local-name()='key']='address1_city']/*[local-
name()='value']"/>
</City>
<State>
<xsl:value-of select="//*[local-name()='KeyValuePairOfstringanyT
ype'][*[local-name()='key']='address1_stateorprovince']/*[local-
name()='value']"/>
</State>
<PostalCode>
<xsl:value-of select="//*[local-name()='KeyValuePairOfstringan
yType'][*[local-name()='key']='address1_postalcode']/*[local-
name()='value']"/>
</PostalCode>
</Address>
</Addresses>
```

30. Next, add a Scripting functoid that leverages **Inline XSLT** and connects to the `PhoneNumbers` node:

```
<PhoneNumbers>
<PhoneNumber>
<Type>Business</Type>
<Number>
<xsl:value-of select="//*[local-name()='KeyValuePairOfstr
inganyType'][*[local-name()='key']='telephone1']/*[local-
name()='value']"/>
</Number>
</PhoneNumber>
</PhoneNumbers>
```

31. Finally, add one more Scripting functoid that uses **Inline XSLT** and connects to the `EmailAddress` node in the destination schema:

```
<EmailAddress>
<xsl:value-of select="//*[local-name()='KeyValuePairOfstri
nganyType'][*[local-name()='key']='emailaddress1']/*[local-
name()='value']"/>
</EmailAddress>
```

32. The final map looks like the following image:

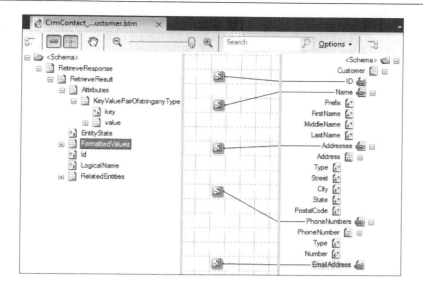

33. This service will be consumed by a BizTalk orchestration, so right-click the BizTalk project and add a new item. Select orchestration and set the name to `QueryCrmCustomer.odx`. This solution could consume the service directly through messaging (without orchestration), but because the generated BizTalk send port will have multiple possible operations to invoke (for example, Create, Retrieve, Update), an orchestration is the easiest way to set that target operation.

34. Create four orchestration messages: `Customer_Input` of type `Chapter3-DynamicsCRM.AccountInt.Customer_XML`, `Customer_Output` of type `Chapter3-DynamicsCRM.AccountInt.Customer_XML`, `ContactRetrieve_Request` of type `Chapter3-DynamicsCRM.AccountInt.organizationservice_schemas_microsoft_com_xrm_2011_contracts_services.Retrieve` and `ContactRetrieve_Response` of type `Chapter3-DynamicsCRM.AccountInt.organizationservice_schemas_microsoft_com_xrm_2011_contracts_services.RetrieveResponse`.

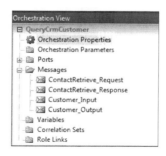

35. Sketch out an orchestration flow that receives a message, transforms a message, sends a request to a service, receives a response, transforms the response, and sends out a final message. The top Receive shape, named **Receive Request**, is associated with the `Customer_Input` message. The Construct shape, named **Construct Query**, builds the `ContactRetrieve_Request` message. The Transform shape uses the **Customer_To_CrmContactQuery** map that was built earlier. The next Send shape, named **Send Request**, uses the `ContactRetrieve_Request` message while the Receive shape that follows, named **Receive Result**, gets back the `ContactRetrieve_Response` message. The next Construct shape, named **Construct Output**, builds the `Customer_Output` message. Its Transform shape uses the **CrmContact_To_Customer** map where the Transform destination is set to `Customer_Output`. Finally, the last Send shape, named **Send Result** is tied to the `Customer_Output` message.

36. Add a one-way orchestration port that receives messages and is tied to the **Receive Request** shape.

37. Add a one-way orchestration port that sends messages and connects to the **Send Result** shape.

38. Create a two-way orchestration port that sends a message and receives a response. Be sure to set the Operation name of this port to **Retrieve**. The operation name here must correspond to the operation name of the Dynamics CRM web service method that is being called.

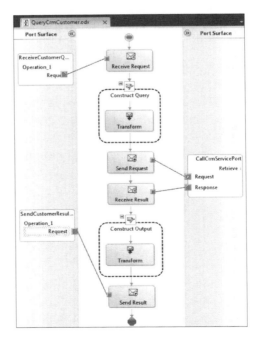

39. Build and deploy the BizTalk project.

We now have the components necessary to configure the messaging ports that complete the solution.

Configuring the BizTalk endpoints

In this part of the exercise, we will configure the BizTalk messaging ports that receive the query request, call Dynamics CRM 2011, transform the response message, and emit the canonical Customer message to disk via a FILE adapter.

1. Open the BizTalk Administration Console and find the **Chapter3** application.

2. Add a new Receive Port (**Chapter3.PickupCustomerQuery**) and Receive Location (**Chapter3.PickupCustomerQuery.FILE**) to the application which will pick up a "query request" message from the file system.

3. Right-click the **Chapter3** application and choose **Import** and then **Bindings**. Point to the OrganizationService_Custom.BindingInfo.xml binding file that was generated by referencing the Dynamics CRM web service and now sits inside the BizTalk project in Visual Studio. When the import is complete, a new send port is displayed.

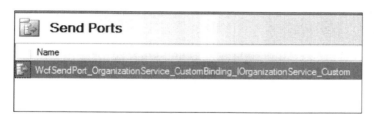

4. Double-click the new send port to observe its settings. Notice that it uses the **WCF-Custom** adapter and applies a custom WCF binding. The service is called using the credentials of the send port's host instance, so we do not need to add credentials to the send port itself.

5. Add a new send port that will emit Dynamics CRM response message. This one-way send port uses the FILE adapter and sends a message to the file system.

6. With the messaging ports in place, we now bind the orchestration to these ports. View the **Orchestrations** folder in the **Chapter3** application and double-click the **QueryCrmCustomer** orchestration.

7. Bind the orchestration to the host, the newly created receive port, the generated send port, and the FILE send port.

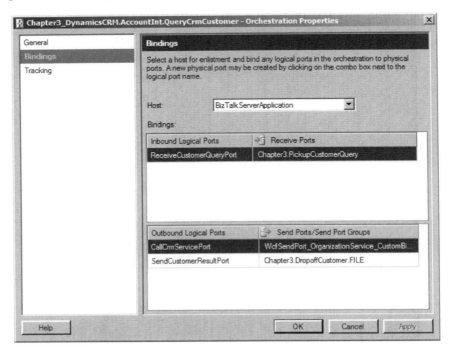

8. Start the receive location, send port, and orchestration.

We now have a channel for picking up the "query" message, a send port that calls Dynamics CRM 2011, and a send port that sends out the service result.

Recall that the primary field in the query message into Dynamics CRM is the ID of the record. Therefore, an XML instance is needed for the Customer message with only the ID value populated.

1. Navigate to your Dynamics CRM 2011 instance and open up the customer record you wish to query. Look at the address in your browser and retrieve the record's GUID and remove the URL encoding.

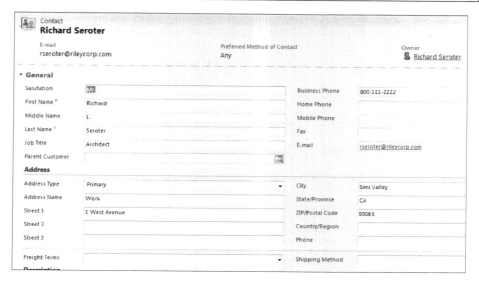

2. Add the record ID to the `ID` field of the generated instance of a `Customer_XML` message.

```xml
<ns0:Customer xmlns:ns0="http://Chapter3-DynamicsCRM.AccountInt.Customer_XML">
  <ID>C210E386-D58A-E011-A552-000C29D4FA55</ID>
  <Name>
    <Prefix />
    <FirstName />
    <MiddleName />
    <LastName />
  </Name>
  <Addresses>
```

3. Copy the XML instance file to the folder being polled by the BizTalk receive location.

4. Observe the file folder where the send port transmits the final message. We should see a message containing the values from Dynamics CRM formatted in the Customer_XML message.

```xml
<ns0:Customer xmlns:ns0="http://Chapter3-DynamicsCR|
  <ID>c210e386-d58a-e011-a552-000c29d4fa55</ID>
  <Name>
    <Prefix>Mr.</Prefix>
    <FirstName>Richard</FirstName>
    <MiddleName>L.</MiddleName>
    <LastName>Seroter</LastName>
  </Name>
  <Addresses>
    <Address>
      <Type>Primary</Type>
      <Street>1 West Avenue</Street>
      <City>Simi Valley</City>
      <State>CA</State>
      <PostalCode>93065</PostalCode>
    </Address>
  </Addresses>
  <PhoneNumbers>
    <PhoneNumber>
      <Type>Business</Type>
      <Number>800-111-2222</Number>
    </PhoneNumber>
  </PhoneNumbers>
  <EmailAddress>rseroter@rileycorp.com</EmailAddress>
</ns0:Customer>
```

What we saw here was how to create mappings to the Dynamics CRM "retrieve" message, how to put the unstructured results of that query into a structured format, and how to set up the BizTalk components necessary to route and invoke the request. Next up, we will see how to add records to Dynamics CRM from BizTalk Server.

Adding New Records to Dynamics CRM from BizTalk Server

We have already seen how the untyped schemas associated with the Dynamics CRM 2011 SOAP endpoint can make mapping a challenge. Specifically, we just saw how to take the untyped message from DynamicsCRM and convert it to a structured, canonical schema. But what about taking a canonical schema and mapping it to an untyped message? In this exercise, we will take the Customer_XML message and map it to the Dynamics CRM Create message and add a record to our DynamicsCRM instance.

Building the BizTalk components

This exercise builds upon the previous one. In this step, we will define a new mapping and build an orchestration that calls the Dynamics CRM Create operation:

1. Right-click the BizTalk project and add a new item. Choose the **Map** type and name the map `Customer_To_CrmContactCreate.btm`.

2. Set the source of the map to the `Customer_XML` message type. For the destination schema, select the `organizationservice_schemas_microsoft_com_xrm_2011_contracts_services` type and pick the `Create` message.

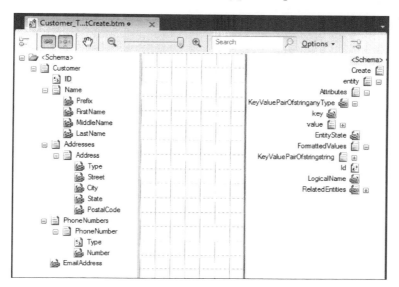

3. In this case, we have to get each source field copied over to the repeating `KeyValuePairOfstringanyType` node. We will leverage the feature of BizTalk Server 2010 that lets you neatly segment map aspects into logical containers called pages. Rename the first page to **Entity Name**.

   Drag a **Value Mapping** functoid from the **Advanced Functoids** tab on the mapping surface. Double click the **Value Mapping** functoid and manually set the value of the first parameter (**Condition**) to **true**, and manually set the **Result** parameter to **contact**.

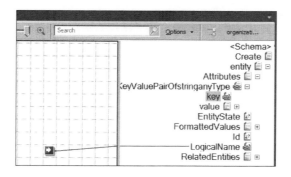

4. Create a new page in the map and name the page **Looping**. While we could choose to build up the destination schema using nothing but custom XSLT, this exercise shows you how to use the BizTalk functoids to make that task a bit easier. If you connect a set of nodes to a **Looping** functoid, and then connect the output of the Looping functoid to a target node, you create an environment that lets us copy the individual nodes from the source into the repeating node of the destination. Drag a **Looping** functoid from the **Advanced Functoids** section of the Toolbox onto the map. Connect the following nodes to it: `Prefix`, `FirstName`, `MiddleName`, `LastName`, `[Address] Type`, `Street`, `City`, `State`, `PostalCode`, `Number`, `EmailAddress`.

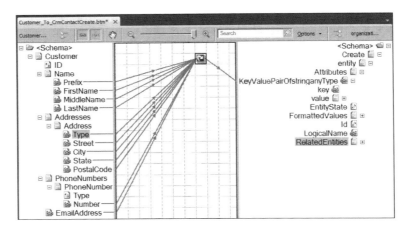

5. Create another map page named **Any Pairs**. On this page, connect the individual nodes to the repeating destination node. However, there are a few caveats. First, the `key` node underneath `KeyValuePairOfstringanyType` expects to hold the name of the Dynamics CRM entity attributes. Our canonical schema does not exactly match the names of the Dynamics CRM entity attributes. Therefore, we have to do a bit of translation to set the right value. In addition, because the `KeyValuePairOfstringanType` can hold any data type as the column value, we must explicitly "type" the `value` node when it is created. For instance, we must add a "string" attribute for string values.

6. Drag the Scripting functoid onto the mapping surface and connect it to the `Prefix` source node and `key` destination node. Set the **Script type** to **Inline XSLT Call Template**. Add the XSLT found below. Note that the `xsi:type` attribute is added to the `value` node and the type is set as `xs:string`:

```
<xsl:template name="SetPrefixValue">
<xsl:param name="param1" />
```

```
<key xmlns="http://schemas.datacontract.org/2004/07/System.
Collections.Generic">salutation</key>
<value xmlns="http://schemas.datacontract.org/2004/07/System.
Collections.Generic" xmlns:xs="http://www.w3.org/2001/XMLSchema"
xmlns:xsi="http://www.w3.org/2001/XMLSchema-instance">
<xsl:attribute name="xsi:type">
<xsl:value-of select="'xs:string'" />
</xsl:attribute>
<xsl:value-of select="$param1" />
</value>
</xsl:template>
```

7. Repeat this process for every source node that previously connected to the looping functoid and make sure to use a different XSLT template name for each script. Excluded from the list is the [Address] Type node which must be handled differently, as we will see shortly. Note that my mapping is as follows:

Source Node	XSLT Template Name	CRM Key Name
Prefix	SetPrefixValue	salutation
FirstName	SetFNameValue	firstname
MiddleName	SetMNameValue	middlename
LastName	SetLNameValue	lastname
Street	SetStreetValue	address1_line1
City	SetCityValue	address1_city
State	SetStateValue	address1_stateorprovince
PostalCode	SetPostalValue	address1_postalcode
Number	SetPhoneValue	telephone1
EmailAddress	SetEmailValue	emailaddress1

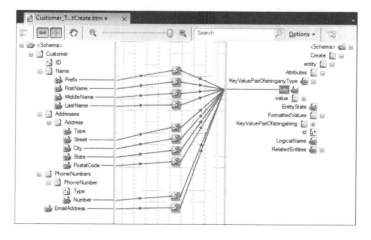

8. Now we are ready to tackle the Address Type attribute which is not a string, but rather an entry within a list of values (called Option Sets). Drag a new Scripting functoid to the mapping surface and set it to use **Inline XSLT Call Template**. Add the following XSLT:

```
<xsl:template name="SetAddrTypeValue">
<xsl:param name="param1" />
<key xmlns="http://schemas.datacontract.org/2004/07/System.
Collections.Generic">address1_addresstypecode</key>
<value xmlns="http://schemas.datacontract.org/2004/07/System.
Collections.Generic"
  xmlns:xs="http://www.w3.org/2001/XMLSchema"
  xmlns:xsi="http://www.w3.org/2001/XMLSchema-instance"
  xmlns:a="http://schemas.microsoft.com/xrm/2011/Contracts">
  <xsl:attribute name="xsi:type"><xsl:value-of
select="'a:OptionSetValue'" /></xsl:attribute>
  <Value xmlns="http://schemas.microsoft.com/xrm/2011/
Contracts"><xsl:value-of select="$param1" /></Value>
  </value>
</xsl:template>
```

9. Connect the `Type` node under the `Address` node to this functoid and connect the other end of the functoid to the `key` node under the `KeyValuePairofstringanyType`.

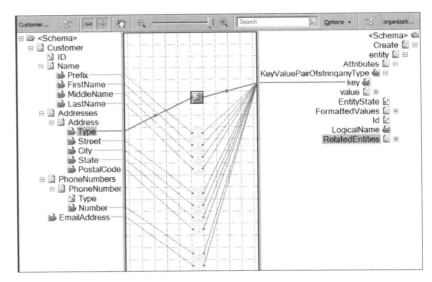

10. With the map complete, the final task is to build an orchestration that consumes the Dynamics CRM service and emits the result. In this case, the result of a call to the Create operation is a GUID representing the new record's unique ID. Add a new orchestration named `CreateCrmCustomer.odx` to this BizTalk project.

11. Create three orchestration messages: `Customer_Input` of type `Chapter3-DynamicsCRM.AccountInt.Customer_XML`, `ContactCreate_Request` of type `Chapter3-DynamicsCRM.AccountInt.organizationservice_schemas_microsoft_com_xrm_2011_contracts_services.Create`, and `ContactCreate_Response` of type `Chapter3-DynamicsCRM.AccountInt.organizationservice_schemas_microsoft_com_xrm_2011_contracts_services.CreateResponse`.

12. Build an orchestration flow that receives a message, transforms a message, sends a request to a service, receives a response, and sends out a final message. The top Receive shape, named **Receive Request**, is associated with the `Customer_Input` message. The Construct shape, named **Construct Create**, builds the `ContactCreate_Request` message. The Transform shape uses the **Customer_To_CrmContactCreate** map that was just built. The next Send shape, named **Send Request**, uses the `ContactCreate_Request` message while the Receive shape that follows, named **Receive Result**, gets back the `ContactCreate_Response` message. The last Send shape, named **Send Result** also uses the `ContactCreate_Response` message.

13. Add a one-way orchestration port that receives messages and is tied to the **Receive Request** shape.

14. Add a one-way orchestration port that sends messages and connects to the **Send Result** shape.

15. Create a two-way orchestration port that sends a message and receives a response. Set the Operation name of this port to **Create**. Recall that the operation name here must correspond to the operation name of the Dynamics CRM web service method being called.

16. Build and deploy the BizTalk project.

We have now built the map and orchestration necessary to successfully call this service.

Configuring the BizTalk endpoints

Our final task is to configure the BizTalk messaging components to send a message to the Dynamics CRM service. We already have a series of reusable ports configured as a result of our last exercise and can leverage those this time around.

1. Open the BizTalk Administration Console and confirm that the updates to our application were successfully deployed. This can be confirmed by looking for our new orchestration under the **Orchestrations** folder beneath the **Chapter3** application.

2. Double-click the orchestration to bind it to messaging ports.

3. Set the host value, and for the initial receive port, reuse the port created in the previous exercise. When a receive port is bound to an orchestration, the resulting subscription looks at both the name of the port and the message type coming in. So, in this case, because we are using a `Customer_XML` message input for both types, we have to un-enlist the previous orchestration to prevent it from picking up this message as well.

4. Set the orchestration to also reuse the send ports from the previous exercise. This includes the generated send port which calls Dynamics CRM, and the port that sends the service result message to the file system.

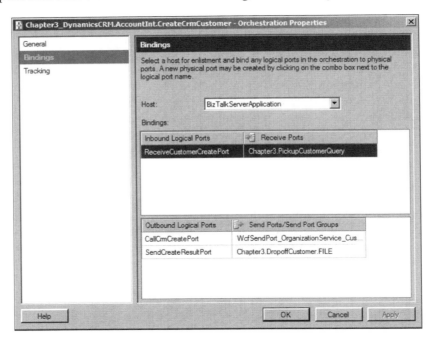

5. Start the orchestration, and ensure that the receive location, send ports, and host are also started. Remember to un-enlist the previous orchestration so that it does not pick up the message as well.

6. Create an XML instance file for the `Customer_XML` message type and populate it with details of a new contact that does not yet exist in Dynamics CRM.

7. Drop this file into a folder being monitored by our FILE receive location.

8. If everything is configured correctly, we should see both a new record in our Dynamics CRM instance, and a file that holds the unique ID of that new record.

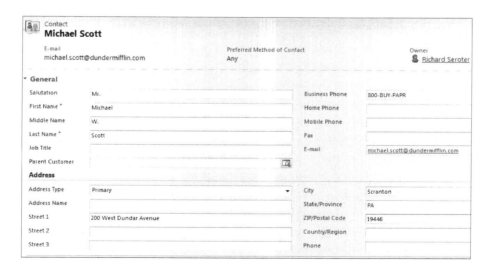

In this exercise, we saw how to create the untyped service request message from a canonical schema and successfully create a record in Dynamics CRM from BizTalk Server.

Using a Dynamics CRM proxy service with BizTalk Server

Setup

The proxy-service strategy requires the installation of the Dynamics CRM 2011 SDK. Make sure to add the XRM assemblies to the Global Assembly Cache of your development machine. In addition, whether or not you are using Dynamics CRM's new claims-based security strategy, you still need to install the Windows Identity Foundation (WIF) components as there is a dependency between the client assemblies and WIF.

Generating a proxy service

The secret to the proxy service is the typed classes that represent the standard and custom entities in the Dynamics CRM application:

1. Within a Windows command prompt, navigate to the `bin` directory beneath the CRM SDK download package.

2. Execute the CrmSvcUtil.exe utility which creates .NET classes for the entities within Dynamics CRM 2011. This utility has a series of command line parameters including:

    a. url – endpoint address of Dynamics CRM Organization service

    b. out – the file name of the generated code

    c. username – name of the user with permission to invoke the Dynamics CRM services

    d. password – password of the user with permission to invoke the Dynamics CRM services

    e. domain – directory domain of the user invoking the Dynamics CRM services

    f. namespace – .NET namespace used in the generated code

Using these parameters, a sample query to generate the early-bound Dynamics CRM class looks like this:

```
CrmSvcUtil.exe /url:http://<server>/<orgName>/XRMServices/2011/
Organization.svc /out:"C:\temp\CrmEntites.cs" /
username:<username> /password:<password> /domain:<domain> /
namespace:Chapter3.CrmProxyService
```

3. The resulting C# class contains definitions for all of the standard and custom entities present in the target Dynamics CRM system. This class allows us to deal only with typed entities and avoid interacting with the raw `Entity` format.

4. In Visual Studio 2010, create a new **Web Site** project of type **WCF Service** and name it `Chapter3-DynamicsCRM.SvcProxy`.

5. Right-click the new project and choose to **Add Existing Item**. Locate the `CrmEntities.cs` class that was generated earlier and include it in this project. Add it to the `App_Code` folder of the project.

6. Once again, right-click the project and choose to **Add New Item**. Select the **WCF Service** type and name it `CrmCustomerProxy.svc`.

7. The contract for this service is displayed, which will contain the data type and operation that BizTalk will invoke. Note that the `CrmEntities.cs` class does not contain WCF serializable types. Therefore, we cannot simply return the Dynamics CRM "customer" type from our service. Define a new class in `ICrmCustomerServiceProxy.cs` that describes a customer. Be aware that we are using a single CRM entity, Customer, in this example. A similar exercise would have to be performed for each entity that we wish to expose to BizTalk.

```
[DataContract(Namespace="http://chapter3/data")]
public class Customer
{
    [DataMember]
    public string NamePrefix { get; set; }
    [DataMember]
    public string FirstName { get; set; }
    [DataMember]
    public string MiddleName { get; set; }
    [DataMember]
    public string LastName { get; set; }
    [DataMember]
    public string PrimaryAddressStreet { get; set; }
    [DataMember]
    public string PrimaryAddressCity { get; set; }
    [DataMember]
    public string PrimaryAddressState { get; set; }
    [DataMember]
    public string PrimaryAddressPostalCode { get; set; }
    [DataMember]
    public string PhoneNumber { get; set; }
```

```
    [DataMember]
    public string EmailAddress { get; set; }
}
```

8. Also in this `ICrmCustomerProxy.cs` file, add the service contract. This contract contains a single operation that takes in a customer object and returns a string containing the new record's unique identifier.

```
[ServiceContract(Namespace="http://chapter3/service")]
public interface ICrmCustomerProxy
{
    [OperationContract]
    string AddCustomer(Customer newCustomer);
}
```

9. Switch to the generated `CrmCustomerProxy.cs` file and add a placeholder for the required `AddCustomer` operation.

10. Before going further, add an assembly reference to this project. Point to the `Microsoft.Xrm.Sdk.dll` that is included in the `bin` folder of the Dynamics CRM SDK download.

11. At the top of the `CrmCustomerProxy.cs` code class, add three references:

```
using Microsoft.Xrm.Sdk;
using Microsoft.Xrm.Sdk.Client;
using System.ServiceModel.Description; //for credentials
using Chapter3.CrmProxyService; //generated class
```

12. When calling the Dynamics CRM WCF SOAP service through code, we have the option of using a special service proxy class included in the SDK (`OrganizationServiceProxy`). By combining this proxy class with a Dynamics CRM WCF behavior (`ProxyTypesBehavior`), we can work solely with typed objects and let those objects get translated to, and from, `Entities` underneath the covers. At the beginning of the `AddCustomer` operation, add the following code, which creates a variable for the service proxy and defines the client credentials object:

```
OrganizationServiceProxy proxy;
ClientCredentials creds = new ClientCredentials();
creds.Windows.ClientCredential =
System.Net.CredentialCache.DefaultNetworkCredentials;
```

13. Define the two variables that will hold our Dynamics CRM contact object and the GUID value that is returned when a new contact is created.

```
Contact newContact;
Guid newContactId;
```

14. We are ready to instantiate the custom service proxy that we used to call the Dynamics CRM service. Notice that our credential object is passed into the constructor. After the proxy is instantiated, add the custom Dynamics CRM WCF behavior to the endpoint:

```
using (proxy = new OrganizationServiceProxy(new
Uri("http://<server>/<instance>/XRMServices/2011/Organization.
svc"),
null,
creds,
null))
{
    proxy.ServiceConfiguration.CurrentServiceEndpoint.
Behaviors.Add(new ProxyTypesBehavior());

}
```

15. Create the mapping between the service's customer definition and the Dynamics CRM contact entity:

```
newContact = new Contact();
newContact.Salutation = newCustomer.NamePrefix;
newContact.FirstName = newCustomer.FirstName;
newContact.MiddleName = newCustomer.MiddleName;
newContact.LastName = newCustomer.LastName;
newContact.Address1_Line1 = newCustomer.PrimaryAddressStreet;
newContact.Address1_City = newCustomer.PrimaryAddressCity;
newContact.Address1_StateOrProvince =
newCustomer.PrimaryAddressState;
newContact.Address1_PostalCode =
newCustomer.PrimaryAddressPostalCode;
newContact.Telephone1 = newCustomer.PhoneNumber;
newContact.EMailAddress1 = newCustomer.EmailAddress;
```

16. Finally, invoke the service, pass in the Dynamics CRM entity, and get the GUID response. Return the string value of the GUID from the service operation:

```
newContactId = proxy.Create(newContact);
```

17. Build the service and deploy it to a local web server. Pull up the service in the browser to ensure that it is configured correctly:

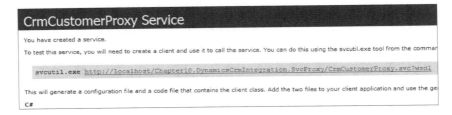

18. If you choose, you may also try and call this service using the WCF Test Client. Make sure that the service sits within an Application Pool that runs with a domain account that has access to Dynamics CRM 2011.

We now have a complete, working proxy service that sits as a façade in front of the actual Dynamics CRM 2011 WCF endpoint. This proxy exposes a clean, typed interface that BizTalk can readily consume, as we will see next.

Building the BizTalk components

In this set of steps, we consume the proxy service from our BizTalk project and create the map necessary for translating our canonical schema to the format expected by the service:

1. Back in Visual Studio 2010, navigate to the existing BizTalk Server project. We will add a reference to this new WCF service and configure the BizTalk component needed to call the proxy service. Right-click the BizTalk project and choose to **Add** and then **Add Generated Items**.

2. Walk through the BizTalk WCF Service Consuming wizard and select the metadata source to be a MEX endpoint. On the following page, set the address to the web address of our WCF service:

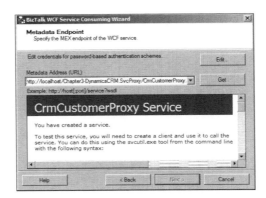

3. Complete the wizard and observe the new artifacts included in our solution. This includes binding files, schemas, and an orchestration:

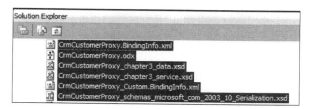

4. Right-click the BizTalk project and add a new item of type **Map** and name the map `Customer_To_CrmContactProxy.btm`.

5. Set the source of the map to the `Customer_XML` and the destination to `Chapter3-DynamicsCRM.AccountInt.CrmCustomerProxy_chapter3_service` and choose the `AddCustomer` root node.

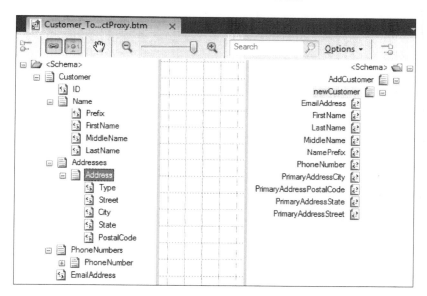

6. Connect the applicable source nodes to the corresponding destination field.

7. We are consuming this service directly from BizTalk messaging and therefore we do not need to build an orchestration to call the proxy service. Build and deploy the BizTalk project to the BizTalk Server.

This set of steps produced the BizTalk artifacts we needed to call the façade service sitting in front of Dynamics CRM. As opposed to the previous exercises where we had to creatively transform untyped schemas, this set of service schemas are strongly typed and easy to work with.

Configuring the BizTalk endpoints

Up next, we are going to configure the BizTalk messaging components that call the service and route the response:

1. Open the BizTalk Administration console and ensure that the new proxy service schemas are part of the **Chapter3** application.

2. When we created a service reference to the proxy service, the BizTalk WCF Service Consuming wizard generated a binding file that defines a send port capable of calling the proxy service. Right-click the **Chapter3** application and choose to import a binding and select the `CrmCustomerProxy_Custom.BindingInfo.xml` file included in our BizTalk project.

3. Open the generated send port. There are no changes needed to the port's configuration, but we will add our new map, and a filter, to this send port. On the **Outbound Maps** tab of the port configuration, select the **Contact_To_CrmContactProxy** map.

4. Switch to the **Filters** tab and add a subscription for the message type of the `Customer_XML` type.

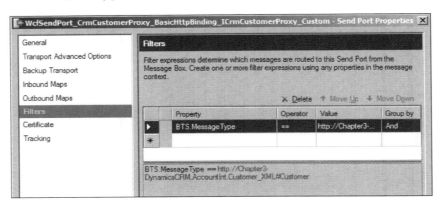

5. Our last configuration item is the send port, which listens for the response from this service call and sends a message to the file system. Create a new one-way, static send port. Set the adapter to FILE and set the location where the send port will send the response message. Go to the **Filters** tab of the port configuration. Here, we will add a subscription to the response message type.

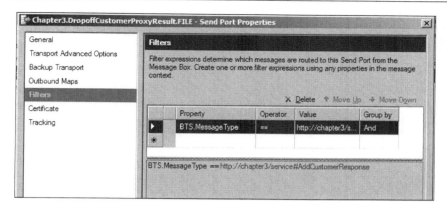

6. Un-enlist all the previously defined send ports and orchestrations in order to eliminate any side effects from using the same `Customer_XML` message type as input.

7. Send a file containing a customer definition into BizTalk Server:

```
- <ns0:Customer xmlns:ns0="http://Chapter3-DynamicsCRM.Acco
    <ID />
  - <Name>
      <Prefix>Mr.</Prefix>
      <FirstName>Jim</FirstName>
      <MiddleName>P.</MiddleName>
      <LastName>Halpert</LastName>
    </Name>
  - <Addresses>
    - <Address>
        <Type>3</Type>
        <Street>200 West Dundar Avenue</Street>
        <City>Scranton</City>
        <State>PA</State>
        <PostalCode>19446</PostalCode>
      </Address>
    </Addresses>
  - <PhoneNumbers>
    - <PhoneNumber>
        <Type>Business</Type>
        <Number>800-BUY-PAPR</Number>
      </PhoneNumber>
    </PhoneNumbers>
      <EmailAddress>jim.halpert@dundermifflin.com</EmailAddress>
  </ns0:Customer>
```

8. As a result, we should see our new record in Dynamics CRM and a file on disk that holds that record's identifier.

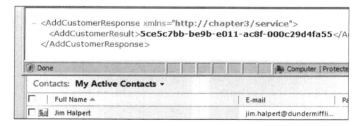

In this exercise, we showed a straightforward way to build a façade, or proxy, service that sits in front of Dynamics CRM 2011 and exposes an easy to use, typed interface. The underlying proxy service takes advantage of the Dynamics CRM SDK so that at no point did we need to work with the base Entity object.

Communicating from Dynamics CRM to BizTalk Server

One can imagine many scenarios where Dynamics CRM either publishes data to BizTalk Server or queries BizTalk-exposed service endpoints. For instance, when a customer requests a refund for a defective product, the call center agent may record this request in Dynamics CRM. After the phone call is over, Dynamics CRM should send a message to a returns processing system which handles the crediting of a customer's account. In another scenario, BizTalk Server may be the host of a data aggregation service which queries three enterprise systems that store "customer" data and aggregates the responses. Dynamics CRM may want to execute that service when a call center agent views a customer record so that they get a fuller picture of that customer's interactions with the company.

There are three viable places where Dynamics CRM can communicate with BizTalk Server. First, a Dynamics CRM form is capable of executing client-side JavaScript at various points in the form lifecycle. One can definitely use JavaScript to invoke web services, including web services exposed by BizTalk Server. However, note that JavaScript invocation of web services is typically synchronous and could have a negative impact on the user experience if a form must constantly wait for responses from distributed services. Also, JavaScript that runs within Dynamics CRM is client-side and tied directly to the page on which it resides. If we programmatically interact with a Dynamics CRM entity, then any code existing in client-side script will not get invoked. For instance, if after an "account" record is created we send a message, via JavaScript, to BizTalk, this logic would not fire if we created an "account" record programmatically.

The second place where Dynamics CRM can communicate with BizTalk Server is through workflows. A workflow in Dynamics CRM is an automated process where a set of steps is executed according to rules that we define. For example, when a sales opportunity is closed, we run a workflow that adds a message to the customer record, notifies all parties tied to the opportunity, and sends a polite email to the lost prospect. Workflows are based on Windows Workflow 4.0 technology and can be built either in the Dynamics CRM application itself or within Visual Studio 2010. The Dynamics CRM web application allows us to piece together workflows using previously registered workflow steps. If we need new workflow steps or need to construct something complex, we can jump into Visual Studio 2010 and define the workflow there. Why would we choose to use a workflow to send a message to BizTalk Server? If you have a long-running process that can either be scheduled or executed on demand, and want the option for users to modify the process, then workflow may be the right choice.

The final strategy for communicating between Dynamics CRM and BizTalk Server is to use plugins. Plugins are server-based application extensions that execute business logic and get tied directly to an entity. This means that they are invoked whether we work in the Dynamics CRM web interface or through the API. I can run a plugin both synchronously and asynchronously, depending on the situation. For instance, if we need to validate the data on a record prior to saving it, we can set a plugin to run before the "save" operation is committed and provide some user feedback on the invalid information. Or, we could choose to asynchronously call a plugin after a record is saved and transmit data to our service bus, BizTalk Server. In the following exercise, we will leverage plugins to send data from Dynamics CRM to BizTalk Server.

Integration to BizTalk Server

In this first walkthrough, we will build a plugin that communicates from Dynamics CRM to a BizTalk Server located. An event message will be sent to BizTalk whenever a change occurs on an Account record in Dynamics CRM.

Setup

This exercise leverages a BizTalk Server project already present in your Visual Studio 2010 solution. We are going to publish a web service from BizTalk Server that takes in a message and routes it to a BizTalk send port that writes the message to the file system.

1. If you have not already done so, go to the code package for this book and navigate to `C:\LOBIntegration\Chapter03\Chapter3-DynamicsCRM` and open the Visual Studio 2010 solution file named `Chapter3-DynamicsCRM.sln`.

2. Find the BizTalk Server project named **Chapter3-DynamicsCRM. AcctRouting** and open it.

3. The book's code package includes a custom schema named `AccountEventChange_XML.xsd` and notice which elements we want from Dynamics CRM 2011 when an account changes. The first element, `EventSource`, is used to designate the source of the change event, as there may be multiple systems that share changes in an organization's accounts.

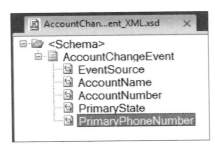

4. This BizTalk project should be set to deploy to a BizTalk application named Chapter3. Build and deploy the project to the designated BizTalk Server.

5. After confirming a successful deployment, launch the BizTalk WCF Service Publishing Wizard. We are going to use this schema to expose a web service entry point into BizTalk Server that Dynamics CRM 2011 can invoke.

6. On the WCF Service Type wizard page, select a **WCF-BasicHttp** adapter and set the service to expose metadata and have the wizard generate a receive location for us in the **Chapter3** application:

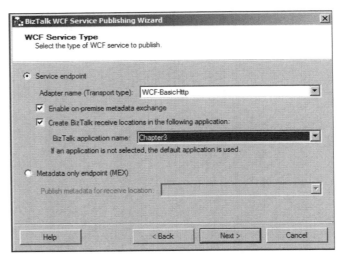

7. On the **Create WCF Service** wizard page, choose to **Publish schemas as WCF service**. This option gives us fine-grained control over the naming associated with our service.

8. On the next page, delete the two-way operation already present in the service definition. Rename the topmost service definition to **AccountChangeService** and assign the service the same name. Right-click the service and create a new one-way operation named **PublishAccountChange**. Right click the **Request** message of the operation and choose the `AccountChangeEvent` message from our BizTalk Project's DLL:

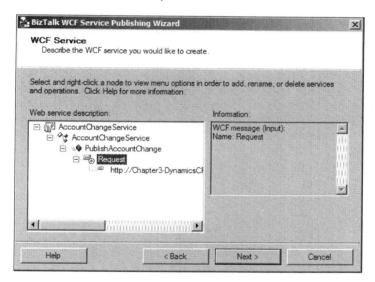

9. On the following wizard page, set the namespace of the service to `http://Chapter3/AccountServices`.

10. Next, set the location of our service to `http://localhost/AccountChangeService` and select the option to allow anonymous access to the generated service. Finally, complete the wizard by clicking the **Create** button on the final wizard page.

11. Confirm that the wizard successfully created both an IIS-hosted web service, and a BizTalk receive port/location. Ensure that the IIS web service is running under an Application Pool that has permission to access the BizTalk databases.

12. In order to test this service, first go to the BizTalk Server Administration Console and locate the **Chapter3** application.

13. Right click the **Send Ports** folder and create a new, static one-way send port named **Chapter3.SendAccountChange.FILE**. Set the send port to use the FILE adapter and select the `FileDrop\DropCustomerChangeEvent` folder that is present in the chapter's code package:

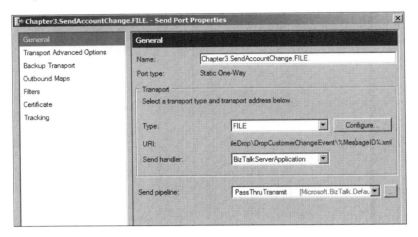

14. This send port should listen for all account change event messages, regardless of which receive location (and system) that they came from. Go to the **Filters** tab of this send port. Set the filter **Property** to **BTS.MessageType** and filter **Value** to `http://Chapter3-DynamicsCRM.AcctRouting.AccountChangeEvent_XML#AccountChangeEvent`.

15. All that remains is to test our service. Open the WCF Test Client application and add a new service reference to `http://localhost/AccountChangeService/AccountChangeService.svc`.

16. Invoke the `PublishAccountChange` method and, if everything is configured correctly, we will see a message emitted by BizTalk Server that matches our service input parameters:

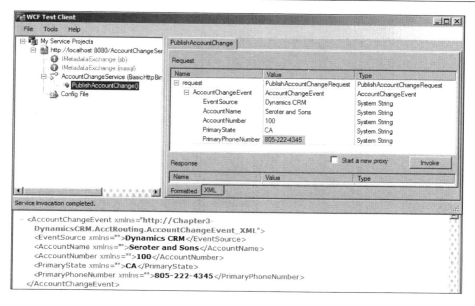

We now are sufficiently ready to author the Dynamics CRM plugin, which calls this BizTalk service.

Writing the Dynamics CRM plugin

A Dynamics CRM plugin is a powerful way to extend the out-of-the-box behavior of the product with custom code. The plugin that we are building for this exercise invokes the service we built above.

Before starting, ensure that you have downloaded the Dynamics CRM 2011 SDK and installed the `microsoft.xrm.sdk.dll` assembly in the Global Assembly Cache.

1. In the existing Chapter3-DynamicsCRM Visual Studio 2010 solution, add a new Class Library project named `Chapter3-DynamicsCRM.AcctPlugin` to the solution.

2. Add a new reference to this project and point to the `microsoft.xrm.sdk.dll` assembly. This assembly contains the interfaces and types that we need to correctly define a plugin.

3. Now, we need a service reference to our BizTalk-generated WCF endpoint. Choose to add a new Service Reference to the project. Point to our previously created service and set the namespace to **AcctChangeSvc**:

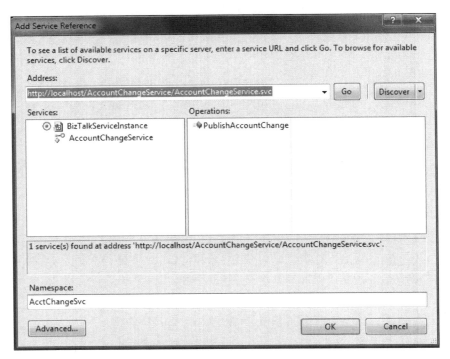

4. Add a new class file named `AccountEventPlugin.cs` to the project.

5. At the top of the new class, add two additional "using" statements pointing to `Microsoft.Xrm.Sdk` and `System.ServiceModel`. These assemblies have all that we need to define the plugin and consume our BizTalk-generated service.

6. The public class should implement the `IPlugin` interface, which has a single required operation, named `Execute`:

```
public class AccountEventPlugin : IPlugin
    {
        public void Execute(IServiceProvider serviceProvider)
        {

        }
    }
```

7. Depending on your use case, you may need to store the result of a successful plugin invocation on a Dynamics CRM record. In this scenario, we will simply log details of our plugin execution to the machine's Event Log. Hence the first line in the Execute operation is as follows:

```
System.Diagnostics.EventLog.
WriteEntry("Application", "Plugin invoked successfully", System.
Diagnostics.EventLogEntryType.Information);
```

8. Next up, we need to acquire context about the data entity being passed to the plugin. The `IPipelineExecutionContext` holds such information in addition to the runtime environment that the plugin is executing in:

```
IPluginExecutionContext context = (IPluginExecutionContext)
serviceProvider.GetService(typeof(IPluginExecutionContext));
```

9. We will be extracting data from an Account, and thus need a variable that references this entity. At the time of declaring this variable, its value is null:

```
Entity accountEntity = null;
```

10. Because one can use a plugin in all sorts of scenarios, some preventative error checking is prudent. To start with, we can ensure that the object that was passed into the plugin is indeed a Dynamics CRM entity. The context object defined earlier contains a set of input parameters containing the data from the request message:

```
if (context.InputParameters.Contains("Target") && context.
InputParameters["Target"] is Entity)
{
}
```

11. If the plugin target is an entity, set the previously defined `accountEntity` variable to the entity passed into the plugin:

```
//retrieve entity from input params
accountEntity = (Entity)context.InputParameters["Target"];
```

12. We could have tied this plugin to any Dynamics CRM entity and therefore should check and make sure that the type of entity passed into the plugin is valid:

```
//if the target account type isn't "account" exit
if (accountEntity.LogicalName != "account")
{
    System.Diagnostics.EventLog.WriteEntry(
"Application",
"Target is not 'account' type",
System.Diagnostics.EventLogEntryType.Error);
    return;
}
```

13. One key thing to realise is that when the "Update" events occur in the Dynamics CRM event pipeline, only the changed fields of an entity are put in the context's property bag. In order to have access to the entire payload of the account entity, we can use an Image. An Image is a representation of an entity either before or after it was saved to Dynamics CRM. There are four fields of the Account entity that we are interested in and those can be retrieved from the PostEntityImages collection that is part of the context. We use the name "PostEventImage" here and will refer to it later when we register this plugin with Dynamics CRM:

```
Entity acctImage = context.PostEntityImages["PostEventImage"];

string acctName = accountEntity["name"].ToString();
string acctNumber = accountEntity["accountnumber"].ToString();
string state = accountEntity["address1_stateorprovince"].
ToString();
string phone = accountEntity["telephone1"].ToString();
```

14. Armed with the necessary data elements, we can now create the WCF service input object. The AccountChangeEvent object is defined as part of the Service Reference established previously:

```
AcctChangeSvc.AccountChangeEvent acct = new AcctChangeSvc.
AccountChangeEvent();
acct.EventSource = "Dynamics CRM";
acct.AccountName = acctName;
acct.AccountNumber = acctNumber;
acct.PrimaryState = state;
acct.PrimaryPhoneNumber = phone;
```

15. We are now ready to invoke the service from code. First, create a reference to the binding type associated with our BizTalk-generated service. In this example, use the BasicHttpBinding without any security settings turned on:

```
BasicHttpBinding binding = new BasicHttpBinding(BasicHttpSecurityM
ode.None);
```

16. Next, an endpoint address is required. Put in the full service URL associated with your BizTalk endpoint:

```
EndpointAddress addr = new EndpointAddress("http://localhost/
AccountChangeService/AccountChangeService.svc");
```

17. This information is all that is needed to instantiate the service client that was defined in our Service Reference:

```
AcctChangeSvc.AccountChangeServiceClient client =
  new AcctChangeSvc.AccountChangeServiceClient(binding, addr);
```

18. Invoke the PublishAccountChange operation and upon success, write a message to the machine's Event Log:

```
client.PublishAccountChange(acct);

System.Diagnostics.EventLog.WriteEntry("Application",
"Service called successfully",
System.Diagnostics.EventLogEntryType.Information);
```

The plugin is now ready for deployment and registration in the Dynamics CRM environment.

Registering the plugin

Microsoft provides a plugin registration tool as part of the SDK. This tool is located in the SDK\Tools\PluginRegistration folder of the SDK. Prior to running the plugin registration tool, copy the Chapter3-DynamicsCRM.AcctPlugin.dll to the <installation directory>\Program Files\Microsoft CRM\server\ bin\assembly on the servers where Dynamics CRM resides. You need to put the assembly here if you want to debug it later or if you are not using the database storage option. If you do choose to store the plugin assembly in the Dynamics CRM database and are not concerned about debugging your plugin, then the assembly may reside anywhere during registration:

1. The plugin registration tool is included in the Dynamics CRM SDK as an example application. Go to the location where we unpacked the SDK and navigate to the tools\pluginregistration folder. Build the project and launch the executable.

2. Connect to the Dynamics CRM 2011 instance.

3. Click the option to register a new assembly:

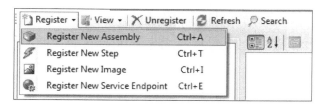

4. Navigate to the Chapter3-DynamicsCRM.AcctPlugin.dll assembly and click **Load Assembly**.

5. Specify the Isolation Mode as **None**. There is an additional option of **Sandbox** that introduces a series of limitations on plugins run in that mode. Sandboxed plugins have limits on access to the file system, Event Log, network, and more. This is a very useful option when offering a hosting environment, as a provider can restrict the types of plugins that each customer in the shared environment can deploy.

6. Next, choose the location to store the plugin. The default option is **Database** but we may also store the file on disk or the Global Assembly Cache. Set the location as **Database**.

7. Click the **Registered Selected Plugins** button to load and register the plugin in the Dynamics CRM database:

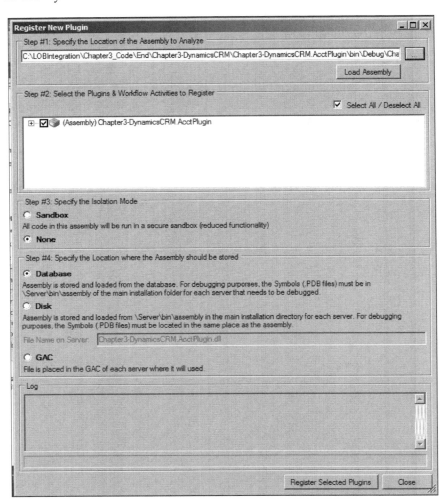

8. Next up, within the **Registered Plugins & Custom Workflow Activities** window, select our new plugin, and choose **Register** and then **Register New Step** from the menu.

9. This window lets us register the event and entity that should trigger our plugin. Set the event, called a **message** in Dynamics CRM, to **Update**. There are many message options, including Create, Close, Merge, Retrieve, and more.

10. Set the **Primary Entity** value to **account**. This is the entity whose message will launch the plugin. Note that by using the **Filtering Attributes** property, we can set which fields on an entity trigger the message.

11. Set the **Eventing Pipeline Stage of Execution** to **Post-operation**. Plugins run within the execution pipeline of entity processing. Plugins that run in the "pre" stage operate before the message is saved to Dynamics CRM. It is a useful place for doing data validation. The "post" stage is a good place for logic that should run after the data is committed to Dynamics CRM. In our case, we want to send the message to BizTalk Server after the entity has been updated. Select the radio button next to **Post-operation**.

12. Finally, set the execution mode. Plugins can run either synchronously or asynchronously. A plugin that validates data before saving it should run synchronously so that the user can be notified if any errors are encountered. In this case, our service should execute after the Dynamics CRM user has finished updating the entity and we do not want to interrupt or delay the user while the BizTalk service is called. Set the **Execution Mode** to **Asynchronous**:

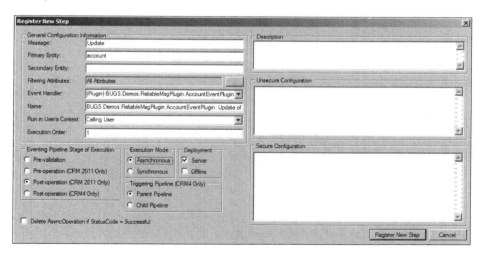

13. With the step registered, our last step is to register an Image. Recall that the Update message only contains the fields that have undergone a change. If we need to access other fields from the entity, we either have to invoke the Dynamics CRM services, or, even better, use an Image that gets passed into the plugin. Select the plugin from the **Registered Plugins & Custom Workflow Activities** window, select the **Register**, and then the **Register New Image** button.

14. Set the **Image Type** as **Post Image**, and set the **Name** and **Entity Alias** to **PostEventImage**. The **Parameters** setting allows us to set which fields on the entity we want available in the Image. Leave this value as **All Attributes**. Finally, click the**Register Image** button.

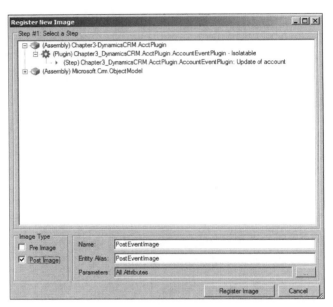

15. At this point, our configuration should look like this:

We have now successfully built a Dynamics CRM 2011 plugin and registered it with the system. This plugin will asynchronously fire after an account record has been saved and pass a complete image within the `IPluginExecutionContext` object.

Testing the plugin

To test this configuration, we simply need to change the details on a specific account. Because we registered this plugin to fire on **any** change to an account entity (vs. filtering which attributes launch the plugin), any changed attribute will do:

1. Open Dynamics CRM 2011 and navigate to the Accounts view.

2. Open any existing account to view its attributes.

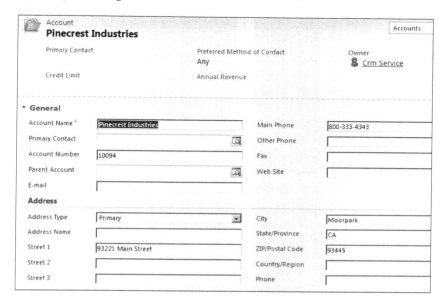

3. Change any one attribute of the account. In the example above, I changed the account number from 10094 to 10095. The plugin should launch nearly immediately. Check the Event Log of the machine hosting Dynamics CRM 2011 and watch for the events signifying success.

4. Next, switch to the folder that BizTalk Server sends the account change events to and confirm that the event was published there.

```
- <AccountChangeEvent xmlns="http://Chapter3-DynamicsCRM.AcctRou
    <EventSource xmlns="">Dynamics CRM</EventSource>
    <AccountName xmlns="">Pinecrest Industries</AccountName>
    <AccountNumber xmlns="">10095</AccountNumber>
    <PrimaryState xmlns="">CA</PrimaryState>
    <PrimaryPhoneNumber xmlns="">800-333-4343</PrimaryPhoneNumber>
  </AccountChangeEvent>
```

This simple test showed how a change in a Dynamics CRM entity could immediately send a message to BizTalk Server for additional processing.

Summary

Microsoft Dynamics CRM 2011 offers a host of options for integration. While it no longer provides a strongly-typed SOAP interface for BizTalk to consume, we have multiple ways to send messages to Dynamics CRM. To send messages from Dynamics CRM to BizTalk Server, we have numerous choices, including the plugin model that we demonstrated in this chapter. As Dynamics CRM 2011 matures in the market, expect to see additional creative ways to integrate it with BizTalk Server.

In the next chapter, we'll understand how to install the WCF-SAP adapter's prerequisite DLLs. Learn about extended, custom and out of the box IDOCs and how to send and receive them.

4

WCF SAP Adapter—Sending and Receiving IDOCs

SAP is a large Enterprise Software company that was established in 1972 in Mannheim, Germany. SAP is an acronym that stands for Systeme, Anwendungen, Produkte, which translates into Systems Applications and Products in English. The company historically has a focus on building business applications as the five original co-founders previously worked for IBM.

SAP provides a comprehensive development platform and licenses domain-specific modules that are tailored towards industry-specific functions. Some of the modules include Human Resources (HR), Finance (FI), Materials Management (MM), Plant Maintenance (PM), Supply Chain Management (SCM), Compatible Units (CU), Utilities (ISU), and Customer Relationship Management (CRM). In addition to these modules, underlying platform components exist called BASIS. BASIS administrators are generally responsible for configuring and maintaining the Relational Database Management System (RDBMS), deploying transports (deployment packages), and configuring access for external systems requesting connectivity to SAP's interfaces.

In this chapter, we will be discussing the following topics:

- What is SAP?
- Why do people use it?
- SAP's market share
- Why do people choose BizTalk to integrate with SAP?
- Challenges that BizTalk Developers may face
- Installation of WCF SAP Adapter
- Pre-requisite files
- SAP DLLs that are required

- 32-bit vs. 64-bit considerations
- WCF-SAP Adapter vs. WCF Custom Adapter
- IDOC Schema Generation
- What are IDOCs?
- Difference between Inbound and Outbound IDOCs
- IDOC deep Dive
- Control Record
- Partner Profile/Program ID
- Extended IDOCs
- Building a BizTalk Application
- Testing a BizTalk Application
- Custom IDOCs
- Flat File IDOC considerations

Why do people use SAP?

Many medium and large-sized businesses have relied upon SAP to provide the software that runs their business. Often times, these organizations have adopted a "Buy" mentality instead of "Build". Many CIOs have gone in this direction since building software may not be the company's core competency. Since SAP also provides a development platform, businesses can often customize SAP functionality that does not align with their internal practices. Customizing SAP happens quite often as every business is different and also regulation differs throughout various jurisdictions around the world.

Since the SAP platform is so comprehensive, most developers, or consultants, will focus on particular modules such as Material Management (MM) or Plant Maintenance (PM). Within each of these modules, SAP resources will specialize in a functional role or in a more technical ABAP role. ABAP , or Advanced Business Application Programming, is a programming language very similar to COBAL. ABAP continues to be the predominate language SAP programmers use to build programs. Recently, Java has started to gain in popularity as SAP has introduced the NetWeaver stack. NetWeaver is SAP's attempt at moving towards a Service Oriented Architecture (SOA), which is very different from the mainframe-like culture that SAP was built upon.

A component of NetWeaver that directly competes with BizTalk is called Process Integration (PI). PI can be used to integrate SAP functions across modules or can also be used to integrate with other external systems. PI has tools similar to BizTalk that include functions like message transformation, business process orchestration, and adapters.

Why do people choose BizTalk to integrate with SAP?

BizTalk often competes with PI when organizations start integrating SAP with other internal and external systems. Some organizations will choose to go the SAP route, others will go the Microsoft route, and some will use a combination of both technologies to solve their integration needs.

Organizations that choose to introduce BizTalk usually do so for some of the following reasons:

- SAP PI resources are scarce and expensive
- Microsoft has an excellent development ecosystem
    - In order to verify this, all one needs to do is start browsing Microsoft's MSDN forums, BizTalkGurus.com, or many of the BizTalk blogs that exist. The amount of BizTalk integration-related information is un-paralleled amongst BizTalk's competitors.
- Consistent development experience
    - Many, if not most, BizTalk developers spent time as .NET programmers before getting involved in BizTalk. While some integration concepts are foreign to .NET programmers, the environment in which they develop their applications is not. Both .NET and BizTalk developers perform their development tasks in Visual Studio. Tasks like adding Service references and schema development are also extremely similar between the two technologies. The development tools on the SAP platform do not possess the sophistication and continual improvement that Visual Studio provides.

- Developer Productivity
  - Microsoft sponsored a Productivity study to determine the Total Cost of ownership between PI and BizTalk. BizTalk performed very favourably against SAP PI. The entire study can be found here: `http://www.microsoft.com/downloads/en/details.aspx?FamilyID=6EC68631-2B4C-485F-83CF-7C26893839C4&displaylang=en`

Another aspect to consider is what other systems you will be integrating with. One of BizTalk's strengths is its ability to integrate well with Microsoft and non-Microsoft platforms. This book in itself is a testament to BizTalk's ability to integrate with so many different platforms. This point is often one that pushes BizTalk over the top for decision makers. BizTalk is able to integrate with SAP reliably, efficiently, cost effectively, and can also integrate with other non-SAP systems. While SAP PI is very capable of integrating with SAP, it just does not do a great job when integrating with non-SAP systems.

Challenges that BizTalk Developers may face

Some of the most challenging obstacles that BizTalk Developers face when integrating with SAP are not technical in nature. Often times, the challenges are related to politics. The perception that many SAP resources have of Microsoft is that Microsoft's systems are unstable, not enterprise ready, and full of security vulnerabilities. Considering that most SAP systems are run on top of UNIX, or derivations of it, these perceptions are not surprising. The reality is that Microsoft has matured in the enterprise space and can compete with the likes of SAP, Oracle, and IBM. Other concerns often involve whether or not the BizTalk Adapter is doing things to the SAP system that it shouldn't be. I recall a few years back a BASIS Administrator who was adamant that no Microsoft "connector" would be connecting to his system. What is important to emphasize in these scenarios is the certification process Microsoft undergoes in order to ensure its related products are certified by SAP. The BizTalk Adapter Pack happens to be one of these technologies that has achieved such a rating by SAP.

Turf wars often develop as SAP resources may feel that an "outsider" is encroaching on their territory. I have worked with a SAP consultant in the past who was adamant that he could perform the integration work by using SAP Data Warehouse/Business Intelligence to move data around. It clearly wasn't the right decision, but the person didn't want to see some of that control passed over to Microsoft.

The reality is whenever you build integrated solutions, across multiple technologies and teams, you need to work as a team to build, test, and troubleshoot the solutions. It requires that developers and architects set aside their biases and egos in order to work as a team. The end result is something that should provide value to the organization and not the individuals involved. Something that I have found that helps in this regard is to try and understand their terminology. If you are the new BizTalk "whiz", they are probably not going to be overly happy to see you there, let alone learn your terminology. But, if you can learn their terminology, it may make the transition smoother.

As a BizTalk developer, you need to establish a positive working relationship with your BASIS administrator(s). Building an IDOC solution will require some effort by the BASIS administrator as they will have to create the BizTalk account, Program ID, or Partner Profile, that will provide access to the various IDOCs that BizTalk will be processing.

Installation of WCF SAP Adapter

The installation of the WCF SAP Adapter was covered in the first chapter; however, there are a few specific details worth mentioning in this chapter.

32-bit vs. 64-bit

If our BizTalk environment is 32-bit, then we do not need to perform any additional actions. If our BizTalk environment is 64-bit, then we need to install both the 32-bit and 64-bit versions of the Adapter. The reason for this is that a lot of the BizTalk tooling remains as 32-bit applications, including Visual Studio and the BizTalk Administration console. So, even though our runtime may be 64-bit, we need the 32-bit version in order to generate schemas and to configure any Receive Locations or Send Ports that will be using the SAP Adapter.

SAP Prerequisite DLLs

Installing the BizTalk Adapter pack is not enough. You need to obtain two packages from the SAP Marketplace. The SAP Marketplace is the equivalent of Microsoft's MSDN and TechNet offerings. It is a place where registered customers and partners can obtain SAP software downloads and technical documentation. SAP Marketplace requires a login and any organization who is paying for SAP support will have one. Most likely our BASIS Administrator will have a login so we may need to ask them to download the packages for us. Also, note that each package is specific to a version of SAP whether it is a Unicode or non-Unicode installation. It is advisable to have a conversation with the BASIS Administrator before any packages are downloaded.

The first package that we need to obtain contains the SAP RFC SDK DLLs. These RFC DLLs get used during design time generation of SAP schemas and during the runtime operations when BizTalk is sending and receiving messages with SAP. Microsoft using these DLLs is a good thing and strengthens our case for having Microsoft handle the integration with an SAP system since we are using SAP code when establishing connections.

The second package is called `R3DLLINST.zip` and contains the Microsoft runtime DLLs. Even though these are Microsoft DLLs, they are still available through the SAP Marketplace.

Within the BizTalk Adapter Pack installation folder, an install guide called `InstallationGuide.htm` exists in the `C:\Program Files\Microsoft BizTalk Adapter Pack(x64)\Documents` folder for 64-bit systems. Similarly, a document will exist on a 32-bit system in the `C:\Program Files\Microsoft BizTalk Adapter Pack\Documents` folder. A table exists that describes the prerequisite DLLs that are required for specific versions of SAP. Microsoft has included a link within each section that will take us directly to the location within the SAP Marketplace to download the package and get more specific information. The SAP client version that we will be using for this chapter is SAP client 7.0 so the URLs that we will follow are:

Download Purpose	SAP Note ID	Download URL
RFC SDK	27517	`http://go.microsoft.com/fwlink/?LinkID=94691`
Microsoft Run Time DLLs	684106	`http://go.microsoft.com/fwlink/?LinkID=94693`

When we navigate to the SAP note for the installing the SAP RFC SDK, we are prompted to download the assemblies from another URL: `http://service.sap.com/swdc`.

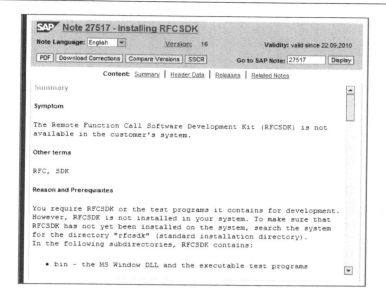

Once we navigate down the website's hierarchy of **Support Packages and Patches - Entry by Application Group - Additional Components - SAP RFC SDK UNICODE - SAP RFC SDK 7.00 UNICODE** we end up with the download section that we are interested in. If we are running a 64-bit environment, then we need both 32-bit and 64-bit packages due to the differences between the 32-bit BizTalk design/admin tools and the 64-bit BizTalk runtime.

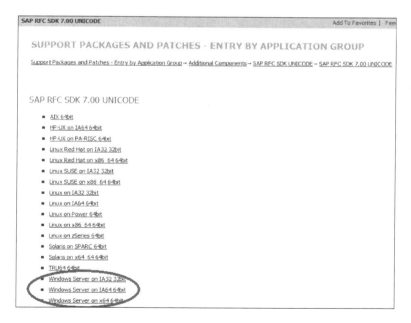

These software packages that exist in the SAP Marketplace have been packaged in a SAP specific package tool called SAPCAR. In order to open these packages, we need to download the SAPCAR tool.

We can download SAPCAR from the same location as where we found the RFC SDK.

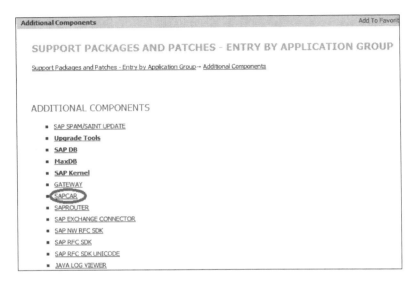

Once again we will need to choose the platform that we will be using when extracting the SAR package.

Once we have SAPCAR downloaded, we need to open a command line prompt and change our directory to the location where we saved the SAPCAR.exe. If we execute a command similar to the one below, we will be able to extract the SAR archive.

```
F:\Dev\SAP>SAPCAR_0-10003696.exe -xfv "RFC_25-20001765.SAR"

SAPCAR: processing archive RFC_25-20001765.SAR (version 2.01)

SAPCAR: 61 file(s) extracted
```

The result of this command being executed is that a folder called rfcsdk is created that will contain several sub folders including a bin and lib folders.

- If we are running a 64-bit BizTalk environment, then we need to copy the SAP DLLs from the 32-bit SAR package and 64 bit SAR package to multiple locations.

- If you are installing both 32 bit and 64 bit Adapters and DLLs, you need to pay close attention to Microsoft's install instructions. The installation instructions that are provided as part of the adapter install specify the following:

  ○ "On a 64-bit computer, the 32-bit version of the DLLs must be added to the `C:\Windows\SysWow64` folder. The 64-bit version of the DLLs must be added to the `C:\Windows\System32` folder." These instructions defy common logic so be sure not to overlook this step. You can also read about this step in the SAP Adapter's Frequently Asked Questions page: `http://msdn.microsoft.com/en-us/library/cc185322(BTS.10).aspx`

In the demo environment for this book, the following 64-bit DLLs and libraries have been copied into the `%WINDOWS%\System32` directory from the `bin` directory that was created in the SAPCAR process.

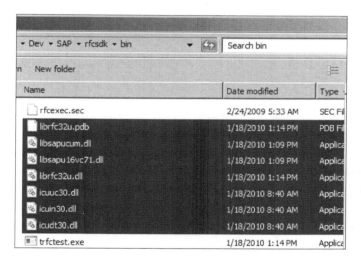

We now need to copy the following libraries from the 64-bit lib directory into the `%WINDOWS%\System32` directory.

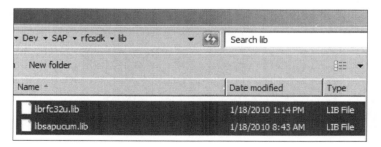

The end result is that the following nine files should all end up in the `%WINDOWS%\`
`System32` directory as illustrated in the following screenshot:

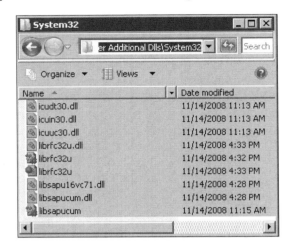

Similarly, the following 32-bit DLLs need to be copied into the `%WINDOWS%\SysWOW64`
directory. The 32-bit DLLs should come from the 32 bit SAR archive that we
previously downloaded.

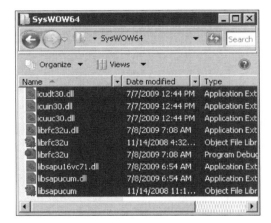

The next set of prerequisite DLLs that we need to deal with are the Microsoft runtime
DLLs. Once again, these DLLs can be retrieved from the SAP Marketplace via the
URL that is specified in the BizTalk Adapter Pack Installation Guide. Navigating
to `http://go.microsoft.com/fwlink/?LinkID=94693` will render the following
page. After reviewing the content that SAP has provided, we want to click on the
Attachments link.

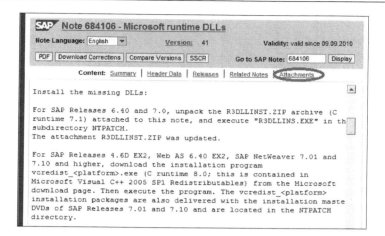

The file that we are interested in is r3dllinst.zip. Click on the link to download this package.

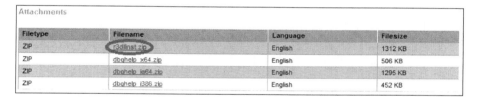

Once we have the `r3dllinst.zip` downloaded, we need to extract this package and will end up with the following files in the `ntpatch` folder:

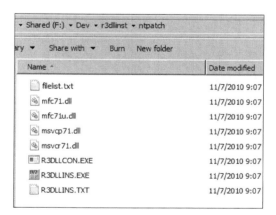

We now want to execute `R3DLLINS.EXE` and should get prompted with the following message. Click **OK** to proceed with the installation of these DLLs.

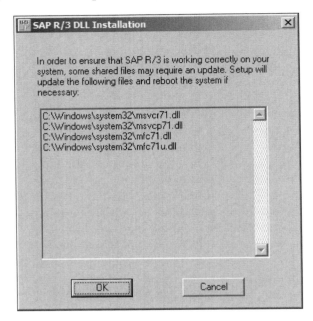

This concludes the prerequisite DLLs that are required in order for the SAP adapter to function properly. We will validate the SAP Adapter functions properly in an upcoming section when we generate IDOC schemas. If we are able to generate Schemas via Visual Studio, then we know our 32-bit installation is complete. We will not know about our 64-bit assemblies until we try to process a message.

WCF-SAP Adapter vs WCF Customer Adapter with SAP binding

When we generate schemas for SAP artifacts, the binding file that is also generated will use the WCF-Custom Adapter with an **SAP Binding Type**. With this binding type selected, we can manipulate any SAP-related property.

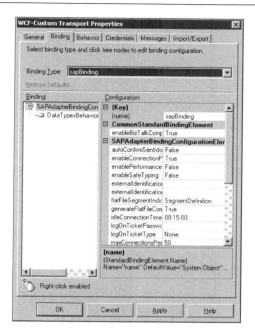

The challenge with using the WCF-Custom Adapter is that when we configure the URI for our SAP server, the interface is not very intuitive. The SAP connection string is confusing at best and one missing key stroke will result in an error.

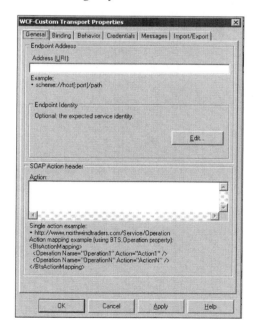

Conversely, the WCF-SAP adapter is a little more intuitive when we configure our SAP URI. By clicking the **Configure** button, we have a well-organized table to populate, which reduces the complexity of providing a valid SAP connection string.

To create a WCF-SAP adapter, we need to perform the following steps:

1. Right mouse click on **Adapters** and then select **New - Adapter**.

2. Click the **Adapter** drop-down list and select **WCF-SAP**. In the **Name** text box, type in **WCF-SAP** and click **OK** button.

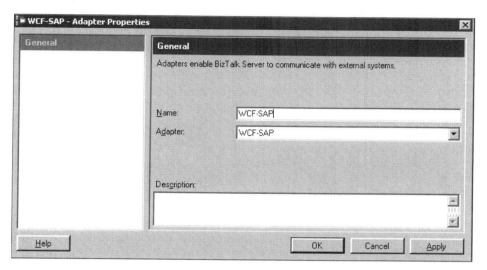

It is important to understand that no matter whether you use the WCF-Custom Adapter or WCF-SAP Adapter, you are not losing functionality. Using the WCF-SAP adapter simplifies the administration tasks that are involved in maintaining our BizTalk environment. Since the WCF-Custom adapter can leverage many different bindings including Oracle, SQL, SAP, and bindings that allow us to connect to the cloud, it is beneficial to explicitly create these adapters to avoid confusion.

Supported SAP configurations

The following SAP configurations are supported. New to BizTalk 2010 is the support for SAP 7. For the purpose of this chapter, the SAP system that is being used is SAP ECC 6.0 but the following versions are supported:

- Supported server versions: SAP 7, SAP ECC 6.0 Unicode, SAP ECC 5.0 Non-Unicode, SAP ECC 5.0 Unicode, SAP R/3 4.7 Non-Unicode, SAP R/3 4.7 Unicode, SAP R/3 4.6c Non-Unicode, SAP ERP 6.0 with EHP 4.0

- Supported client versions: SAP RFC SDK 7.11 UNICODE, SAP RFC SDK 7.1 UNICODE, SAP RFC SDK 7.0 UNICODE, SAP RFC SDK 6.4 UNICODE

IDOC schema generation

With the installation and configuration of the SAP Adapter out of the way, we are now going to focus on IDOCs. We will be exploring the following features of IDOCs:

- What are IDOCs
- How to Generate IDOC schemas and understanding important properties

What are IDOCs?

IDOC stands for **Intermediate Document** and is a SAP specification that is used for exchanging information within SAP systems and with external systems such as BizTalk. SAP resources think of IDOCs much like BizTalk resources think about XSD schemas. The difference being that IDOC structures resemble flat files whereas XSD schemas are based upon XML.

SAP has a consistent structure that includes a Header segment that contains metadata associated with the IDOC. The Header is consistent across all IDOC types but the body of the IDOCs will be different based upon the function that the IDOC supports. SAP has specific IDOC structures for different system functions. An HR Timesheet IDOC is going to look very different from a Purchase Order. Each IDOC will have segments that are specific to the IDOC. We can think of segments much like we think of XML Nodes. If you ask an SAP resource if the IDOC has repeating nodes, they may not understand your question. But, if you ask if an IDOC has repeating segments, they will instantly understand.

How to generate IDOC schemas

Now that we have some basic knowledge of IDOCs, let's go ahead and generate an IDOC to gain a better understanding. Much like we previously generated Schemas for SQL Server, we will be leveraging the Consume Adapter Service. We can launch this wizard by right mouse clicking on our BizTalk project and selecting **Add – Add Generated Items…Consume Adapter Service**.

1. We are now in familiar territory having used this wizard in previous chapters. This time around we want to select the **sapBinding** from the **Select a binding** dropdown.

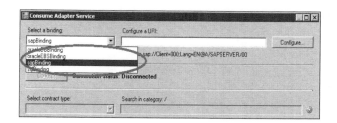

2. We now need to configure a URI and can do so by clicking the **Configure** button. The first area that we need to address is the **Security** tab. Within this tab, we have a few different options when it comes to **Client credential type**:

   ° None

   ° Windows

   ° Username

   ° Certificate

I am going to go out on a limb and suggest that we will never run into a situation where we don't have to provide credentials so we will not be using **None**. The SAP system that is being used for this walkthrough does not reside on the **Windows** platform so that is not an option. If your SAP system supports Windows Authentication then using this type of authentication is worth considering. There are no specific requirements around proving our identity so **Certificate** is not required. This leaves us with providing a standard **Username** and **Password**. Generally, these credentials are assigned by a SAP Security Administrator and sometimes a BASIS Administrator. These are the same type of credentials that users provide when accessing SAP through the SAP GUI except with additional privileges.

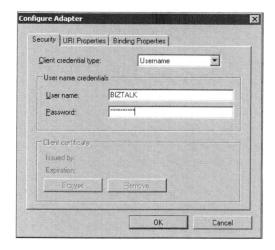

3. The next tab that we want to focus on is the **URI Properties.** The base properties that we need to populate include:
   - Application Server Host
   - System Number
   - Client

The **Application Server Host** is the name of the physical SAP Application server, or more likely a virtual DNS alias. This value will most likely be unique across the various SAP landscapes, that is, DEVELOPMENT/TEST/ PRODUCTION.

The **System Number** is a unique numerical identifier for a particular instance of SAP. **Client**, in this context, is used to separate data within an SAP system. For instance if you have subsidiaries sharing an SAP system, but want to have segregated data, then you could create multiple clients that will allow you to distinguish one company's data from another. If you are familiar with Dynamics CRM, **Client** would be the equivalent of an Organization. This number will most likely be the same across the various SAP landscapes but you may have multiple values in co-hosting situations. These are all values that you will most likely get from a BASIS Administrator.

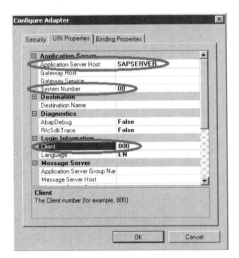

4. The final tab that we need to be concerned with is the **Binding Properties** tab. Within this tab, we will specify some attributes related to how BizTalk will interact with SAP. It is important to note that many of these settings can be changed within the BizTalk Administration console when you are ready to configure your application. Within the next screenshot, we will concentrate on two particular properties:

○ **ReceiveTimeout** – Probably one of the most important production properties to set. This property specifies the duration that BizTalk will wait for an inbound message before shutting down. The default value is 10 minutes which is hardly enough time. If we don't modify this setting, we may have some undesirable results in a Production environment when BizTalk stops listening for IDOCs once this threshold has been exceeded. The maximum value is 24.20:31:23.6470000 (24 days). To learn more about this property, please see the following blogpost: `http://kentweare.blogspot.com/2010/03/biztalk-adapter-pack-sap-binding.html`

○ **EnableBizTalkCompatibilityMode** – Specifies whether the BizTalk Layered Channel Binding Element should be loaded which will allow BizTalk transactions to flow to SAP. This value should always be set to true when using the WCF-SAP Adapter in BizTalk.

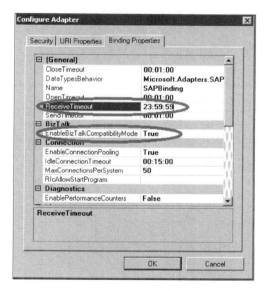

5. There are some additional properties within the **Binding Properties** tab that are of interest to us:

   ° **EnableSafeTyping** – Not all SAP data types have .NET data type equivalents. By enabling safe typing, BizTalk will have "looser" requirements about types when trying to bind an SAP data type to a .NET data type. It is important to understand how this property may change the behavior of your app. If you are expecting a Date from SAP, it is quite possible that the data will be converted to a string when this property is set to True. Speaking from personal experience, I have not had to set this property to true when integrating with IDOCs but have had to change the property when calling RFCs and BAPIs.

   ° **GenerateFlatFileCompatibleIDOC** – This property specifies whether the **<appinfo>** node should include segment types, or segment definitions, for parsing flat file IDOCs. By setting the property to True, it does not mean that you have to use Flat Files in order to process the IDOCs. It is a good idea to leave this value set to true as it provides you flexibility in the future to use Flat File if so desired.

   ° ReceiveIDOCFormat – Previously with the SAP Adapters that were based upon the .NET Connector, you had to process the IDOC as a Flat File. This is no longer the case with the WCF version of the Adapter. We now have the opportunity to send and receive messages as XML without the use of Flat File Schemas and Pipelines. If we specify **Typed** then we will receive the message as an XML message. We also have the ability to specify String or RFC. If we want to use a Flat File Schema/Pipeline then we need to specify String. If we want to receive the IDOC as a WCF message with RFC parameters then we want to specify RFC. Do note that these properties can be modified when we configure our receive location inside of the BizTalk Administration console.

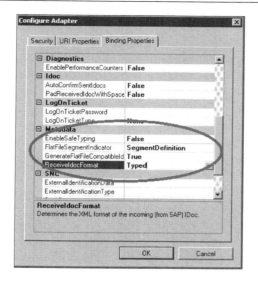

6. Now that we have our configuration set, click the OK button to return to the main wizard.

7. As long as we have configured the Wizard properly, we can now click the **Connect** button to establish a connection to SAP.

8. The next question that we need to ask ourselves is whether this is an Inbound or Outbound operation. It is important to remember the context in which this question is being asked. The question is being asked from a BizTalk perspective. Will this IDOC be an Outbound Operation from BizTalk or an Inbound Operation to BizTalk? Since we are sending an IDOC to SAP then we will want to specify a **Client (Outbound operations)**.

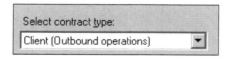

9. If we wanted to receive an IDOC from SAP, we will want to specify Service **(Inbound operations):**

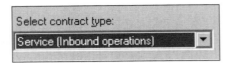

10. The next area to focus on is the **Search in category** function. In order for this function to work we need to specify the **Select a category** as we cannot search SAP's entire **BAPI, IDOC, RFC,** and **TRFC** catalogue. For the purpose of this demonstration, we will select IDOC.

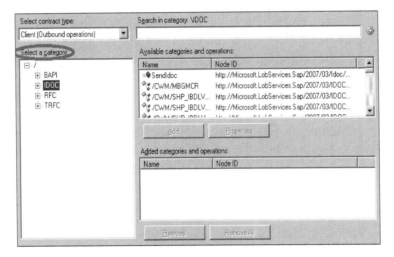

11. Within this text box, we can provide wild card searches and then click on the green arrow to execute the search. In this case, we can provide the term **CONF,** which will search for Confirmation IDOCs.

12. We will see our results populated in the **Available categories and operations:** list. The particular IDOC that we are interested in is the **CONF32** IDOC. Once we have this IDOC selected, we can click **Add** and then the IDOC will be added to the **Added categories and operations:** list box.

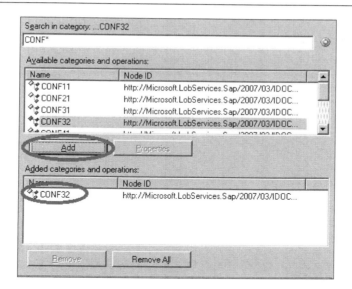

13. With the old, .NET Connector-based adapter one IDOC equaled one BizTalk XSD schema. This is no longer the case. The Consume Adapter Service Wizard will generate multiple schemas for each IDOC. The reason for this is the Wizard will create schemas for specific SAP types that then get imported into a Master, or Parent, Schema. If you have many IDOCs within your solution this can get very confusing unless you provide a **Filename Prefix**. If we provide a prefix, like **CONF32**, all schemas will start with this prefix, which will allow us to organize and differentiate our schemas.

14. Once we have provided this prefix, we can click the **OK** button and our IDOC schema will get generated.

15. While this method is convenient, it comes with some baggage. When you click the OK button, it will download every version of the IDOC from your SAP system. This may leave you with way more schemas than you are interested in and may also result in timeouts from the Consume Adapter Server Wizard as there is just too much data to retrieve.

16. Another option that we have is to browse the IDOC catalogue and find the exact version of the IDOC that we are interested in. As you can see by the following image, there are many different versions of the IDOC within our SAP systems. Select the version of the IDOC that you are interested in, click the **Add** button. Had we used the steps previously mentioned by downloading all versions, our BizTalk Solution would have become extremely bloated. By browsing to the exact version that we are interested in, we will only download that version and any supporting schemas that contain the complex types.

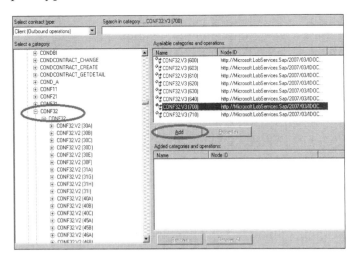

17. We now have an opportunity to provide a **Filename Prefix**. If we do not provide a Prefix, the wizard will provide a very generic filename that will not differentiate it from other SAP schemas. We should use a descriptive prefix so that we can easily differentiate this schema from other schemas that we will have in our solution. We can click the OK button to have the schemas added to our BizTalk solution.

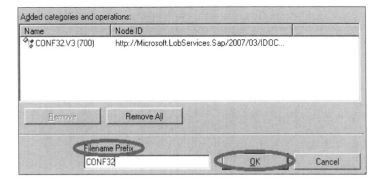

18. We will now find that six artifacts have been added to our solution. The main schema that we are interested in is `CONF32IDOCOperation.CONF32.700.3.Send.xsd`. The remaining schemas are there to support sending the IDOC and we also have a binding file that contains the values that we used to configure the Consume Adapter Service Wizard.

19. The Consume Adapter Service Wizard allows us to generate a single IDOC schema or multiple IDOCs at the same time. When dealing with multiple schemas, we need to be careful that the IDOCs do not share underlying common types that could lead to compilation errors. In order to avoid these compile time errors, we can check the **Generate unique schema types** check box. By doing so we will increase the number of schemas that are added to our solution. The additional schemas will include unique namespaces, which allows us to avoid the compile time errors.

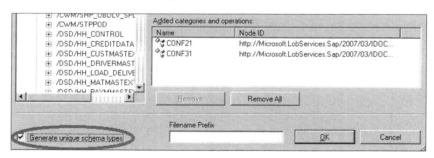

 Note: New for BizTalk 2010 is the ability for the SAP URI to be saved between launches of the Consume Adapter Service Wizard. Previously, we would have had to populate the entire URI configuration each time we wanted to generate Schemas. This is a significant timesaver and extremely convenient feature that has been added. Please be aware that if you are using Username as the client credential type that you will still need to provide the password each time you run the wizard.

IDOC Deep Dive

It is now time to take a closer look into the structure of IDOCs to better understand some of the segments that a BizTalk Developer must understand.

In each IDOC schema, you can expect the following elements:

- EDI_DC40
- SAP table(s), that is, E2CONF5
- guid

The EDI_DC40 node is also referred to as the Header node, or record. Within this node we will discover several fields that we need to populate including:

Element Name	Purpose
IDOCTYP	The basic structure of the IDOC.
CIMTYP	The structure of the custom extension. If an SAP basic structure is extended, a name must be given for the extension.
MESTYP	A logical representation of the message. The name should provide a business contextual meaning.
SNDPOR	Sending System Port
SNDPRN	Sending System/Partner
SNDPRT	Sender Partner Type
RCVPRT	Receiver Partner Type
RCVPRN	Receiving System/Partner
IDOCTYP	The basic structure of the IDOC

Depending upon the IDOC there may be one or more SAP tables that are represented within the IDOC. In the case of the CONF32 IDOC, there is only one called **E2CONF5**. Within this segment, or node, there are a number of fields that we need to populate.

Element Name	Purpose
LDATE	Logical date/actual date of the confirmation. In our situation we are just going to provide the current date.
BUDAT	Posting date of the confirmation. In our situation we are just going to provide the current date.
LTIME	Logical time/actual time of the confirmation. In our situation we are just going to provide the current time.
ERTIME	Entry time of the confirmation. In our situation, we are just going to provide the current time.
ARBPL	Work center
AUFNR	This field is where the Order Number for the job is submitted.
VORNR	Order Numbers, usually have an Operation associated with them so we can leverage this field to provide the Operation Number.
ISMNW	The duration of the work that was performed.

Finally, a GUID element exists that associates itself with the SAP transaction ID (TID). We can provide our own GUID, or let the adapter provide a GUID.

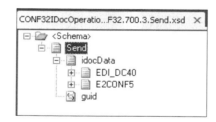

Building a BizTalk application – Sending IDOC

The application that we are going to build will receive Vehicle Timesheets from our Work Order Management system, transform the data and construct a CONF32 Confirmation IDOC. You may be asking yourself "Vehicles have Timesheets"? Yes they do! This scenario is an example of a real world solution where we have employees in the Energy sector out working on the maintenance of energy infrastructure. Much like we would expect to track the time that an employee spends on a job, we also want to track the time of equipment that has been used. A Vehicle makes up a significant portion of the overall costs on the job and therefore we want to ensure these costs are recorded in SAP. The, out-of-the-box, CONF32 IDOC allows us to send this information to SAP without customization.

1. The first task that we are going to take on is generating the **CONF32** IDOC. To simplify this process, we can leverage the steps discussed in the *How to Generate IDOC schemas* section in this chapter. The end result is that we should have the following schemas:

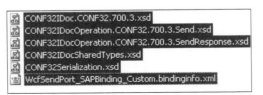

2. The next area that we need to focus on is generating a schema that represents the XML that the Work Order Management system will be sending. A simple schema called `VehicleTime.xsd` exists in this chapter's source code.

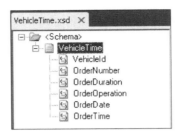

3. We now need to construct a map called `VehicleTime_to_CONF32.btm`. Within this map, we will have two tabs. The first tab that we are going to build is the **Control Record** tab. Within this tab, we need to provide SAP with metadata about the IDOC that we are about to send. SAP will use this information to determine how it should process the IDOC. SAP will also use the Partner information provided to determine if the BizTalk user that is submitting the IDOC has the appropriate permissions to do so.

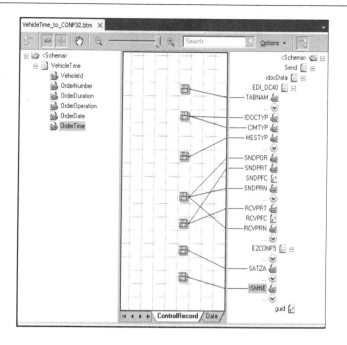

4. The following table contains the values that have been provided to each node. This information is generally static, but it is a good idea to store this information in a common Helper class so that if you have to make a change you can do so in one place. For the purpose of this chapter, we will simply embed this information with String Concatenate functoids. Do note that some values like **SNDPOR**, **SNDPRN**, and **RCVPRN** will most likely be different on your SAP system.

Node	Value
/EDI_DC40/TABNAM	EDI_DC40
/EDI_DC40/IDOCTYP	CONF32
/EDI_DC40/CIMTYP	CONF32
/EDI_DC40/MESTYP	CONF32
/EDI_DC40/SNDPOR	MTSIDOC
/EDI_DC40/SNDPRT	LS
/EDI_DC40/SNDPRN	MTSIDOC
/EDI_DC40/RCVPRT	LS
/EDI_DC40/RCVPRN	MTSIDOC
/E2CONF5/SATZA	I20
/E2CONF5/ISMNE	H

5. The next tab that we want to create is the **Data** tab. Within this tab, we will focus on the data that is being passed from the Work Order Management system and perform any formatting required for SAP.

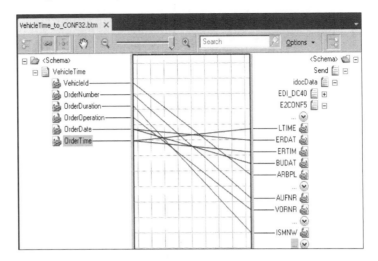

 Note: A new feature of the BizTalk 2010 mapper is the ability to display only nodes that are currently mapped. To enable this feature, click on the **Switch to relevance tree view for destination schema** button. When selected, the BizTalk mapper will only display nodes that are currently being mapped. This feature is very helpful when mapping SAP IDOCs that have many nodes.

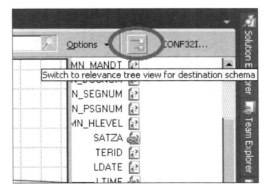

6. With the BizTalk Map complete we can focus on the BizTalk Orchestration that will be responsible for orchestrating the events between the Work Order Management System and SAP. The Orchestration will be responsible for the following functions:

   a. Receiving the Work Order Management request that includes the Vehicle Time.

   b. Transforming this request into the SAP CONF32 IDOC request.

   c. Receiving the SAP CONF32 IDOC Response.

   d. Writing the SAP CONF32 IDOC Response to disk so that we can verify whether the exchange with SAP was successful.

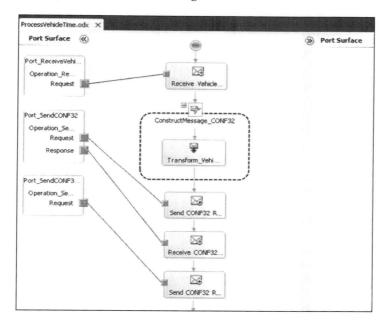

7. Since we are not using a Flat File schema and will opt to use the SOAP messaging capability of the SAP adapter, we can now deploy our application by right mouse clicking on the solution and selecting Deploy Solution.

8. Once inside the BizTalk Administration Console, we will discover that an application called Chapter04-SAPIDOCs now exists.

9. Within this application, we can find a Receive Port called
    ReceiveVehicleTimeSheet and a Receive Location called
    ReceiveVehicleTimeSheetFromDisk. This Receive Location will use the
    FILE adapter, the **BizTalkServerApplication** Receive handler and the
    XMLReceive Receive Pipeline.

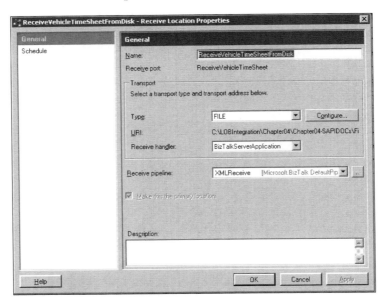

10. We will have two Send Ports with the first one being the Send Port that will
    be used to communicate with SAP. The Consume Adapter Wizard generated
    a binding file that we could use to generate a Send Port automatically. The
    issue with this approach is that the binding file will use the WCF Custom
    adapter, which does not allow us to manipulate the SAP connection details
    easily. Since we often create our SAP IDOC schemas in non-Production
    environments, it is not likely that we will be able to take full advantage of the
    generated Binding file anyways as our targets will be different within each
    BizTalk environment.

11. The name of the SAP Send port is **SendCONF32IDOC.** It will use the WCF-
    SAP custom adapter, the **BizTalkServerApplication** Send Handler, the
    XMLTransmit Send pipeline, and the **XMLReceive** pipeline. By clicking the
    Configure button, we can further explore the properties that are exposed by
    the SAP Adapter.

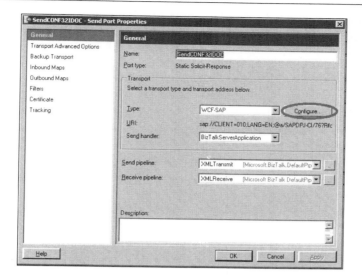

12. The **General** tab will expose our **Endpoint Address** and **SOAP Action header**. To further explore the **Address URI** we can click on the **Configure** button.

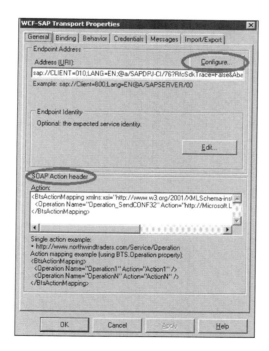

13. The configure button on the **General** tab is one of the key differentiators between using the WCF-Custom adapter, with SAP Binding, and the WCF-SAP adapter. As you can see in the following image the WCF-SAP Adapter provides us more options when configuring our SAP configuration. The key properties that we want to populate are:

   a. **Application Server Host**

   b. **System Number**

   c. **Client**

14. If you are unsure of the values for your organization, please contact your BASIS administrator.

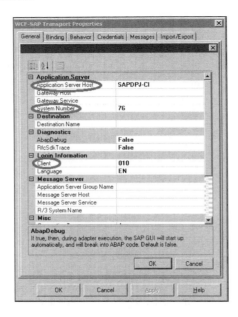

15. The next tab that we need to be concerned with is the **Credentials** tab. On this tab we will provide the BizTalk credentials that will be used to communicate with SAP. We do have the ability to specify a Username/Password combination or an SSO Affiliate application. For the purposes of this chapter, we will simply provide a Username/Password.

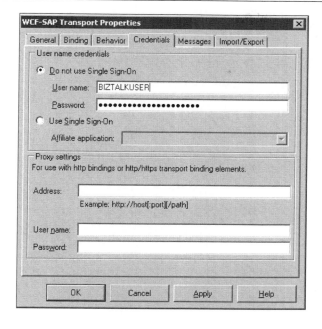

16. The next Send Port that we need to create is the Send Port that will write the SAP IDOC response to disk. The name of this Send Port is **SendIDOCResponseToDisk**, and it will use the **FILE** Adapter, a Send Handler of **BizTalkServerApplication,** a Send Pipeline of **PassThruTransmit**.

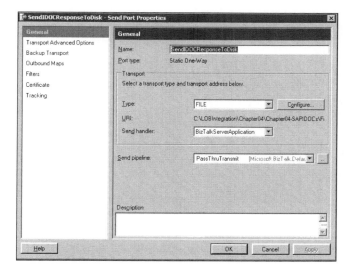

17. We now need to configure our Orchestration to use the Receive Port and Send Ports that we just created.

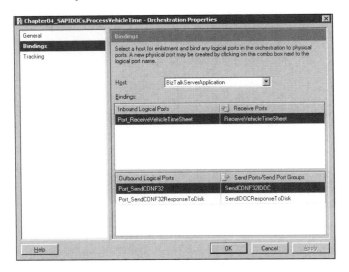

18. We can now start our application so that it is ready for Application Testing.

Testing BizTalk Application

Our Application Testing involves copying and pasting our sample file inside the hot folder as configured in the Receive Location. The file contents will include:

- **VehicleID**
- **Order Number**
- **Order Duration**
- **Order Operation**
- **Order Date**
- **Order Time**

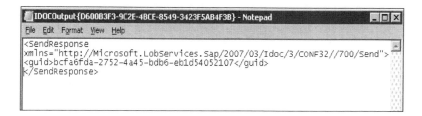

1. To initialize the test, copy and paste the `VehicleTimeSample.xml` file as found in the `C:\LOBIntegration\Chapter04\Chapter04-SAPIDOCs\FileDrop`folder.

2. BizTalk will consume this file and begin to process the file.

3. Once BizTalk has communicated with SAP, SAP should return a response to BizTalk.

4. BizTalk will take this response and generate a file called `IDOCOutput{GUID}.xml`.

Custom IDOCs

The previous example included an "out of the box" CONF32 SAP IDOC. While the idea of being able to integrate with SAP out of the box is extremely compelling, the reality is it just isn't realistic to expect an out of the box IDOC for each integration scenario that your organization is interested in. Most organizations will attempt to use the out of the box IDOCs before looking to build a custom IDOC. When forced to build, there are a few options that SAP Developers have:

- Extend existing IDOCs.
- Copy an IDOC structure and modify as you see fit.
- Start a new IDOC from Scratch.

Extending an IDOC involves keeping an IDOC structure intact, but adding additional segments that are required in your scenario. This is an ideal solution when you are only missing a few segments and want to leverage SAP's existing efforts.

If SAP has an IDOC that is somewhat similar to your scenario, you can copy that existing structure and then add or remove segments as required.

While SAP does provide a rich platform in which to run your business on, it is impossible for them to envision every integrated scenario. This leaves us the option of custom building an IDOC that addresses our unique integration scenario.

BizTalk is able to integrate with SAP through all three of these mechanisms. Using the out of the box IDOCs is the preferred option as it requires no customization and you can ensure of support by SAP in future versions. If you write a custom IDOC and it performs functions that conflict with SAP's upgrade path, your organization will be on its own in order to resolve any issues.

When generating a custom IDOC, there is nothing special that needs to occur from a BizTalk perspective. We continue to use the Consume Adapter Service Wizard just as we would if we were trying to generate a schema for an out-of-box IDOC.

 Note: If the SAP developer who built the custom IDOC says the IDOC is available but you do not see it in the list of available IDOCs, within the Consume Adapter Service Wizard, ask them to ensure that the IDOC has been released.

Below is an image of a custom IDOC. As you can see, it does not look all that different from an SAP out of box IDOC. The schema will have both **idocData** and **EDI_DC40** nodes. The remaining nodes, or segments, have been built by the SAP developer.

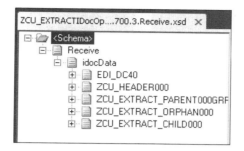

Much like the out of the box IDOCs, our custom IDOC schemas will also inherit shared types.

Receiving a custom IDOC from SAP

1. The following walkthrough will describe what is involved in receiving a custom IDOC, or standard IDOC for that matter. The source code for this walkthrough is not included in the book's source code as building a custom IDOCs inside of SAP is outside the scope of this book. This walkthrough has been included in this chapter since a custom scenario is very likely to occur when integrating with SAP but will vary depending upon how SAP has been implemented within your organization.

2. When receiving typed IDOCs there is a configuration that is required in order to process messages successfully. When we deploy our BizTalk application that includes any IDOC schemas, we need to add a reference to the **Microsoft.Adapters.SAP.BiztalkPropertySchema.dll**.

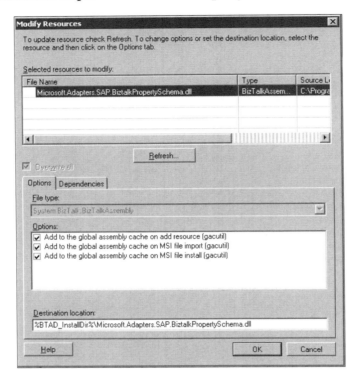

3. If you fail to add this reference, you can expect the following runtime error in the event viewer when trying to process an SAP IDOC:

   ```
   "System.Exception: Loading property information list by
   namespace failed or property not found in the list. Verify that
   the schema is deployed properly."
   ```

4. Since this error is only raised during the first time you receive an IDOC, adding this resource reference is something that you will want to include in any deployment scripts.

5. With the appropriate reference in place, we can proceed to configuring our BizTalk application that consists of Receive and Send Ports. A lesser known fact is that when exchanging IDOCs you do have the option of specifying a one-way or two-way port. IDOC responses typically provide the Transaction ID from SAP so unless you are interested in tracking this information, it may not be necessary to use a two-way port.

6. Deploy your BizTalk application that includes any custom IDOC schema(s).

7. Create a one way Receive Port called **ReceiveCustomIDOC** and a Receive Location called **ReceiveCustomIDOCFromSAP**. We are going to use the **WCF-SAP** Adapter, the **BizTalkServerApplication** Receive handler and the **XMLReceive** Receive Pipeline.

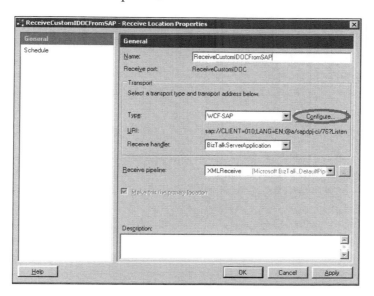

8. Click the **Configure** button so that we can provide the SAP connection information.

9. Once in the WCF-SAP Transport Properties dialog, we want to click the **Configure** button to provide the SAP connection information.

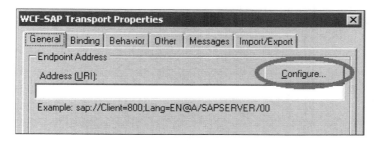

10. Much like the SAP Send port in our previous example, we need to provide the **Application Server Host**, **System Number**, and **Client**.

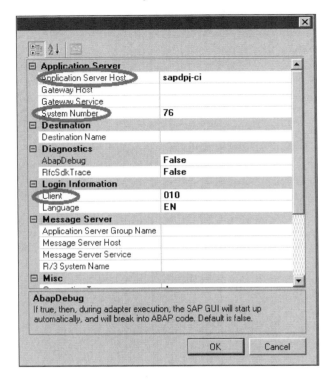

11. If we scroll down, we will discover a few additional properties that are not included in Send Port configurations:

   a. **Gateway Host** – Depending upon the configuration of your SAP system, this may be the same value as the Application Server Host.

   b. **Gateway Service** – This value generally begins with "sapgw" followed by the System Number.

   c. **Program Id** – Is a value that will be provided by your BASIS admin. It may also be referred to as the Partner Profile and acts as an authorization container for SAP IDOC interfaces. For instance, within this **WOMIDOC Program ID** configuration in SAP, entries will exist for this Custom IDOC that we are about to receive. Also, our BizTalk user will be granted access to send or receive these types of IDOCs. If BizTalk tried to send in an IDOC that it did not have permissions for, SAP would accept the message but would not process it.

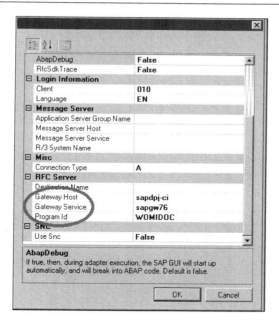

12. The next tab that we need to address is the **Other** tab. This tab provides us with our various credential options. Once again we will use Username/Password as our authentication type.

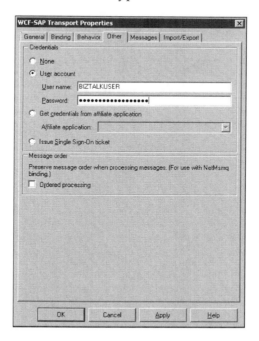

13. With our Receive Port configured, it is now time to focus on our Send Port. In this simple scenario, we are not going to have an Orchestration process this message but rather have a Send Port subscribe to this Receive Port and write the contents of the IDOC to a file folder. The name of this Send Port is **SendCustomIDOCToDisk**. It will use the **FILE** Adapter, the **BizTalkServerApplication** Send Handler, and the **PassThruTransmit** Send pipeline.

14. Within the Filters Property, we want to create a subscription against our **ReceiveCustomIDOC** Receive Port. What this will allow us to do is process any message that is received through our Receive Port and have it written to the URI that is specified in our Send Port.

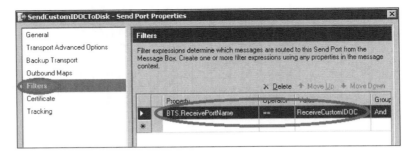

15. At this point, with both our Receive Port and Send Port configured, we can enable both the Send Port and Receive Location.

Testing BizTalk Application—Receiving custom IDOC

When integrating SAP with BizTalk, this part of the process almost always gets difficult. The reason for this is that BizTalk will listen for SAP messages. There is no way where you can tell BizTalk to go retrieve an IDOC from SAP. You can think of it much like hosting a Web Service; a client system must initiate the request. In this case, the client is SAP.

SAP is a very large system with many screens or transactions that need to be called in order to initiate an IDOC being sent to BizTalk. The end result is that you almost always need to work as a team or memorize a complex set of steps to generate an IDOC. This process may become frustrating to both the BizTalk and SAP developer as minor bugs are worked out.

An approach that may be beneficial to both the SAP Developer and BizTalk developer is to have an SAP resource generate an initial IDOC and have BizTalk process the IDOC. If the BizTalk developer needs to perform additional tests, or even load tests, against his interface he can do this by using an SAP transaction called "WE19". This transaction will reprocess both incoming and outgoing IDOCs.

If we want to resend an IDOC to BizTalk, we need to know the IDOC number for the original IDOC and then we can resubmit the message form SAP to BizTalk. In order to get the IDOC number, we will use a transaction called "WE02". Most SAP developers will have access to these two transactions so it should not be too much of a stretch for BizTalk Developers to get the same access for these transactions. Other than trying to process too many messages, in load test scenarios, there is not much damage that a user can do with these two transactions.

Let's now walkthrough the process of browsing WE02, getting an IDOC number, and then using that IDOC number in WE19 to submit an IDOC to BizTalk.

1. Once you have logged into the SAP GUI, type WE02 into the navigation text box and hit *Enter*.

2. In WE02, we have the ability to restrict the time frame that we would like to query upon. If your organization processes a lot of IDOCs you will want to ensure this query window is small. Once we have specified our query timeframe, we can click on the **Execute** button, which is represented as a Clock with a green check mark.

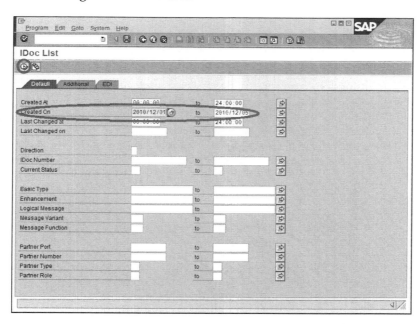

3. When the query results have been returned, we will see a list of IDOCs that have been sent or received recently. On the left-hand side of the screen, we can refine our results by clicking on **Inbound** or **Outbound** IDOCs. We even have the ability to click on the particular IDOC type that we are interested in if we want to focus just on that type. Also worth noting is the various columns that are included in this display. The **Status** and **Status code** columns are useful for knowing the success/failure of your IDOC and the **Direction** column is useful for distinguishing whether the IDOC was inbound or outbound.

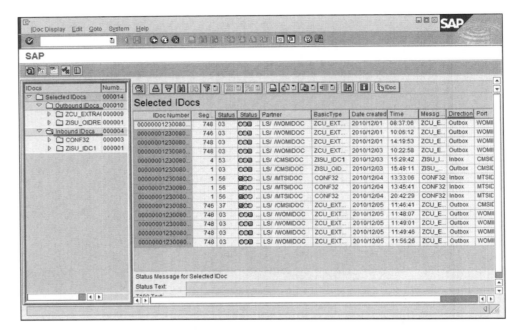

4. The primary reason that we are in the WE02 transaction is to obtain the IDOC number of a previous IDOC that was sent. The easiest way to obtain it is to note the value of the IDOC that we are interested in by scanning the **IDOC Number** column.

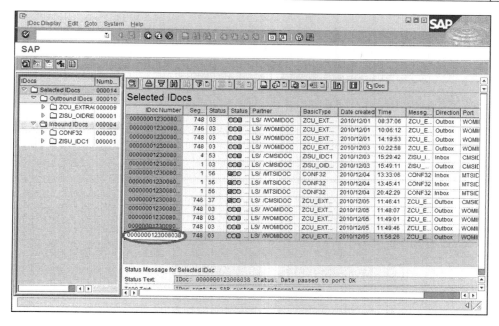

5. Once we have an IDOC Number, we can navigate to the WE19 transaction and populate the **Existing IDOC** text box, without leading zeros. To execute the transaction, click on the **Execute** button.

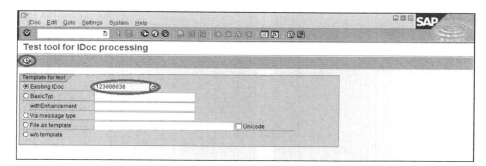

6. Segments of the IDOC will now be displayed. We now need to decide what we would like SAP to do with this IDOC. If this was an Inbound IDOC then we would click the **Standard inbound** button. Since this is an Outbound IDOC, we will click the **Standard outbound processing** button. It is important to note that SAP is not reprocessing this message. It is simply taking a copy of the original message and sending it through a port to a BizTalk server. There is no additional re-processing that will take place within SAP when this message is sent to BizTalk.

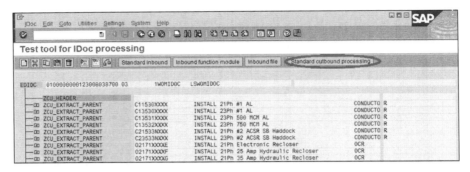

7. We now have the opportunity to specify how many copies of the IDOC we would like to send to BizTalk. In our scenario, we will choose **1** copy and click on the green **checkmark**. This feature does provide an interesting opportunity for BizTalk developers when wanting to load test their application. If you do decide to use the WE19 transaction to load test your BizTalk application, ensure that you are communicating with your BASIS team in order to mitigate any performance issues in SAP.

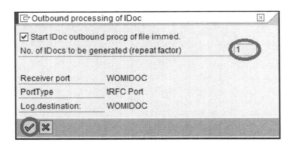

8. SAP will now submit this message and display a confirmation message.

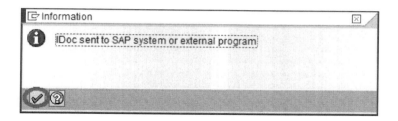

9. As expected, BizTalk will receive this message and send it to a file drop. When we open the file, we will see the IDOC represented in XML-based upon the XSD schema that was generated by the Consume Adapter Service wizard.

```
- <Receive xmlns="http://Microsoft.LobServices.Sap/2007/03/Idoc/3/ZCU_EXTRACT//700/Receive">
  - <idocData>
    + <EDI_DC40 xmlns="http://Microsoft.LobServices.Sap/2007/03/Types/Idoc/3/ZCU_EXTRACT//700">
    + <ZCU_HEADER000 xmlns="http://Microsoft.LobServices.Sap/2007/03/Types/Idoc/3/ZCU_EXTRACT//700">
    + <ZCU_EXTRACT_PARENT000GRP xmlns="http://Microsoft.LobServices.Sap/2007/03/Types/Idoc/3/ZCU_EXTRACT//700">
    + <ZCU_EXTRACT_PARENT000GRP xmlns="http://Microsoft.LobServices.Sap/2007/03/Types/Idoc/3/ZCU_EXTRACT//700">
    + <ZCU_EXTRACT_PARENT000GRP xmlns="http://Microsoft.LobServices.Sap/2007/03/Types/Idoc/3/ZCU_EXTRACT//700">
    + <ZCU_EXTRACT_PARENT000GRP xmlns="http://Microsoft.LobServices.Sap/2007/03/Types/Idoc/3/ZCU_EXTRACT//700">
    + <ZCU_EXTRACT_PARENT000GRP xmlns="http://Microsoft.LobServices.Sap/2007/03/Types/Idoc/3/ZCU_EXTRACT//700">
    - <ZCU_EXTRACT_PARENT000GRP xmlns="http://Microsoft.LobServices.Sap/2007/03/Types/Idoc/3/ZCU_EXTRACT//700">
      - <ZCU_EXTRACT_PARENT000>
          <DATAHEADERCOLUMN_SEGNAM>ZCU_EXTRACT_PARENT000</DATAHEADERCOLUMN_SEGNAM>
          <DATAHEADERCOLUMN_MANDT>010</DATAHEADERCOLUMN_MANDT>
          <DATAHEADERCOLUMN_DOCNUM>0000000123008039</DATAHEADERCOLUMN_DOCNUM>
          <DATAHEADERCOLUMN_SEGNUM>000012</DATAHEADERCOLUMN_SEGNUM>
          <DATAHEADERCOLUMN_PSGNUM>000000</DATAHEADERCOLUMN_PSGNUM>
          <DATAHEADERCOLUMN_HLEVEL>02</DATAHEADERCOLUMN_HLEVEL>
          <CU_ID>C23533NXXX</CU_ID>
          <CU_ACTION>INSTALL</CU_ACTION>
          <CU_CATEGORY>2</CU_CATEGORY>
          <CU_DESCRIPTION>3Ph #2 ACSR SB Haddock</CU_DESCRIPTION>
          <CU_TYPE>CONDUCTOR</CU_TYPE>
```

Receiving flat file IDOCs

If we closely examine the message the BizTalk received from SAP in the previous scenario, we will notice something interesting about the namespace. The DOCREL (Document Release) version is included in the namespace of the schema that we generated as part of the Consume Adapter Service Wizard.

```
<Receive xmlns="http://Microsoft.LobServices.Sap/2007/03/Idoc/3/ZCU_EXTRACT//700/Receive">
- <idocData>
  + <EDI_DC40 xmlns="http://Microsoft.LobServices.Sap/2007/03/Types/Idoc/3/ZCU_EXTRACT//700">
  + <ZCU_HEADER000 xmlns="http://Microsoft.LobServices.Sap/2007/03/Types/Idoc/3/ZCU_EXTRACT//700">
  + <ZCU_EXTRACT_PARENT000GRP xmlns="http://Microsoft.LobServices.Sap/2007/03/Types/Idoc/3/ZCU_EXTRACT//700">
  + <ZCU_EXTRACT_PARENT000GRP xmlns="http://Microsoft.LobServices.Sap/2007/03/Types/Idoc/3/ZCU_EXTRACT//700">
  + <ZCU_EXTRACT_PARENT000GRP xmlns="http://Microsoft.LobServices.Sap/2007/03/Types/Idoc/3/ZCU_EXTRACT//700">
  + <ZCU_EXTRACT_PARENT000GRP xmlns="http://Microsoft.LobServices.Sap/2007/03/Types/Idoc/3/ZCU_EXTRACT//700">
  + <ZCU_EXTRACT_PARENT000GRP xmlns="http://Microsoft.LobServices.Sap/2007/03/Types/Idoc/3/ZCU_EXTRACT//700">
    - <ZCU_EXTRACT_PARENT000>
        <DATAHEADERCOLUMN_SEGNAM>ZCU_EXTRACT_PARENT000</DATAHEADERCOLUMN_SEGNAM>
```

If we examine the Context properties that are populated when we receive an IDOC from SAP, we will discover that SAP is sending the DOCREL of the IDOC that is being sent.

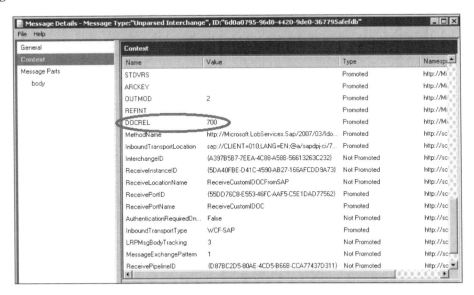

So what is the big deal? It is not a big deal, until the next time your organization performs an SAP upgrade. If your new SAP version will increment the DOCREL number, then your BizTalk subscription will be invalid since your subscription will be looking for the version 700 document and SAP will be sending version 710 (or other number).

One way to mitigate this situation is to use a flat file pipeline which allows us, as developers, to control the namespace of the message being received. This approach will survive upgrades as long as the IDOC structure does not change.

This type of schema versioning situation should get exposed during Integration testing of an SAP upgrade. However, having been through SAP upgrades before, I would not want to be the reason for X many days/weeks/months of effort to resolve a DOCREL schema versioning issue.

Using flat file pipelines when integrating with SAP IDOCs is not a new concept as it was the only way to receive IDOCs when using the legacy .NET Connector based adapter prior to the BizTalk Adapter Pack. There is some additional overhead in that you need to create additional pipelines, but avoiding DOCREL issues may be worth the minor annoyance.

For additional information related to this issue, please visit the following blog post: `http://kentweare.blogspot.com/2010/01/biztalk-adapter-pack-20-sap-adapter.html`

Summary

In this chapter we learned about SAP, how their software is used, some of the challenges in integrating with it, Standard and Custom IDOCs, and some of the SAP GUI transactions that help a BizTalk developer when building integrated solutions.

SAP usually represents an organization's System of Record, or crown jewel. Adding the ability to efficiently integrate with SAP will open up many new corporate opportunities that could result in a competitive advantage for your organization.

While integrating with SAP requires some underlying prerequisite knowledge, once an organization gets the first interface implemented, additional interfaces can be implemented very quickly as the foundational components have already been established and can continue to be leveraged. BizTalk is very capable of integrating with SAP in mission critical situations and should not be discounted due to SAP administrator paranoia.

As I am sure you are starting to recognize, integrating with SAP is a very large topic and could warrant an entire book being dedicated to it let alone one chapter. With this in mind, an additional chapter has been included in this book that deals with integrating SAP in a synchronous pattern using Remote Functions Calls (RFCs) and BAPIs. You can read all about the capabilities of RFCs and BAPIs in *Chapter 5*.

5

WCF SAP Adapter RFCs and BAPIs

In the previous chapter, we discussed the various situations where you would use IDOCs when integrating with SAP. In this chapter, we are going to continue to investigate other SAP integration technologies including RFCs and BAPIs.

In this chapter, we will be discussing the following topics:

- Overview of SAP RFCs and BAPIs
- RFCs/BAPIs vs. IDOCs
- Schema generation
- Custom vs. out-of-box RFCs/BAPIs
- RFC walkthrough
- BAPI walkthrough
- Tips, pitfalls, and troubleshooting

Overview of SAP RFCs and BAPIs

The terms RFC and BAPI are often used interchangeably, especially by non-SAP resources. Technically, they are very similar but operate at two different levels of detail. Over the course of this next section, we will further discover the similarities and differences between these two technologies.

RFCs

RFC stands for Remote Function Call and is the standard SAP interface when exchanging data across SAP systems or between non-SAP systems and SAP systems. You can think of an RFC much like a C# method, the difference being SAP provides an interface that allows for communication with SAP systems. There are three different types of RFCs:

RFC Type	Description
Synchronous RFC	As the name implies, this type of RFC utilizes request-response connectivity when exchanging information between SAP and SAP systems or SAP and Non-SAP systems. This is probably the most popular type of RFC due to the popularity of Request-Response requirements.
Transactional RFC (tRFC)	"Transactional RFCs (tRFCs) are RFCs that are invoked as part of a logical unit of work (LUW). On an SAP system, a LUW contains all of the steps necessary to complete a business or programming task. A tRFC represents a way of invoking an RFC; it is not a unique SAP artifact."
	This RFC was previously known as an Asynchronous RFC and for a good reason. Once the request is sent from a client, SAP will process this data and associate a unique Transaction ID. This ID and corresponding data will be stored in SAP, which allows a disconnected client to receive the information when it comes back online. This ID is also used when calling theRfcConfirmTransID operation, which will confirm the tRFC call and allows SAP to remove the current entry from its database.
	tRFCs guarantee that all Logical Units of Work (LUW) will be executed but cannot guarantee the order of transactions will be maintained throughout execution. Also note, there is a performance hit when using this method.
Queued RFC (qRFC)	If you need to guarantee that several transactions, either inbound or outbound, are executed in order then qRFC provides in order, once only delivery. Much like other ordered delivery scenarios, there is a performance hit when using this method.
	Note: qRFC client functionality has been deprecated from BizTalk as of Microsoft BizTalk Adapter 3.0. For further information related to qRFC, please refer to this link:
	`http://msdn.microsoft.com/en-us/library/cc185531(BTS.10).aspx`

The scope of this book focuses on Synchronous RFCs. For more information on tRFCs, please refer to MSDN: `http://msdn.microsoft.com/en-us/library/cc185268(v=BTS.10).aspx`

BAPIs

The simplest way to describe a Business Application Programming Interfaces (BAPI) is a RFC-enabled function module. A function module is a logical grouping of domain specific functions that belong together. For instance, we may have a Human Resources (HR) function module that will contain all available HR operations. The key difference between BAPIs and RFCs are the levels of detail in which they operate. You can think of BAPIs as operating a Business Process level where as an RFC will be operating at a lower, or more granular, level.

RFCs/BAPIs vs. IDOCs

A question that comes up regularly is when to use RFCs/BAPIs versus IDOCs. It really comes down to a few factors:

- Is your integration scenario synchronous or asynchronous?
- Does an out-of-box interface exist?
- Are you trying to chain multiple events/processes together?
- Does your process require SAP Workflow?

Synchronous vs asynchronous

Synchronous scenarios are better suited to leveraging RFCs/BAPIs due to their immediate request/response mechanisms. For example, take the situation where SAP is the system of record for customers within your organization, but you have chosen to use Dynamics CRM/XRM for a specific application. We do not want to manually key in customer information in both systems if we don't have to. So we can build an interface that will query SAP to retrieve the master data for an existing customer in our organization. In this situation, we would not want to use an IDOC, if we are expecting an immediate response, as BizTalk would send the IDOC in and then have to wait for a response from SAP asynchronously. When SAP does send the response back to BizTalk, we may have to correlate this response with the request that was sent into SAP so that BizTalk can provide a correct response to the calling application.

Conversely, if your scenario does not require an immediate response, like a fire and forget scenario, then using an asynchronous mode provides some additional breathing room to get a message to SAP. In a Work Order Management (WOM) system that provides order updates to SAP, the WOM system wants the updates to make it to SAP, but does not need immediate feedback that the message was sent. For instance, if our SAP system has a regular maintenance window to perform a backup, we don't want our WOM system to be interrupted during this planned outage. BizTalk can use its out-of-box retry mechanism to reliably deliver this message to SAP.

Does an out-of-box interface exist?

This scenario can go either way. Not all interfaces are created equally. For example, an IDOC may exist that allows you to submit employee time records where as an RFC/BAPI may not and vice versa. The ability to use an out-of-box interface and reduce, or prevent, SAP customization is a valid situation to choose one type of interface over another.

Are you trying to chain multiple events/processes together?

Earlier in this chapter, we introduced the concept of Logical Units of Work. If you have multiple units of work that logically tie a business process together, then using an RFC/BAPI is a better choice due to the ability to commit and rollback transactions. IDOCs are separate entities that are not related to each other.

Workflow

If you need to execute SAP Workflow as part of an integrated scenario, then using IDOCs is a better alternative. You do not want BizTalk in the middle of a Request-Response situation, with a client, while SAP is executing workflow. This risk here is the execution SAP Workflow can be somewhat unpredictable based upon workflow load and priority.

Schema generation

If you have read some of the previous chapters, you have become very familiar with the Consume Adapter Service Wizard. With this in mind, we will briefly review this wizard in order to cover the RFC/BAPI material.

Outbound operations

When performing Client Outbound operations (from BizTalk), we have the ability to select the following contract types:

- BAPI
- IDOC
- RFC
- TRFC

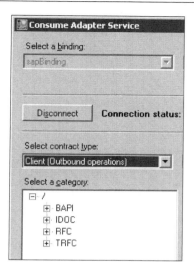

If we expand the BAPI node, we will discover that our schemas are sorted based upon their functional role in the SAP system.

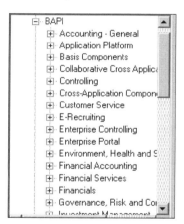

Inbound Operations

When performing Service Inbound Operations (to BizTalk), we have the ability to select the following contract types:

- IDOC
- RFC
- TRFC

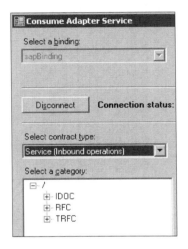

Calling RFCs/tRFCs hosted in BizTalk

If you recall, one of the key differences between RFCs and BAPIs is the Business Object Repository. BizTalk does not store these Business Objects anywhere so it is not possible for BizTalk to host a BAPI as the underlying function module will not be available.

What is interesting about BizTalk hosting an RFC is that SAP could consume it and would not even know that it is calling an external system as opposed to another SAP system. Obviously, the BASIS administrator that is configuring the endpoint would, but Microsoft is leveraging SAP's RFC SDK to ensure interoperability. This architecture also presents some interesting opportunities if your organization was against customizing SAP. You could abstract this functionality away from SAP and have it implemented in a more agile environment like BizTalk. Perhaps your organization does not have the ABAP skillset, or resource bandwidth, to code an RFC and chooses to leverage a BizTalk skillset instead.

A more practical, and likely, use of RFCs being hosted in BizTalk is data residing outside of SAP and SAP needs to obtain this information in a synchronous fashion. In this case, SAP would call a BizTalk hosted RFC, and BizTalk would retrieve the downstream information and return it back to SAP.

A real world example of BizTalk hosting an RFC is an Energy company that needed to retrieve Meter Reads from an External system via Web Services. This company did not have the SAP experience or technology stack to support calling external Web Services securely from SAP. These external Web Services used complex types, were secure, and were hosted in the partner's data center. The solution to this problem included BizTalk hosting an RFC that SAP could call on demand. In turn BizTalk would fetch the required Meter Read information from this external system and return the results back to SAP in a format that SAP was expecting.

Custom objects

If we are looking for custom objects (for example RFC), we will find them in the \ RFC\OTHER hierarchy. SAP best practices indicate that whenever you have a custom object, you prefix it with the letter 'Z'. This is a great concept, especially for non-SAP resources whose first language is not German. While the documentation and naming conventions are improving, there are still a lot of tables, fields, and programs that use German words or acronyms that make absolutely no sense to an English speaking BizTalk person. By leveraging this practice of prefixing custom objects with "Z", both SAP and Microsoft resources can easily identify custom objects.

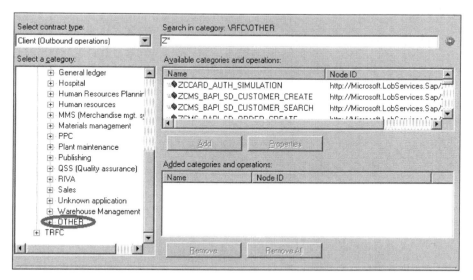

Transactions

When calling BAPIs that perform Create, Update, or Delete operations, it is necessary to generate schemas for two additional operations:

- **BAPI_TRANSACTION_COMMIT**
- **BAPI_TRANSACTION_ROLLBACK**

Calling either of these operations is required since we may be manipulating multiple sets of data and we either want all of the data to be successful or none of it to be successful.

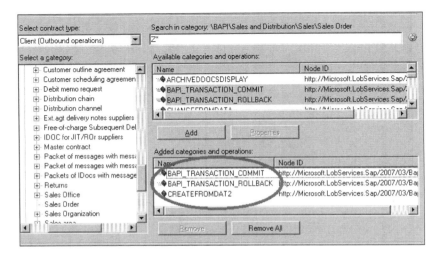

For convenience purposes, we will generate all of these schemas at the same time. It is important to note that the **BAPI_TRANSCTION_COMMIT** and **BAPI_TRANSACTION_ROLLBACK** operations are generic and can be used in conjunction with other BAPIs. If you plan on having multiple BAPI integration scenarios within your environment, placing these schemas in a common project may be a more sustainable solution.

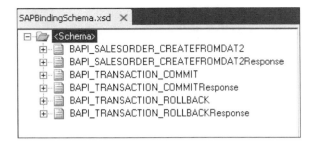

Custom vs. out-of-box RFCs/BAPIs

During a recent project, I worked with an SAP team to determine which interfaces we could leverage to address our business requirements. Unfortunately, this was a very exhaustive exercise. Unless people on the project have used the out-of-box RFC/BAPI before, there is usually an element of trial and error to determine whether or not an interface is a good fit. It is easy to browse the SAP interface catalogue (via Consume Adapter Service Wizard) using keywords to locate a suitable interface only to be disappointed that it doesn't quite fit your scenario. For instance, we were interested in finding a customer in SAP by calling a BizTalk interface from Dynamics CRM. We found a BAPI called BAPI_CUSTOMER_FIND that "should" be a perfect fit. Unfortunately, this BAPI did not return all of the master data that we needed. Another BAPI called BAPI_CUSTOMER_GETDETAIL could be used in conjunction with the FIND BAPI to address our requirements. This meant that we would have to call two BAPIs to accomplish our goal of extracting Customer information from SAP.

As architects, we needed to start evaluating our options to determine which option is the best course of action. In this circumstance, we opted to write a custom BAPI to provide the search function and return the appropriate fields that CRM was looking for. We felt that we could have BizTalk making a series of consecutive calls, but opted for a cleaner "Wrapper" BAPI approach. The term "Wrapper" BAPI is something that we came up with to describe wrapping multiple system calls in one BAPI. Within this BAPI, the SAP developer is responsible for trapping errors that occur across calls and ensuring that transactions are committed or rolled back as deemed necessary. SAP resources also claim that they can insert more debug and tracing statements that will aid in supporting the system in the long term. Another reason for leveraging the Wrapper BAPI is that the call from Dynamics CRM was synchronous. We didn't want CRM "locked up" waiting for a response from BizTalk, while BizTalk was making multiple calls to SAP.

Now that we have introduced some SAP terminology and discussed some of the decisions that Developers and Architects face when integrating with SAP, let's jump into some actual scenarios where we call both a RFC and BAPIs.

Building a BizTalk application—RFC walkthrough

The scenario that we are going to walk through involves a Quoting system for an Energy company. Customers will engage the Energy company to build infrastructure so that they can power their plant/office/home/farm and so on. The Quoting system is built upon a Dynamics CRM/XRM platform. As part of this quoting system, we need to be able to factor in the amount our materials will cost us when providing a quote to our customer. Some of SAP's strengths reside in Supply Chain Management and Material Management so it makes sense to continue to leverage this functionality in SAP. In our scenario, SAP is the system of record for all Material Management. As the cost of materials fluctuate over the course of a year, due to changes in commodity markets, the average moving price will follow suit. We do not want to be over-quoting or under-quoting our customer so we need to acquire the moving average price for our materials before providing a quote to a customer.

1. The RFC that we are going to use is called **BAPI_MATERIAL_GET_ DETAIL** and it is available out of the box. Wait a minute! I thought we were discussing RFCs in this walkthrough, ao why does it start with "BAPI"? Well, remember earlier in the chapter, we discussed that all BAPIs are RFCs and since the schemas were generated from the **\RFC** category, I am considering this an RFC.

2. When generating schemas, it is a good practice to use the **Filename Prefix**. My personal preference is to use the name of the BAPI as the **Filename Prefix**; this way there is no confusion inside of Visual Studio.

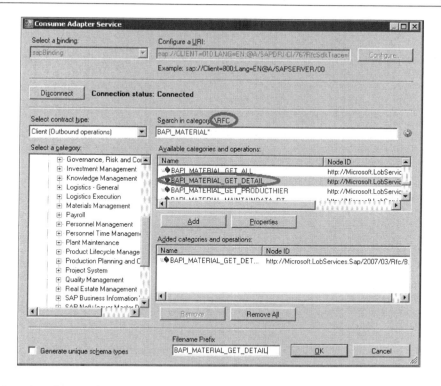

3. Inside of Visual Studio, we will find two schemas generated called:
   BAPI_MATERIAL_GET_DETAILRfc.xsd and **BAPI_MATERIAL_GET_
   DETAILTypes.xsd**.

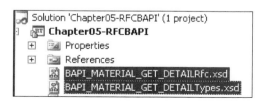

4. Inside the **BAPI_MATERIAL_GET_DETAILRfc.xsd** schema, we will discover that both request and response records exist. The **BAPI_MATERIAL_GET_DETAILTypes.xsd** schema simply contains the underlying SAP data types.

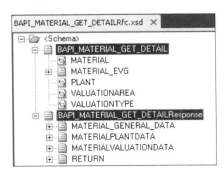

5. Next, we want to build a schema that our CRM system can populate. The name of this schema is called **MaterialDetailRequest.xsd** and it contains three elements. For simplicity purposes, all fields are of type string.

Field Name	Purpose
MaterialID	The identifier used to distinguish different materials.
Plant	The location where goods are produced or provided from. In our situation, we would consider a warehouse a Plant.
ValuationArea	There are two types of Valuation Areas: Company and Plant. Since costs may differ depending upon which plant they are coming from, it could impact the price. Suppose you had a plant, or warehouse, in a remote area. There may be additional transportation costs in retrieving a particular material from that plant. Conversely, if you had a centralized warehouse then you may want to use a Company level cost that would be consistent across materials. In our example, we are going to use Plant level and will provide the Plant ID as our value in this Request message.

Note: it is a best practice to not expose your system generated schemas to consuming clients. In the case of SAP, the schemas that are generated are generally not user/developer friendly, and we do not want to pass down that complexity to teams that may not be as strong in system integration as a BizTalk or Middleware team. We also do not want to have to manage client interfaces breaking should a change to an SAP schema change. For instance, if we would have exposed the old SAP adapter schemas to our client consuming systems and then decided to upgrade the BizTalk interfaces to support the new WCF-SAP adapter, we would have significant, unnecessary, changes to the client application as well.

6. We now want to create a map called **MaterialDetailRequestDisk_ to_MaterialDetailRequestSAP.btm** that will transform our **MaterialDetailRequest** into our **BAPI_MATERIAL_GET_DETAIL** request.

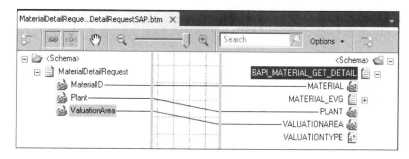

7. Next, we need to build a map that will transform the **BAPI_MATERIAL_GET_DETAILResponse** into a **MaterialDetailResponse** that we can send back to our calling CRM system. The map to do this is called **MaterialDetailResponseSAP_to_MaterialDetailResponseDisk.btm**. The nodes that are being mapped are as follows:

BAPI_MATERIAL_GET_DETAILResponse	MaterialDetailResponse
/MATERIAL_GENERAL_DATA/MATL_DESC	MaterialDescription
/MATERIAL_GENERAL_DATA/MATL_TYPE	MaterialType
/MATERIAL_GENERAL_DATA/BASE_UOM	UnitOfMeasure
/MATERIAL_GENERAL_DATA/NET_WEIGHT	NetWeight
/MATERIAL_GENERAL_DATA/CREATED_ON	MaterialCreateDate
/MATERIAL_GENERAL_DATA/LAST_CHNGE	MaterialLastUpdated
/MATERIALVALUATIONDATA/MOVING_PR	MovingPrice
/MATERIALVALUATIONDATA/PRICE_UNIT	PriceUnit
/MATERIALVALUATIONDATA/CURRENCY	Currency

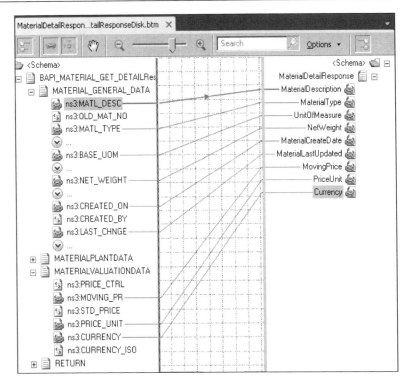

8. In order to coordinate all of these events, an orchestration called **ProcessGetMaterialDetails.odx** is required. Inside this orchestration, the following events take place:

   a. We receive an instance of the Material Detail Request.

   b. Transform the Material Detail Request into a SAP BAPI_MATERIAL_ GET_DETAIL Request.

   c. Send the BAPI_MATERIAL_GET_DETAIL Request to SAP and receive the BAPI_MATERIAL_GET_DETAIL Response.

   d. Transform the BAPI_MATERIAL_GET_DETAIL Response into a Material Detail Response.

   e. Send the Material Detail Response back to the calling application.

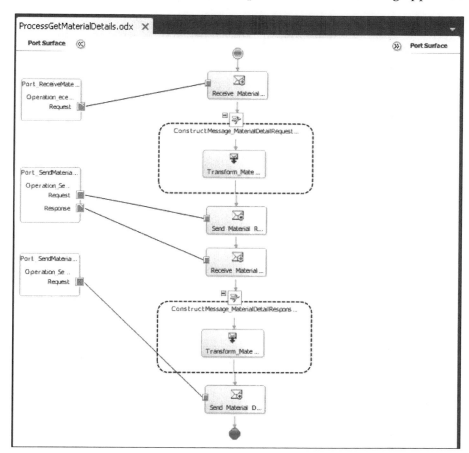

9. With our signed key in place, called **Chapter05-RFCBAPI.snk**, we can right mouse click on the Chapter05-RFCBAPI solution and deploy our application.

10. Once inside the BizTalk Administration console, we will discover an application called Chapter05-RFCBAPI.

11. We need to create a Receive Port called **ReceiveMaterialDetailRequest** that has a Receive Location called **ReceiveMaterialDetailRequestFromDisk.** This receive location will use the **FILE** Adapter, the **BizTalkServerApplication** Receive handler, and the **XMLReceive** Receive pipeline.

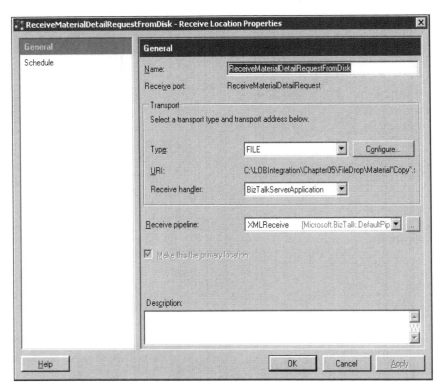

12. Two Send Ports are required for this solution. The first one that we want to address is the SAP two-way send port called **SendMaterialDetailRequestToSAP.** This Send Port will use the **WCF-SAP** adapter, the **BizTalkServerApplication** Send handler, the **XMLTransmit** Send pipeline, and the **XMLReceive** Receive pipeline.

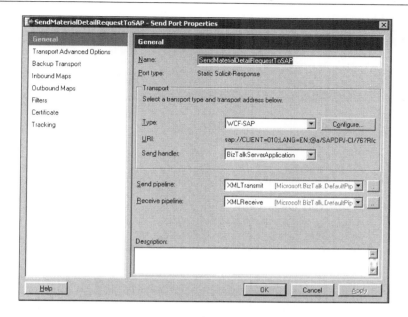

Note: Much like Chapter 4, I have opted to use the WCF-SAP adapter as opposed to the WCF-Custom adapter that uses a SAP Binding. Using the WCF-SAP adapter is really a personal preference. I like the cleaner interface that is available when populating SAP connection information and it differentiates itself from other WCF-Custom ports that are being used to connect to SQL Server and Oracle. The downside of this approach is the additional effort required when extracting the values included in the binding file that is generated when you use the Consume Adapter Service Wizard and including them in your new ports.

13. Click on the **Configure** button to edit the SAP-specific properties.

14. Click the **Configure** button again to edit the SAP URI. Much like our IDOC configuration in Chapter 4, we want to populate the following values:

    a. **Application Server Host**

    b. **System Number**

    c. **Client**

15. If you are unsure of the values for your organization, please contact your BASIS administrator.

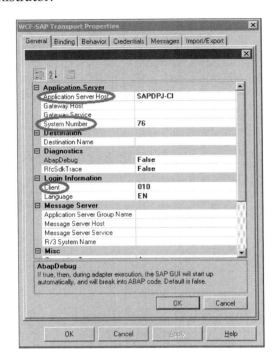

16. Click the **OK** button to close this dialog.

17. Our **SOAP Action Header's Action** value must match the name of the logical operation that we provided within our Orchestration. With this said, we need to provide the following Action within our Send Port.

```
<BtsActionMappingxmlns:xsi="http://www.w3.org/2001/XMLSchema-
instance" xmlns:xsd="http://www.w3.org/2001/XMLSchema">
<Operation Name="Operation_SendMaterialDetailRequestToSAP"
Action="http://Microsoft.LobServices.Sap/2007/03/Rfc/BAPI_
MATERIAL_GET_DETAIL" />
</BtsActionMapping>
```

18. In the **Binding** tab, I want to highlight two properties:

    a. EnableBizTalkCompatibilityMode – This value should always be set to True when calling SAP operations from BizTalk.

    b. EnableSafeTyping – Since not all .NET and SAP types are created equally, we occasionally need to loosen some constraints around dates. For example, if optional dates are being returned from an RFC/BAPI, we may experience the following error: `Microsoft.ServiceModel.Channels.Common.XmlReaderGenerationException: An error occurred when trying to convert the byte array [30-00-30-00-30-00-30-00-30-00-30-00-30-00-30-00] of RFCTYPE RFCTYPE_DATE with length 8 and decimals 0 to XML format`. To work around this, we can set the **EnableSafeTyping** property to **True**. By doing so, the WCF-SAP adapter will expose SAP DATS values as strings instead of DateTime.

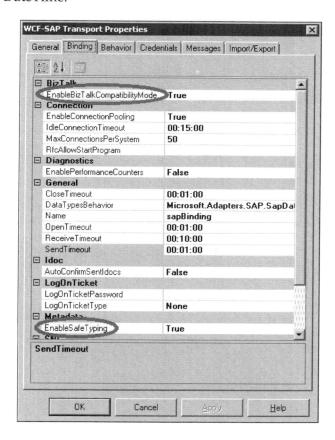

19. On the **Credentials** tab, we need to provide our SAP credentials. In this scenario, we are using **Username/Password** credentials.

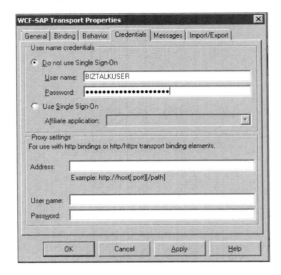

20. The next Send port that we address will send our Material Detail Response to disk where it can be consumed by the calling application. The name of this Send port is **SendMaterialDetailsResponseToDisk**. The Send port will use the **FILE** Adapter, **BizTalkServerApplication** Send handler and the **PassThruTranmit** Send pipeline. You can obtain the binding file for this solution in the C:\LOBIntegration\Chapter05\BindingFiles of the source code so that you do not have to type out this entire configuration manually.

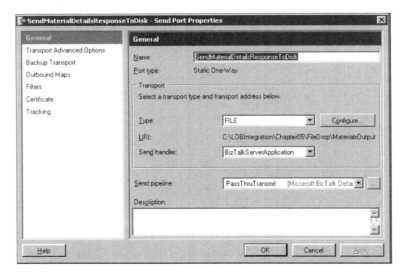

21. In order to start our application, we must bind our orchestration to the Physical Receive and Send ports that we just created.

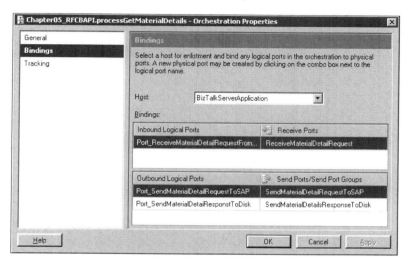

Testing BizTalk application—RFC walkthrough

1. With our application now built and deployed, we are ready to begin testing by performing the following steps: After bouncing the BizTalkServerApplicationHost instance(s) and starting the application, we can process an instance of our `MaterialDetailRequest.xsd`. A sample file called `MaterialDetailRequest.xml` has been included in the `C:\LOBIntegration\Chapter05\FileDrop` folder. To process this file, we need to simply copy and paste the file.

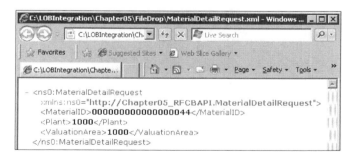

Note: The values that have been provided in this sample file represent master data that exists in the SAP system that was used to build this solution. These values will probably not be valid in your SAP system. It is recommended that you consult an SAP resource within your organization so that they can provide you with data that exists in your system.

2. BizTalk should consume this file, contact SAP, receive a response from SAP, and write the results back out to the same folder.

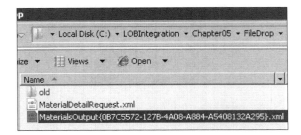

3. When we inspect the **MaterialsOutput{GUID}.xml** file, we will discover information pertaining to the Material we are interested in including the **Moving Price**.

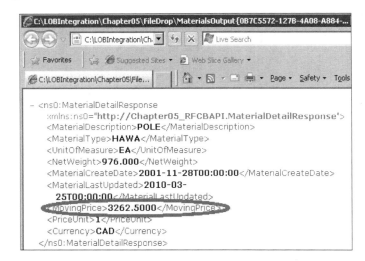

In this example, we used asynchronous messaging between our calling client and BizTalk. Using asynchronous communication in this scenario gives us a little more breathing room when communicating with SAP. Calling the SAP RFC, in this situation, is a very quick operation (~2 seconds), but for some reason if SAP is down, we have time to retry calling SAP.

If we had a synchronous scenario with our client application, then we would not have much time to retry calling SAP before the client times out. In these synchronous situations, I recommend setting the SAP's Send port retry value to 0 and then ensure I return a response back to the client indicating that SAP was not available. This provides a few benefits:

- We are not trying to retry connecting to SAP when the client has already timed out and severed its connection to BizTalk.

- If SAP is down, BizTalk will be able to immediately detect this situation and send a negative acknowledgement message back to the client application. Otherwise, we would not know this until BizTalk had exhausted its retry threshold.

- Client system can then provide a clear, user friendly error message to the client indicating that there is a problem.

Building a BizTalk application—BAPI walkthrough

We are now going to expand on our RFC scenario and update our existing Chapter05-RFCBAPI project. Once our customer receives a quote from our quoting system and has decided to proceed with our company doing the work, we want to leverage SAP's Sales and Distribution capabilities. SAP also has strengths in Sales and Financials so instead of trying to build that functionality in our Quoting system we want to take advantage of SAP's core capabilities in this area.

The Quoting system will create a Sales Order request, and provide information about the customer, and the materials associated with the job. In return, SAP will create the sales order that can be used for billing purposes and return an order number back to the Quoting system.

Let's begin our solution by generating our SAP schemas:

1. Once again, we are going to leverage an out-of-the-box interface called **CREATEFROMDAT2b**, which can be found in the **\BAPI\Sales and Distribution\Sales\Sales Order** category. As previously discussed in the Schema Generation section of this chapter, we also need to include **COMMIT** and **ROLLBACK** operations since we will be creating data in SAP. We will generate all schemas at the same time for convenience purposes.

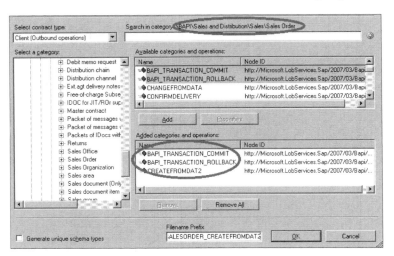

2. Once again, we do not want to expose our SAP Request to our Quoting system so we are going to expose a more user friendly schema called **CreateSalesOrderRequest.xsd**. Inside this schema, we will find the following elements. All elements are strings with the exception of **isCommitted**, which happens to be a Boolean.

Field Name	Purpose
/Header/ DocumentType	Also referred to as Order Type. Typical values are OR(English value) or TA (German value).
/Header/ SalesOrganization	Organizational unit within Logistics, which structures the company according to its sales requirements.
/Header/ DistributionChannel	The distribution channel determines how materials or services are sold and how they are distributed to customers, for example, retail, wholesale, self-collection.
/Header/Division	The division is an organizational unit in Logistics in the R/3 System.
/Header/SalesOffice	The Sales Office or Sales area responsible for this transaction.

Field Name	Purpose
/Header/ RequestedDate	The date that the products, or services, are required by.
/Header/PurchaseNo	Text that describes the Purchase Number.
/Header/Currency	The currency that the transaction will take place in.
/Material/MaterialID	The ID of the Material item that we would like to include in our purchase order.
/Material/TargetQU/	Target unit of measure.
/Partner/PartnerRole	A business partner role is used to classify a business partner in business terms. The roles you assign to a business partner reflect the functions it has and the business transactions in which it is likely to be involved.
/Partner/Number	A number used to identify a customer.
isCommitted	This field is for demonstration purposes. It will trigger whether or not we want to commit the order or roll the order back. In order to easily determine whether or not this value is true or false, this field has been marked as a distinguished field.

3. Our next step is to create a map that will transform our **CreateSalesOrderRequest** from our quoting system to our **SALESORDER_ CREATEFROMDAT2** SAP BAPI call. The name of this map is called **CreateSalesOrderRequest_to_SALESORDER_CREATEFROMDAT2. btm.** The following image contains the detailed mapping instructions. Note that the Material node is a recurring node so a looping functoid has been added to ensure the correct amount of **BAPISDITM** nodes are created in the destination message.

4. We also want to ensure that the **BAPIRET2** node is instantiated so that SAP can return any errors. **BAPIRET2** is a common table that is used for returning the status of the BAPI that was just executed. Even if you are calling a custom BAPI, it is a good practice to return this node. In order to provide this node in our request message, we will simply drag a link from root node to the **BAPIRET2** node.

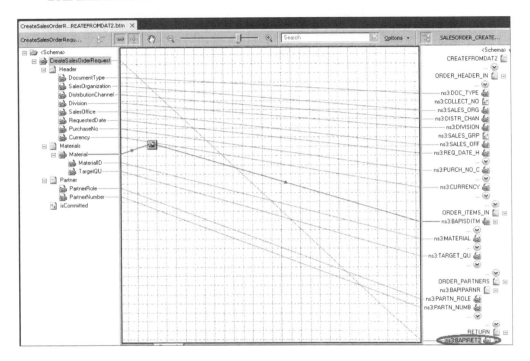

5. Once we have sent our SALESORDER_CREATEFROMDAT2 request to SAP and received a response, we are going to need to provide our Quoting system with a response message. A schema called **CreateSalesOrderResponse.xsd** has been created to handle this responsibility. Inside this schema, we will find three elements. **CustomerNumber** and **SalesOrderNumber** are strings while **isCommitted** is a Boolean.

Field Name	Purpose
CustomerNumber	Since we will be using asynchronous messaging between the Quoting system and BizTalk, we want to provide the customer number that the Sales Order belongs to.
SalesOrderNumber	This is the identifier that SAP will provide when a Sales Order has been successfully created.
isCommitted	This field is also for demonstration purposes and will provide an indicator to the quoting systems as to whether the transaction was committed or rolled back. We will also mark this field as a distinguished field so that we can conveniently update this flag within our `ProcessCreateSalesOrder.odx` orchestration.

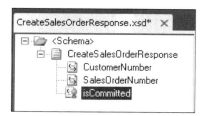

6. The map responsible for transforming the SAP Response into the Quoting System response is called **SALESORDER_CREATEFROMDAT2Response_to_CreateSalesOrderResponse.btm**.

7. Since the **isCommitted** field is not being returned from SAP, we will set an initial value of true from a String Concatenate functoid and subsequently update this flag in a Message Assignment shape within our `ProcessCreateSalesOrder.odx` orchestration.

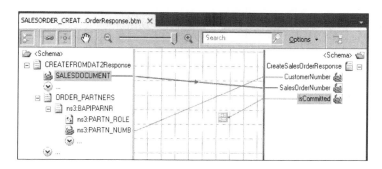

8. In the Schema Generation section of this chapter, we discussed when Creating, Updating, and Deleting data via a BAPI that we need to either Commit or Rollback the transaction. In order to satisfy the requirement of committing the transaction, we need to create a map that will instantiate an instance of a **BAPI_TRANSACTION_COMMIT** message. The source message for this map can really be anything as we are not using any of the message body payload data in the Commit message. With this in mind, the **CreateSalesOrderRequest** message should work. A map called **CreateSalesOrder_to_BAPI_TRANSACTION_COMMIT.btm** has been included in the source code for this chapter that will satisfy our needs.

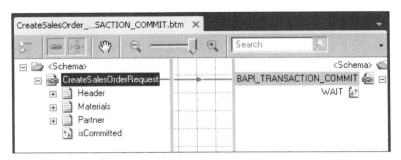

9. Similarly, we need to create a map that deals with Rollback scenarios. A map called **CreateSalesRequest_to_BAPI_TRANSACTION_ROLLBACK.btm** has been created for this purpose and it follows the same logic as the Commit map.

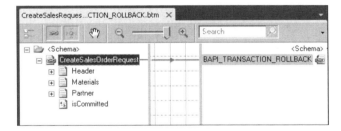

10. We are now at the point where we can assemble all of these artefacts within an orchestration called **ProcessCreateSalesOrder.odx**. Since this orchestration is larger than the other orchestrations in the SAP chapters, we will break it down into several parts.

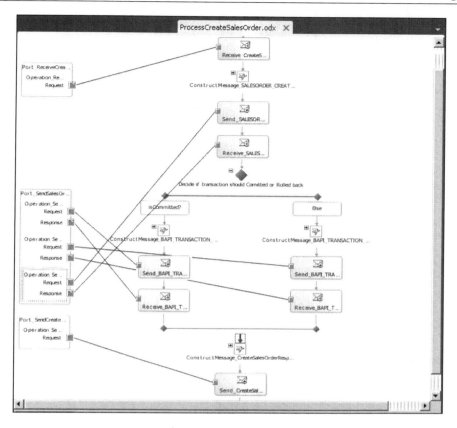

11. Our initial steps will involve the following actions:

    a.   Receiving an instance of our CreateSalesOrderRequest message.

    b.   Transforming our CreateSalesOrderRequest message into our SALESORDER_CREATEFROMDAT2 SAP Request message.

    c.   Updating the message context to set the **ConnectionState** to "OPEN". By setting it to OPEN, we are instructing the adapter to open a new channel for the transaction. In order to set this message context, we need to add an assembly reference for `Microsoft.Adapters.SAP. BiztalkPropertySchema.dll`. You can find this dll in the following locations:

        i.   **32 bit:** `C:\Program Files (x86)\Microsoft BizTalk Adapter Pack\bin`

        ii   **64 bit:** `C:\Program Files\Microsoft BizTalk Adapter Pack(x64)\bin\`

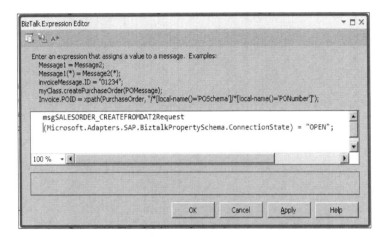

    e.   Send the **SALESORDER_CREATEFROMDAT2Request** to SAP.

    f.   Receive the **SALESORDER_CREATEFROMDAT2Response** from SAP.

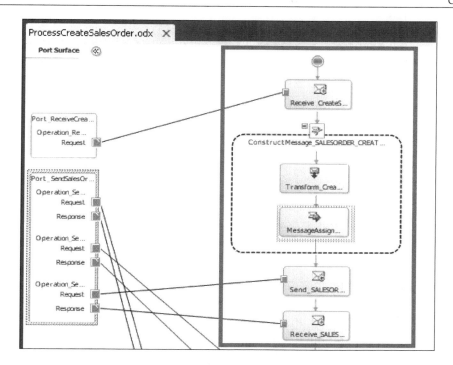

12. We now want to perform a check to determine whether or not we should be committing the transaction in SAP. To do this, we will add a Decide shape to the orchestration and then check to see if our Request message has its **isCommitted** flag set to true:

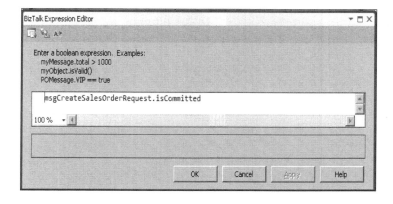

a. If `msgCreateSalesOrderRequest.isCommitted` is set to true, then we will proceed with calling a transformation that will convert our CreateSalesOrderRequest message into an instance of our **BAPI_ TRANSACTION_COMMIT** message.

b. Once this message has been transformed, we need to update its message context properties in a Message Assignment shape. Within this shape, we want to set the **ConnectionState** property to **"CLOSE"**. By setting this property to **CLOSE**, we are instructing the adapter to commit the transaction and close the channel.

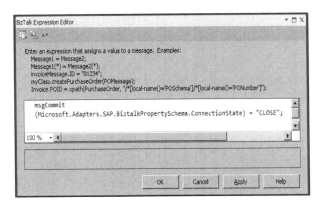

c. We now want to send our **BAPI_TRANSACTION_COMMIT** message to SAP.

d. Once the transaction has been committed, SAP will send us a response message acknowledging that the transaction has been completed.

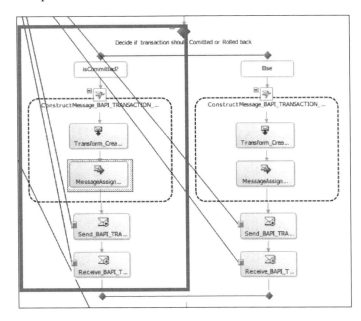

13. If `msgCreateSalesOrderRequest.isCommitted` is set to false, we want to rollback the transaction instead of committing the transaction.

    a.   In order to rollback the transaction, we need to create an instance of a **BAPI_TRANSACTION_ROLLBACK** message by transforming our CreateSalesOrderRequest message.

    b.   Once this message has been transformed, we need to update its message context properties in a Message Assignment shape. Within this shape, we want to set the **ConnectionState** property to **"ABORT"**. By setting this property to **ABORT**, we are instructing the adapter to abort the transaction and close the channel.

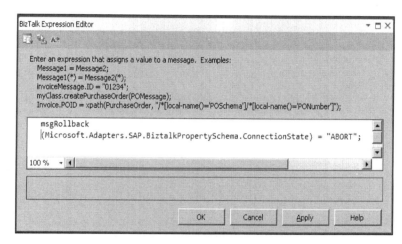

    c.   We now want to send our **BAPI_TRANSACTION_ROLLBACK** message to SAP.

    d.   Once the transaction has been aborted, SAP will send us a response message acknowledging that the transaction has been canceled.

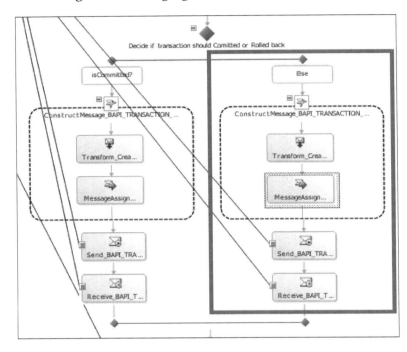

14. The remaining steps include transforming our SALESORDER_ CREATEFROMDAT2Response into our CreateSalesOrderResponse that we will send to our Quoting system.

    a.   For demonstration purposes, we added a flag on the CreateSalesOrderResponse message to indicate whether or not Commit flag was set. In a Message Assignment shape, we will simply assign the value that was populated in the CreateSalesOrderRequest message.

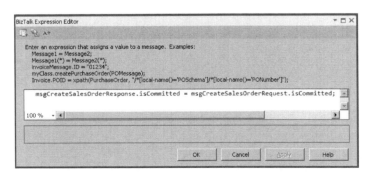

b. Send a CreateSalesOrderResponse message back to the Quoting System.

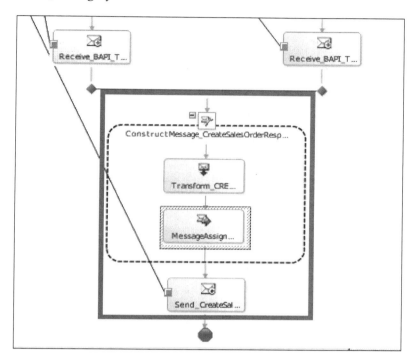

15. Since we have updated our Chapter05-RFCBAPI solution, we do not need to re-add a strong name key; we can right mouse click on our Visual Studio solution file and deploy our application.

16. Inside the Chapter05-RFCBAPI application, we need to add a Receive Port that will receive messages from our Quoting system called **ReceiveCreateSalesOrderRequests.** We now need a Receive Location for this Receive Port called **ReceiveCreateSalesOrderRequestsFromQuotingSystem** that will use the **FILE** Adapter, the **BizTalkServerApplication** Receive handler, and the **XMLReceive** Receive pipeline. Since we are sharing a hot folder with the previous example, we need to provide a file mask of **CreateSales*Copy*.xml.**

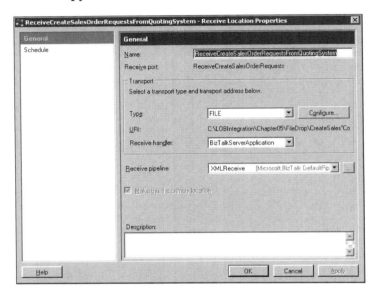

17. We now need to create our Send ports. The first Send port that we will create will be used to communicate with SAP. The Send port that we will create is called **SendCreateSalesOrdersToSAP** and is responsible for sending the BAPI_SALESORDER_CREATEFROMDAT2, BAPI_TRANSACTION_COMMIT, and BAPI_TRANSACTION_ROLLBACK messages.

18. This Send port will use the **WCF-SAP** adapter, the **BizTalkServerApplication** Send handler, the **XMLTransmit** Send pipeline, and the **XMLReceive** Receive pipeline.

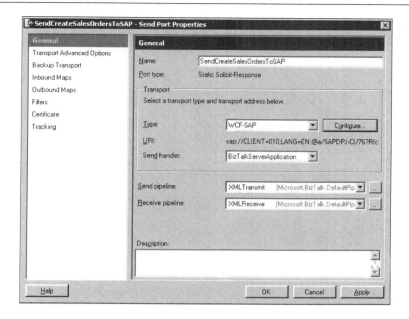

19. Click on the **Configure** button to edit the SAP specific properties.

20. Click the **Configure** button again to edit the SAP URI. Much like our IDOC configuration in Chapter 4, we want to populate the following values:

    a. **Application Server Host**

    b. **System Number**

    c. **Client**

21. If you are unsure of the values for your organization, please contact your BASIS administrator.

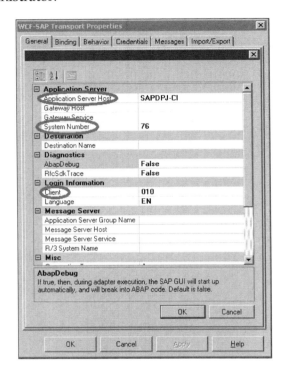

22. Click the **OK** button to close this dialog.

23. We now need to update the **SOAP Action header** with the names of the operations that were created in our Orchestration. Since this Send port is responsible for Sending the Create Sales Order, Commit, and Rollback messages, we will need three entries in this text box:

```
<BtsActionMappingxmlns:xsi="http://www.w3.org/2001/XMLSchema-
instance" xmlns:xsd="http://www.w3.org/2001/XMLSchema">
<Operation Name="Operation_SendCreateSalesOrderCommit"
Action="http://Microsoft.LobServices.Sap/2007/03/Bapi/BUS2032/
BAPI_TRANSACTION_COMMIT/BAPI_TRANSACTION_COMMIT" />
<Operation Name="Operation_SendCreateSalesOrderRollback"
Action="http://Microsoft.LobServices.Sap/2007/03/Bapi/BUS2032/
BAPI_TRANSACTION_ROLLBACK/BAPI_TRANSACTION_ROLLBACK" />
<Operation Name="Operation_SendSalesOrderRequestsToSAP"
Action="http://Microsoft.LobServices.Sap/2007/03/Bapi/BUS2032/
CREATEFROMDAT2/BAPI_SALESORDER_CREATEFROMDAT2" />
</BtsActionMapping>
```

24. On the **Binding** tab, we want to ensure that
    EnableBizTalkCompatibilityMode and **EnableSafeTyping** are set to **True**.

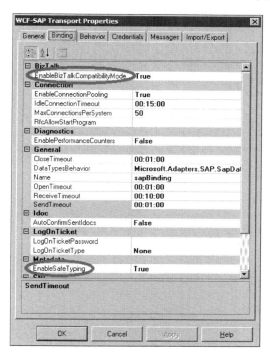

25. On the **Credentials** tab, we need to provide our SAP credentials. In this scenario, we are using **Username/Password** credentials.

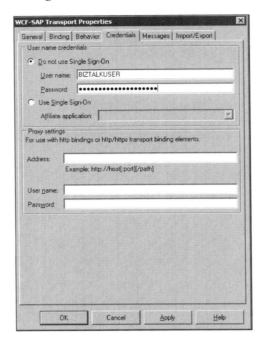

26. The final Send port that we need to create will take care of sending our Sales Order status back to the Quoting System. The Send port is called **SendCreateSalesOrderResponsesToQuotingSystem**, and uses the **FILE** Adapter, the **BizTalkServerApplication** Send handler, and the **PassThruTransmit** Send Pipeline. You can obtain the binding file for this solution in the `C:\LOBIntegration\Chapter05\BindingFiles` of the Source code so that you do not have to type out all of this configuration.

27. Lastly, we need to bind our **ProcessCreateSalesOrder** orchestration to the physical Receive and Send Ports that we just created.

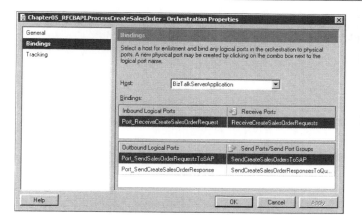

28. We can now bounce our BizTalkServerApplication Host instance and start our application.

Testing BizTalk application—BAPI walkthrough

With our application built and deployed, we are now ready to test our application by performing the following steps:

1. Create a copy of our sample file called `CreateSalesOrderRequest_Commit.xml` from the `C:\LOBIntegration\Chapter05\FileDrop` folder and paste it into this same folder. This file contains the **isCommitted** flag set to true so BizTalk will attempt to commit this transaction.

2. BizTalk will receive this file and then create the sales order in SAP, commit the transaction, and then send a response to our quoting system called **SalesOrderResponse{GUID}.xml**. This document will contain our **SalesOrderNumber** that was just created in SAP.

3. To execute a rollback scenario, we can copy and paste the `CreateSalesOrderRequest_Rollback.xml` as found in the `C:\LOBIntegration\Chapter05\FileDrop` folder. The difference between this file and the `CreateSalesOrderRequest_Commit.xml` is the **isCommitted** flag is set to **false**.

4. When this file is processed through BizTalk a sales order will be created and a Sales Order Number will be returned. The difference is that this transaction is rolled back instead of committed. Also, in our response message to our Quoting system, our **isCommitted** flag is set to **false**.

Here is a table outlining some helpful SAP GUI transactions when manipulating Sales Orders:

SAP Transaction	Purpose
VA01	Create Sales Order
VA02	Change/Modify Sales Order
VA03	Display Sales Order

Tips, pitfalls, and troubleshooting

Using RFCs and BAPIs provide BizTalk developers with another tool for our toolboxes. Below is a list of tips, issues, and behaviors that I have run into while integrating with RFCs and BAPIs:

1. RFCs and BAPIs can handle large amounts of data. While I am not aware of a specific upper limit, I have, by accident, called an RFC that returned over 100 MB of data. This isn't to say that calling an RFC that returns 100 MB is a good idea, but it means that it is possible.

2. Always check with your SAP counterpart to see if you need to provide leading zeros when providing the ID for a specific object. In our Material walkthrough, we need to provide leading zeros in order for the operation to be called successfully.

3. When calling an RFC or BAPI, if the response from SAP is missing a particular segment, or re-occurring node, it may be due to the lack of that node being present in the request document. A perfect example of this behavior was the BAPIRET2 node in our preceding sample. Much like leading zeros, this behavior does not appear to be entirely consistent to me.

4. Using the RFC trace tool may also provide visibility into issues as they occur. The RFC trace tool gets extremely granular and can provide you with details around the message payloads that are being sent back and forth. For more information regarding this trace tool, please read the Troubleshooting section at the following link: http://msdn.microsoft.com/en-us/biztalk/ee705492.

5. It is always beneficial to get "sample" data from an SAP resource before spending a lot of time trying to debug your BizTalk solution. Once you have valid data, you will spend less time troubleshooting and more time developing/testing your solution. The RFC/BAPI could be failing for a variety of reasons and an SAP resource is in a better position to determine what is occurring than a BizTalk resource.

6. When performing BAPI transactions, you must do so using a single host instance. If this situation applies and you need High Availability then you should look at Clustered Host instances. This will allow you to have a single host instance running at one time, but in the event of a system failure, you will have a passive node that can become the active node and continue processing automatically.

7. When a BAPI creates or updates a record, those changes cannot be read by another BAPI instance until the changes are committed.

8. When executing BAPI transactions, you need to manipulate these objects using the same connection. Please refer to `http://msdn.microsoft.com/en-us/library/cc185482(v=BTS.10).aspx` for a breakdown of all Connection States.

Summary

In this chapter, we continued to learn about SAP and BAPI/RFC synchronous processing. We learned about committing and rolling back transactions and some of the tips, tricks, and pitfalls that BizTalk developers face when communicating with SAP.

From the past two chapters, you have seen that integrating with SAP is a vast topic as SAP is such a rich platform. However, integrating with SAP is a great value add for BizTalk Server as business processes hosted in SAP typically represent mission critical services.

In the next chapter, we are going to switch gears and learn about how BizTalk can integrate cloud and on-premise services by leveraging Microsoft's AppFabric Service Bus.

6
BizTalk Integration with Windows Azure AppFabric Service Bus

In today's business environment, organizations need the ability to quickly and securely integrate with an ever-changing set of business partners. Successfully exposing local services to other departments or entire organizations can require a Herculean effort of networking and security. How can you securely expose services that are buried deep behind firewalls and network routers? What measures can we take to avoid a brittle security model that falls apart when partners are added or a situation changes? It is possible to build this type of distributed application today, but it requires a significant investment in infrastructure and multiple concessions by all parties involved.

In this chapter we will cover:

- What is included in Microsoft's cloud computing integration platform named Windows Azure AppFabric

- The problems that AppFabric Access Control services and the AppFabric Service Bus are intended to solve

- How to leverage your on-premises BizTalk Server to securely consume Windows Azure AppFabric messages and publish to the Windows Azure AppFabric cloud environment

What is Windows Azure AppFabric?

Windows Azure AppFabric is part of Microsoft's Windows Azure cloud offering, which is a set of Microsoft-hosted capabilities for building solutions. AppFabric is a "platform as a service" (PaaS) solution that acts as middleware in the cloud. This middleware includes features for secure cloud messaging (Service Bus), unified access control across federated identity stores (Access Control), distributed application cache (Caching), and BizTalk-like integration services (Integration). The Caching and Integration offerings are expected to be released in the latter half of 2011. For the purposes of this chapter, the focus will be on the Service Bus and Access Control services.

AppFabric Access Control

AppFabric Access Control services use "claim transformation" to create a federated security strategy for connected applications. In the sections below, we look at the problems we face when attempting to unify an identity model, and how the AppFabric Access Control service can help.

Problem scenarios

"Who are you and what can you do?" This is the fundamental question of application security. Many of our applications decide to answer this question through locally stored credentials and roles but this leads to a messy, difficult-to-manage security landscape.

While many organizations standardize on an internal identity provider such as Microsoft's Active Directory, it can prove challenging to try and maintain a single identity provider when your organization is expected to interact with a wide array of external parties. One solution is to explicitly add external accounts into the internal Active Directory, but this requires significant maintenance and may give external users more access to internal applications than was intended. What we need is a way to allow each organization to use their own identity providers while enabling a clean way to transform those identities and credentials into something that our own systems can understand. Ideally, our systems should get out of the business of managing credentials and permissions and be able to trust a unified third party instead.

The solution

The AppFabric Access Control (AC) service provides a cloud-based engine for transforming claims from one trusted identity provider to another. The AC service has a trust relationship with specified issuers, whether that is an enterprise directory like the Active Directory of our partner, or a web identity provider like Google, Facebook, or Windows Live ID.

Those providers send a set of "claims" to the AC service. A **claim** is a set of information about a user's identity. A security token may contain claims with your name, email address, job title, and date of hire. If the AC service trusts the issuer who provided those claims, then those values can be considered trustworthy by consumers of those claims.

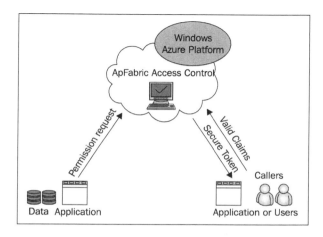

For example, my application could require a user to be authenticated and also require a particular user role (for example, "Manager") to execute an operation. This application could be built to accept claims as its identity input. One can imagine that building applications to accept these issuer-specific claims from every issuer would be a mess to build and a nightmare to maintain. However, this is where the power of claims transformation becomes apparent. My application requires a specific claim and the AC service performs transformation from all the individual issuers to my single output claim type. In this way, our application code is completely decoupled from a specific identity provider and instead can authorize a whole host of parties by transforming their claims to the single format that is expected. The AppFabric AC acts as a "claim broker" as it receives claims from multiple sources and transforms them to the output format we need.

This is a powerful concept and one that will be fully demonstrated in the coming pages.

Service Bus

The AppFabric Service Bus allows us to expose web services to the cloud in a secure fashion and without unnecessarily opening network ports or changing any infrastructure considerations.

Problem scenarios

Connecting two distributed parties is by no means an easy feat. We've been solving this problem for years through the use of Electronic Data Exchange(EDI) and Value Added Networks (VAN), company-to-company VPNs, FTP, and a series of other mechanisms. In each case, the communication required specialized software or significant changes to each organization's infrastructure landscape. To make this happen, firewall ports must be opened, user accounts get created in the target organization's directory, certificates may get exchanged, and so forth. In addition, when an organization opens up a VPN for a partner, they may be unknowingly enabling access to a whole host of applications that the partner is not meant to see.

The solution

The AppFabric Service Bus introduces a novel way to selectively and securely expose on-premises WCF endpoints to the cloud.

Let us look at two of the major components of the Service Bus. First, we have a global addressing service that allows us to own a namespace (for example, "Contoso") and define URIs underneath it. This global namespace can front a distributed set of services that are geographically distributed and hosted in different environments and containers. The URIs built in the cloud namespace act as a central reference point for the internal services that sit behind it.

A second, and primary, component of the Service Bus is the Relay Service, which includes the set of WCF bindings that make it possible for any WCF service to listen on the cloud namespace address. Even non-WCF services (for example, ASMX services, non-.NET clients) are capable of receiving messages through the Relay Service. Service clients call the cloud endpoint and the request is relayed down to the internally-hosted service.

The Service Bus leverages some familiar base bindings as well as introducing some new ones. For instance, many standard WCF bindings (**BasicHttpBinding, WebHttpBinding, Ws2007HttpBinding, NetTcpBinding**) all have equivalent Relay bindings (**BasicHttpRelayBinding, WebHttpRelayBinding, Ws2007HttpRelayBinding, NetTcpRelayBinding**). In addition to those Relay bindings, there are two addition bindings that are unique to the Service Bus. The **NetOneWayRelayBinding** performs a one-way communication over TCP from the cloud to the client. The **NetEventRelayBinding** is a broadcast binding that is also one way, but allows multiple services to listen on the cloud endpoint. You might use this binding if you want a client service request to be sent to multiple services.

Publishing Service Bus messages to BizTalk Server

BizTalk Server 2010 is a straightforward recipient of Azure Service Bus messages. For the foreseeable future, organizations will continue to maintain significant on-premises software investments while looking to the cloud for expansion of their application portfolio. Architects will have to pay particular attention to integration between on-premises software and cloud platforms. Extending BizTalk Server through the Azure Service Bus opens up a host of possibilities and helps leverage the scalability and accessibility of the cloud while exploiting prior software investments.

Scenario description

The remainder of this chapter walks through a complete solution scenario that demonstrates how to send messages through the Service Bus into BizTalk Server and back from BizTalk Server to the Service Bus.

In this scenario, we represent the fictitious company named **WatsonBSafe**. This company manages building access security for organizations that subscribe to their service. They own the technology that scans employee badges and allows entry into both buildings and rooms within a company's office buildings. WatsonBSafe has many clients who each publish their employee registries to them as well as explicit requests for access rights to be granted to client employees.

Riley Semiconductor is one of WatsonBSafe's customers. The relationship between these organizations is many years old and a VPN had been set up so that Riley Semiconductor could interface with the WatsonBSafe user access provisioning system. WatsonBSafe also interfaces back with Riley Semiconductor to discover which training courses are required for access to a particular building.

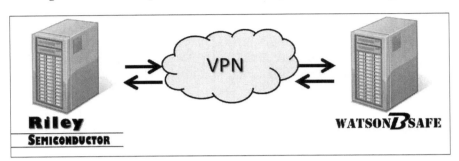

WatsonBSafe wants to move away from this model, but will do so in stages. First, they want to eliminate the need to provision accounts for Riley Semiconductor users and instead rely on claims from Riley's building access provisioning system. Therefore, this solution starts by demonstrating how to apply claims-based authorization to an on-premises BizTalk endpoint.

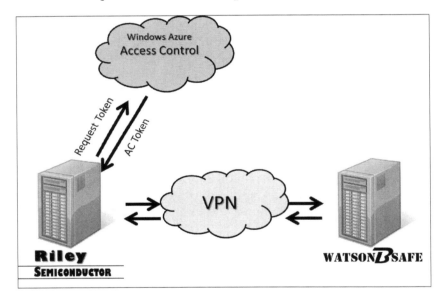

After achieving this, we will shift our endpoint to the cloud, eliminate the VPN, and establish a fully secure cloud exchange.

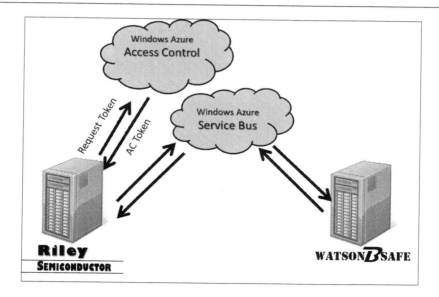

There is a starter solution in the code that accompanies this book. In the Chapter 6 folder, you can find a Visual Studio 2010 solution named `Chapter6.BuildingAccessManagement.sln`. Open this solution prior to building the components below.

Building the BizTalk solution components

We need to create a single message schema to start with, and then configure our BizTalk and service endpoints.

Defining message schemas

Our first step is to build the schema definition describing the request for access and then create a web service that accepts a message of that type.

1. Open the `Chapter6.BuildingAccessManagement.sln` solution and create a new BizTalk project named `Chapter6.BuildingAccessManagement.BizTalk`.

2. Configure the project with a strong name key and set it to deploy to a BizTalk application named **Chapter 6**.

3. Add a new schema named `AccessRequestEvent_XML.xsd` to the BizTalk project.

4. Construct the schema with the fields outlined below and each data type set to "string".

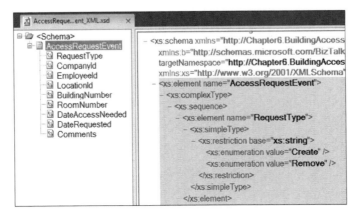

5. Next, define a Promoted Field so that we can later route on the **CompanyId** field. Add a Promoted Property Schema named `BuildingAccess_Prop.xsd` to the project.

6. Add a field named **CompanyID** to the property schema.

7. Map the **CompanyId** field in the `AccessRequestEvent_XML.xsd` to the **CompanyID** field in the property schema.

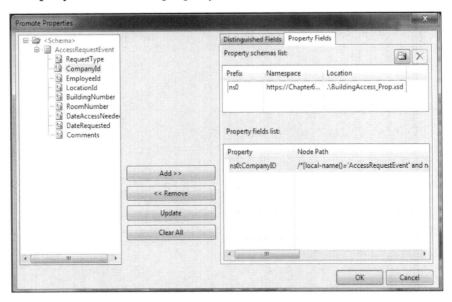

8. Build and deploy the BizTalk application.

Exposing a service endpoint

Next up, we take our schema and use it to expose an on-premises service endpoint. This schema is used to construct two distinct services to expose the "Request Access" and "Revoke Access" operations. Why do we have two services instead of a single service with two operations? We want the option to add fine-grained authorization control to these operations and cannot do so easily if we only have a single receive location, which is what the BizTalk WCF Service Publishing Wizard produces for each individual service solution.

1. In Visual Studio 2010, go to the **Tools** menu and launch the **BizTalk WCF Service Publishing Wizard** to build the first service endpoint that we need.

2. Choose the **WCF-CustomIsolated** adapter and select the **Enable on-premise metadata exchange** and **Create BizTalk receive locations in the following application** options.

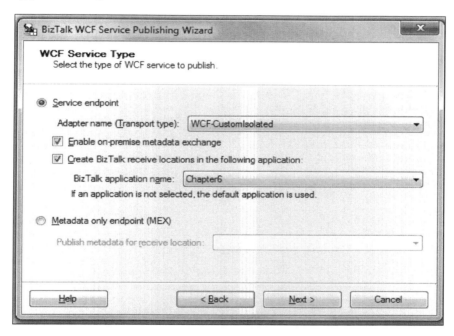

3. Next, choose to publish schemas as a web service. This option lets us manually build out a service definition as opposed to using an orchestration to generate the service's name, operation name, and message types.

4. Skip the option to build a Service Bus endpoint on the following wizard pane. At this stage, we are only exposing the service to local consumers, per our first use case. In a future step, when we simulate the elimination of the VPN between the two companies, we will "cloud enable" our endpoint.

5. Now, we have the option to manually shape our service definition for the **RequestAccessService**.

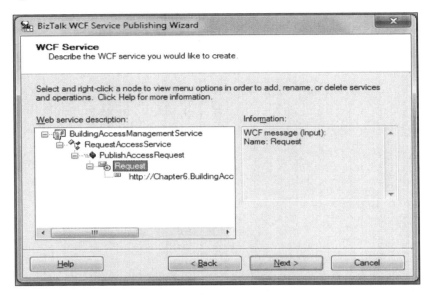

6. After defining our service, set the target namespace to `http://Chapter6/BuildingAccessManagement`.

7. Deploy the service at this address: `http://localhost/RequestAccessService`.

8. Complete the wizard and verify a successful deployment by confirming that the new service exists in IIS and is associated with an Application Pool that runs under an account with permission to publish to the BizTalk MessageBox database.

9. If we dig a bit into our wizard-generated service, we see a few interesting things. First, when you open the svc file you see that `CustomWebServiceHostFactory` was used instead of the standard WCF `ServiceHost`. This leads to the second interesting point. Look at the `web.config` file and notice a very sparse `system.serviceModel` section. There is no specific endpoint definition for the web service. This is because the `CustomWebServiceHostFactory` mentioned earlier pulls in the receive location configuration details to configure the service. The endpoint that you will find in the `web.config` file's `system.ServiceModel` is a definition of our Metadata Exchange (MEX) endpoint.

10. Switch to the BizTalk Server Administration Console and open the **Chapter 6** application.

11. Find the wizard-generated receive location, open it, and set the binding to **BasicHttpBinding**.

12. Start the receive location and browse to the service address and notice a working metadata link.

13. With the "Request Access" service complete, we once again walk through the BizTalk WCF Service Publishing Wizard to build a "Revoke Access" service produced.

14. Select the same adapter (**WCF-CustomIsolated**) as the last walkthrough of the wizard and once again choose to build a service from schemas.

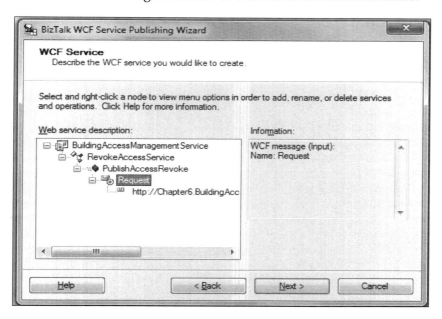

15. Set the target namespace of the service to `http://Chapter6/BuildingAccessManagement`

16. Set the deployment address of this service to `http://localhost/RevokeAccessService`

17. Complete the wizard and confirm success by finding the service in IIS, setting a valid Application Pool, and setting the binding on the generated receive location to **BasicHttpBinding**.

18. With our inbound service channels defined, we now need a send port that subscribes to our published content. Define a new one-way, static send port that emits our messages to disk. The subscription for this send port is based on the message type property.

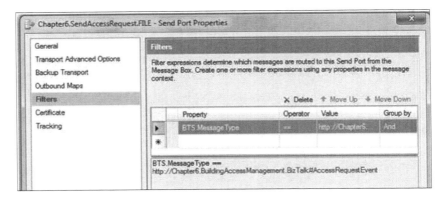

We now have the base components for the first part of our solution. Next, we will define the Azure AppFabric Access Control (AC) service settings to overlay granular authorization to our internal service endpoints.

Building the Access Control Service Components

The AC service can take claims provided by one party and translate them to claims needed by another party. For this part of the solution, we define a set of AC rules that govern permission to send messages to the BizTalk service endpoint.

1. First, we need our credentials to manage our AC Security Token Service (STS), which is responsible for issuing valid tokens. Visit `http://windows.azure.com` and record the **Management Key Name** and **Current Management Key** for a previously-created service namespace. These values are needed to access and manage our STS.

2. Download and open the Azure platform AppFabric SDK (version 1.0 available at `http://bit.ly/9kEVfh`) and navigate to the AcmBrowser application within the Access Control samples (`AccessControl\ExploringFeatures\Management\AcmBrowser`). Compile and run the AcmBrowser application.

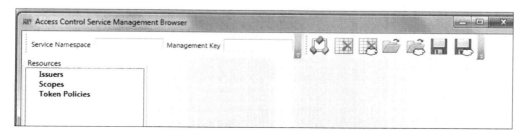

3. Within the AcmBrowser, enter valid AC credentials into the **Service Namespace** and **Management Key** and click the **Load from Cloud** button to confirm connectivity.

4. Create a new Issuer that represents the WatsonBSafe company. Right-click the **Issuers** node and choose **Create**.

5. Set the **Display Name** and **Issuer Name** to **WatsonBSafe** and generate keys.

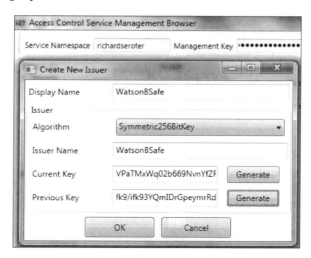

6. We need an additional Issuer for each vendor who is communicating with us. When vendors call our services, they use their unique issuer and we will map their Issuer claims to the claims understood by our application. Create another Issuer named **Riley Semiconductor**.

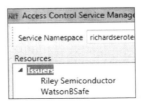

7. Right-click on the **Token Policies** menu item to create a **Token Policy**, which is responsible for signing tokens and applying a designated token lifetime. The new Token Policy is named WatsonBSafe Token Policy and has a 3600 second timeout along with a generated Signing Key.

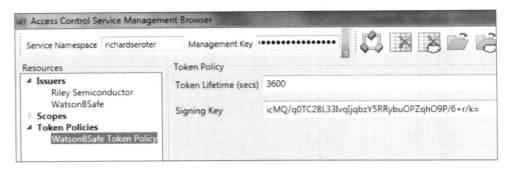

8. With the Issuer and Token Policy in place, we define a **Scope** by right-clicking the **Scopes** menu item and creating a new scope. An AC Scope is a collection of rules that dictate token-issuing behavior for a designated resource. Set the scope's name, **appliesTo** URI (which identifies which resource these rules should apply to) and token policy. Earlier, we built two individual services that deal with "building access management" but now we can define a single logical resource to which we apply rules. Specifically, define a logical resource (**appliesTo** value) named `http://localhost/` `BuildingAccessManagementService` that is used by the two previously-built services to validate incoming claims.

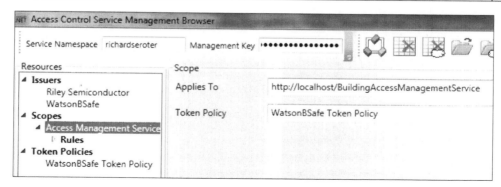

9. The most important part of the scope is the actual rules that drive the claim issuing behavior. We have services that both create and revoke employee access permission to company buildings, and we want to limit who can execute those actions. Any employee is allowed to submit a request for building access, but only site managers have permission to revoke access. Before constructing the claims that govern service authorization, we will build a simple rule that passes along the email address of the vendor to our service.

10. First, underneath our new scope, create a **PassThrough** rule that takes the email address of the vendor and copies the provided value to a selected output claim named **PartnerContactEmail**.

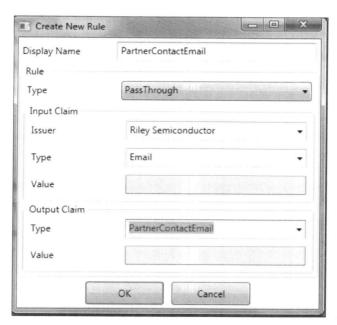

11. Next, create the rules that our services will use to accept or reject the vendor data. Underneath the same scope, create a rule named **ActivityPermission_Create** of type **Simple** and set the **Issuer** to **Riley Semiconductor** with a **Type** of **Group** and a **Value** of **Employee**. What we just did was define an input claim where we are checking if our Issuer (our vendor) gave us a "Group" claim indicating that the service caller is an employee. The output claim type is **ActivityPermission** with a value of **Create**.

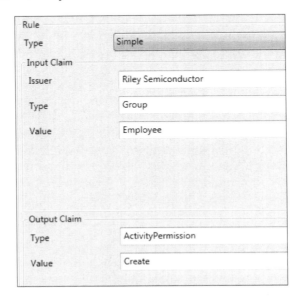

12. Define another rule named **ActivityPermission_Remove** that uses a claim type of **Group** but has a value of **SiteManager**. The output claim is of type **ActivityPermission** and has a value of **Revoke**. You can imagine when we have a dozen vendors that being able to map a diverse set of input claims to a single output claim is a powerful concept!

13. Save your changes to the AC STS by clicking the **Save to Cloud** button on the AcmBrowser application toolbar.

What we have done here is define a set of rules that our services can now leverage when confirming that the service caller is authorized to perform the action requested.

Building the Token Validator WCF behavior

With our claims defined, we now need a way to actually validate the claims sent to our service. In this exercise, we build a validator component that is deployed as a WCF endpoint behavior and rejects invalid inbound tokens. This is a reusable component, so we want to avoid hard-coding any values and instead rely on runtime configuration to provide the claim types that we need to validate.

1. Add a new .NET class library project named `Chapter6.ClaimValidationBehavior` to our existing Visual Studio 2010 solution. Add references to **System.Web**, **System.ServiceModel**, and **System.ServiceModel.Web**.

2. Within the code package provided for this book chapter, you will find a `TokenValidator.cs` file that was taken from the AppFabric SDK. This class does much of the heavy lifting of validating the token's signature, expiration date, issuer, and more. It also contains an operation to retrieve the claims from the token so that we can see if they match what the service demands. Add this class to our new .NET project.

3. Add a new class named `ClaimInspector.cs` to the project.

4. At the top of the class, add the following "using" statements:
   ```
   using System.ServiceModel;
   using System.ServiceModel.Web;
   using System.ServiceModel.Dispatcher;
   //for http response property
   using System.ServiceModel.Channels;
   //for copied TokenValidator object
   using Microsoft.AccessControl.SDK.ACSCalculator.
   AuthorizationManager;
   using System.Net;
   ```

5. Ensure that the `ClaimInspector` class is public and add an inheritance from the WCF `IDispatchmessageInspector` interface.

6. Define a series of member variables that will be set by the constructor and used later in the inspector class:
   ```
   private string serviceNamespace;
   private string trustedTokenPolicyKey;
   private string acsHostName;
   private string trustedAudience;
   private string claimType;
   private string claimValue;
   ```

7. Next, create a public constructor that takes in values and sets the member variables.

```
public ClaimInspector(string serviceNamespace, string
trustedTokenPolicyKey, string acsHostName, string trustedAudience,
string claimType, string claimValue)
        {
this.serviceNamespace = serviceNamespace;
this.trustedTokenPolicyKey = trustedTokenPolicyKey;
this.acsHostName = acsHostName;
this.trustedAudience = trustedAudience;
this.claimType = claimType;
this.claimValue = claimValue;
        }
```

8. The `IDispatchMessageInspector` interface requires two mandatory operations (`AfterReceiveRequest` and `BeforeSendReply`) but before we populate those operations, we want a helper function that examines the inbound HTTP header for valid tokens using our **TokenValidator** object.

```
private bool CheckValidToken()
{
bool isValid = true;
    //instantiate the TokenValidator
TokenValidator tv =
new TokenValidator(
acsHostName,
serviceNamespace,
trustedAudience,
Convert.FromBase64String(trustedTokenPolicyKey));

// get the HTTP authorization header
string authorizationHeader = WebOperationContext.Current.
IncomingRequest.Headers[HttpRequestHeader.Authorization];

    //if the header is missing return false
if (string.IsNullOrEmpty(authorizationHeader))
    {
return false;
    }

    // validate the token and return false if validation fails
if (!tv.Validate(authorizationHeader))
    {
return false;
    }
```

```
    // extract claims from header
    Dictionary<string, string> claims =
tv.GetNameValues(authorizationHeader);

    // look for requested claim
string permValue = "";
    //if the required claim is missing, return false
if (!claims.TryGetValue(claimType, out permValue))
    {
return false;
    }

    // check for the matching claim value
if (permValue != claimValue)
    {
return false;
    }
    //if all checks succeed, return success
returnisValid;
 }
```

9. The `AfterReceiveRequest` operation can now validate the token through the helper function.

```
public object AfterReceiveRequest(
ref System.ServiceModel.Channels.Message request,
IClientChannel channel,
InstanceContext instanceContext)
        {
            //check claims using helper function
bool isValid = CheckValidToken();

if (isValid == false)
            {
request = null;

return "access denied";
            }

return null;
        }
```

10. The value returned from this operation is automatically used as a context parameter in the BeforeSendReply operation. Before we send a reply to the caller, we check to see if the request should be denied and if so, return an HTTP 401 status code ("unauthorized").

```
public void BeforeSendReply(
ref System.ServiceModel.Channels.Message reply,
object correlationState)
        {
//if invalid claim
if (correlationState!= null &&correlationState.ToString() ==
"access denied")
{
HttpResponseMessageProperty httpResponse =
new HttpResponseMessageProperty();
httpResponse.StatusCode =
System.Net.HttpStatusCode.Unauthorized;
reply.Properties["httpResponse"] = httpResponse;
        }
    }
```

11. Our message inspector is now done and we can move on to build the actual WCF behavior that our service will leverage. Create a new class file named ClaimVerificationBehavior.cs.

12. Add the following "using" statements to the top of the class:

```
using System.ServiceModel;
using System.ServiceModel.Description;
```

13. Ensure that the ClaimVerificationBehavior class is public and set it to inherit from the IEndpointBehavior interface and define the following member variables:

```
public class ClaimVerificationBehavior : IEndpointBehavior
    {
private string serviceNamespace;
private string trustedTokenPolicyKey;
private string acsHostName;
private string trustedAudience;
private string claimType;
private string claimValue;
```

14. Like before, our public constructor will accept the values needed to set our member variables:

```
public ClaimVerificationBehavior(
string serviceNamespace,
string trustedTokenPolicyKey,
string acsHostName,
string trustedAudience,
string claimType,
string claimValue)
        {
this.serviceNamespace = serviceNamespace;
this.trustedTokenPolicyKey = trustedTokenPolicyKey;
this.acsHostName = acsHostName;
this.trustedAudience = trustedAudience;
this.claimType = claimType;
this.claimValue = claimValue;
        }
```

15. The final part of the behavior is the interface-required `ApplyDispatchBehavior` operation which adds our `ClaimInspector` object to the list of message inspectors that WCF applies upon message receipt.

```
public void AddBindingParameters(ServiceEndpoint endpoint,
System.ServiceModel.Channels.BindingParameterCollection
bindingParameters)
        {}

public void ApplyClientBehavior(ServiceEndpoint endpoint, System.
ServiceModel.Dispatcher.ClientRuntime clientRuntime)
        {}

public void ApplyDispatchBehavior(ServiceEndpoint endpoint,
System.ServiceModel.Dispatcher.EndpointDispatcher
endpointDispatcher)
        {
endpointDispatcher.DispatchRuntime.MessageInspectors.Add(new Clai
mInspector(serviceNamespace, trustedTokenPolicyKey, acsHostName,
trustedAudience, claimType, claimValue));
        }

public void Validate(ServiceEndpoint endpoint)
        {}
```

16. The final piece of this puzzle is the object that allows us to configure this behavior as part of a configuration binding. Create a new class named `ClaimBehaviorExtension.cs`.

17. Add the following three "using" statements to the class:

```
using System.ServiceModel;
using System.ServiceModel.Configuration; //for extension element
using System.Configuration; //for configurationproperty
```

18. This public class should inherit from the WCF `BehaviorExtensionElement` interface.

19. Create a series of public properties that we can set on our service configuration.

```
//default constructor
public ClaimBehaviorExtension(){}


[ConfigurationProperty("serviceNamespace", IsRequired=true)]
public string ServiceNamespace
  {
get { return base["serviceNamespace"].ToString(); }
set { base["serviceNamespace"] = value; }
  }


[ConfigurationProperty("trustedTokenPolicyKey", IsRequired=true)]
public string TrustedTokenPolicyKey
  {
get { return base["trustedTokenPolicyKey"].ToString(); }
set { base["trustedTokenPolicyKey"] = value; }
  }


[ConfigurationProperty("acsHostName", IsRequired=true)]
public string AcsHostName
  {
get { return base["acsHostName"].ToString(); }
set { base["acsHostName"] = value; }
  }


[ConfigurationProperty("trustedAudience", IsRequired=true)]
public string TrustedAudience
  {
get { return base["trustedAudience"].ToString(); }
set { base["trustedAudience"] = value; }
  }


[ConfigurationProperty("claimType", IsRequired=true)]
public string ClaimType
  {
```

```
get { return base["claimType"].ToString(); }
set { base["claimType"] = value; }
 }


[ConfigurationProperty("claimValue", IsRequired=true)]
public string ClaimValue
 {
get { return base["claimValue"].ToString(); }
set { base["claimValue"] = value; }
}
```

20. Next, set the `BehaviorType` property to the .NET type of the actual custom behavior class.

```
public override Type BehaviorType
  {
    get
    {
    returntypeof(ClaimVerificationBehavior);
    }
  }
```

21. Finally, describe the `CreateBehavior` operation that instantiates our custom claims inspector behavior and passes in all the values that the service defines in its configuration settings.

```
protected override object CreateBehavior()
        {
return new ClaimVerificationBehavior(
ServiceNamespace,
TrustedTokenPolicyKey,
AcsHostName,
TrustedAudience,
ClaimType,
ClaimValue);
        }
```

At this point, we have our claims defined in the AppFabric AC and a new WCF behavior that can validate claims. Up next, configuring BizTalk Server 2010 to use our custom behavior and validate the incoming service calls.

Configuring the BizTalk Service to verify claims

BizTalk Server 2010 has clear extension points for WCF and can leverage service and endpoint behaviors in its processing pipeline.

1. Sign the custom WCF behavior with a strong name key and add it to the Global Assembly Cache (GAC) of the server(s) with BizTalk Server installed.

2. For BizTalk Server to find custom behaviors, they must be added to the `machine.config` file of the server(s). On my server, this file is located at `C:\Windows\Microsoft.NET\Framework\v4.0.30319\Config\machine.config`. If you are running a 64 bit machine, don't forget to also open and add to the 64-bit `machine.config` file as well (`C:\Windows\Microsoft.NET\Framework64\v4.0.30319\Config\machine.config`).

3. In the `behaviorextensions` section of the `machine.config` file(s), add the following block (changing the public key token per your signing key).

   ```
   <add name="ClaimValidationBehavior" type="Chapter6.
   ClaimValidationBehavior.ClaimBehaviorExtension, Chapter6.
   ClaimValidationBehavior, Version=1.0.0.0, Culture=neutral,
   PublicKeyToken=<your public key>"/>
   ```

4. If you have the BizTalk Server Administration Console open, close, then reopen it to avoid any caching problems.

5. Browse to the receive location for the **RequestAccessService**.

6. Visit the **Behaviors** tab under the adapter configuration and add a new **EndpointBehavior**. Our **ClaimValidationBehavior** should be listed and available for selection.

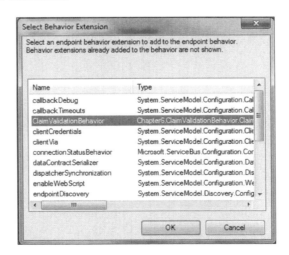

7. Once we add the behavior to the receive location configuration, we can view the exposed properties and set them per our AppFabric AC values.

Property	Value	Comment
acsHostName	Accesscontrol.windows.net	
claimType	ActivityPermission	This is from the AC output claim
claimValue	Create	Also from the output claim
serviceNamespace	richardseroter	Use the value of your AppFabric namespace

trustedAudience	`http://localhost/`
	
	`BuildingAccessManagementService`
		From the AC scope "appliesTo" value

trustedTokenPolicyKey	`<insert your token policy key>`	From the AC TokenPolicy

8. Save the receive location configuration.

We have now configured BizTalk Server 2010 to validate AppFabric AC claims. Notice that we have yet to extend our endpoints to the cloud, but, we can still use the claims even for on-premises-to-on-premises scenarios.

Building the service consumer

To test our configuration we need a valid service consumer. Within the Visual Studio 2010 starter project provided for this chapter, you should find a Windows Forms project named `Chapter6.ServiceConsumer.WinUI`.

1. Open the `Chapter6.ServiceConsumer.WinUI` project and add a service reference to `http://localhost/RequestAccessService/RequestAccessService.svc`.

2. Add project references to **System.Web**, **System.ServiceModel**, and **System.ServiceModel.Web**.

3. Add the following "using" statements to the code of the form:

```
using System.ServiceModel;
using System.ServiceModel.Web;
using System.Web;
using System.Net;     //for HttpWebRequest
using System.IO;      //for Streaming
```

4. Add a helper function named `BuildToken` to the form's code. Tokens are requested in a few ways, and I will demonstrate here how to do a simple, yet effective, request.

```
private string BuildToken()
{
 //get the scope resource from the form
 string wrap_scope = HttpUtility.UrlEncode(txtScope.Text);
 //get the AC issuer name from the form
 string wrap_name = txtIssuerName.Text;
 //get the AC issuer key from the form
 string wrap_password =
HttpUtility.UrlEncode(txtIssuerKey.Text);

 //build token request
 //NOTE: if you don't pass in the correct (or any) input claims,
 get HTTP 400 error (bad request)
 string tokenReq = "wrap_scope=" + wrap_scope + "&wrap_name=" +
 wrap_name + "&wrap_password=" + wrap_password +
 "&Email=riley@hotmail.com&Group="+ cbSubmitterType.SelectedItem;

 //create web request to AC endpoint
 HttpWebRequest req =
(HttpWebRequest)WebRequest.Create(
 "https://your namespace.accesscontrol.windows.net/WRAPv0.9");
 req.ContentType = "application/x-www-form-urlencoded";
 req.Method = "POST";

 //stream the token request string
 using (Stream reqStream = req.GetRequestStream())
 {
  var bytes = Encoding.UTF8.GetBytes(tokenReq);
  reqStream.Write(bytes, 0, bytes.Length);
  reqStream.Close();
 }

 //get the token result
 var response = (HttpWebResponse)req.GetResponse();
 var token = new StreamReader(response.GetResponseStream()).
ReadToEnd();

 //remove the "wrap_access_token" prefix
 string splitToken = token.Split('&').Single(value => value.
StartsWith("wrap_access_token=", StringComparison.
OrdinalIgnoreCase)).Split('=')[1];
 string tokenHeader = HttpUtility.UrlDecode(splitToken);

 return tokenHeader;
}
```

5. Create a click event for the form's **btnSubmit** button. This click event first gets a token through our `BuildToken` method and then proceeds to build up the WCF channel stack necessary to invoke our service. First though, simply emit the result of the `BuildToken` method to ensure that we can successfully return a token from the AppFabric AC service.

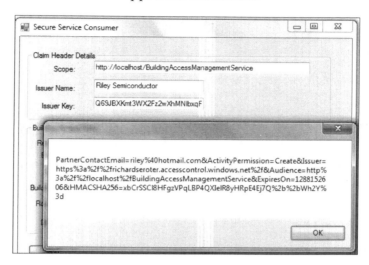

6. With a token in hand, we can proceed to define our WCF binding and endpoint objects.

```
BasicHttpBinding binding = new BasicHttpBinding();
EndpointAddress address = new EndpointAddress("http://localhost/
RequestAccessService/RequestAccessService.svc");
```

7. Next, we define the WCF channel factory for this binding and address.

```
ChannelFactory<RequestAccessSvc.
RequestAccessServiceChannel> factory =
    new ChannelFactory<RequestAccessSvc.
    RequestAccessServiceChannel>(binding, address);

 RequestAccessSvc.RequestAccessServiceChannel proxy = factory.
CreateChannel();
```

8. Finally, we open our proxy, add our token to the outgoing HTTP authorization header, build the message payload, and invoke the service.

```
using (new OperationContextScope((IClientChannel)proxy))
 {
  //pass in token in service header
  WebOperationContext.Current.OutgoingRequest.Headers.
Add(HttpRequestHeader.Authorization, tokenHeader);
  try
```

```
{
  //build payload
  RequestAccessSvc.PublishAccessRequestRequest req =
      new RequestAccessSvc.PublishAccessRequestRequest();

  req.AccessRequestEvent =
new RequestAccessSvc.AccessRequestEvent();
  req.AccessRequestEvent.EmployeeId = txtEmpId.Text;
  req.AccessRequestEvent.LocationId = txtLocation.Text;
  req.AccessRequestEvent.CompanyId = "Riley Semiconductor";
  req.AccessRequestEvent.BuildingNumber = txtBuilding.Text;
  //TODO reader, conditionally set this value
  req.AccessRequestEvent.RequestType = RequestAccessSvc.
AccessRequestEventRequestType.Create;
  req.AccessRequestEvent.RoomNumber = txtRoom.Text;
  req.AccessRequestEvent.DateRequested = "2010-10-29";
  req.AccessRequestEvent.DateAccessNeeded = dtNeeded.Text;
  //call service
  proxy.PublishAccessRequest(req);
}
catch (Exception ex)
{
MessageBox.Show("Error: " + ex.Message);
}
finally
{
    ((IClientChannel)proxy).Close();
    MessageBox.Show("Done!");
}
```

9. You may notice that like the receive location exercise above; these steps are only dealing with the Create service and not the Revoke one. You can feel free to add those steps to your solution, but it is unnecessary to configure this when proving the point of this exercise.

10. Build the application and make sure that the **Scope, Issuer Name**, and **Issuer Key** values match our AppFabric AC values.

11. Create a new request and set the **Submitter Type** to **Employee**. This is a valid group assignment for the service caller so we should see the message go through BizTalk and get emitted to the location specified in our previously-built send port.

12. Submit the same request again, except this time, set the Submitter Type property to Site Manager. Upon submission, you should receive an error back saying that the HTTP request is unauthorized. Also, there should be no message emitted to disk since there was not a successful publication to BizTalk.

The token does have a lifetime associated with it, so realistically we could have cached the token on the client and used it for a period of time until a refreshed token was required. You have now built a BizTalk Server 2010 service endpoint with rich authorization controls. Well done!

Creating Service Bus Access Control permissions

To complete this portion of our example solution, we want to extend this on-premises BizTalk Server endpoint to the Azure cloud through the Azure AppFabric Service Bus. Recall from our use case that the two partners first eliminated the need to use a single identity provider, and now they are ready to eliminate their VPN and communicate through the cloud-based Service Bus relay.

Earlier we configured the AppFabric AC service for a particular scope and set of access rules. The AppFabric Service Bus has its own Secure Token Service that governs who can send to and receive from the Service Bus. You can see on the AppFabric portal that there are two distinct STS endpoint addresses: one for the Service Bus and one for the Access Control Service.

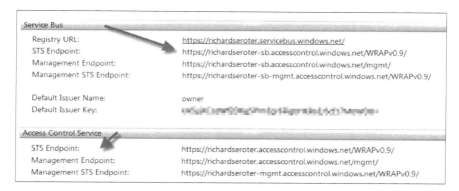

In this next exercise, we configure the Service Bus STS for our WatsonBSafe company and our partner, Riley Semiconductor.

1. In the AcmBrowser application, enter the namespace of the Service Bus STS and owner key. Note that the namespace for the Service Bus STS is the AppFabric namespace PLUS the "-sb" suffix. For instance, my Service Bus STS namespace is **richardseroter-sb**. Load the current configuration from the cloud.

2. You may notice that many demonstrations of the AppFabric Service Bus use the "owner" issuer name and management key for both listening to and sending to the cloud. In the real world, you would never hand out your namespace administration credentials, but rather, define specific scopes and issuer permissions that restrict senders and receivers to a given domain. We will add specific issuers and a new scope to this STS to reflect our solution scenario. Note that we won't add any service authorization rules because our previous Access Control settings will be applied to cloud transmissions as well.

3. Add a new issuer for **WatsonBSafe**, and another for **Riley Semiconductor**.

4. The default scope is at the namespace root for the Service Bus STS. This is too broad, so we will define a scope at a level below the root. Set our scope's **AppliesTo** parameter to `http://<your namespace>.servicebus.windows.net/RequestAccessService` and reuse the existing Service Bus token policy. You may notice that this scope is for a physical service address while the AC STS used a logical one. In this case, the Service Bus will be issuing claims for a specific address that wishes to bind to the cloud, so an exact match is required.

5. Create a new rule named **Listen**. This rule's input claim uses the **WatsonBSafe** issuer and has a type of **Issuer** and a value of **WatsonBSafe**. The output claim is of type **net.windows.servicebus.action** and has a value of **Listen**. Basically, it says that if the service knows the issuer name and key for this issuer, then they have permission to listen at the requested service URL.

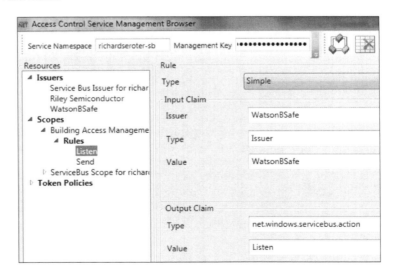

6. Define a second rule named **Send** whose input claim uses the **Riley Semiconductor** issuer with a **Type** of **Issuer** and **Value** of **Riley Semiconductor**. The output claim has a type of **net.windows.servicebus. action** and a value of **Send**. Like before, if the service client knows the issuer name and secret key for the issuer, then they are allowed to send requests to the Service Bus endpoint.

7. Save this configuration to the Service Bus STS.

You have now configured the AppFabric Service Bus STS with more granular Issuers and a specific resource that our service can bind to and that clients can invoke.

Reconfiguring a BizTalk solution to use Service Bus binding

If you wanted BizTalk Server to listen to the cloud prior to the release of **BizTalk Server 2010 AppFabric Connect for Services**, you had to manually configure a **WCF-CustomIsolated** endpoint that used a Service Bus binding. This wasn't a particularly challenging thing to do; however, there was a problem in getting metadata easily shared since the Service Bus bindings don't fully respect the `serviceMetadata` WCF behavior that is often used to share a WSDL for a service. The updated service-generation wizard for BizTalk Server 2010 takes care of this problem by producing cloud-visible MEX endpoints.

What we can do is rebuild our previously-built, BizTalk-generated services, but this time, choose the option to extend our endpoints to the cloud. Note that for the purpose of future-cloud-enablement, we previously created two distinct services earlier rather than one service with two endpoints. The new wizard doesn't support that concept of two service endpoints in the same solution, so we needed two distinct service projects. For this example, we will only rebuild (and cloud enable) the **RequestAccessService**.

1. From within Visual Studio 2010, start the BizTalk WCF Service Publishing Wizard and choose the **WCF-CustomIsolated** adapter. Also choose to have a metadata endpoint and a receive location in the **Chapter 6** application.

2. On the next wizard page, choose the option to **Add a Service Bus endpoint.** If you do not see this option, verify that you have indeed installed the BizTalk Server 2010 Feature Pack.

3. Choose the option to build a web service from schemas.

4. Rebuild the service to look the same as our initial **RequestAccessService** did.

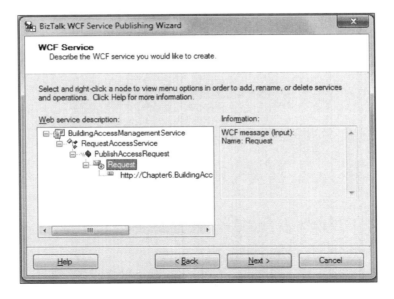

5. Set the target namespace of the service to `http://Chapter6/ BuildingAccessManagement`

6. Set the deployment location to `http://localhost/RequestAccessService` and make sure to select the option to overwrite the existing service.

7. The subsequent wizard page shows up because we earlier chose the option to build a Service Bus endpoint.

8. Choose the **BasicHttpRelayBinding** and enter your personal Service Bus namespace value in the **Service Namespace** field. Also, choose the option to **Enable metadata exchange on cloud**. This means that we have a distinct cloud endpoint in our service that exposes the metadata description. You can also choose to make this service discoverable in your Service Bus namespace's ATOM feed if you so choose.

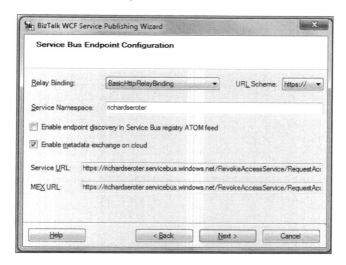

9. After defining our Service Bus endpoints, we choose the service authentication parameters. In our case, we use the WatsonBSafe issuer and associated issuer key. The configuration below shows that pulling the service metadata does not require client authentication, but actually invoking the service requires the caller to authenticate with the Service Bus.

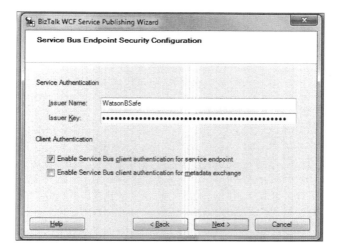

10. Complete the wizard which overwrites our existing web service and receive location. Go into the BizTalk Administration console, find the generated receive location and reset the binding to **BasicHttpBinding** (NOT the cloud relay binding) and re-add our custom claim authorization behavior using the previously outlined values.

11. Find the wizard-generated web service and investigate the `web.config` file. Notice that we now have three total endpoints: one for the on-premises metadata exchange, one for the cloud metadata exchange, and one for the cloud relay. Instead of leveraging the receive location configuration to define the service endpoint, the wizard added the cloud-required settings to the Azure AppFabric web service endpoint. However, this means that our custom authorization behavior will NOT get automatically applied to our cloud relay endpoint. The behavior must be manually added to the AppFabric endpoint as it will not be pulled from the receive location's configuration.

12. Find the endpoint behavior named `sharedSecretClientCredentials` and add a configuration block for our custom behavior using identical values as our receive location behavior.

```
<ClaimVerificationBehavior
serviceNamespace="<your namespace>"
trustedTokenPolicyKey= <your key here>
acsHostName="accesscontrol.windows.net"
trustedAudience="http://localhost/BuildingAccessManagementService"
claimType="ActivityPermission"
claimValue="Create" />
```

13. Save the `web.config` file and browse the service endpoint in the browser and confirm that our endpoint is configured correctly.

Reconfiguring the Service Consumer to use Service Bus Binding

All that's left to do now is call our service through the cloud relay. The steps below outline the changes to the client code to make this happen.

1. To call our new cloud endpoint in the `Chapter6.ServiceConsumer.WinUI` Windows Forms project, we have a few changes to make to the existing code. First, add a reference to the `System.ServiceBus.dll` and a "using" statement in the form's code. Then, in the form's button click event, redefine the `binding` variable using a `BasicHttpRelayBinding` type.

```
BasicHttpRelayBinding binding = new  BasicHttpRelayBinding(EndToEn
dBasicHttpSecurityMode.Transport,  RelayClientAuthenticationType.
RelayAccessToken);
```

2. Next, change the endpoint address to now point to the cloud-hosted endpoint.

```
EndpointAddress address = new EndpointAddress("https://
richardseroter.servicebus.windows.net/RequestAccessService/
RequestAccessService.svc");
```

3. In order to pass in our Service Bus authentication token that gives us the claims necessary to invoke the service, we need to define a `TransportClientEndpointBehavior`. We are using the `SharedSecret` credential type and passing in our vendor credentials for the Service Bus.

```
TransportClientEndpointBehavior sbBehavior =
        new TransportClientEndpointBehavior();
sbBehavior.CredentialType =
TransportClientCredentialType.SharedSecret;
sbBehavior.Credentials.SharedSecret.IssuerName =
"Riley Semiconductor";
sbBehavior.Credentials.SharedSecret.IssuerSecret =
"HwWbATe00bCpxszylPdJoVns+FNfJCdgK21UErcWJAE=";
```

4. Finally, after our channel factory definition, we add our endpoint behavior.

```
factory.Endpoint.Behaviors.Add(sbBehavior);
```

5. Save and compile the client application.

If we use the correct sender ("Employee") when submitting a message to the cloud endpoint, then we see the message travel through BizTalk Server and come to rest on the file system. If we try and call the service with an invalid sender type ("Site Manager"), then we receive the HTTP 401 error.

In this demonstration, we saw how to build a custom authorization manager and apply it to an on-premises BizTalk-generated web service. It was then fairly easy to come along later and extend that on-premises service with cloud endpoints. This is a powerful scenario for extended existing, internal endpoints through the cloud to a select group of external users.

Publishing BizTalk Server messages to the Service Bus

BizTalk Server 2010 is a straightforward consumer of Azure Service Bus messages. As more organizations introduce cloud solutions into their enterprise architecture, we will see an increasing need to seamless orchestrate these endpoints with on-premises data and systems. A cloud service can be invoked by BizTalk Server quite easily and makes BizTalk a valuable asset when integrating between clouds or between on-premises and the cloud.

Scenario description

In this scenario, we continue our work with the WatsonBSafe and Riley Semiconductor organizations. If you recall from the last exercise, WatsonBSafe has a need to query the Riley Semiconductor's training system so that they can uncover which courses are required by an employee before access is granted to a building or room. The training service is exposed through the Service Bus and needs to be invoked by BizTalk Server 2010.

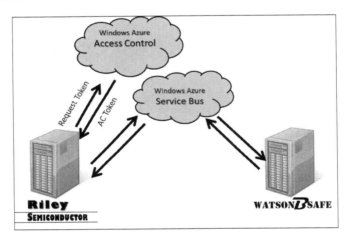

Solution design

For this solution, we will use BizTalk Server's **WCF-CustomIsolated** adapter alongside a Service Bus binding to call the training service. Because this service only looks up data and does not require granular security, we will not apply any security above and beyond the standard Service Bus authentication process.

Building the Access Control Service components

The first thing we need is the Service Bus STS configuration for our vendor's training service. In our previous demonstration, WatsonBSafe was hosting a service that Riley Semiconductor was sending to. Here, the roles are reversed.

1. Open the AcmBrowser application and log in to the Service Bus STS using your namespace (plus "-sb" suffix) and default issuer key.

2. Add a new Scope named **TrainingServices** and set the scope's **Applies To** URL to `http://<your namespace>.servicebus.windows.net/ TrainingServices`

3. Create a new rule named **Listen** where the input claim **Issuer** is **Riley Semiconductor**, the **Type** is **Issuer**, and the **Value** is **Riley Semiconductor**. The output claim type is **net.windows.servicebus.action** with a value of **Listen**.

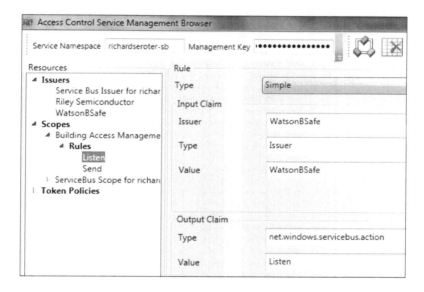

4. Define a second rule named **Send** that uses the **WatsonBSafe** Issuer, has a Type of **Issuer**, and a Value of **WatsonBSafe**. The output claim type is **net. windows.servicebus.action** with a value of **Send**. This rule issues a token allowing the service consumer to call the service if they know the credentials for the WatsonBSafe Issuer.

5. Save the Service Bus STS configuration back to the cloud.

6. Return to Visual Studio 2010 and open the `Chapter6.TrainingService` project that exists in the solution.

7. Open the `web.config` file for the service and make the following changes:

    a. Complete the endpoint address for each endpoint under `system.ServiceModel/services/service` by filling in your own Service Bus namespace.

    b. Set valid issuer secrets for the two behaviors at `system.serviceModel/behaviors/endpointBehaviors`.

8. Build and deploy the TrainingService and view the service in the browser to ensure a successful binding to the cloud.

Our TrainingService is now complete and ready for BizTalk Server to invoke it.

Building the BizTalk solution components

We are going to build a few BizTalk components for calling the TrainingService and combining its result with the access request message in order to emit a single message containing both the employee requesting access and the training required for access to be granted.

1. Open the existing BizTalk Server project in the Visual Studio 2010 solution.

2. Create a new schema named `AccessRequirements_XML.xsd`. This schema holds a combination of access request details and required training courses related to the access request. All of the elements have a data type of "string."

3. Ensure that the schema above has the `Course` node set to be unbounded to support an unlimited number of assigned courses.

4. Now we are ready to reference our cloud-hosted TrainingService and produce the BizTalk artifacts needed to call the service. Right-click the BizTalk project in Visual Studio 2010 and choose to **Add Generated Items**. Select the option to **Consume WCF Service**.

5. When prompted, put in the MEX address for the service (for example, `https://<your namespace>.servicebus.windows.net/TrainingServices/TrainingService.svc_mex`) and click the **Get** button. You will likely see an error but that has no negative impact. A MEX query is done via SOAP, and this wizard is only doing a simple HTTP GET request. Therefore, the error is expected.

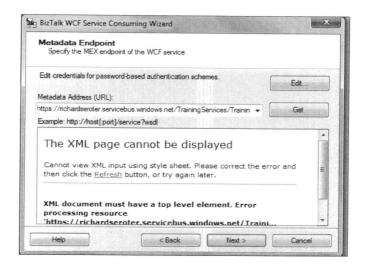

6. Complete the BizTalk WCF Service Consuming Wizard and notice that the wizard adds schemas, an orchestration, and a binding file to the BizTalk project.

7. Create a new orchestration named `VerifyRileyAccessRequirements.odx` in the BizTalk project. This orchestration listens for building access requests from the Riley Semiconductor company and calls back through the cloud to the Riley Semiconductor's training system to look up required training for the requested building. We would conceptually have one orchestration for each partner, or, could alternately build a more loosely coupled orchestration that relies more on send port maps for destination specific formats. In this scenario, we'll build vendor-specific orchestrations.

8. Define four orchestration-level messages:

   a. **AccessRequestInput** of type **Chapter6.BuildingAccessManagement. BizTalk.AccessRequestEvent_XML**

   b. **EmployeeTrainingOutput** of type **Chapter6. BuildingAccessManagement.BizTalk.AccessRequirements_XML**

     c.   **TrainingServiceRequest** of multi-part type **Chapter6. BuildingAccessManagement.BizTalk.ITrainingService_ GetTrainingForBuildingAccess_InputMessage**

     d.   **TrainingServiceResponse** of multi-part type **Chapter6. BuildingAccessManagement.BizTalk.ITrainingService_ GetTrainingForBuildingAccess_OutputMessage**

9. Add a filter on the initial receive shape of the orchestration. This filter will ensure that only messages from Riley Semiconductor come into this orchestration.

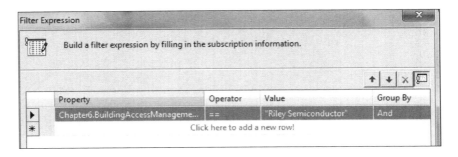

10. After the topmost receive shape, add a **Construct/Transform** block that is responsible for building the service's request message.

11. Double-click the **Transform** shape and choose the option to create a new map named **BizTalk.AccessRequest_To_TrainingServiceRequest**. This map should start with the **AccessRequestInput** message and output the **TrainingServiceRequest** message.

12. Within the map, connect the **LocationId**, **BuildingNumber**, and **RoomNumber** to the corresponding nodes in the target schema. Save the map and return to the orchestration.

13. Add a **Send** shape and **Receive** shape below the previous **Construct** shape. These new shapes are responsible for calling the TrainingService and receiving the response message. Set the **Send** shape to use the **TrainingServiceRequest** message and the **Receive** shape will use the **TrainingServiceResponse** message.

14. Create a new, configured port on the **Port Surface** portion of the orchestration. For the **Port Type** value, choose to use an existing port type and point to the one created by the service reference. Our orchestration should look like the following image:

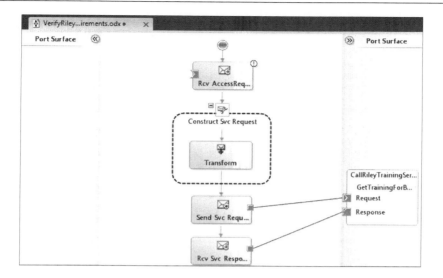

15. Next, we need to mash up our original message with the result of the service call. Add a new **Construct/Transform** block at the bottom of the orchestration.

16. Double-click the **Transform** shape and create a new map named **AccessRequestTrainingResponse_To_EmployeeTrainingOutput**.

17. The input to the map is BOTH the **AccessRequestInput** and **TrainingServiceResponse** message and outputs the **EmployeeTrainingOutput** message. You may remember that you can create multi-part maps in BizTalk Server, but only from within an orchestration. You cannot create a multi-part map from within the Mapper itself.

18. Connect the relevant source nodes to the destination nodes.

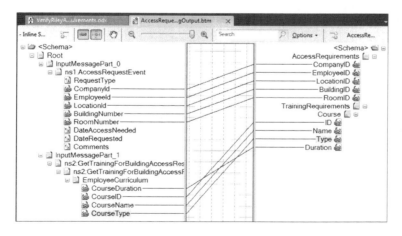

19. Add a final send shape that uses the **EmployeeTrainingOutput** message.

20. Define an orchestration receive port for the initial **Receive** shape and an orchestration send port for the last **Send** shape. The topmost orchestration receive port should be **Direct Bound**, which means that it listens to the MessageBox for data instead of being bound to a messaging port.

21. Build and deploy the updated BizTalk solution.

We now have all the compiled components necessary to consume the cloud service from BizTalk Server. Next, we need to configure the BizTalk messaging components to communicate with Windows Azure AppFabric.

Configuring BizTalk Solution to use Service Bus bindings

Our final exercise is to configure the BizTalk messaging components.

1. Switch to the BizTalk Server Administration Console and find the **Chapter6** application.

2. We need two messaging ports. First, we need the two-way send port that calls the TrainingService through the Service Bus. Instead of manually building this port, we can use the binding file that the BizTalk WCF Service Consuming Wizard produced. Right click the **Chapter6** application and choose **Import**, then **Bindings**, and navigate to the `TrainingService_Custom.BindingInfo.xml` file residing in the folder with our BizTalk project code.

3. After the binding is imported, we can see a new Send Port in the application. Opening that port shows us the cloud address, cloud binding, and valid WCF action.

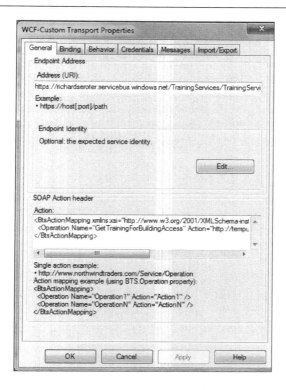

4. Switch to the **Behaviors** tab and add a new Endpoint Behavior. Find the **TransportClientEndpointBehavior** and set the valid "send" credentials for the Service Bus. In our case, this is the WatsonBSafe issuer and secret key from the Service Bus STS.

5. Our final messaging port is a one-way send port that transmits the final message from the orchestration. Create a file send port that emits a message to the file system.

6. With the messaging ports complete, we can complete our orchestration binding. Go to our orchestration in the Chapter6 application and match the **Outbound Logical Ports** to the appropriate **Send Ports / Send Port Groups**.

7. Start the send ports and orchestration.

We can test the entire end-to-end solution by starting our client application and submitting a new building access request. Select building 10 for the first request and notice that the output message has no training requirements for the user. If you send another request and use building 41, you should see a message with two courses assigned to the user.

Summary

As more and more organizations begin to rely on the cloud for mission critical applications, the need for straightforward integration solutions will increase. In this chapter, we first saw how we can send messages from the cloud to our on-premises BizTalk Server with minimal effort. The majority of work we performed was around building a reusable WCF behavior that can validate tokens and overlay an authorization layer across our services. Prior to the availability of Windows Azure AppFabric, this sort of integration would have only been possible by either exposing BizTalk Server to the Internet through a reverse proxy, or, by using hardware/software to allow partners to directly access an internal service bus. Now, with minimal effort, we selectively exposed individual endpoints to any authorized, Internet-accessible client.

Besides just sending to the cloud, we also need the ability to consume cloud services. We saw that it was very easy to consume a cloud endpoint in the same way that BizTalk consumes on-premises services. One can imagine the exciting possibilities of orchestrating messaging solutions that combine internal and external data in a seamless manner.

In the following chapter, we'll see how to build integrated SharePoint solutions using the Windows SharePoint Services Adapter and InfoPath.

7
Integrating with SharePoint 2010

Microsoft SharePoint Server is a platform that allows people to collaborate through interactive Web technology. Teams can manage sets of documents through project lifecycles, capture structured and non-structured data that can be leveraged in reporting functions, and build composite business applications.

For many, SharePoint is not considered a Line of Business (LOB) system. It has historically been considered a document management system. So, why is it included in this book? The reality is that SharePoint is constantly being used as a LOB system as organizations continue to make investments in the technology. No longer is SharePoint just a storage location for Word documents and PowerPoint presentations. SharePoint is very much a platform much like BizTalk. The difference being that SharePoint is a Collaboration platform whereas BizTalk is an Integration Platform, among other things. SharePoint includes an underlying framework called SharePoint Foundation. Developers can take advantage of APIs and Web Services to build custom applications on top of the platform. For organizations that like to "buy" before "building", this is an attractive offer. Even if your organization has an appetite for custom development, we can still build custom applications inside of SharePoint using ASP.Net, JQuery, Windows Workflow Foundation (WF), and Windows Communication Foundation (WCF).

Do note that SharePoint 2010 utilizes .NET 3.5 so we are unable to take advantage of the latest WF and WCF features that are available in .NET 4.0.

Organizations are starting to build composite applications on the SharePoint platform. These applications are generally standalone applications, but as more organizations look to leverage SharePoint, they often need to get information into or out of SharePoint and that is where using BizTalk adds value.

A common scenario that is emerging involves the use of SharePoint in situations where the System of Record could be used, such as an ERP system. SharePoint allows for Rapid Application Development and in many situations solutions can be built through configuration. Organizations are increasingly pressured to build solutions quickly and cost effectively, which makes SharePoint an attractive option. End users may also prefer the user interface to that of an ERP. SharePoint's user interface, especially in SharePoint 2010, closely aligns to the user interfaces that you will find in the Office product suite. This eases end user adoption and acceptance and provides a consistent experience across applications that users frequently access. One of the new features available in SharePoint 2010 is the Office Ribbon. So love the ribbon or hate the ribbon, you will have a consistent experience across Microsoft's Office Suite and SharePoint.

Systems of Record applications, such as ERPs, generally require the data that has been collected in SharePoint applications. Organizations that designate Systems of Record, generally do not want data being modified and stored in other systems where information cannot be reconciled or reported upon. In order to keep your System of Record in sync with your other systems, you either need to integrate the systems or have the end user key data into multiple systems. Both Enterprise Architects and end users do not want to have this information entered into multiple locations as it leads to data integrity issues and is laborious. Using BizTalk to integrate these systems prevents this extra manual effort, while providing repeatable, robust data synchronization between the various systems.

In the rest of this chapter, we will cover the following topics:

- SharePoint and BizTalk Integration: Why SharePoint is better with BizTalk
- Understanding the components of SharePoint Integration
- Installation of Windows SharePoint Services Adapter
- Windows SharePoint Services Adapter
- Receiving documents from SharePoint
- Sending documents to SharePoint

SharePoint and BizTalk integration: Why SharePoint is better with BizTalk

SharePoint is better with BizTalk as it extends SharePoint's reach into the enterprise. No longer is it an isolated system that requires manual input from users. While it is possible to integrate SharePoint without BizTalk, BizTalk has built-in features that reduce the amount of time it takes to integrate systems with SharePoint. Integration can be accomplished using the Windows SharePoint Services (WSS) Adapter, which is included in the BizTalk installation, and by interacting with SharePoint's out-of-the-box Web Services.

Organizations have found some clever ways to enhance or extend the functionality of SharePoint with other systems via BizTalk. We will now walk through some of these different scenarios that demonstrate how we can use SharePoint and BizTalk together to provide real value to your organization.

Capturing equipment replacement images

Problem: As a Utility Distribution company is replacing their traditional meters with Automated Metering meters, a regulatory requirement exists to store the current meter read information for both the old and new meters. This information needs to be retained for a specific period of time in case of billing discrepancies. When one of these discrepancies exists, a Customer Service Representative needs to be able to easily search for these images.

Solution: As field workers complete their meter installs, images are synced onto a network folder location where BizTalk has its FILE adapter watching. As files are being consumed, by BizTalk, the images will move through a Send Pipeline where the file names are parsed and metadata about the image is retrieved and placed in Windows SharePoint Services Adapter Context properties. This metadata will be added to the SharePoint columns within the Document Library where they can be sorted on and grouped on.

These images could easily be stored on a network file share, but there are a few advantages of using this solution:

- Metadata can be added for these images which will improve the search experience.

- Due to SharePoint indexing, search will execute quicker than scanning a network folder, which may include tens of thousands of images to hundreds of thousands of images.

- Information Policies can be implemented in SharePoint that will clean up unnecessary files after regulatory compliance periods have been met.

Vehicle maintenance lists

Problem: When field vehicles have maintenance work completed on them, this information needs to be recorded for both financial and regulatory purposes in the company's System of Record, which happens to be an ERP. Mobile workers want to complete this information quickly and accurately so that they can get back to actually getting "real" work done.

Solution: Inside of SharePoint, we can create a simple Custom List. You can think of a Custom List much like an Excel spreadsheet with the difference being, the data in a Custom List is stored within a SharePoint database. Field workers can input the required vehicle maintenance information into the Custom List without entering many keystrokes. Having these field workers logging into a complex ERP system is both time consuming and has training implications. Accessing the SharePoint List is as simple as launching a bookmarked site within Internet Explorer and leveraging Windows Authentication so that no additional credentials have to be provided.

This information needs to get to the ERP for financial and reporting purposes; BizTalk is able to consume SharePoint's Web Services on a regular basis and retrieve this information, and construct an equivalent flat file that can be loaded in the ERP system. An in depth walkthrough of this scenario is included in Chapter 8.

Some of the benefits of using this solution are:

- Simple user interface to input Vehicle Maintenance details
- No additional credentials need to be provided to application
- Little training required for end users since they are all familiar with the Office 2010 suite

Field incident reporting

Problem: Whenever a field worker is involved in an accident or environmental event, this information must be tracked for regulatory purposes. Once again, this information needs to be captured in the organization's System of Record, which happens to be an ERP. The ERP system does allow users to complete this information via a Graphical User Interface (GUI) form within the ERP system, but requires users to complete 12 different tabs, which is very time consuming.

Solution: Once again, we want to ensure that the solution is easy to use for field workers, does not require an abundance of key strokes or mouse clicks, and does not require a lot of training. By leveraging InfoPath forms stored in SharePoint, employees can access these forms from the field, and submit them to SharePoint where someone in the office validates this information before submitting the information to the ERP. Once the data has been validated, BizTalk will listen for these InfoPath requests and transform the InfoPath message before submitting the information to the ERP system via a BizTalk Adapter.

Some of the benefits of using this solution are:

- Increased employee productivity as they no longer need to fill out 12 tabs within the ERP application
- Reduced training costs
- Single Sign On capabilities

Understanding the components of SharePoint and BizTalk integration

For many developers integrating with SharePoint may be a confusing endeavour. This in part is related to the required components that must be present in order for integration to occur between these two systems.

Out of the box, BizTalk includes an adapter called the Windows SharePoint Services adapter. This is the adapter that you use when communicating with SharePoint Document and Form Libraries.

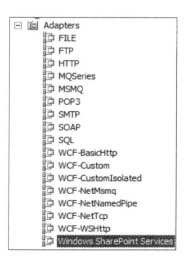

Using this BizTalk adapter on its own is not enough. In order for this adapter to properly function, we need to also install the Windows SharePoint Services Adapter Web Service. This Adapter Web Service is available on the BizTalk installation CD, but the Windows SharePoint Services Adapter Web Service needs to be installed on the SharePoint server. If you are co-hosting BizTalk and SharePoint on the same server, then you would install it on this same server. If you have a remote SharePoint server then this Adapter Web Service only needs to be installed on the SharePoint server and not on the BizTalk server.

 When integrating with remote SharePoint installations, both the BizTalk Server and SharePoint Server must exist on the same domain.

If SharePoint is not detected on the server that you are trying to install the Adapter Web Service, you will not be able to install this component as the option will be disabled in the Setup application.

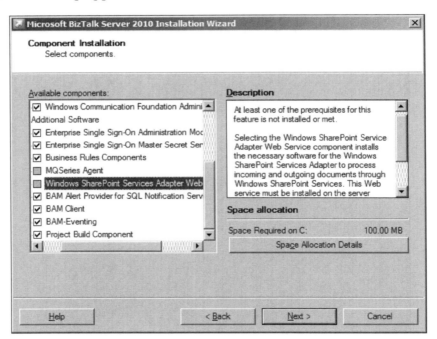

Installation of Windows SharePoint Services Adapter Web Service

Since the Windows SharePoint Services adapter is installed when you install the BizTalk runtime, we are solely going to focus on installing the Windows SharePoint Services Adapter Web Service.

Below are the supported configurations when integrating BizTalk 2010 and SharePoint. Please refer to `http://technet.microsoft.com/en-us/library/bb743377(BTS.70).aspx` for additional information.

SharePoint Version	Comments
SharePoint 2010/SharePoint 2010 Foundation	SharePoint 2010 Foundation is a free, foundational component that SharePoint 2010 runs on top of.
Microsoft Office SharePoint Server (MOSS) 2007/Windows SharePoint Services (WSS) 3.0 SP2	WSS 3.0 SP2 is a free, foundational component that MOSS 2007 runs on top of.

 Both SharePoint 2010 Foundation and Windows SharePoint Service 3.0 SP2 are free of charge provided you run them on a licensed version of Windows.

1. Once we have SharePoint installed, or have access to an existing SharePoint environment, we can install the Windows SharePoint Services Adapter Web Service from the BizTalk installation media. The installation process will detect that SharePoint is installed as you can select the Windows SharePoint Services Adapter Web Service option.

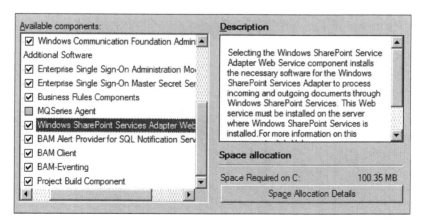

2. We will now be prompted to confirm whether we would like to proceed installing the Windows SharePoint Services Adapter Web Service. Click on the **Install** button to continue.

 Even though the SharePoint product team has moved away from the Windows SharePoint Services branding, the BizTalk team continues to call this component the Windows SharePoint Services Adapter Web Service even though you may be connecting to a SharePoint 2010 environment which now leverages SharePoint Foundation.

3. Like many BizTalk components, there are two aspects to every implementation: installation and configuration. We will now proceed to configure the Windows SharePoint Services Adapter Web Service by selecting the **Launch BizTalk Server Configuration** checkbox and clicking on the **Finish** button.

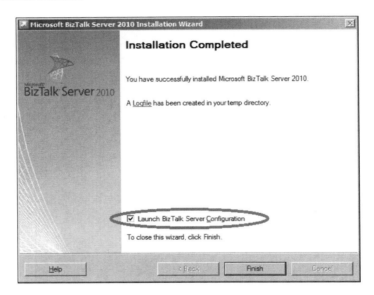

4. We now want to enable Windows SharePoint Services Adapter on this computer. In order to enable this adapter, we need to provide a Windows Group that the Host Instance user is a member of. In the following configuration, a group in Active Directory called **SharePoint Enabled Hosts** has been created and a BizTalk Host instance user account called **btslcl** has been added to this group. Each Host Instance runs under the context of a user who has the required permissions to perform BizTalk tasks such as interacting with other end point systems and the BizTalk Message Box among other things.

5. We also need to provide the name of the Windows SharePoint Services/ Foundation site where this Adapter Web Service will be deployed to. In this case, we are selecting the name of our SharePoint website which happens to be called **SharePoint-LOB-8080**.

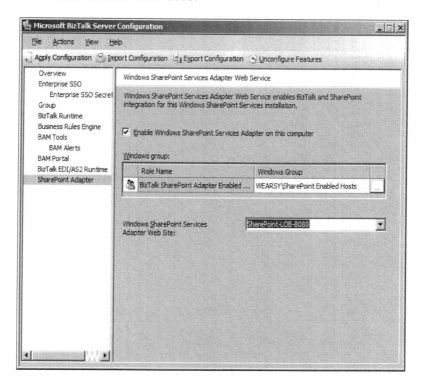

6. At this point, we are ready to click on the **Apply Configuration** button to complete the Adapter Web Service installation.

7. We should now see the confirmation of the Adapter being configured successfully. Click on the **Finish** button to complete this task.

Note: Native 64 bit support

SharePoint 2010 exclusively supports 64 bit operating systems. With this in mind, we also need to ensure that IIS, on the server that is hosting the Adapter Web service, is running in 64 bit Native mode. Otherwise, we may be presented with the following error when applying the configuration settings.

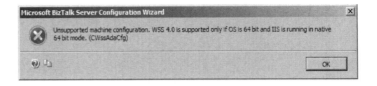

To enable 64 bit Native mode, run the following commands, as an Administrator, from the Command Prompt:

```
C:\inetpub\AdminScripts>cscript adsutil.vbs SET
W3SVC/AppPools/Enable32bitAppOnWin64 0

C:\inetpub\AdminScripts>%SYSTEMROOT%\Microsoft.NET\
Framework64\v2.0.50727\aspnet_regiis.exe -i
```

8. Once the configuration has been applied successfully, we can navigate to Internet Information Services (IIS) Manager and discover that an Application called **BTSharePointAdapterWS** has been created.

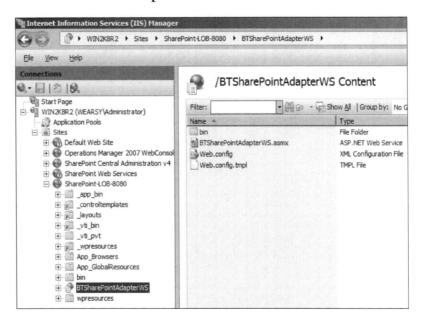

9. Within this IIS application, a Web Service called `BTSharePointAdapterWS.asmx` exists. This is the Web Service that the Windows SharePoint Adapter leverages when communicating with SharePoint Services. If you try to launch this Web Service in a Web Browser, you will be prompted with an error. This error is a display error only and will not disrupt BizTalk interacting with SharePoint.

Server Error in '/BTSharePointAdapterWS' Application.

Request format is unrecognized.

Description: An unhandled exception occurred during the execution of the current web request. Please review the stack trace for more information about the error and where it originated in the code.

Exception Details: System.InvalidOperationException: Request format is unrecognized.

Source Error:

```
An unhandled exception was generated during the execution of the current web
request. Information regarding the origin and location of the exception can be
identified using the exception stack trace below.
```

Stack Trace:

```
[InvalidOperationException: Request format is unrecognized.]
   System.Web.Services.Protocols.WebServiceHandlerFactory.CoreGetHandler(Type type, HttpConte
   System.Web.Services.Protocols.WebServiceHandlerFactory.GetHandler(HttpContext context, Str
   System.Web.Script.Services.ScriptHandlerFactory.GetHandler(HttpContext context, String req
   System.Web.MaterializeHandlerExecutionStep.System.Web.HttpApplication.IExecutionStep.Execu
   System.Web.HttpApplication.ExecuteStep(IExecutionStep step, Boolean& completedSynchronous]
```

 Note: Enabling or disabling this error message is really a personal preference. By leaving the error message in place, it gives the impression that there is something wrong with the service. As developers, we generally like to browse the services that we are connecting to. If we connect and get an error message then we tend to think something is wrong. Leaving this error message enabled will not impact connectivity with SharePoint, provided you complete the remaining steps correctly.

10. In order to get rid of this error message, you need to modify the `Web.config` file that exists in the same folder as the `BTSharePointAdapterWS.asmx` web service.

```
<webServices>
    <protocols>
        <!-- Commented out line below to resolve bad request
                                                    error-->
        <!--<remove name="Documentation"/>-->
    </protocols>
</webServices>
```

11. Once we have made this change to the `web.config` file, we can refresh our web browser and will be presented with the Service Operations.

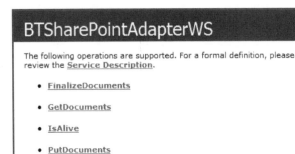

12. The `BTSharePointAdapterWS.asmx` Web Service exposes four Web Methods:

   ○ **FinalizeDocuments**
   ○ **GetDocuments**
   ○ **IsAlive**
   ○ **PutDocuments**

The Windows SharePoint Services Adapter will call these methods when interacting with SharePoint. The implementation of these Web Services is abstracted from BizTalk developers making integrating with SharePoint a great experience.

Each Web Method has a distinct purpose, so let's further investigate each method.

FinalizeDocuments

When receiving documents from SharePoint, the default behavior of the adapter is to remove the file from the source location. This behavior models that of the FILE and FTP Adapters in order to prevent an endless loop and message duplication. If a person has loaded a message, or document, in SharePoint then there is a good chance that they do not want to lose the message entirely when BizTalk picks it up. To avoid this situation, Microsoft has included a property in the Adapter called Archive Location URL. This feature will store a copy of the message that is currently being processed and place it into a different Document or Forms library. The Archive Location URL feature leverages the FinalizeDocuments Web Method to accomplish the archival of messages that are being processed.

GetDocuments

The GetDocuments Web method is used by the Windows SharePoint Services Adapter when retrieving documents from SharePoint. The Windows SharePoint Services Adapter is a polling adapter by nature. The Polling Interval property will determine how frequently the adapter should connect to SharePoint. The Adapter will call this Web Service during each poll of the adapter and if documents exist, they will be retrieved using this Web Service.

IsAlive

The IsAlive Web method is a simple ping web service that allows BizTalk to determine whether SharePoint is online.

PutDocuments

Whenever a document is uploaded to SharePoint, the Windows SharePoint Services Adapter will do so leveraging this Web Service.

Note: Multi-Node Deployments

If your organization has a SharePoint farm that includes multiple roles and servers, BizTalk can still support this deployment. Simply install the Windows SharePoint Services Adapter Web Service on each Front End server within the SharePoint farm. When providing URLs, as part of the Adapter configuration, ensure that you use the URL for the Network Load Balancer (NLB) that is front loading these requests.

Windows SharePoint Services Adapter configuration

Now that the Windows SharePoint Services Adapter and Adapter Web Service have been installed, we will further investigate some of the properties that can be used when integrating with SharePoint.

Receive Adapter

The following image will further illustrate the configuration for the SharePoint Services Receive Adapter.

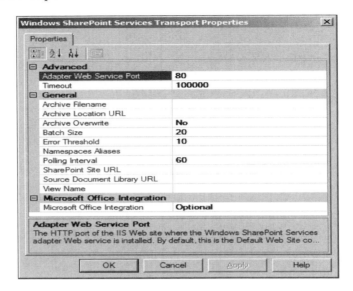

Adapter Web Service port

The default port for IIS Web Applications is 80. If we want to run multiple websites on one IIS Server, then we would want to separate these websites by having IIS listen on a different port. If you have chosen to do this, then you will need to populate this property with the correct port value. The examples in this book will leverage port 8080 since the SharePoint site that was created for this book is running on port 8080. In situations where we are co-hosting BizTalk and SharePoint services on one server we are very likely to encounter this situation, especially if we have the BAM Portal installed in the Default website. If this is the case, then we need to separate our SharePoint site from our Default site, so one of these sites will have to run on a non-standard port.

Note: Another option is to create another website that uses port 80 but also leverages host headers. If we create a DNS alias for our server, we can then reference this alias as a host header and have multiple sites listening on port 80. IIS will then look at the http header when determining which site should be responsible for handling the request. To learn more about host headers, please refer to the following link: http://technet. microsoft.com/en-us/library/cc424952.aspx.

Archive File Location URL

When Documents are retrieved from SharePoint, they will be deleted from SharePoint to prevent an endless loop. Populate this property with the location of another Document or Forms Library for the archival of the message. If the configured Archive File Location is unavailable or configured incorrectly, BizTalk will attempt to retrieve the source document. However, BizTalk will not process the document until the Archive File Location issue has been resolved. The source document will remain in the SharePoint library in order to prevent message loss.

Batch Size

Since the Receive Adapter is a polling adapter you may want to throttle the number of Documents that BizTalk retrieves from SharePoint in a single batch.

Namespaces Aliases

If we plan on using XPath for populating other SharePoint columns, such as Archive Filename, we need to provide the namespace of the message that we are expecting. For instance we could extract a value from the message body using XPath and use it as part of the name of the file that we are archiving.

Polling Interval

The interval, in seconds, that we would like BizTalk to connect to SharePoint to determine if there are any outstanding messages available for consumption.

SharePoint Site URL

The base URL, for the SharePoint site, that BizTalk will connect to. For example if we have created a Document Library and the entire URL is `http://localhost:8080/sites/BizTalkLineOfBusiness/Completed%20Forms/` then we would populate the SharePoint Site URL with `http://localhost:8080/sites/BizTalkLineOfBusiness/` and would subsequently populate the SharePoint Document Library URL with Completed%20Forms/.

Note: Spaces and Special Characters

SharePoint Document and Forms Libraries may contain spaces in their names. Like any other HTTP Address that includes a space in it, URL encoding is required to translate the space into a character sequence. This sequence is represented as %20. Inside the BizTalk configuration, you can specify either a space, by pressing the space bar key, or by providing %20. Whenever you export your BizTalk binding files, you will always find that spaces are represented as %20.

View Name

Unlike the FILE Adapter, the Windows SharePoint Services Adapter does not support file masks. By default, BizTalk will retrieve all documents from a Document, or Form Library, when it connects. In order to avoid this scenario, we can provide a View Name and BizTalk will only retrieve records that meet the criteria of that view. For example, imagine we have an Office Supplies Approval Process that has been implemented in SharePoint. An employee may fill out an InfoPath form and save it to a SharePoint Form Library. Since this purchase needs to be approved by the employee's supervisor, we do not want BizTalk to pick up this Office Supply request until it has been approved. We can construct a view in SharePoint and it will only display approved Office Supply requests. We will then have BizTalk connect to this view to retrieve these approved requests. This allows employees and supervisors to work from within the same Form library, but have BizTalk only retrieve forms that have been approved.

Send Adapter

Now, we will further explore the configuration for the SharePoint Services Send Adapter.

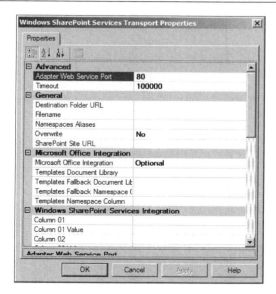

Adapter Web Service Port

The port of the Web Application where our Windows SharePoint Services Adapter Web Service has been deployed.

SharePoint Site URL

The base URL for the SharePoint site that you would like to connect to. For example if we have created a Document Library and the entire URL is `http://localhost:8080/sites/BizTalkLineOfBusiness/Completed%20Forms/` then we would populate the SharePoint Site URL with `http://localhost:8080/sites/BizTalkLineOfBusiness/` and would subsequently populate the SharePoint Document Library URL with `Completed%20Forms/`.

Namespaces Aliases

If we plan on using XPath for populating other SharePoint columns, such as Filename, we need to provide the namespace of the message that we are expecting. For instance we could extract a value from the message body using XPath and use it as part of the name of the file that we are archiving. We can also populate SharePoint columns with this information as well.

Microsoft Office Integration

One of the key value adds to SharePoint and BizTalk integration is the functionality that can be leveraged from InfoPath. For instance, we can create SharePoint columns and then populate those columns using either data from InfoPath fields or data that has been populated in a BizTalk Adapter context property. Enabling this property will allow for InfoPath pre-processing instructions to be enabled. These pre-processing instructions also allow for XML messages that have been deposited in SharePoint to have an association with a form. When you click to launch the XML message that was deposited, SharePoint will find its related template and launch the form with the XML data embedded. It is important to note that as BizTalk is processing these types of messages, it does not have visibility into the form template mark up. It is strictly dealing with the underlying XML form data and does not actually receive the form template mark up.

Template Document Library

When an XML message has been sent to a SharePoint library and we want to associate it with a particular InfoPath form, we can populate this property so that SharePoint knows where to find the matching Form template.

Templates Namespace Column

This is the name of the SharePoint column that stores the namespace of the InfoPath solution.

SharePoint Columns

The Windows SharePoint Services Adapter exposes properties that when populated will be inserted into the corresponding column in a SharePoint Library. For instance if we have an Approver scenario, we can create a column in the SharePoint Library and when BizTalk inserts a message into this Library, it can take data from the message body, or from the Send Port configuration, and insert that data into the SharePoint column. The column context property works much like key/value pairs. We need to insert the name of the column in the "Column XX" property and then the related value in the "Column XX Value" property. There is an upper limit of 16 columns that can be populated.

Other Considerations

Context Properties

Much like other adapters, the Windows SharePoint Services Adapter context properties are also available inside Orchestrations. This becomes extremely useful when building dynamic send port scenarios.

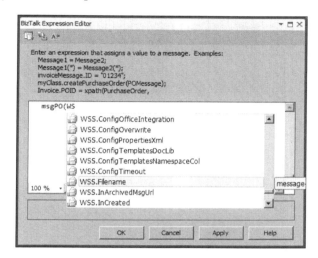

Windows SharePoint Services Adapter is a one-way adapter

When configuring Receive Locations or Send Ports that use the Windows SharePoint Services Adapter, we can do so using One Way Receive Locations or One Way Send Ports. What is interesting about this scenario is that we know that the Adapter leverages two way web services. This is not saying that BizTalk will be unaware of any failures that occur when SharePoint is not available or there are other runtime issues like security failures. These errors continue to get caught and reported by BizTalk. However, if you look in the Tracked service instances, within the BizTalk Administration console, you will only find one record for each connection to SharePoint.

Once again, Microsoft is abstracting a lot of the complexities involved in calling web services for us. Another benefit of Microsoft's architecture is there are no SharePoint Proxy classes that are required within our Orchestrations when we use the Windows SharePoint Services Adapter. This provides us with a loosely coupled design in our solutions. If we have projects that currently leverage the FILE Adapter, we can easily change Receive Locations or Send Ports to use the Windows SharePoint Services Adapter without recompiling our solutions. We simply need to change the Adapter Type in the BizTalk Administration Console.

Receiving documents from SharePoint

The scenario that we are going to build is a Vacation Request Approval System using InfoPath, BizTalk, and SharePoint 2010 Foundation. An employee will fill out the form and submit it to a Forms Library in SharePoint where it will be ready for approval by the employee's supervisor. Once the vacation has been approved, BizTalk will consume this form, archive it, and then use the FILE adapter to deliver the approved Vacation Request to an ERP system. The ERP system requires this information to be in a Comma Separated Value (CSV) file.

> Note: The examples in this chapter assume you have an existing SharePoint site in place. The following links describe how to create SharePoint sites for WSS 3.0 SP2 and SharePoint 2010 Foundation:
>
> WSS 3.0 SP2:
>
> `http://technet.microsoft.com/en-us/library/cc288969(office.12).aspx`
>
> SharePoint 2010 Foundation:
>
> `http://technet.microsoft.com/en-us/library/cc263094.aspx`

The foundation for this solution is a schema called `InfoPath_Vacation_Approval.xsd`. We will use this schema as a Message Type within the BizTalk solution, but we will also use this schema to build an InfoPath form. The end result is that when the Approval Form is submitted to SharePoint, and picked up by BizTalk, we will have a strongly typed message inside of BizTalk.

This schema is part of the Chapter7-ReceivingDocuments solution that is part of this book's source code.

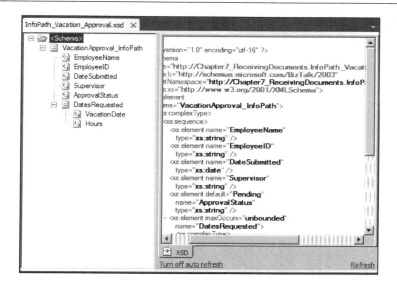

Building InfoPath Form and SharePoint Forms Library

In order to design a form based upon this schema, we need to open Microsoft InfoPath Designer. This example will utilize InfoPath 2010, but this solution should also work with previous versions of the InfoPath product:

1. Double click on **XML or Schema** from **Advanced Form Templates**.

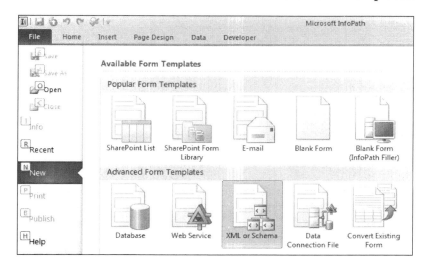

2. Browse to the location of the **InfoPath_Vacation_Approval.xsd** schema and click the **Next** button.

3. When prompted with whether we want to add another XML Schema or XML Document to the main data source we want to select **No** and then click the **Finish** button.

4. In the right hand portion of the following screenshot, we will notice that the fields and nodes that were created in our XSD Schema are now available to be inserted on our InfoPath form:

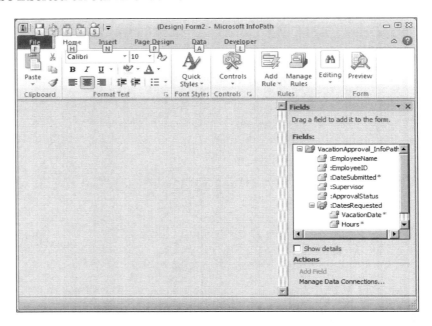

5. We now have the opportunity to design the form to conform with any look and feel, or design standards that our organization may have.

6. Once we have completed the design of the form, we want to publish the form to a SharePoint Forms Library. To do this, click on **File – Publish – SharePoint Server**.

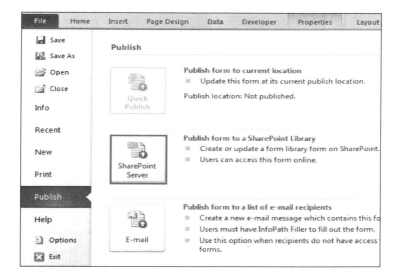

7. Provide the URL to the SharePoint site that you would like to deploy this form to and click the **Next** button.

8. For this example, we want to choose to publish this form to a **Form Library** and then click the **Next** button.

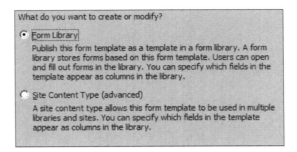

9. We now want to **Create a new form library** and then click the **Next** button.

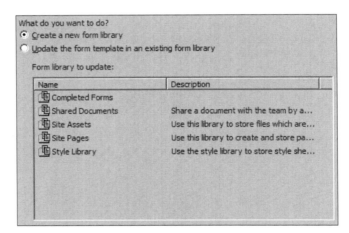

10. Provide a name for this new form library such as **Vacation Approval** and then click the **Next** button.

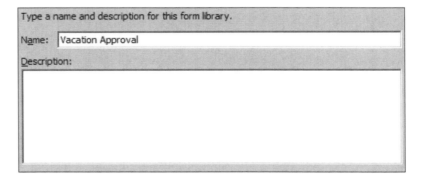

11. Specify the **Employee Name, Supervisor**, and **Approval Status** as fields that we would like to see displayed in the form library.

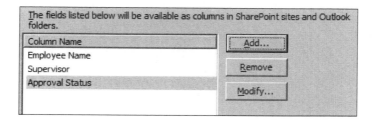

12. Publish and verify that our form library was deployed successfully. Note that we should see the **Vacation Approval** link under libraries and we should see the **Employee Name, Supervisor,** and **Approval Status** columns in the upper-right-hand corner of the browser.

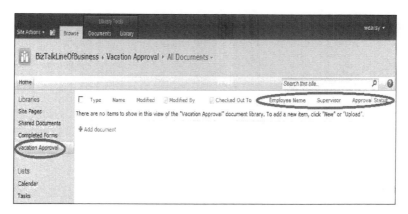

13. Click on the **Add document** link.

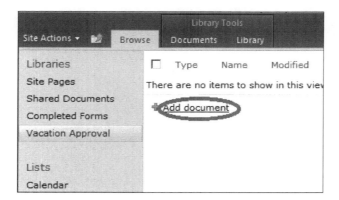

14. The form that we previously designed gets launched.

15. We now need to go back into the form and modify where the form should be submitted to after an employee has completed the form. We have a couple of options when it comes to submitting a form to a SharePoint library:

    ○ Using the **Submit Form** button that is part of the native InfoPath client

    ○ Adding a button control to the form and then attaching a **Submit Form** action to the button

16. We will now add the submit form functionality through the InfoPath client by clicking on **File –Info – Submit Options –To SharePoint Library.** This allows us to leverage the out-of-the-box functionality without any additional configuration or scripting.

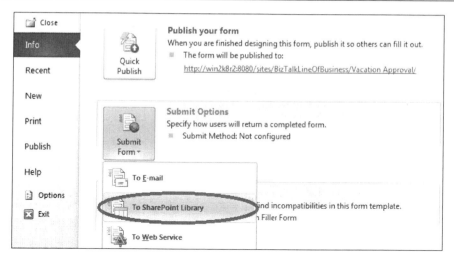

17. We need to provide the URL of our Forms Library and the name of the form that will be used when the form is submitted. It is a good idea to use a macro and leverage unique data from the form to avoid duplicate file names. Once these text boxes have been populated, click the **Next** button to continue.

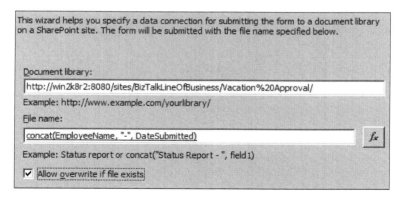

18. Provide a name for this data connection that describes the type of data that is being submitted and then click the **Finish** button.

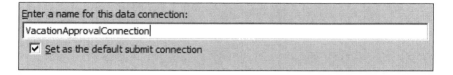

19. If our form location has not changed since we initially published the form, we can select **Quick Publish** to upload this latest version of the form to SharePoint.

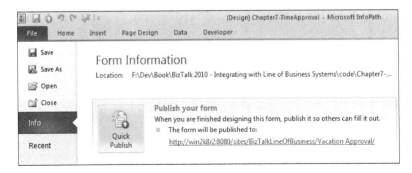

20. When we launch a new form by clicking on the **Add Document** link, we will now have an option to **Submit** the form.

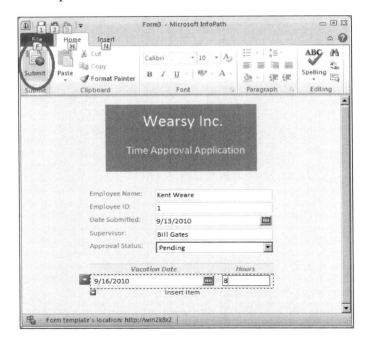

21. Once submitted, we will see the InfoPath form has been added to the Forms Library and metadata has been populated inside the SharePoint columns.

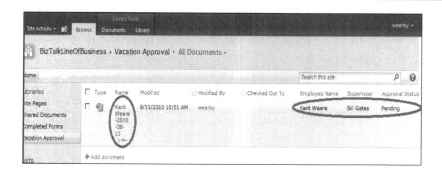

Creating SharePoint view

At this point, we can configure BizTalk to consume messages from this Forms Library, but the Vacation Request has not been approved. We only want consume InfoPath Forms that have been approved.

1. In order to achieve this requirement, we need to create a view within this Forms Library and then we will configure BizTalk to only retrieve documents that satisfy the requirements of this view.

2. To create a view, select **Library** from the **Library Tools** menu and then click on **Create View**.

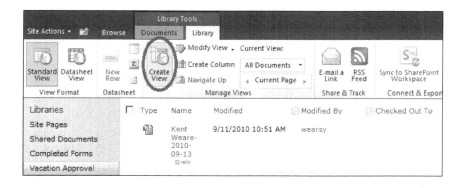

3. Select **Standard View**.

4. Provide an appropriate View Name such as **Approved Vacation Requests** and then click on the **OK** button.

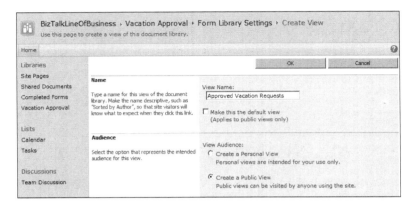

5. Now, scroll down to the **Filter** Section. We only want to display forms that have an **Approval Status** that is equal to **Approved**.

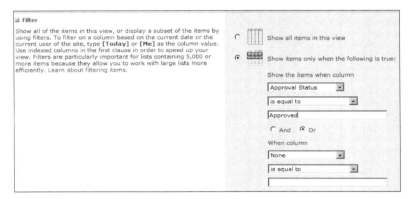

6. In the default view called **All Documents**, we can see all documents regardless of their **Approval Status**.

7. If we change the view to **Approved Vacation Requests,** we will not find any documents listed since no Vacation Requests have been approved.

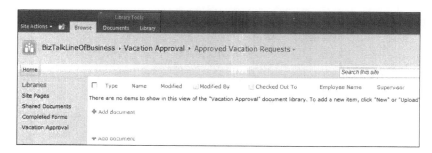

Creating SharePoint archive library

BizTalk can leverage these same views that allow documents to be in various states. If we provide a View within the Receive Location configuration, BizTalk will only retrieve documents that satisfy the conditions of that view.

We also want to ensure that we have an archived copy of successful vacation requests. To do this, we will create another Forms Library called **Archived Vacation Requests**.

1. Click on the **Libraries** link in your SharePoint site.

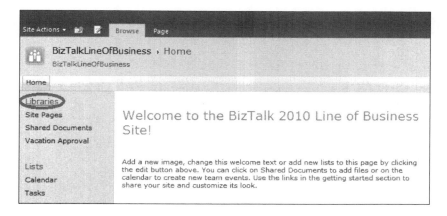

2. Click on the **Create** link.

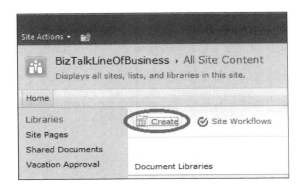

3. Select **Form Library**, provide a Form Library Name such as **Archived Vacation Requests**, and click **Create**.

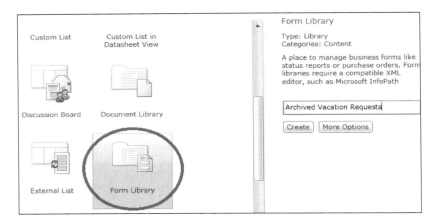

4. We now have a Forms Library called **Archived Vacation Requests**.

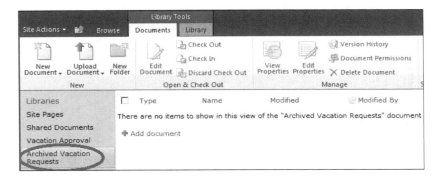

5. Now, whenever BizTalk picks up an approved Vacation Request, it will make an archive copy of the form in this Forms Library. Up until this point, we have performed the following actions:

   ° Designed a schema that we can use to design an InfoPath form
   ° Designed an InfoPath form
   ° Created a Forms Library
   ° Published the InfoPath form and created custom columns
   ° Updated the form to submit to our Forms Library

Building the application

We will now focus on the BizTalk portion of this solution. Once approved, this Vacation Request information needs to be submitted to the organization's HR system, which happens to be an ERP system. This ERP system is expecting a flat file much like the one below.

1. A copy of this file may be found in the `FlatFile` folder of this chapter's source code.

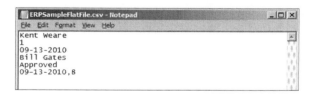

2. We now need a flat file schema that is capable of assembling a flat file for our ERP system. Included in the solution is a Flat File schema called `ERP_Vacation_Approval_FF.xsd`.

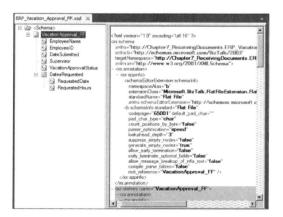

3. A flat file schema does not provide much value without a pipeline to assemble, in our case, or disassemble a message from an XML format to a flat file format or vice versa. Within our solution, a Send Pipeline called `SendVacationApproval.btp` exists to take an XML message that has been created inside of BizTalk and assemble a flat file for consumption by an ERP system. The **Document Schema** property within this schema is assigned to the flat file schema, `ERP_Vacation_Approval_FF.xsd` that we previously created.

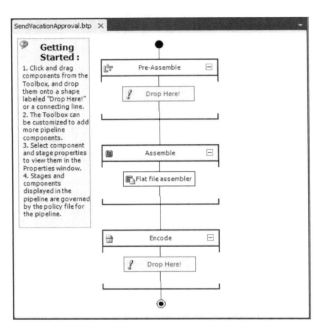

4. Now that we have both source (InfoPath) and destination (ERP) schemas created, we want to create a map to perform the transformation between these two messages. The name of this map in our solution is `InfoPathVacationRequests_to_ERPVacationRequests.btm`.

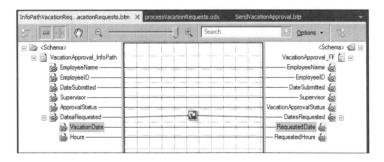

5. The BizTalk artifact that brings all of these components together is an orchestration called `processVacationRequests.odx`. Within this orchestration, we will find the following features:

   ○ Receiving an XML InfoPath message

   ○ Transforming the InfoPath message to an ERP message

   ○ Sending the ERP Message to the ERP System

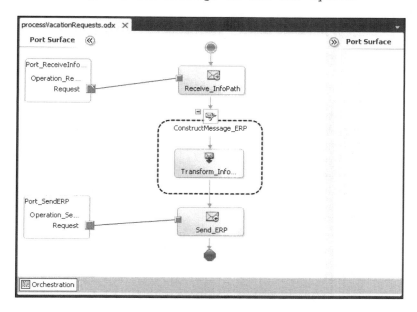

6. We now need to deploy our solution by right mouse clicking on the solution name and clicking on **Deploy Solution**.

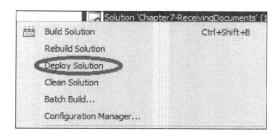

7. When we launch the BizTalk Server Administration Console, we will discover that an application called **Chapter7-ReceivingDocuments** has been created. We will now walk through the various configuration settings for the **Receive Locations**, **Orchestrations**, and **Send Ports**.

 Note: You can find a copy of the solution's binding file in the `Bindings` folder found in this chapter's source code. Please be aware that the binding files include references to the 8080 port that was used to demonstrate this chapter's functionality. If your SharePoint Server is using a different port, you will need to update your configuration.

8. Within the Receive Locations Node, we will find a Receive Location called `ReceiveInfoPathVacationRequest`. This Receive Location will use the Windows SharePoint Services Adapter, use the default **BizTalkServerApplication** Host, and the **XMLReceive** Pipeline.

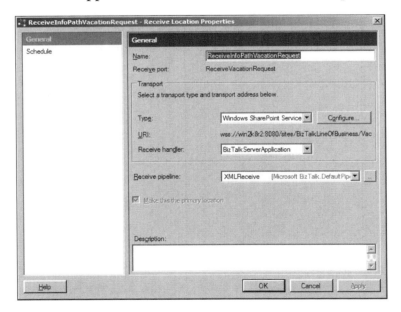

9. By clicking on the **Configure** button, we can further explore the receive location's configuration.

Below is a table that describes the significant adapter properties:

Property	Value	Comment
Adapter Web Service Port	8080	On the server that was used to build this solution, the SharePoint site was created on port 8080 since this server also has the BAM Portal installed. If you have installed SharePoint as your Default website then your port will be 80.
Timeout	100000	The amount of time, in milliseconds, that the Adapter has before it times out.
Archive File Name	%XPATH=// ns0:VacationApproval_ InfoPath/ EmployeeName%-%XPATH=// ns0:VacationApproval_ InfoPath/ DateSubmitted%.xml	We can use values from the message that has been received to determine the name of the file that will be placed in the archive. Here, we are using the name of the employee and the date that the employee submitted the form.
Archive Location URL	Archived%20 Vacation%20Requests	This is the library where Archived Vacation requests will be stored.
Namespace Alias	ns0="http://Chapter7_ ReceivingDocuments. InfoPath_Vacation_ Approval"	This is the namespace of the `InfoPath_Vacation_Approval.xsd` schema that was used when building the InfoPath form.
Polling Interval	60	The time interval, in seconds, that BizTalk will connect to the SharePoint library to check to see if new Vacation Requests have been approved.
SharePoint Site URL	http:// win2k8r2:8080/sites/ BizTalkLineOfBusiness/	The location of the SharePoint site that is used to host the Forms Library where Vacations Requests are created and stored.
Source Document Library	Vacation Approval	The name of our Form Library where Vacation Requests are created and stored.
View Name	Approved Vacation Requests	The name of the view that BizTalk will use to determine which forms can be consumed.

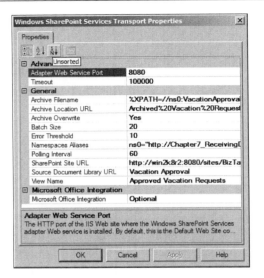

Note: The BizTalk Host instance user for the Receive Location that will be connecting to SharePoint requires "Contributor" access to the document or form library. For additional information regarding SharePoint permissions, please refer to the following link: `http://technet.microsoft.com/en-us/library/cc721640.aspx`

10. Our Send Port will leverage the FILE Adapter to deliver the approved flat file vacation request to a file drop that our ERP system is capable of consuming from. Since the ERP system is expecting a flat file, we need to ensure that our custom Send Pipeline is being used. The pipeline that we want to use is **Send Vacation Approval**.

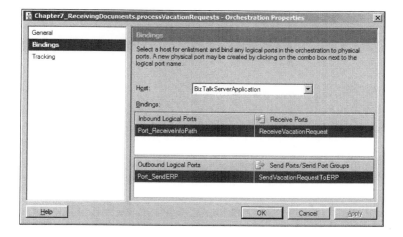

11. The configuration for the **processVacationRequests** orchestration is very straightforward:

    ○ We have one Receive Port for receiving the InfoPath Forms from SharePoint

    ○ A Send Port that we will use to send the Approved Vacation Requests to the ERP system

    ○ The Host we will use is **BizTalkServerApplication.** Remember to restart this Host Instance, before trying to execute the sample application.

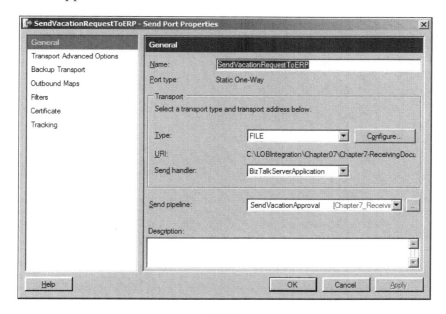

Testing the application

At this point, we are ready to validate our solution. To test our solution, we need to perform the following:

1. Navigate to your SharePoint document library and select **Add Document.**

2. Populate the InfoPath form and click the **Submit** button.

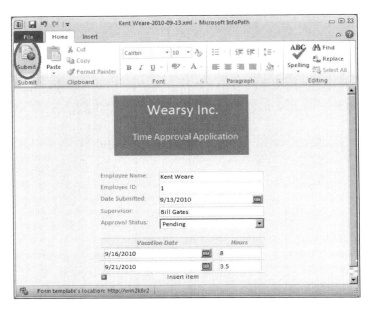

3. You should now have a document stored in your form library that has an Approval Status of **Pending**.

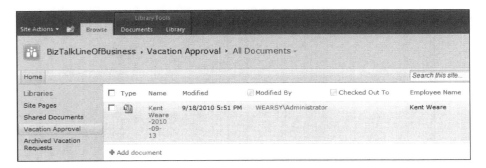

4. Open this existing form, set the **Approval Status** to **Approved**, and then click the **Submit** button.

5. We will momentarily see that the **Approval Status** of the InfoPath has changed to **Approved**.

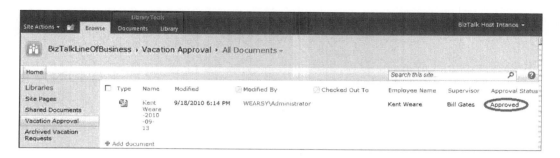

6. Since the **Approval Status** has changed to **Approved**, BizTalk will now consume this message and write it to our folder location.

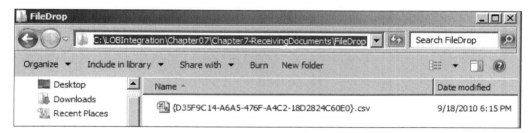

7. If we open up the file, we will determine that it matches the format that the ERP system is expecting.

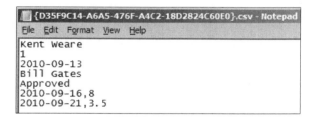

Sending documents to SharePoint

In this scenario, we have a Work Order Management system that employees use to manage their job, or tasks, for an Oil and Gas company. A legal requirement for this organization is they must record any safety incidents that occur in the field for their employees. Employees will use this Work Order Management system to update the statuses of their jobs, but will also record any Field incidents. The problem with capturing this information in the Work Order Management system is that it has been designed for the field and is not conducive for office employees that may be required to track these incidents to ensure regulatory compliance.

The solution to this problem is to allow the field staff to input the incident data in the Work Order Management system, but to feed this info into SharePoint where it can be tracked by office employees. The Work Order Management system will output an XML file that we will load into a SharePoint Form library.

Since we do not want office employees reviewing XML documents, we will load this information into an InfoPath form, which will allow for a nice user interface for our office employees.

Another benefit of having this information in SharePoint is that we can apply an Information Policy which will set the stale date of the document and automatically purge it if the date of the document exceeds the document's expiration date.

Creating the SharePoint Forms Library

In the Receiving Documents walkthrough, we had the InfoPath client create a Forms Library for us. This time around we will manually create a Content Type, a Forms Library, and the SharePoint Columns. A Content Type is a template that we can use to base content on. It allows us to set a default document type within the SharePoint library so if we want to create a new document from the SharePoint ribbon, by default it will be the type that we based the Content Type upon.

1. Before we create a Content Type, we need to create an InfoPath form that we can base the Content Type upon. We will once again start with an XSD schema. In this particular case, the name of the schema that we will be using is **WorkOrderManagmentIncident_InfoPath.xsd**, which can be found in the Chapter7-SendingDocuments solution.

2. We then want to design an InfoPath form based upon the **WorkOrderManagmentIncident_InfoPath** schema much like we did in the Receiving Documents from SharePoint section in this chapter. The difference being that we will not publish this form to SharePoint, nor will we submit the form to SharePoint as we are basically using InfoPath as a viewer for these documents and will not be modifying them.

3. We now need to create a Content Type and associate this InfoPath form with it. To do this, click on the **Site Actions** drop down and then click on **Site Settings.**

4. Now, we need to click on the **Site Content Types** from the **Galleries** grouping.

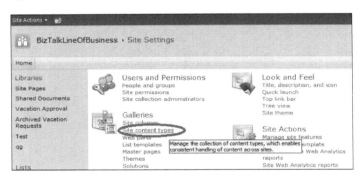

5. Click on the **Create** button.

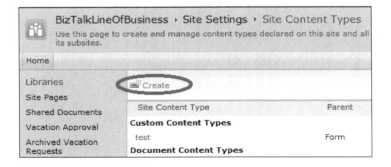

6. Provide a **Name**, the **Parent Content Type**, and then the select the group that this site content should belong to. In this case, we should use **Custom Content Types**.

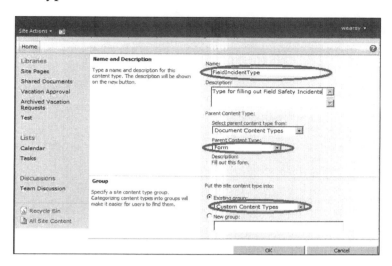

7. As we saw in the Receiving Documents sample from this chapter, SharePoint columns become a valuable tool for associating metadata to documents inside SharePoint. By populating SharePoint columns, we can now search, sort, and create views based upon the information contained within the columns.

   ° We will now associate columns to our particular Content Type so that when we add our Content Type to our document library, these columns will be available for us to populate using the Windows SharePoint Services Adapter. Click on the **Add from new site column** link.

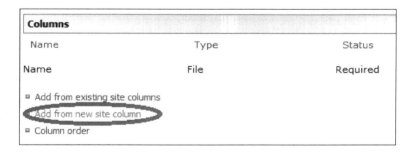

8. We will now go ahead and create columns for the **Incident Date**, **Incident City**, and **Incident Plant** using the data below. Otherwise, we will use the default values.

Column Name	Data Type	Max Number of Characters
Incident Date	Date and Time	N/A
Incident City	Single line of text	50
Incident Plant	Single line of text	10

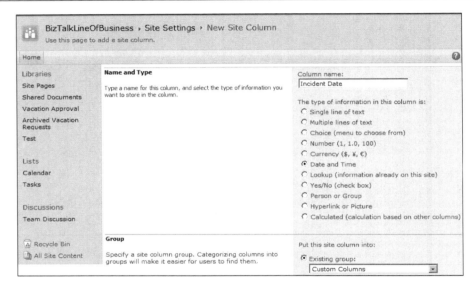

9. Once we have completed our Content Type, it should look like the following screenshot:

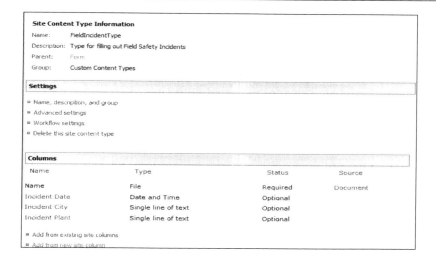

10. We now need to associate a particular InfoPath form with this Content Type. Click on **Advanced Settings** to launch the wizard responsible for this function.

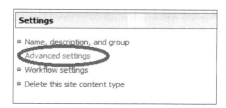

11. Browse to the location of your form and select it. Also, ensure that the Content Type is not set to read only.

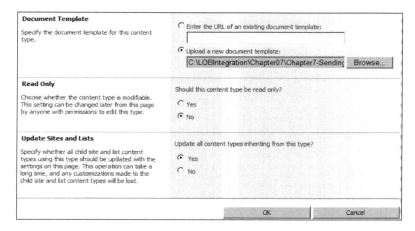

12. At this point, we are ready to create a new Form Library and then associate this Content Type with our newly created document library. To create a new document library, click on **Site Actions** and then **More Options.**

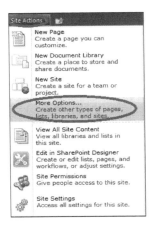

13. Select **Form Library** and then provide a name and click the **Create** button.

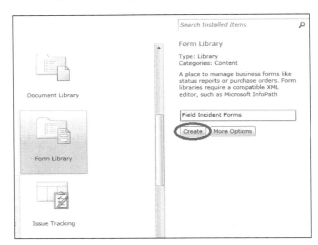

14. We also want to set the default template for our Form Library. We need to modify the default template setting and can do so by clicking on **Library Settings**.

15. Once in the Form **Library Settings** page, click on the **Advanced Settings** link.

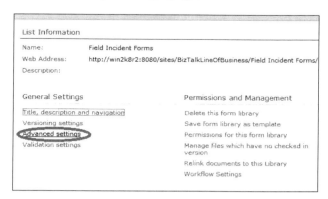

16. Within this screen, we want to set the **Template URL**. By setting the document template, when BizTalk loads a document into this Forms Library, SharePoint will automatically try to associate the uploaded file with this template.

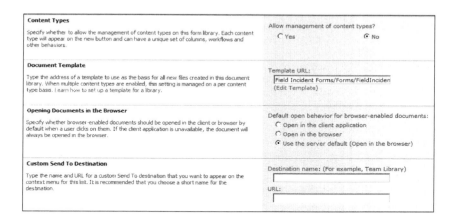

Note: We do not need to provide the entire path of the Document Template. We only need to provide the path after the base site.

For example, the base URL of our site is:

`http://win2k8r2:8080/sites/BizTalkLineOfBusiness/`

So, for the location of the Document Template, we only need to provide the name of the Folder(s) and the name of the template.

`Field Incident Forms/Forms/FieldIncidentType/`
`Chapter7-WorkOrderManagement_Incident.xsn`

17. If we want to be able to browse the file system that the SharePoint libraries utilize, click on **Library** and then **Connect & Export.** This will launch Windows Explorer and take us to the folder where our document library files are stored. To make things a little easier, ensure that hidden files and folders can been seen within Windows Explorer in order to view the **Forms** folder.

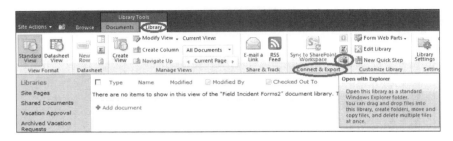

18. If we navigate to our Forms Library and click on the **New Document** button, we now have our Field Incident Template launched by default.

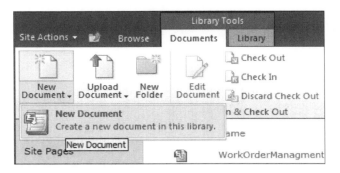

19. We now need to add columns from the FieldIncidentType that we previously created. We can do this by clicking on the **Add from existing site columns** link from the **Form Library Settings** page.

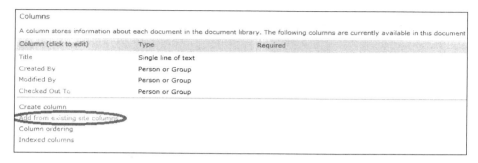

20. Select **Custom Columns** from the **Select site columns from**: dropdown and then add **Incident City, Incident Date,** and **Incident Plant** to the **Columns to add:** combo box and click on the **OK** button.

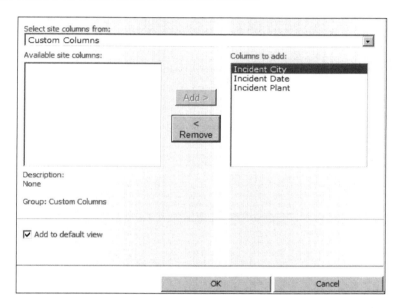

21. We will now see these columns being displayed in the Form Library.

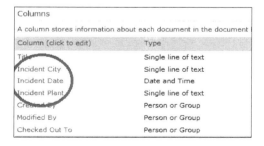

22. Up until this point we have performed the following actions:

    - Designed a schema that we can use to design an InfoPath form
    - Designed an InfoPath form
    - Created a Content Type
    - Created a Form Library
    - Set a template for the Form Library
    - Modified the Form Library's view to include custom columns that we specified in the Content Type

Building the BizTalk application

With the SharePoint configuration complete we now need to focus on the BizTalk portion of the solution. As part of the BizTalk solution we need to perform the following steps:

    - Establish a schema for the message that we will be receiving from the Work Order Management System
    - Create a map to transform this Work Order Management data into the InfoPath Schema type data
    - Set a Windows SharePoint Services Adapter context property so that the name of the original file name is maintained
    - Send the message to SharePoint and configure the Windows SharePoint Services Adapter so that we can populate the content type columns that we previously configured

1. The message structure for the file that the Work Order Management system uses is pretty similar to the structure of the InfoPath schema. The difference being that the Work Order Management system uses attributes instead of elements.

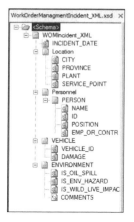

2. The map that we will use is pretty straightforward as the schema structures are pretty similar.

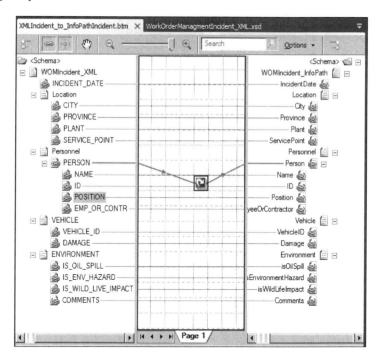

3. Once we have transformed the incoming Work Order Management message, to the InfoPath Message, we need to modify the InfoPath message in a Message Assignment Shape. The intention of this Message Assignment shape is to retrieve the name of the incoming message so that we can maintain the name of the file once it is published to SharePoint. By default, the SharePoint adapter will use a GUID as the file name if you do not provide a static or dynamic file name.

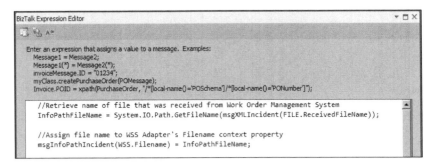

 Note: New for BizTalk 2010, is a feature that has been on a lot of Developer's want lists for a long time: an expandable expression editor! I never could understand why we were constrained to work in a fixed window, but glad to see this feature has finally been added.

4. In this example, we have manipulated the Adapter Context properties from within an orchestration. We also have access to these properties from within a Custom Pipeline component. This allows for messaging only solutions to also take advantage of the great features available in the Windows SharePoint Services Adapter. For a full feature walkthrough of manipulating the SharePoint Adapter's context properties, please see Kent Weare's blog post: `http://kentweare.blogspot.com/2010/01/sharetalk-integration-sharepointbiztalk_16.html`

   ° Overall, our orchestration is pretty simple. We receive a message, transform it, update it to set an Adapter context property, and then send it to SharePoint.

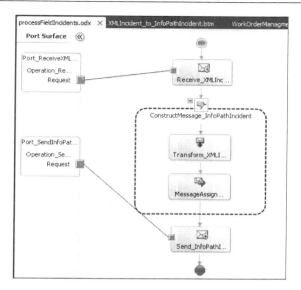

5. We are now ready to deploy our application by right mouse clicking on the solution name and clicking on **Deploy Solution**.

6. In the BizTalk Administration Console, we should now see an application called Chapter7-SendingDocuments. We now need a receive location that will pick up the file from the Work Order Management System. The name of this receive location is **ReceiveXMLIncident**. It will use the **FILE** adapter, the **BizTalkServerApplication** Receive handler and the **XMLReceive** Receive pipeline.

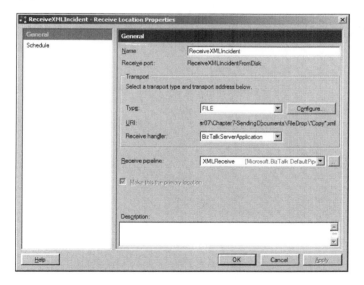

7. The configuration for the Send Port is much more interesting than the other parts of the application. The Send Port will take advantage of the Windows SharePoint Services adapter by leveraging the BizTalkServerApplication Host Instance and a PassThruTransmit Send Pipeline.

8. If we click on the **Configure** button we can further explore the Adapter's configuration settings.

9. The configuration for our `processFieldIncidents.odx` is pretty straightforward. We have a receive port, which we will receive the Field Incidents from and a Send Port that will be used to send the InfoPath messages to SharePoint. We are once again using the default host instance **BizTalkServerApplication.**

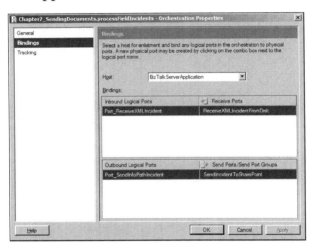

Property	Value	Comment
Adapter Web Service Port	8080	On the server that was used to build this solution, the SharePoint site was created on port 8080 since this server also has the BAM Portal installed. If you have installed SharePoint as your default web site then your port will be 80.
Destination Folder URL	Field Incident Forms	The Form Library that we will deposit these InfoPath documents to.
Namespace Alias	ns0="http://Chapter7_ SendingDocuments. WorkOrderManagmentIncident_ InfoPath"	This is the namespace of the `WorkOrderManagment Incident_ InfoPath.xsd` schema that was used when building the InfoPath form.

Property	Value	Comment
SharePoint Site URL	http://localhost:8080/sites/ BizTalkLineOfBusiness/	The location of the SharePoint site that is used to host the Forms Library where Field Incident Forms are created and stored.
Microsoft Office Integration	Yes (InfoPath Form Library)	This instructs SharePoint to try to load this document with an InfoPath template.
Column 01	Incident City	The name of the SharePoint column that we created while establishing the FieldIncidentType content type.
Column 01 Value	%XPATH=//ns0:WOMIncident_ InfoPath/Location/City%	This is an XPath expression that will retrieve the City of the incident from the payload of our message.
Column 02	Incident Plant	The name of the SharePoint column that we created while establishing the FieldIncidentType content type.
Column 02 Value	%XPATH=//ns0:WOMIncident_ InfoPath/Location/Plant%	This is an XPath expression that will retrieve the plant of the incident from the payload of our message.
Column 03	Incident Date	The name of the SharePoint column that we created while establishing the FieldIncidentType content type.
Column 03 Value	%XPATH=//ns0:WOMIncident_ InfoPath/IncidentDate%	This is an XPath expression that will retrieve the date of the incident from the payload of our message.

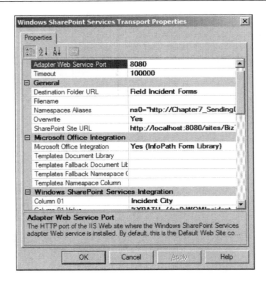

 Note: The BizTalk Host instance user for the Send Port that will be connecting to SharePoint requires "Contributor" access to the document or form library.

Testing the application

With our application configured, we can now start it up and execute a test to ensure that it works correctly.

1. We want to drop a message similar to the one below in our Receive location's folder. A sample of this message may be found in the `Chapter7-SendingDocuments\FileDrop\` folder of this chapter's source code.

```xml
- <ns0:WOMIncident_XML INCIDENT_DATE="2010-10-10"
    xmlns:ns0="http://Chapter7_SendingDocuments.WorkOrderManagmentIncident_InfoPath">
    <Location CITY="Regina" PROVINCE="Saskatchewan" PLANT="2135"
    SERVICE_POINT="23" />
- <Personnel>
    <PERSON NAME="Kurt Weare" ID="9999" POSITION="Area Foreman"
    EMP_OR_CONTR="Employee" />
  </Personnel>
    <VEHICLE VEHICLE_ID="J400" DAMAGE="Front End Damage to Truck" />
- <ENVIRONMENT IS_OIL_SPILL="false" IS_ENV_HAZARD="false"
    IS_WILD_LIVE_IMPACT="true">
    <COMMENTS>While travelling back from Oilfield install, a moose ran into the road
    and I couldn't stop in time to avoid him. Extensive damage to the front end of
    the truck has occurred.</COMMENTS>
  </ENVIRONMENT>
</ns0:WOMIncident_XML>
```

2. BizTalk should pick this file up, transform it into the format that InfoPath is expecting, and send it to SharePoint. During this process, BizTalk should also populate SharePoint columns using data from the message's payload.

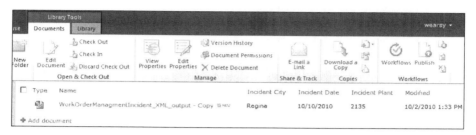

3. Notice that in the **Type** column, it contains an InfoPath icon. What this means is that SharePoint has determined that the data within this document, is a match for an InfoPath template that can be found within this Forms Library. What makes this demonstration interesting is that nowhere in BizTalk have we specified an InfoPath template name. In fact BizTalk has no idea that this data matches a template as we did not have to provide any Processing instructions like we had to do in BizTalk 2006. To validate this, turn the **Track Message Bodies** feature of this Send Port on and look at the content of the message. Nowhere will you find any indication that this data belongs to an InfoPath Template.

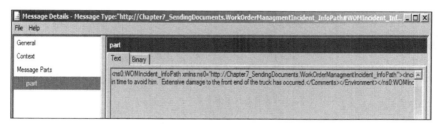

4. When we click on the link for this document, we will also discover that our InfoPath client is loaded and our XML message is loaded into our InfoPath template.

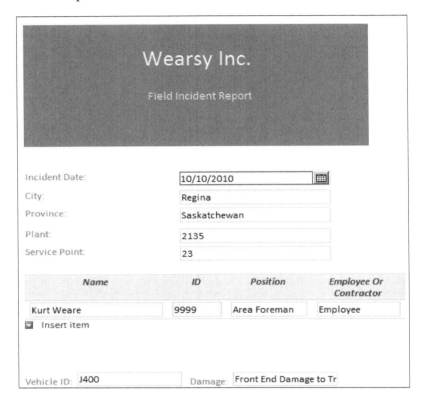

Summary

In this chapter, we have seen two examples that demonstrate the tight integration between InfoPath, SharePoint, and BizTalk. In the first scenario we received timesheet requests from field employees and sent only approved requests off to our payroll system. In the second scenario, we demonstrated a Work Order Management system outputting Field Incidents that were loaded into SharePoint. These scenarios demonstrate the tight integration that allows us to build compelling solutions. This enables us, as BizTalk developers, to quickly build robust solutions that have high visibility within the business.

We have also been able to extend SharePoint to our enterprise and brought our enterprise to SharePoint which allows IT to capitalize on previous investments. SharePoint is no longer an island where data gets created and becomes stale. With BizTalk and its suite of Adapters, we can extend SharePoint functionality to any system that BizTalk is capable of communicating with.

The combination of the Windows SharePoint Services Adapter and Windows SharePoint Services Adapter Web Service provide a comprehensive solution when integrating with Document and Form Libraries. However, there is a limitation, in the sense that the Windows SharePoint Adapter can only integrate with Document and Form Libraries. If we want to communicate with other SharePoint features such as Lists, we are unable to do so with the Adapter. Fear not, options do exist when communicating with Lists, and they are discussed in the next chapter.

8
Integrating with SharePoint 2010 Web Services

In Chapter 7, both the Sending and Receiving walkthroughs demonstrated SharePoint integration with the Windows SharePoint Services (WSS) Adapter. These demonstrations really highlighted SharePoint's strengths including forms management and collaboration in an environment that end users are familiar with: Microsoft Office.

The problem with the Windows SharePoint Services Adapter is that it is very document and forms library centric. The adapter is very good when interacting with these libraries, but we inevitably will be asked the question of whether BizTalk can manipulate a Custom SharePoint List. The answer to this question is Yes and No. The adapter itself does not support manipulating Custom Lists, but since SharePoint exposes the functionality of manipulating lists as a Service, BizTalk can integrate with SharePoint via that mechanism.

In this chapter, we will cover:

- SharePoint List overview
- SharePoint's List Web Services
- Consuming SharePoint List scenario walkthrough
- Creating Custom SharePoint Lists
- Custom list GUIDs
- Building BizTalk application
- Deploying and configuring BizTalk application
- Testing BizTalk application
- Other ways to integrate with SharePoint

SharePoint List overview

SharePoint Lists represent a foundational component of SharePoint. It is nearly impossible to avoid a list in some manner while working with SharePoint. Technically speaking, a Document/Form library is a type of list, but for the purpose of this discussion we are going to exclude Document/Form libraries from this category. A list often resembles a database table in its structure and behavior. Lists have columns and metadata that can be attached. A difference being that a list has a Graphical User Interface (GUI) that can be manipulated by users.

SharePoint ships with lists out of the box such as the Calendar and the Task List. Our discussion is going to focus Custom Lists. **Custom Lists** allow us to configure specific fields that are relevant to our business process.

An example of a Custom List is illustrated below called BizTalk Environments. It is a simple list that can be used to track the various endpoints that your BizTalk servers are connected to.

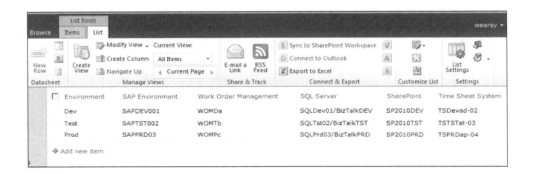

SharePoint's List Web Services

With MOSS 2007/Windows SharePoint Services 3.0, you only had one option when manipulating lists through Web Services. An out-of-the-box Web Service called `Lists.asmx` allows you to manipulate list data through a variety of Web methods. The following image illustrates many of the Web methods that the `Lists.asmx` Web Service exposes:

Lists

The following operations are supported. For a formal definition, please review the <u>Service Description</u>.

- <u>AddAttachment</u>
- <u>AddDiscussionBoardItem</u>
- <u>AddList</u>
- <u>AddListFromFeature</u>
- <u>AddWikiPage</u>
- <u>ApplyContentTypeToList</u>
- <u>CheckInFile</u>
- <u>CheckOutFile</u>
- <u>CreateContentType</u>
- <u>DeleteAttachment</u>
- <u>DeleteContentType</u>
- <u>DeleteContentTypeXmlDocument</u>
- <u>DeleteList</u>
- <u>GetAttachmentCollection</u>
- <u>GetList</u>

You will find the `Lists.asmx` Web Service in the `_vti_bin` folder of a Custom List. For example, here is the location of the `lists.asmx` Web Service that we would use if we were going to manipulate the BizTalk Environments List that was previously described.

```
http://localhost:8080/sites/BizTalkLineOfBusiness/Lists/BizTalk%20
Environments/_vti_bin/lists.asmx
```

> Note: You only need to provide the port number (:8080) if you have set up SharePoint on a non-standard port.

SharePoint 2010 and SharePoint 2010 Foundation introduce another way of consuming list data and that is through a WCF RESTful service. This allows us to consume a RESTful endpoint and use the data from our list as an Atom feed.

REST stands for **Representational State Transfer** and is a flexible software architecture for distributed systems based upon HTTP. A detailed synopsis of REST is outside the context of this book.

> For a more detailed explanation of REST, please visit the following link: `http://en.wikipedia.org/wiki/Representational_State_Transfer`

We can point our web browser at the `ListData.svc` service and provide the name of our BizTalk Environments List. In turn, all of the data that exists in our list will be returned as an Atom feed. This service requires permissions just like any other resource within a SharePoint site. This service cannot be called anonymously so if you want to manipulate this list via BizTalk, ensure your host instance user has contribute access. We also have the ability to provide REST queries to return subsets of data within our list, much like a database query. In addition to reading data via this interface, we can also perform inserts and updates.

We can find the `ListData.svc` in the `_vti_bin` folder beneath our site. Unlike the WSS adapter, if our List Name contains a space, we need to remove it instead of providing the HTML equivalent of the space key: %20.

```
http://localhost:8080/sites/BizTalkLineOfBusiness/_vti_bin/ListData.
svc/BizTalkEnvironments
```

When we enter this URL into our browser and click Enter, we will receive an XML response which includes our BizTalk Environment data that was captured in the list.

It is worth noting the BizTalk WCF Adapter does not support these RESTful interfaces out of the box. When BizTalk consumes a RESTful List Service, it is unable to parse some of the XML. Within the `<entry m:etag="W/"1"">`tag, a nested quotation "" exists, which BizTalk considers to be invalid XML. The end result is this message gets suspended in the Receive Pipeline. If using the WCF Endpoint was imperative, we could write a custom Pipeline Component that would remove this additional quotation mark before the message is sent to the Message Box. For the purpose of this book, we will focus on the `Lists.asmx` as there is no additional coding required when interacting with this service.

```xml
<?xml version="1.0" encoding="utf-8" standalone="yes" ?>
<feed xml:base="http://win2k8r2:8080/sites/BizTalkLineOfBusiness/_vti_bin/ListData.svc/"
  xmlns:d="http://schemas.microsoft.com/ado/2007/08/dataservices"
  xmlns:m="http://schemas.microsoft.com/ado/2007/08/dataservices/metadata" xmlns="http://www.w3.org/200
  <title type="text">BizTalkEnvironments</title>
  <id>http://win2k8r2:8080/sites/BizTalkLineOfBusiness/_vti_bin/ListData.svc/BizTalkEnvironments/</id>
  <updated>2010-10-03T21:59:19Z</updated>
  <link rel="self" title="BizTalkEnvironments" href="BizTalkEnvironments" />
  <entry m:etag="W/"1"">
    <id>http://win2k8r2:8080/sites/BizTalkLineOfBusiness/_vti_bin/ListData.svc/BizTalkEnvironments(1)</id>
    <title type="text">Dev</title>
    <updated>2010-10-03T11:35:03-06:00</updated>
    <author>
      <name />
```

Since `Lists.asmx` Web Service is based upon the classic ASMX style Web Services, we have two BizTalk adapter options when it comes to consuming this service:

- SOAP
- WCF-BasicHttp

The SOAP Adapter has been deprecated as of BizTalk 2009 and continues to be deprecated in BizTalk 2010. While it is still a supportable scenario to use this Adapter, it is in our best interest to avoid it if possible since this Adapter will disappear in a future version of BizTalk. Please refer to the official MSDN documentation for more details: `http://msdn.microsoft.com/en-us/library/aa559720(BTS.70).aspx`

The WCF-BasicHttp Adapter supports consuming both WCF and traditional ASMX Web Services. This Adapter was introduced in BizTalk 2006 R2 and continues to be a reliable Adapter in BizTalk 2010 when consuming Web/WCF Services. The scenario that we will develop is based upon the WCF Adapter.

When using the `Lists.asmx` Web Service, we need to leverage a technology called Collaborative Application Mark-up Language (CAML). CAML is an XML-based mark-up language that is used to manipulate SharePoint via Web Services, the Client Object Model, or SharePoint APIs. Within the context of this book, we will cover CAML at a high level as this book is not intended to be a comprehensive CAML resource.

Consuming SharePoint List scenario walkthrough

The real world scenario we are going to walk through is a Vehicle Maintenance List. Field Employees will use this list to populate any maintenance information related to their company vehicle. Much like the scenarios in Chapter 7, we don't want field employees logging into our ERP system as the user experience is not conducive to Field employees who are in the field performing their day to day responsibilities for the company.

The information populated in the SharePoint List still needs to make it to our ERP system. This information is tracked by the Finance and Regulatory departments so it is important that this information is exchanged with our system of record. A common challenge that BizTalk developers face, is the ability to schedule a process to launch an orchestration. Most BizTalk scenarios begin with BizTalk receiving a message and in turn, that message instantiates an orchestration. In our scenario, this is not the case and since you cannot begin a BizTalk orchestration by sending a message, we need to trigger a message to launch the BizTalk orchestration. We have a couple of options:

- BizTalk Scheduled Task Adapter
- SQL Server Polling Adapter

The BizTalk Scheduled Task Adapter is an open source adapter that is available on codeplex; http://biztalkscheduledtask.codeplex.com. The adapter allows you to schedule a trigger message that will instantiate an Orchestration at a set time.

The SQL Server Adapter, either WCF or traditional, can be used in a similar fashion as the BizTalk Scheduled Task Adapter as it can be scheduled to execute every X minutes/hours/days. For some environments, running open source, or community, executables is prohibited so with this in mind, we will leverage the WCF-based SQL Server Adapter.

Another benefit of using the SQL Server Adapter, either traditional or WCF based, is the need to store the SharePoint List GUID for the SharePoint List that we would like to communicate with. We can store this GUID in a SQL Server table and retrieve this value from the database, prior to consuming our SharePoint List data. As we move this solution from various environments (Development/Test/Production), we possess some portability as each SharePoint environment will have a unique List GUID.

Once we have the GUID for the SharePoint List, we are going to use this GUID when we construct a CAML query. We will then send this query to the `Lists.asmx` service. We expect the CAML query will return the results of the Vehicle Maintenance List. The result of this query will be mapped to a Flat File format that the ERP system is expecting.

Creating Custom SharePoint List

 Note: The following example assumes you have an existing SharePoint site in place. The following links describe how to create SharePoint sites for WSS 3.0 SP2 and SharePoint 2010 Foundation:

WSS 3.0 SP2:

```
http://technet.microsoft.com/en-us/library/
cc288969(office.12).aspx
```

SharePoint 2010 Foundation:

```
http://technet.microsoft.com/en-us/library/cc263094.
aspx
```

We need to create a Custom List where our field workers can input their data related to their Vehicle Maintenance. BizTalk will later connect to this list and retrieve the data so that it can be sent to our ERP system.

1. We can create a Custom List by clicking on the **Lists** link underneath the **Home** menu in the SharePoint Ribbon.

2. We now want to click on the **Create** link.

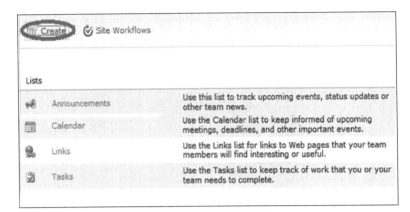

3. Select **Custom List**, provide a list name of **Vehicle Maintenance**, and click the **Create** button.

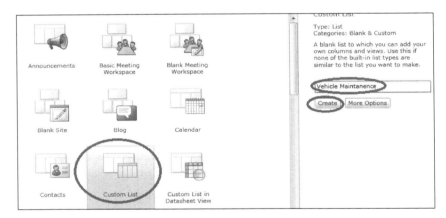

4. We now have an empty list and want to create our Custom Columns by clicking on the **Create Column** button.

5. Add the following columns to the list:

    ◦   Title (system generated)

    ◦   Location

    ◦   StartTime

    ◦   EndTime

    ◦   Unit

    ◦   OdometerReading

- ○ Item
- ○ For simplicity, we will keep the data types as **Single line of text** and use the default properties

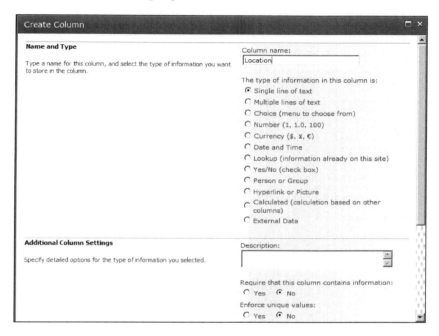

In the preceding example, we created columns that did not include spaces in their name. This was done intentionally as SharePoint maintains internal values for field names and then an external name which is displayed on GUIs. Under the hood, SharePoint will always use the internal name. Having internal column names that include spaces will create runtime issues that may be difficult to debug. For this reason, it is always a good idea to create your column names without spaces and then rename them after the fact if you require more user friendly column names.

6. When complete, we can populate our list by clicking on the **Add new item** link.

7. Once complete, our list should look like the following:

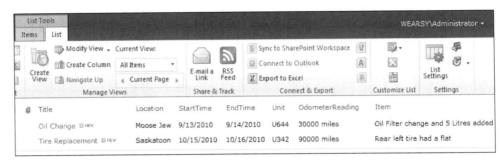

Custom List GUIDs

SharePoint heavily relies upon the use of GUIDs when identifying lists. List GUIDs are unique for each environment. So if we create a Custom List in a test environment, it will have a different value than a Custom List in a Production environment.

1. The first step in retrieving our List GUID is on the **List Settings** page. We can navigate to the settings by clicking on the **List Settings** button.

2. We need to determine what the GUID is for the list that we just created. We can accomplish this by right mouse clicking on the **Title, description, and navigation** link and click on **Copy Shortcut.**

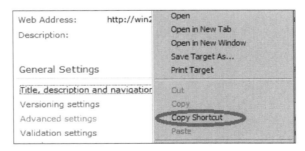

3. Paste this value into an editor such as Notepad. We end up with a URL that looks something like the following: `http://localhost:8080/sites/BizTalkLineOfBusiness/_layouts/ListGeneralSettings.aspx?List=%7B27E9BDCE%2D0D87%2D451C%2DB6C9%2D053C246517AE%7D`

   ○   Our Encoded List GUID is the value after "?List="

4. Since this GUID value is still encoded, we want to decode it using a URL Decoder tool. We can use a free service on `http://www.albionresearch.com/misc/urlencode.php` to decode our GUID. The initial value of %7B27E9BDCE%2D0D87%2D451C%2DB6C9%2D053C246517AE%7D gets converted into our actual GUID of **{27E9BDCE-0D87-451C-B6C9-053C246517AE}**. Conversely, if you wanted to perform this conversion yourself, '%7B' has the equivalent of '{', '%2D' has the equivalent of '-' and '%7Dg' has the equivalent of '}'.

5. We now want to take this GUID Value and insert it into our custom SQL Server table. This table is called **Lists** and contains one column called **ListGUID**. A SQL script exists in this chapter's source code that will generate the appropriate **SharePointList** database, **Lists** table, and **ListGUID** column.

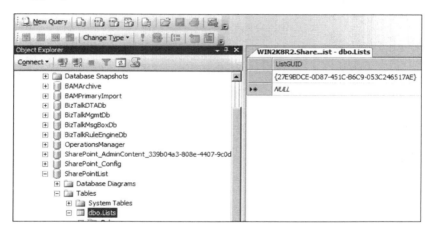

Building BizTalk application

In this section, we will discuss the BizTalk components required in order to build out a solution that will consume a Custom SharePoint list and generate a flat file.

Generating schemas for SharePoint Web Service

In order for BizTalk and SharePoint to effectively communicate with each other, we need a contract between the two systems. We will establish this contract by generating schemas for the SharePoint Web Service by using the Consume Adapter Service Wizard. This will ensure that when BizTalk sends a request to SharePoint, it is able to understand the request and provide a response that BizTalk is expecting. Before generating our SharePoint schemas, we need to do one thing and that is add the schema that allows us to communicate with the database table that we previously created.

1. Now that we have the Database structure in place, we can use the Consume Adapter Service Wizard to generate our `GetListGUIDTypedPolling.xsd`. Detailed instructions on how to generate this schema are not covered in this chapter as Typed Polling is covered in *Chapter 2, WCF SQL Server Adapter*.

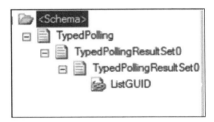

2. The Web Service exposes a Web Service Description Language (WSDL) much like most other Web Services. We want to consume this WSDL using the Consume WCF Service wizard. We can launch this wizard by right mouse clicking on the **Chapter8-ManipulatingLists** project and selecting **Add**.

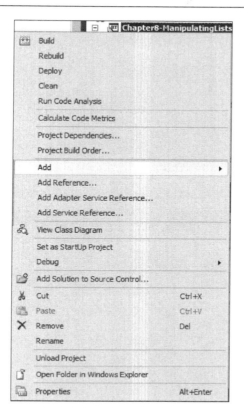

3. We now want to select **Add Generated Item.**

4. From the **Add Generated Items** screen, we want to select **Consume WCF Service** and click the **Add** button.

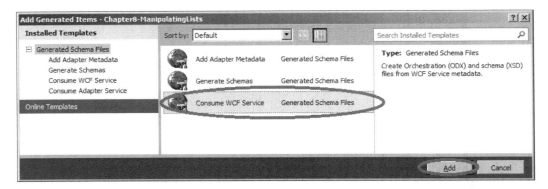

5. Click the **Next** button to proceed with the BizTalk WCF Service Consuming Wizard.

6. Ensure the **Metadata Exchange (MEX) endpoint** is selected and click **Next** button.

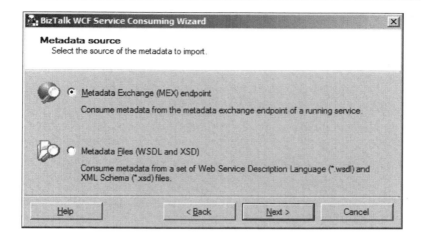

7. In the **Metadata Address (URL),** we need to provide the location of our `Lists.asmx` Web Service. For example: `http://localhost:8080/sites/BizTalkLineOfBusiness/Lists/VehicleMaintanence/_vti_bin/lists.asmx`. In this case, **BizTalkLineOfBusiness** is the name of the SharePoint site, **Lists** is the location of all lists within this site, and the name of the list we are trying to consume is called **VehicleMaintanence**. Since the `Lists.asmx` is not specific to any Custom List, we can generate the schemas from any `Lists.asmx` endpoint and use it against any list. By providing the URL of the `Lists.asmx` endpoint, we can click on the **Get** button and view all of the Web Methods that make up the `Lists.asmx` Web Service.

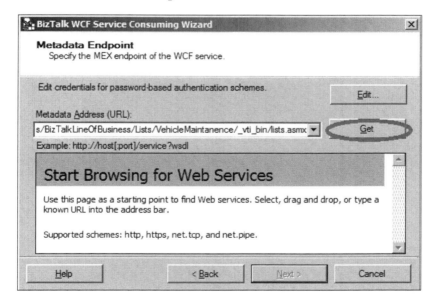

8. Click **Next** to proceed.

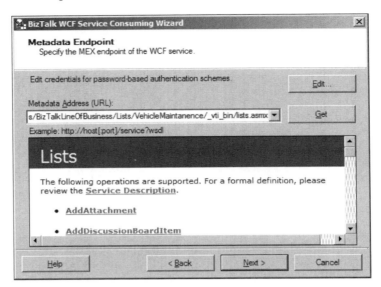

We are now in a position to import the schemas associated with our Web Service and can do so by clicking the **Import** button.

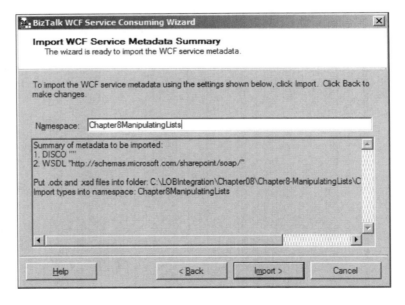

9. We will find that five artifacts have been added to our solution:

Artifact Name	Purpose
`Lists.BindingInfo.xml`	A binding file that can be used with the WCF-BasicHttp Adapter.
`Lists.odx`	A template Orchestration that includes the Multi-part Message Types and Port Types required when communicating with SharePoint. We do not want to delete this orchestration: the Multi-part Message Types and Port Types will be required when configuring our Logical Port.
`Lists_Custom.BindingInfo.xml`	This binding file is similar to the `Lists.BindingInfo.xml` with the difference being this binding is for the WCF-Custom Adapter that will use a basicHttpBinding. Fundamentally, this Adapter, with this binding, will work the same as the WCF-BasicHttp Adapter. The WCF-Custom Adapter allows for more options, including security, when configuring our Send Port.
`Lists_microsoft_com_wsdl_types.xsd`	This schema provides underlying support for the `Lists_schemas_microsoft_com_sharepoint_soap.xsd` schema when interacting with the `Lists.asmx` Web Service.
`Lists_schemas_microsoft_com_sharepoint_soap.xsd`	This is the most critical artifact of the set as it provides the structures that are required when communicating with all of the various Web methods contained within our Lists Web Service.

10. When we download these artifacts, an issue appears in the **Lists_schemas_microsoft_com_sharepoint_soap.xsd** schema at compile time. The error we get is as follows:

⊗	163	Node "<Schema>" - Schema reference "" is not a valid reference or does not exist in the current project.	Lists_schemas_microsof	1	1

There appears to be a bug in the **Consume WCF Service** Wizard in that it inserts a schema import node that does not contain a **schemaLocation**.

```
<?xml version="1.0"?>
<xs:schema xmlns:tns="http://schemas.microsoft.com/sharepoint/soap/" elementFormDefault=
    <xs:import schemaLocation="" namespace="http://www.w3.org/2001/XMLSchema" />
    <xs:import schemaLocation=".\Lists_microsoft_com_wsdl_types.xsd" namespace="http://mic
    <xs:element name="GetList">
      <xs:complexType>
        <xs:sequence>
          <xs:element minOccurs="0" maxOccurs="1" name="listName" type="xs:string" />
        </xs:sequence>
      </xs:complexType>
    </xs:element>
    <xs:element name="GetListResponse">
      <xs:complexType>
        <xs:sequence>
          <xs:element minOccurs="0" maxOccurs="1" name="GetListResult">
            <xs:complexType mixed="true">
              <xs:sequence>
                <xs:any />
              </xs:sequence>
            </xs:complexType>
          </xs:element>
        </xs:sequence>
```

11. We can work around this bug by removing the first **<xs:import />** node with no issues. In order to remove this line, open a text editor such as Notepad or edit the XSD file in Visual Studio by right mouse clicking on it, selecting **Open With**, and then selecting **XML Editor**.

```
Lists_schemas_micro...sharepoint_soap.xsd  X   Lists_microsoft_com_wsdl_types.xsd      Lists.odx      Utility.cs
    <?xml version="1.0"?>
  <xs:schema xmlns:tns="http://schemas.microsoft.com/sharepoint/soap/" elementFormDefault="qua
      <xs:import schemaLocation=".\Lists_microsoft_com_wsdl_types.xsd" namespace="http://micros
    <xs:element name="GetList">
      <xs:complexType>
        <xs:sequence>
          <xs:element minOccurs="0" maxOccurs="1" name="listName" type="xs:string" />
        </xs:sequence>
      </xs:complexType>
    </xs:element>
    <xs:element name="GetListResponse">
      <xs:complexType>
        <xs:sequence>
          <xs:element minOccurs="0" maxOccurs="1" name="GetListResult">
            <xs:complexType mixed="true">
              <xs:sequence>
                <xs:any />
              </xs:sequence>
            </xs:complexType>
          </xs:element>
        </xs:sequence>
      </xs:complexType>
```

Orchestration initialization

Consuming SharePoint List data requires BizTalk to submit a request and then
wait for a response. Prior to BizTalk sending this request, we need to instantiate
our Orchestration by receiving a trigger message. We will now configure BizTalk
to receive this trigger message from SQL server so that we can launch our
Orchestration.

1. With our WCF-SQL and Web Service schemas downloaded, we now want
   to build our solution by dragging a logical **Receive Port** and **Receive Shape**
   onto our Orchestration. When a message is processed through this port,
   it will initialize this Orchestration, which will allow us to connect to the
   SharePoint Custom List. The logical port is a **one-way** port and will have
   a **Port Binding** of **Specify later**. We then want to configure the **Receive
   Shape** to accept a message called **msgSQLConfiguration** that has a type of
   Chapter8ManipulatingLists.GetListGUIDTypedPolling.TypedPolling.
   This receive shape should also have its Activate property set to True. The
   message that will be received is the result of our Polling query that is
   specified in our Receive Location. This message will contain the GUID for the
   SharePoint List that we want to interact with.

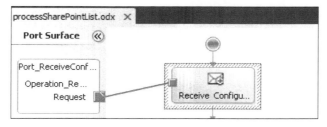

2. The schema for the message that we want to provide to SharePoint is called **Lists_schemas_microsoft_com_sharepoint_soap.xsd.** Within this schema, we will discover many nodes that represent the XML structures that need to be passed to the various Web methods that are available in the `Lists.asmx` Web Service. The structure we are most interested in is the **GetListItems** node. We will use this message to retrieve the data from our Custom List. In order to use this schema, we need to create a message in our Orchestration called **msgGetListItemsRequest** that has a type of **Chapter8ManipulatingLists. GetListItemsSoapIn**.

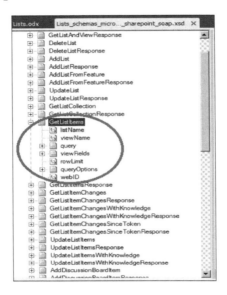

Mapping SharePoint request

With our orchestration launched, it is now time to pass the GUID that we received from our polling call to SQL Server and provide it, and other supplementary data, to the SharePoint request message. The request message provides SharePoint with instructions on what data BizTalk is expecting back from the SharePoint List.

In order to populate our SharePoint Request message, we need to be able to retrieve the GUID from the **msgSQLConfiguration** message and provide it to the SharePoint Get List Item Request message. This transformation occurs in a map called **SQLConfiguration_to_GetListItemsRequest.btm,** which is provided in the source code as part of this book.

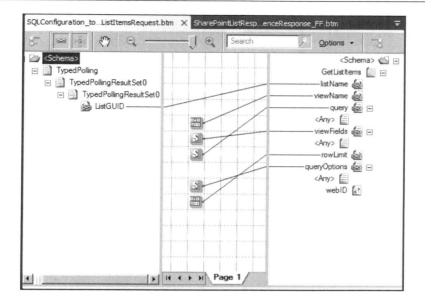

1. At this point, we need to finish populating the SharePoint List Request message. This message must follow the CAML structure that SharePoint is expecting. The request message is comprised of seven message parts.

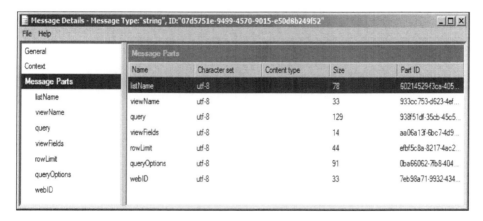

2. We will populate each of these message parts from within the **SQLConfiguration_to_GetListItemsRequest.btm** map. In the **listName** node, we want to populate the GUID for our Custom List. In this case, we are going to leverage the **ListGUID** element in the **msgSQLConfiguration** message by mapping this node to the **listName** node.

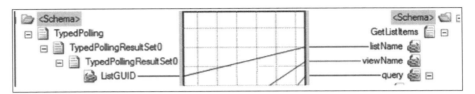

3. For the **viewName** property, we are simply going to assign an empty string value via a **String Concatenation** Functoid. In our scenario, we are not leveraging SharePoint views.

4. In the **query** node of the SharePoint Request message, notice the type of node that it is expecting: **<Any>.** Within the context of this schema, this means it is a loosely typed node and is expecting us, the developer, to provide valid CAML mark up. This CAML mark up will then get executed against our Custom List. If we wanted to filter the SharePoint List based upon a set of criteria, we would do so here. Since we are interested in all data stored within the list, we will look for all records where the **ID** field is greater than 0. Since ID is a system column, it is guaranteed to be there and IDs always start at number 1 so we will always have records returned if they exist in the list.

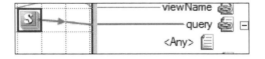

5. In order to populate this CAML query, we can leverage a **Scripting Functoid** and have it return XML from an XSLT Call Template. We can configure this **Scripting Functoid** by right mouse clicking on it and selecting **Configure Functoid Script.**

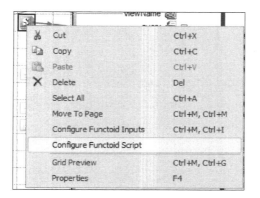

6. Once inside the configuration of the Functoid Script, we can set our **Select Script** type to **Inline XSLT Call Template** and provide the following XSLT mark-up:

```
<xsl:template name="Query">
    <Where>
        <Gt>
            <FieldRef Name='ID'/>
            <Value Type='Number'>0</Value>
        </Gt>
    </Where>
</xsl:template>
```

 Note: We also have the option to write a .NET Helper method that will return XML and assign it to this node.

7. The next message part that we need to populate is the **queryOptions** element. We will follow the same pattern for this element as we did for the Query element. We will configure **a Scripting Functoid** to call a **XSLT Template**. The purpose of this element is to provide constraints in our query such as including mandatory columns. In our scenario, we are not going to force mandatory columns to be returned.

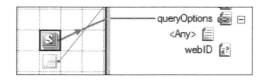

8. The Inline XSLT Call Template will contain the following XSLT mark-up:

```
<xsl:template name="QueryOptions">
    <QueryOptions>
        <IncludeMandatoryColumns>FALSE</IncludeMandatoryColumns>
    </QueryOptions>
</xsl:template>
```

9. The **rowLimit** message part provides the ability to restrict the number of rows we are interested in being returned from the SharePoint List. This message part does not require an XML node, so we can simply provide a numerical literal from a **String Concatenate** functoid.

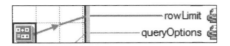

10. In our scenario, we will provide a value of 1000 inside the **String Concatenate** functoid.

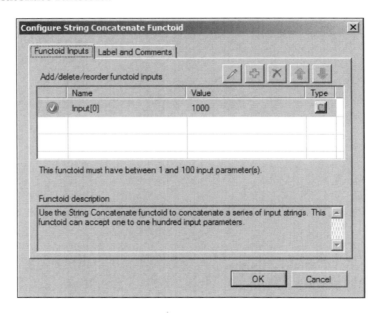

11. The next message part that we need to take care of is **viewFields**, which provides the ability to restrict the amount of fields returned by the CAML query. In our scenario, we are going to return all user-created and system-generated fields. Once again, we will leverage a **Scripting Functoid** that calls an XSLT Call Template.

12. In the XSLT Call Template call, we will provide the following XSLT mark up:

```
<xsl:template name="ViewFields">
  <ViewFields></ViewFields
</xsl:template>
```

13. If we wanted to manipulate a list in the root website, we can provide the GUID of the parent site in the **webID** node even though the `Lists.asmx` Web Service could be in a child site. In our scenario, we can simply not map the node and provide no instructions.

14. At this point, we have populated our SharePoint Get List Items Request message and are ready to send it to SharePoint. In order to do this we want to take advantage of a Logical Port that the Consume WCF Service Wizard has provided us with. When creating our logical port we want to ensure that we are using an existing port type called **Chapter8ManipulatingLists.ListSoap**.

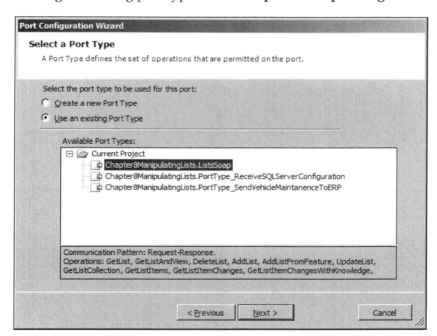

15. Once we have the logical port configured, we will discover that all of the various Web methods that have been exposed are added to our orchestration. The Web method that we are interested in is **GetListItems**. If you are interested in learning more about the other Web methods that are provided by this Web Service, please visit the following web page: `http://msdn.microsoft.com/en-us/library/ms774517(v=office.12).aspx`

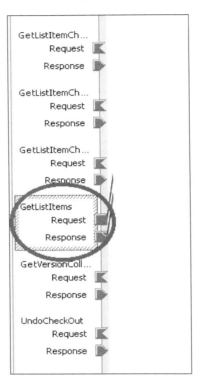

16. We can then drag the **Request** operation up to a **Send Shape** and the **Response Operation** to a **Receive Shape**.

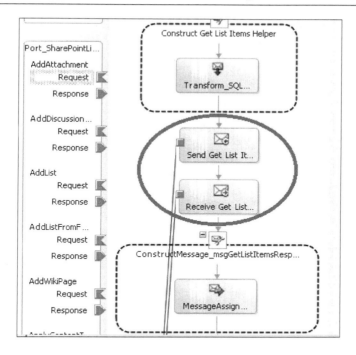

17. The **Send Shape** will be sending a message called **msgGetListItemsRequest**, which has a type of **Chapter8ManipulatingLists.GetListItemsSoapIn**.

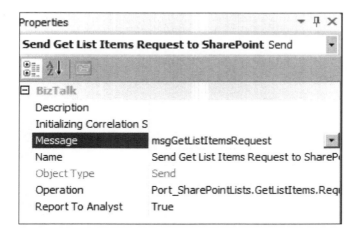

18. The Receive Shape will be receiving a message called **msgGetListItemsResponse**, which has a type of **Chapter8 ManipulatingLists.GetListItemsSoapOut**.

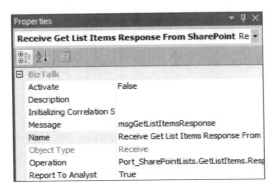

19. Now that we have created a logical send port and wired up a **Send Shape**, we can send a Get List Items Request to SharePoint and receive a response message back from SharePoint. The problem we will run into is the response message coming back from SharePoint has an untyped segment. What this means is SharePoint is aware of the structure that it is sending back, but BizTalk is not. The reason why BizTalk is not aware is because the structure for the **GetListItemsResponse** contains an **<Any>** node meaning that unstructured XML will be returned. The reason why Microsoft has chosen the **<Any>** node is they have no idea how many columns our Custom List has, so they leave the structure loose to accommodate more scenarios.

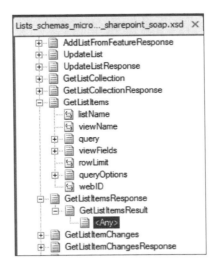

20. Included in the **SampleDocs** folder of this chapter's source code is an example of SharePoint's response in a file called `Sample_Response_From_Lists.xml`.

```xml
<GetListItemsResponse xmlns="http://schemas.microsoft.com/sharepoint/soap/">
- <GetListItemsResult>
    <listitems xmlns:s="uuid:BDC6E3F0-6DA3-11d1-A2A3-00AA00C14882" xmlns:dt="uuid:C2F41010-65B3-11d1-A29F-
    00AA00C14882" xmlns:rs="urn:schemas-microsoft-com:rowset" xmlns:z="#RowsetSchema">
    - <rs:data ItemCount="2">
        <z:row ows_Attachments="0" ows_LinkTitle="Oil Change" ows_Location="Moose Jaw" ows_StartTime="9/13/2010"
          ows_EndTime="9/14/2010" ows_Unit="U644" ows_OdometerReading="30000 miles" ows_Item="Oil Filter change and 5
          Litres added" ows_ModerationStatus="0" ows__Level="1" ows_Title="Oil Change" ows_ID="1" ows_UniqueId="1;#
          {98176F45-44B7-49EF-B718-646D634368E6}" ows_owshiddenversion="2" ows_FSObjType="1;#0"
          ows_Created_x0020_Date="1;#2010-10-03 21:09:21" ows_Created="2010-10-03 21:09:21"
          ows_FileLeafRef="1;#1_.000" ows_PermMask="0x1b03c4312ef" ows_Modified="2010-10-03 21:10:09"
          ows_FileRef="1;#sites/BizTalkLineOfBusiness/Lists/Vehicle Maintanence/1_.000" ows_MetaInfo="1;#" />
        <z:row ows_Attachments="0" ows_LinkTitle="Tire Replacement" ows_Location="Saskatoon" ows_StartTime="10/15/2010"
          ows_EndTime="10/16/2010" ows_Unit="U342" ows_OdometerReading="90000 miles" ows_Item="Rear left tire had a
          flat" ows_ModerationStatus="0" ows__Level="1" ows_Title="Tire Replacement" ows_ID="2" ows_UniqueId="2;#
          {53627805-CB8F-478C-BBC4-C49DBD577213}" ows_owshiddenversion="1" ows_FSObjType="2;#0"
          ows_Created_x0020_Date="2;#2010-10-03 21:11:31" ows_Created="2010-10-03 21:11:31"
          ows_FileLeafRef="2;#2_.000" ows_PermMask="0x1b03c4312ef" ows_Modified="2010-10-03 21:11:31"
          ows_FileRef="2;#sites/BizTalkLineOfBusiness/Lists/Vehicle Maintanence/2_.000" ows_MetaInfo="2;#" />
    </rs:data>
  </listitems>
 </GetListItemsResult>
</GetListItemsResponse>
```

SharePoint's unstructured responses

The problem with receiving an unstructured message segment is it is very difficult to transform this data into a response that we can send to our ERP system. We have a couple of options we can pursue at this point:

- Write a series of XPath statements that can retrieve the values needed for the ERP system
- Use this sample message to generate a Schema we can use later in a BizTalk Map to transform the data returned from SharePoint into a format the ERP system can process

Writing a lot of XPath statements is error prone and difficult to debug. With the second option, we can leverage the BizTalk Mapper tool. In order to do so, we will generate a Schema that we can use to structure these responses from SharePoint and then transform these responses into a message that our ERP can consume.

1. In order to create a schema for the structure being returned from SharePoint, we can use the **Generate Schemas** feature that is part of the **Add Generated Items** Wizard.

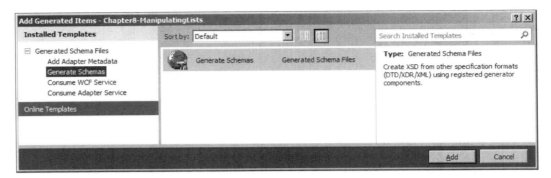

2. Once we are in the **Generate Schemas Wizard**, we want to ensure that our **Document Type** is set to **Well Formed XML (Not Loaded)** and then we can browse for a sample file. The sample file that we can use is called Sample_ Response_From_Lists.xml and can be found in the **SampleDocs** folder in this Chapter's source code. Once we have found this document we can click on **OK** to proceed to the next step.

 The sample file has been provided for your convenience. If you want to generate your own sample message from SharePoint, send in your SharePoint List request and then write the response message to your file system.

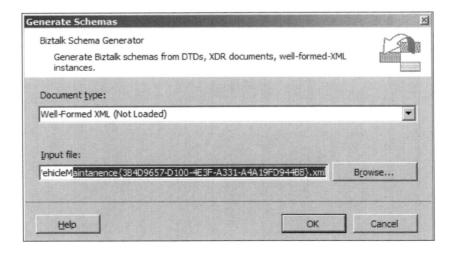

3. Three schemas have been added to our project. These schemas have been renamed to better reflect their purpose.

 Note: When renaming these schemas, ensure you update the references inside the schema by opening the schema in a text editor. We need to update the **<xs:import>** element within `SharePointListResponseParent.xsd` to reflect the new name for `SharePointListResponseChildData.xsd` schema.

```
SharePointListResponseParent.xsd  ×  Lists_schemas_micro..._sharepoint_soap.xsd
      <?xml version="1.0" encoding="utf-16"?>
    □ <xs:schema xmlns:rs="urn:schemas-microsoft-com:rowset" xmlns:dt="uuid:C2F41010-
        <xs:import schemaLocation=".\SharePointListResponseChildData.xsd" namespace="
    □    <xs:annotation>
    □      <xs:appinfo>
    □        <references xmlns="http://schemas.microsoft.com/BizTalk/2003">
            <reference targetNamespace="urn:schemas-microsoft-com:rowset" />
            <reference targetNamespace="#RowsetSchema" />
          </references>
```

We also need to update the **<xs:import>** element within `SharePointListResponseChildData.xsd` to reflect the new name for `SharePointListResponseChildRow.xsd` schema.

```
SharePointListResponseChildData.xsd  ×  SharePointListResponseChildRow.xsd      SharePointListResponseParent.xs
      <?xml version="1.0" encoding="utf-16"?>
    □ <xs:schema xmlns:tns="urn:schemas-microsoft-com:rowset" attributeFormDefault="
        <xs:import schemaLocation=".\SharePointListResponseChildRow.xsd" namespace="#
    □    <xs:element name="data">
    □      <xs:complexType>
    □        <xs:sequence>
            <xs:element maxOccurs="unbounded" xmlns:q1="#RowsetSchema" ref="q1:row"
          </xs:sequence>
          <xs:attribute name="ItemCount" type="xs:unsignedByte" use="required" />
        </xs:complexType>
      </xs:element>
```

4. The next modification we will make is to update the **Target Namespace** of the **SharePointListResponseParent.xsd** schema. Open this schema, select the **Schema** folder and then update the **Target Namespace** to: http://Chapter8ManipulatingLists.SharePointListResponseParent. The reason we need to do this is when we generated this schema, we did so using the output from the SharePoint Get List Items Response, which includes SharePoint's Target Namespace. If we do not make this change, we will have two schemas with the same Target Namespace within our project. This will result in a runtime error since BizTalk will not know which schema to match the incoming message to.

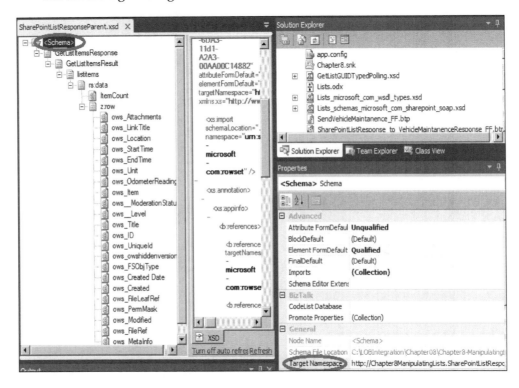

5. We now need to be able to cast the result from SharePoint to an instance of a message based upon our **SharePointListResponseParent. xsd** schema. In order to do this, we will create a new message called **msgGetListItemsResponseHelper** that is of type **Chapter8ManipulatingLists.SharePointListResponseParent**. We will then add a **Message Assignment** shape to our orchestration and set the **Message Constructed** property to **msgGetListItemsResponseHelper**.

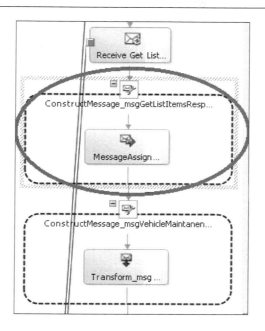

6. Within this **Message Assignment** shape, we are going to leverage a Helper method that exists in our Helper C# Project called `Chapter8ManipulatingLists.Utility`.

```
//We want a typed response document so that we can map to
//the flat file message for our ERP
msgGetListItemsResponseHelper = Chapter8ManipulatingLists.Utility.
toXML(msgGetListItemsResponse);
```

7. The `toXML` method will simply accept the Get List Items Response message from SharePoint, update the Target Namespace so that it matches our **msgGetListItemsResponseHelper** Target Namespace, and return the message back to BizTalk so that it can be cast against the **msgGetListItemsResponseHelper's** schema. The Utility class is fairly straightforward with one method, `toXML`:

```
using System;
using System.Collections.Generic;
using System.Linq;
using System.Text;
using System.Xml;

//needed to receive message from BizTalk
using Microsoft.XLANGs.BaseTypes;
namespace  Chapter8ManipulatingLists
{
```

```
public static class Utility
  {

Public static XmlDocument toXML(XLANGMessage msgXlang)
    {
//Want to receive a typed BizTalk message as an XML Document

XmlDocument xmlMessage = (XmlDocument)msgXlang[0].
RetrieveAs(typeof(System.Xml.XmlDocument));

try
    {
//Need to override Target Namespace to use our custom schema
instead of the SharePoint response message's Target Namespace

xmlMessage.DocumentElement.SetAttribute("xmlns", "http://
Chapter8ManipulatingLists.SharePointListResponseParent");
    }
catch (XLANGsException xlngEx)
    {
throw xlngEx;
    }

//Return message back to BizTalk
Return xmlMessage;
    }
  }
}
```

ERP flat file

Our ERP system, like many others, has a strict requirement that we must provide the Vehicle Maintenance data as a flat file. BizTalk has a rich tool set that allows us to easily address this requirement.

1. Now that we have a typed response message from SharePoint, we can transform it into the format that our ERP system is expecting. We will once again leverage the BizTalk Mapper to provide this functionality. The map that will take care of this for us is called **SharePointListResponse_to_ VehicleMaintanenceResponse_FF.btm**.

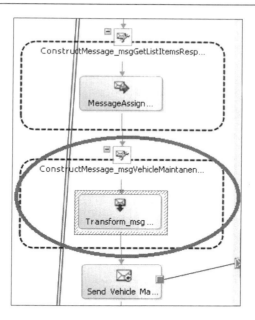

2. The schema for the ERP message that we will be using is called **SharePointListVehicleMaintanence_FF.xsd** and it is a Flat File Schema. A sample of the message that we want to generate exists in the `SampleDocs` folder that may be found this chapter's sample code. The name of the file is called **Vehicle_Maintanence_For_ERP.csv**.

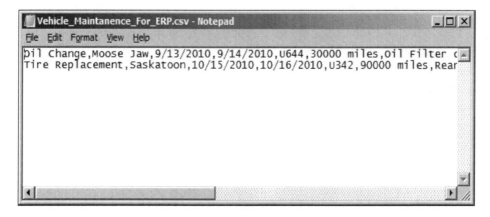

3. You will notice the structure of the flat file schema resembles the Custom SharePoint List that we previously created.

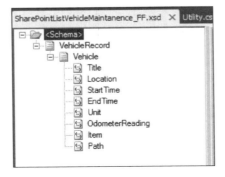

4. Since this is a flat file schema, we will also need a flat file pipeline to assemble this message as it is moving through the Send Port. The Send pipeline that will take care of this for us is called **SendVehicleMaintanence_ FF.btp**. Inside the **Assemble** stage, we want to drag a **Flat File assembler** component onto the pipeline's surface. We then want to set the **Document schema** to our flat file schema: **Chapter8ManipulatingLists. SharePointListVehicleMaintanence_FF**.

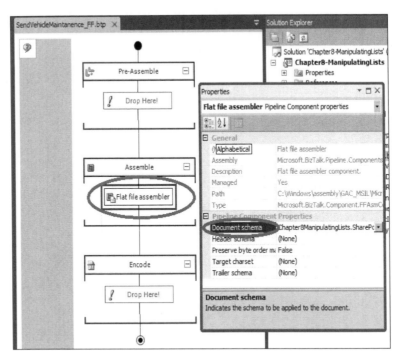

5. We now want to drop a **Send** shape onto the orchestration and create a Logical Send Port. In the **Send** shape, we want to specify a message called **msgVehicleMaintanence_FF**, which has a type of **Chapter8ManipulatingLists.SharePointListVehicleMaintanence_FF** and a logical **Send Port** that is one-way and that has a port binding that is set to **Specify Later**.

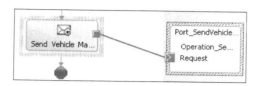

Deploying and configuring the BizTalk solution

We are now ready to deploy and configure our BizTalk solution.

1. To deploy our solution, right mouse click on it and then click on **Deploy Solution.**

2. Inside the BizTalk Admin console, we should find an application called **Chapter8-ManipulatingLists.** A binding file called `Chapter8-ManipulatingLists.xml` exists for this solution in the `Bindings` folder within this Chapter's source code. If we import this file, we will discover that we have one Receive Port, one Receive location, and two Send Ports. Do note that the endpoints that are included in this binding file may not match the targets on your machine.

3. Our Receive Port, called **RetrieveSharePointGUIDs**, has one Receive Location called **RetrieveSharePointGUIDsFromSQL**. The Receive Location will use the WCF-Custom Adapter, the **BizTalkServerApplication** Host Instance, and the **XMLReceive** pipeline.

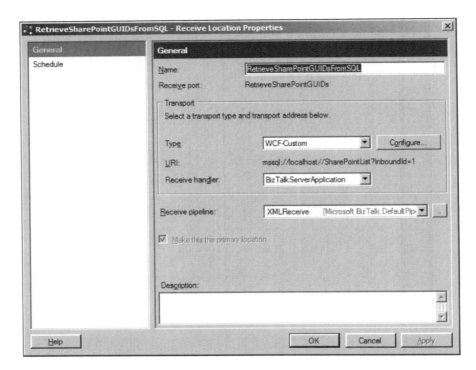

 Note: We can also use the WCF-SQL Adapter in this solution as well. Since the Consume Adapter Service Wizard specifies WCF-Custom Adapter in the binding file that it automatically generates we will use it. Essentially, both adapters are leveraging the sqlBinding so the underlying functionality is the same.

4. Within this Receive Location, we need to provide an **Address (URI)**. In this case, we can provide the following: `mssql://localhost//SharePointList?InboundId=1`. **Localhost** represents the Database Server hosting the **SharePointList** database. We also have to provide a unique **InboundId** for this connection in the event we have multiple polling Receive Locations configured to use this same database. For more information regarding the **InboundId** property, please refer to Chapter 2.

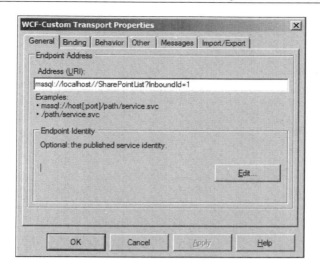

5. In the **Binding** tab, there are a few properties that we need to modify which are described below:

Property Name	Property Value	Description
Binding Type	sqlBinding	Since we are using the WCF-Custom Adapter, we need to provide a binding and since we are connecting to a SQL Server, we need to provide **sqlBinding**.
inboundOperation Type	TypedPolling	Our scenario uses TypedPolling as we are expecting a strongly typed message returned from our **pollingStatement** query.
polledData Available	Select count(*) from Lists	This property needs a query that when executed will determine whether or not to proceed with executing the **pollingStatement**. If this query does not return any data then the **pollingStatement** query will not be executed.
pollingIntervalIn Seconds	30	The interval in which we want to contact our SQL Server to retrieve data. This value is probably not valid in a production scenario, but for our demonstration purposes it will work. In a production scenario, we may not want to poll this frequently since each poll puts some stress on the database.
pollingStatement	Select ListGUID from Lists	This query will return the GUID that we will use when contacting SharePoint in order to retrieve our Custom List data.

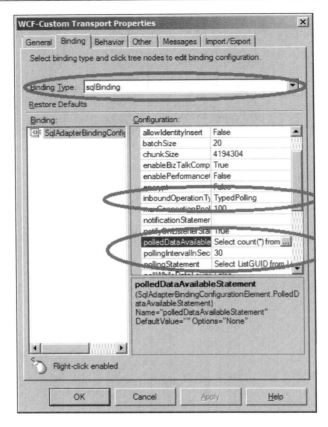

6. The remaining properties that have been set are default values for **the WCF-Custom** Adapter that uses the **sqlBinding**.

7. Our send port that we will use to communicate with SharePoint is called **cfSendPort_Lists_ListsSoap_Custom**. This send port will also use the **WCF-Custom** Adapter, the **BizTalkServerApplication** Host Instance, the **PassThruTransmit** Send Pipeline, and the **XMLReceive** Receive Pipeline.

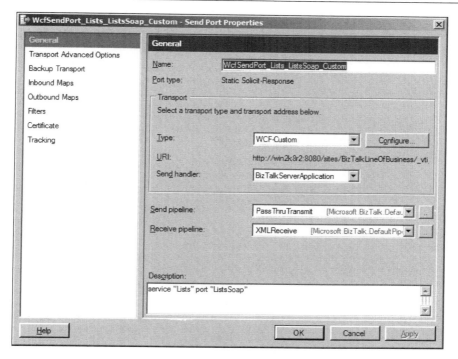

8. We now need to specify the URL of our `Lists.asmx` Web Service and our **Soap Action** header. The URL that is provided below represents the URL that was used to build this example. You will need to update this URL to reflect your SharePoint server. When we used the Consume WCF Service Wizard, it also generated a Binding file that we can use to populate our send port. One of the key benefits of this approach is the generated Binding file will include all of the **Soap Action Headers** including **GetListItemChanges** as follows:

```
<Operation Name="GetListItems" Action="http://schemas.microsoft.
com/sharepoint/soap/GetListItems" />
```

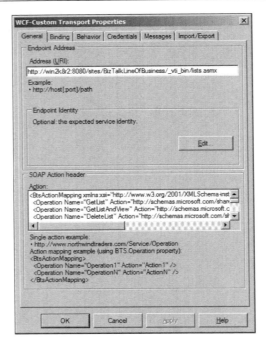

9. On the **Binding** tab, there are a few significant properties that we need to modify, which are described as follows:

Property Name	Property Value	Description
Binding Type	**basicHttpBinding**	This binding is our best option when consuming classic ASP.Net ASMX Web Services.
Security	**mode=Transport CredentialOnly**	Since the data that we are consuming is not sensitive we do not require any special message-based security for this scenario. We do need to provide credentials for SharePoint so that we can be authenticated and authorized in order to manipulate SharePoint Lists. In this scenario, our BizTalk Host Instance account will be passed. Our BizTalk Host instance account also requires Contribute access to the site that we are connecting to.
Security-Transport	**clientCredential Type=Ntlm**	Since our BizTalk Server and SharePoint Server exist in the same domain, we can utilize Ntlm credential types.

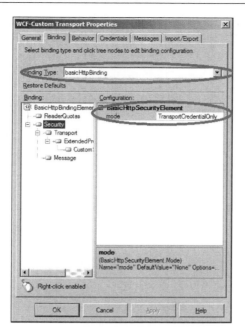

10. In the **Behavior** tab, we need to ensure that we have an **EndpointBehaviour** that has a type of **clientCredentials** and enable Windows **Impersonation**.

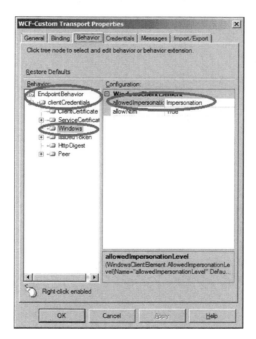

11. The remaining settings for this send port leverage the WCF-Custom Adapter's default properties for the basicHttpBinding.

12. Our final send port is responsible for sending our flat file to our ERP System. The name of this send port is **SendVehicleMaintananceListToERP**. It will leverage the **FILE** Adapter, the **BizTalkServerApplication** Host Instance, and our custom **SendVehicleMaintanence_FF** pipeline.

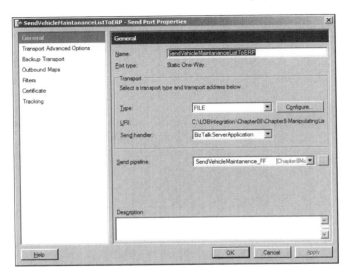

13. We now need to configure our Orchestration so we can set our Host Instance and link our Logical Ports with our Physical Ports.

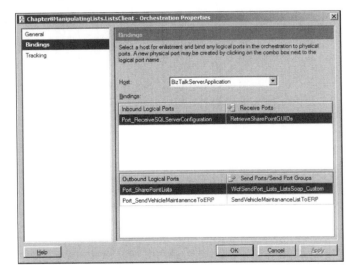

Testing BizTalk application

Before enabling our BizTalk application, let's go back to our List to ensure we have some data that we can retrieve via the SharePoint `Lists.asmx` Web Service.

1. Once we are at the list, we can add new records by clicking on the **Add new item** link.

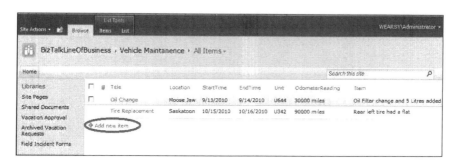

2. SharePoint provides a nice interface for us to add data to our Custom List.

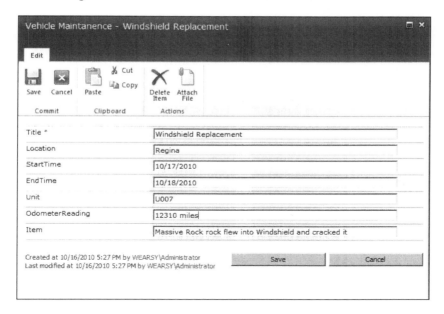

3. We now have three records that BizTalk should process once our application has been started.

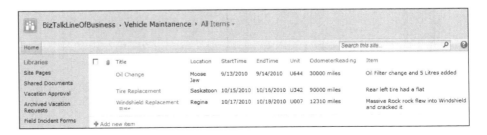

4. Let's now **Start** our application. Within 30 seconds, we should see a flat file generated for our ERP System to consume.

5. If we navigate to our ERP folder, we find that a CSV file has been generated for us.

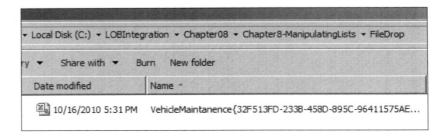

6. We can now open this file with a text editor like Notepad or Microsoft Excel. When we do so, we will discover that the three records in our custom SharePoint List are now included in this CSV file.

	A	B	C	D	E	F	G
1	Oil Change	Moose Jaw	9/13/2010	9/14/2010	U644	30000 miles	Oil Filter change and 5 Litres added
2	Tire Replacement	Saskatoon	10/15/2010	10/16/2010	U342	90000 miles	Rear left tire had a flat
3	Windshield Replacement	Regina	10/17/2010	10/18/2010	U007	12310 miles	Massive Rock rock flew into Windshield and cracked it

Note: Unlike the Windows SharePoint Services Adapter, the data that was retrieved from this Web Service has not been deleted. If we were interested in retrieving only the new records that have been added to our list since the last time we polled the database, we would have to implement this solution ourselves. This situation could easily be managed by adding a column to our SQL Server database that stored the **ID** of the record that we lasted retrieved. We would then use this **ID** as criteria in our CAML query.

Other ways to integrate with SharePoint

In the past two chapters, we have reviewed two ways that BizTalk can integrate with SharePoint: by leveraging the out-of-the-box Windows SharePoint Services Adapter and by consuming SharePoint's out-of-the-box Web Services. There are a couple other ways to integrate with SharePoint that we should also be aware of.

SharePoint Client Object Model

New in SharePoint 2010 is the SharePoint Client Object Model. The Client Object Model is primarily comprised of two assemblies called `Microsoft.SharePoint.Client.dll` and `Microsoft.SharePoint.Client.Runtime.dll`. When using these libraries, we need to reference them within our projects. This Client Object Model can be referenced by JavaScript, Silverlight, and the .NET CLR. The Client Object Model still relies upon CAML, much like the Web Services do, and the data being returned from SharePoint is also untyped, much like it is from the Web Services. The Client Object Model has the ability to manipulate Webs, Lists, List Items, Content Types, Fields, and External Lists.

If we wanted to leverage this Client Object Model from BizTalk, we would create a Helper .NET Assembly and then add the reference to the Object Model from within this Helper project. BizTalk would interact with this Helper Assembly through an Expression shape or Pipeline component. A benefit of this approach would be increased performance as we are avoiding the MessageBox and are communicating directly with SharePoint. A downside of this approach is we are avoiding the MessageBox and are responsible for the configuration of the service call. In the event that SharePoint is offline, or an error is raised, we need to deal with these situations ourselves. BizTalk provides in-depth tracking, message retries, and configuration that makes our jobs as developers much easier. By creating solutions that avoid these BizTalk core functions, we run the risk of developing solutions that are difficult to support.

SharePoint REST services

Earlier in this chapter, we discussed the inclusion of RESTful services in SharePoint 2010. Even though the BizTalk WCF-Custom Adapter has trouble processing the XML that is returned from these services, we can still get BizTalk to interact with these services with the help of WCF Data Services. From within a .NET Helper project, we can consume a WCF Data Service and can manipulate these lists. We will still be in the same situation as the Client Object Model when it comes to message retries, tracking, and configuration. However, we will have the advantage of consuming typed data that is returned from the Atom feeds.

Business Connectivity Services (BCS)

Another interesting feature of SharePoint 2010 is the Business Connectivity Services or BCS, which is not to be confused with America's College Football Bowl Championship Series that shares this same acronym. BCS is an update of a SharePoint 2007 feature called Business Data Catalogue (BDC). With BDC, SharePoint has the ability to consume data from external systems via Web Services and Database connections. For example, if we want to consume data from a SQL Server database, we could configure BDC to consume this data and display it as a list within SharePoint. This is an ideal solution when needing data from systems of record like ERPs. An example of how we can use this technology is being able to create a List of Employees within SharePoint, without maintaining the data in two places. We can simply use the BDC to retrieve Employee information for use within SharePoint. It is important to note that BDC/BCS does not copy the data; it is just referencing the data from the source system.

In addition to all of the functionality that the BDC provided, BCS provides the ability to write to data sources as well. This allows us to leverage SharePoint's User Interface to modify the data in other systems such as ERPs and CRMs. In addition to writing via Database connections, we can also write to .NET objects and Web/WCF Services. In many Database Scenarios, we can get away with these types of functions without writing any code. Interacting with .NET objects and Web Services will in all likelihood involve some code to be written.

Determining the right solution

So how do we know which approach to take? It really comes down to architectural direction from within our own organizations. If one of our architectural tenants includes reducing the amount of custom coding within our systems, then using BizTalk has a strong case.

If your organization is not adverse to custom coding and perhaps does not already have a BizTalk license, then using some of these other techniques outside of BizTalk has a lot of merit.

Summary

In this chapter, we discovered other ways we can integrate with SharePoint using the out-of-the-box Web Services that SharePoint provides. We were also introduced to other techniques that can be used to interact with SharePoint 2010 including the SharePoint Client Object model, RESTful services, and Business Connectivity Services.

In the next chapter, we will be moving away from SharePoint but continuing to discuss integration with ERP systems. This time instead of focusing on a generic ERP system, we will be investigating what is involved when integrating with Microsoft's ERP system Dynamics AX.

Microsoft Dynamics AX

9

In this chapter, we'll discuss integrating with Microsoft Dynamics AX 2009 using the BizTalk Dynamics AX adapter. It will be a complete walkthough for the configuration setup in the Dynamics AX 2009 Application Integration Framework (AIF)module and related set up for batch jobs. We'll complete two BizTalk applications that will demonstrate both synchronous and asynchronous forms of integration and show the benefits of using the AIF module.

The completed solutions are included in the code for this chapter. In the first walkthough example, we'll create a BizTalk application to populate the exchange rates table. In the second walkthough example, we'll create a BizTalk application that retrieves messages from Dynamics AX 2009 via the AIF Queue. Also included is a console application that demonstrates how to leverage the .NET business connector to integrate with Dynamics AX 2009.

We will specifically cover:

- What is Dynamics AX?
- Methods of integration with AX
- Installing the adapter and .NET Business Connector
- Configuring Dynamics AX 2009 Application Integration Framework for BizTalk Adapter
- Synchronous walkthrough example — Currency Exchange Rates
- Asynchronous walkthrough example — Dynamics AX message outflow
- Other development and configuration notes

What is Dynamics AX?

Microsoft Dynamics AX (formally **Microsoft Axapta**) is Microsoft's Enterprise Resource Planning (ERP) solution for mid-size and large customers. Much like SAP, Dynamics AX provides functions that are critical to businesses that can benefit from BizTalk's integration. Microsoft Dynamics AX is fully customizable and extensible through its rich development platform and tools. It has direct connections to products such as Microsoft BizTalk Server, Microsoft SQL Server, Exchange, and Office.

Often Dynamics AX is compared to SAP All in One. Those who are familiar with SAP are also familiar with high cost of implementation, maintenance, and customization associated with it. A Microsoft Dynamics AX solution offers more customizability, lower maintenance costs, and lower per-user costs than SAP. ERP implementations often fail in part due to lack of user acceptance in adopting a new system. The Dynamics AX user interface has a similar look and feel to other widely used products such as Microsoft Office and Microsoft Outlook, which significantly increases the user's comfort level when dealing with a new ERP system. For more information on Dynamics AX 2009 and SAP, please see http://www.microsoft.com/dynamics/en/us/compare-sap.aspx

Methods of integration with AX

Included with Dynamics AX 2009, Microsoft provides two tools for integration with Dynamics AX:

- Dynamics AX BizTalk Adapter
- .NET Business Connector

The BizTalk adapter interfaces via the **Application Interface Framework Module** (AIF) in Dynamics AX 2009, and the .NET Business Connector directly calls the Application Object Tree (AOT) classes in your AX source code.

The AIF module requires a license key, which can add cost to your integration projects if your organization has not purchased this module. It provides an extensible framework that enables integration via XML document exchange. A great advantage of the AIF module is its integration functionality with the BizTalk Dynamics AX adapter. Other adapters include a **FILE adapter** and **MSMQ**, as well as Web Services to consume XML files are included out of the box. The AIF module requires a fair amount of setup and configuration, which we will discuss later in this chapter. Other advantages include full and granular security, capability of synchronous and asynchronous mode integration mode, and full logging of transactions and error handling.

The Microsoft BizTalk AX 2009 adapter can execute AX actions (exposed functions to the AIF module) to write data to AX in both synch and asynch modes. Which mode is used is determined by the design of your BizTalk application (via logical ports). A one-way send port will put the XML data into the AIF queue, whereas a two-way send-receive port will execute the actions and return a response message. Asynch transitions will stay in the AIF queue until a batch job is executed. Setting up and executing the batch jobs can be very difficult to manage, something which we will discuss later in this chapter. Pulling data from AX can also be achieved using the BizTalk adapter. Transactions pushed into the same AIF queue (with an OUTBOUND direction in an async mode) can be retrieved using the AX adapter which polls AX for these transactions.

The .NET Business connector requires custom .NET code to be written in order to implement it. If your business requirements are for a single (or very small amount) of point-to-point integration data flows, then we would recommend using the .NET Business Connector. However, this often requires customizations in order to create and expose the methods. Security also needs to be handled with the service account that the code is running under. We'll touch on this later in this chapter and we've provided a working example with the source code for this chapter.

Installing the adapter and .NET Business Connector

The Microsoft BizTalk adapter for Dynamics AX 2009 and the .NET Business Connector are installed from your Dynamics AX Setup install setup under **Integration** on the **Add or Modify components** window. Each component is independent of one another; however the BizTalk adapter leverages components of the business connector. You are not required to install the Dynamics AX client on the BizTalk server. When installed in BizTalk adapter, you can simply select all the defaults from the install wizard. For the .NET business connector, you'll be prompted for the location of your Dynamics AX instance. This will be used only as a default configuration and can easily be changed.

Configuring Dynamics AX 2009 Application Integration Framework for BizTalk Adapter

Configuration of the AIF module involves several steps. It also goes a long way to increasing your understanding of the granularity of Dynamics AX setup and security considerations that were taken into account for integration of what can be highly sensitive data.It is recommended that this setup be done with Admin level security, however, only full control of the AIF module is required. This setup is almost identical in version prior to Dynamics AX 2009; minor differences will be noted.

1. All AIF setup tables can be found in Dynamics AX under **Basic | Setup | Application Integration Framework**.

2. The first step is rather simple, however critical. In the **Transport Adapters** form, add in a new entry selecting **Adapter Class** drop down **AifBizTalkAdapter**, select **Active**, and **Direction** will be **Receive and Respond**. You also notice there are two other out-of-the-box adapters: FILE and MSMQ. This is a one-time setup that is effective across all companies.

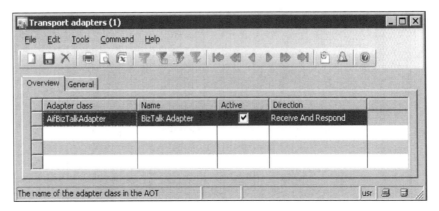

3. Next, using the **Channels** form, set up an active channel for your specific BizTalk server. Select a meaningful and identifiable **Channel ID** and **Name** such as **BizTalkChannelID** and **BizTalkChannel**. Select the **Adapter** to **BizTalk Adapter**, check **Active**, set **Direction** to **Both**, **Response channel** equal to the Channel ID of **BizTalkChannelID**. Set the **Address** to your BizTalk Server (**I2CDARS1** as shown below).

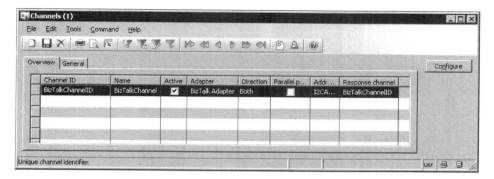

4. Then, click **Configure** to bring up the **BizTalk Adapter configuration** form. Again, set the **Server name** to the name of your BizTalk Server instance.

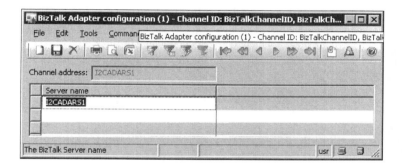

5. This configuration is required for secure connectivity during runtime. It is also required in order for Visual Studio to connect to your Dynamics AX 2009 instance when using the schema import wizard (we'll do this later in this chapter). This is also a one-time setup across all companies.

6. Now, in this step, we will set up a local endpoint from the **Local endpoints** form. Each company that your BizTalk application requires connectivity with will require a local endpoint. Select the **Company** you want to configure (**CDF** in our case) and type in **CDFLocalEndpoint** as shown.

> We recommend using this type of naming convention (**Company** + 'LocalEndpoint'), as often your BizTalk applications will need to specify this value. Often, the incoming message will contain data to determine which company it is intended for, thus, you'll need to dynamically determine the local endpoint during runtime. See the walkthrough example later in this chapter where we'll need to send currency exchange rates to multiple Dynamics AX companies.

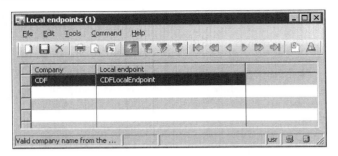

7. Next, we need to create an endpoint from the **Endpoints** form. The endpoint links together our local endpoint, BizTalk channel, BizTalk service account, and active Dynamics AX actions. Again, each company will require a local endpoint and thus we'll use the same naming conversion.

8. We'll start by typing in the **Endpoint ID** to **CDFEndpoint** and select the **Local endpoint ID** to **CDFLocalEndpoint**.

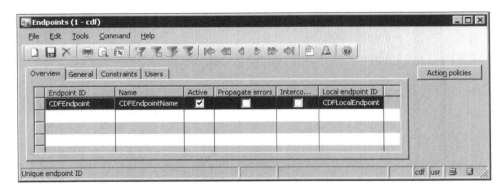

9. On the **General** tab, specify the **Outbound channel ID** to **BizTalkChannelID**, which we created above. This will also allow asynchronous outbound messages to be retrieved from Dynamics AX 2009 using the BizTalk adapter.

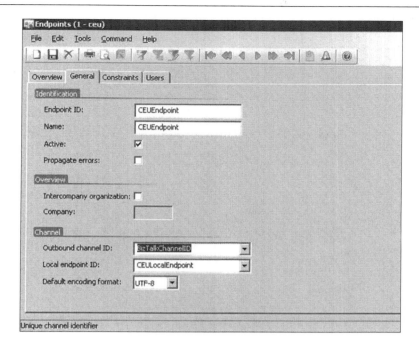

10. On the **Constraints** tab, we'll check **No constraints**. If required, you can specify constraints such as Customer and Vendor. Now, set the record to **Active** from the **General** tab and save.

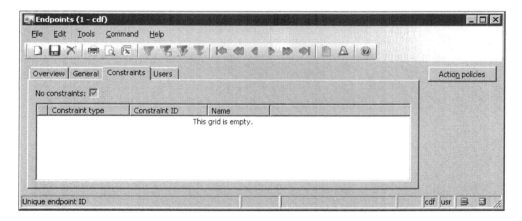

11. On the **Users** tab, we'll add the AX BizTalk user (linked to the Active Directory account that our BizTalk host instance is running under) by selecting **User type** to **User**, and then selecting the AX BizTalk (**cdar** in the example shown) user. Thus, all the records in AX will have this account as created by user. Depending on your integration requirements, this user may also need other associations such as employee.

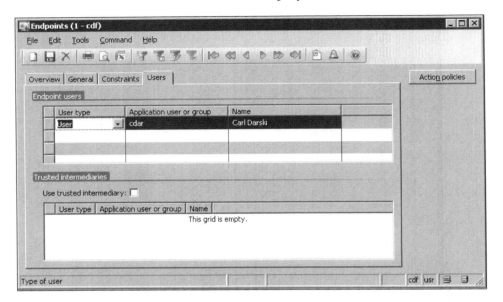

12. The next thing to do (after we have the AIF base configuration setup complete in AX) is to determine which **AIF Services** we are going to use. This will allow us to know what services to and thus which we need to enable. Each service has several actions associated with it. If there are no services out of the box with actions that meet our needs, we can either customize existing services or create our own. This is where the speed and ease of customizations in Dynamics AX are of great advantage.

 Note: Prior to AX 2009 actions were not grouped in services, thus no AIF Services table existed.

13. For this example, (we'll use this later in this chapter) we must use the out-of-the-box service **LedgerExchangeRatesService**. So, we will enable this service in the **AIF services** form as shown in the following screenshot:

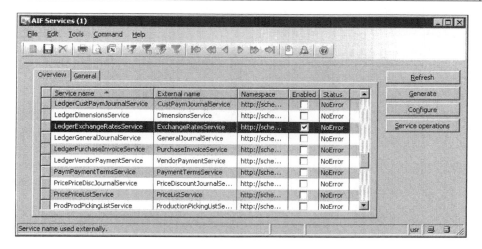

14. On the **AIF Services** form, we can examine the AX schema(s) for each by highlighting a **Service name**, clicking **Service operations**, selecting a specific **Action**, and then clicking **Parameter schema**. Actions include **create**, **delete**, **find**, **findkeys**, **read**, and **update**. Select the **SalesOrderService** and notice that there is no outbound schema for **delete** and **update** actions because these do not return a message.

A basic record in the Exchange Rates table only requires three fields: (1) Currency code, (2) Exchange Rate, and (3) From Date. We don't typically specify an end date as AX logic handles this when the next day's rate is entered.

Each AIF service will have its own security key associated with it. You must give the DynamicsAX BizTalk user account that access by assigning user permission to the required security keys in Dynamics AX 2009. In prior versions of Dynamics AX 2009, (where the AIF did not have services) security permissions had to be handled manually. This can be done by creating a security group with the permission needed to execute each AIF action and associating the Dynamics AX BizTalk user with the group.

1. Now that the AIF service is enabled, we can go over to the **Actions** form and see the four actions that are enabled. These are the actions that are a part of the AIF **LedgreExchangeRatesService** service. Notice we can't enable any default action individually without enabling the service (in previous versions of Dynamics AX each individual action was required to be enabled).

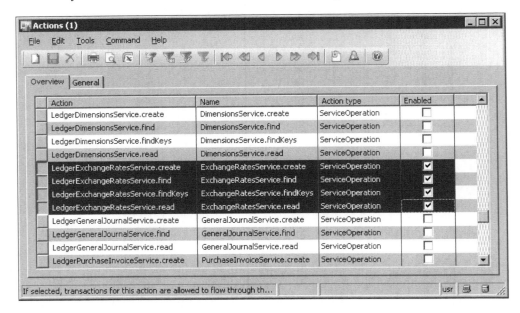

2. For each Dynamics AX company, you'll need to enter a currency relative to the base currency. Thus if you have one company whose currency is USD based, and another that's CAD based, then you'll need to enter a rate in each company for each currency. The USD-based company will require a USD/CAD rate to be entered, and the CAD-based company will need a CAD/USD rate entered. Thus, you'll need to repeat the following AIF **Actions** setup for each company's **Endpoint** if you're using the **LedgerExchangeRatesService** AIF Service.

3. Now, we go back to the **Endpoints** form and click on **Action policies** to bring up the **Endpoint Action Policies** form. Although we have activated the **LedgerExchangeRatesService**, the **Endpoint Action Policies** are action-specific, thus we need to create a record for each. Here, we'll select the **Action ID** to **LedgerExchangeRatesService.create** from the drop down; set the **Status** to **Enabled**, and **Logging Mode** to **Log All**. Now, we need to save the record. This will enable the **Configure** button on this form as shown in the following screenshot:

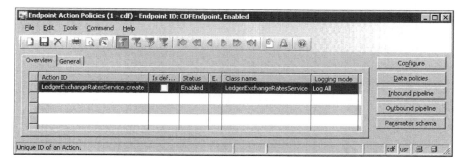

4. Next, click **Configure** to bring up the **Parameter Data Policies** window.

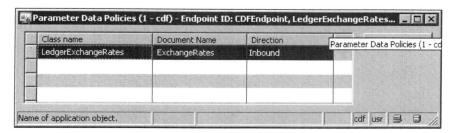

5. Click on **Data policies**; that will bring up the **Endpoint Action data policies** form. You'll notice that only the required fields are enabled. Here, we can get very granular in our security and data policies; however, with more complex AX actions this can get very tedious. Thus, simply click **Set** and then click **Enable all**.

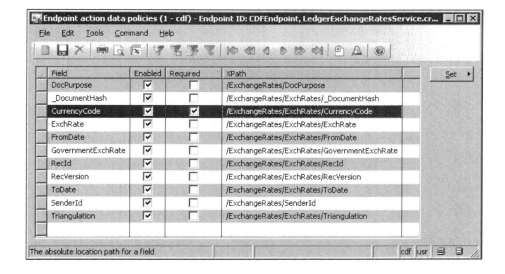

If you add customization to any Dynamics AX services, adding a new field for example, you need to (1) update the AIF Services by hitting the Refresh button (as in the figure above) and (2) enable the field in the Endpoint action data policies table.

Typically, an integration policy would be not to override the value in the Exchange Rate table (based on currency & date) if it already exists. In fact, if we attempt to send a duplicate rate, AIF will throw an error. We could simply catch and ignore this error; however, this would be introducing unnecessary clutter in the AIF exception log. Since we can expose this table to AX business users, we want to limit as much as possible the amount of errors that are thrown from the AIF module.

6. So, before we attempt to push an exchange rate we want to query AX so as to see if a particular rate already exists. To do this, we can use the out-of-the-box action **LedgerExchangeRates.find**. Note that the schema for the action will return a list of exchange rates. So now we'll need to repeat the above steps to enable this **Action** in the AIF **Actions** form, add it to the **Action policies** of our AIF **Endpoint**, and enable all the fields in the **Endpoint Action data policies** form. This completes the configuration of the AIF module in Dynamics AX in order to do the examples in this chapter that are next.

Synchronous walkthrough example—currency exchange rates

The best way to understand the behavior and setup required to use the Dynamics AX BizTalk adapter is to walk through a full example. A common requirement for many companies that use Dynamics AX is to populate the currency exchange rates. Typically, this needs to be daily when the closing rates are published. The **Exchange Rates(General ledger | Setup Exchange rates)** table in AX is not a shared table across companies, thus depending how your organization is set up; you may or may not need to populate the Exchange rate table using multiple companies with multiple rates. We'll further explain this shortly in the following example. We've found this to be an excellent practical example to begin with when learning to create integration applications with BizTalk and the Dynamics AX AIF module.

For this example, we are going to assume that we have twocompanies in our Dynamics AX implementation; one that is Canadian Dollar (CAD) based, and one that is United States Dollar(USD) based. Thus, we will need to repeat the AIF setup procedure (shown previously in this chapter) in order to use the **LedgerExchangeRates.create** and **LedgerExchangeRates.find** actions in both companies. For the remainder of this example, we'll refer to these as **daxCADCompany** and **daxUSDCompany**. The complete solution, titled **Chapter9-AXExchangeRates,** is included with the source code for this chapter.

Dynamics AX schemas

We'll start by creating a new BizTalk project, **Chapter9-AXExchangeRates**, in Visual Studio. After the AIF actions setup is complete (as shown previously in this chapter), the next step is to generate the required schemas that are needed for our BizTalk application. This is done by right clicking on the BizTalk project in Visual Studio 2010, click **Add**, highlight and click **Add Generated Items**. This will bring up the **Add Generated Items** window, under the **Templates** section — **Visual Studio installed template**, select **Add Adapter Metadata**, and click **Add**. This will bring up the **Add Adapter Wizard** window (shown in the following screenshot), so we'll simply select **Microsoft Dynamics AX 2009** and click **Next**. Now, we'll need to fill in the AX server instance name (**AX 2009-SHARED** in our example) under **Server name**, and the **TCP/IP Port** number (**2712,** which is the default port number, but this can differ). Now, click **Next** from the BizTalk Adapter for Microsoft Dynamics AX Schema Import Wizard window.

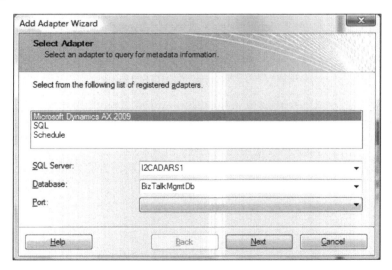

Specify the connection information in the next step.

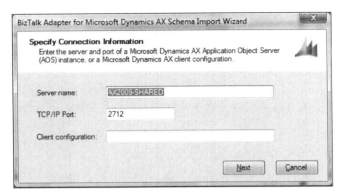

In the next window, you should see all the active AIF services. Note that since the AIF services table is a global table, so you will see all the active services in your Dynamics AX instance. This does not mean that each endpoint, thus each company, is configured to accept the actions that each AIF service listed has available. This is the point where you first verify that your connectivity and AIF setup is correct. An error here using the wizard typically is due to an error in the AIF channel configuration.

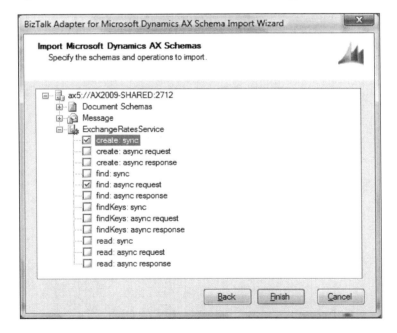

In the wizard window above, you can see the AIF services that are enabled. In our case, the **ExchangeRatesService** is the only service currently enabled in our Dynamics AX instance. Under this service, you will see three possible modes (**sync**, **async request**, and **async response**) to perform these actions. All three will actually produce the same schemas. Which mode and action (**create**, **find**, **findkeys**, or **read**) we use is actually determined by the metadata in our message we'll be sending to AX and the logical port configurations in our orchestration. Now, click **Finish**.

Now in the project solution, we see that the wizard will generate the two artifacts. The first **ExchangeRates_ExchangeRates.xsd** is the schema for the message type that we need to send when calling the **LedgerExchangeRates.create** action and it is also the same schema returned in the response message when calling the action **LedgerExchangeRates.find**. Since we are actually dealing with the same AX table in both actions, Exchange Rates, both actions will in part (one will be the inbound message, the other will be the outbound message) require the same schema.

The second artifact, **BizTalk Orchestration.odx**, is also generated by default by the wizard. In the orchestration view, we can see that four **Multi-part Message Types** were also added to the orchestration. Rename the orchestration to something more meaningful such as **ProcessExchangeRates.odx**.

Now that we have defined our message type that will be returned in our response message, we need to define what the request type will be. Notice from the orchestration view that two messages, **ExchangeRatesService_create_Response** and **ExchangeRatesService_find_Request,** have types which Visual Studio has in error 'does not exist or is invalid'.

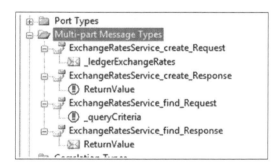

For the out-of-the-box *find* action, we need the message type **DynamicsAX5. QueryCriteria**. The other message type is return by AX when calling a create action is **DynamicsAX5.EntityKey** (if we called a createList action, the returned message would be of type **DynamicsAX5.EntitiyKeyList**).

The schemas for these message types are in the **Microsoft.Dynamics.BizTalk. Adapter.Schemas** assembly, which can be found in the bin directory of the install location of the BizTalk adapter. Add this reference to the project in Visual Studio. Then, re-select the appropriate message type for each Message Part that is invalid from the Select Artifact Type window as shown.

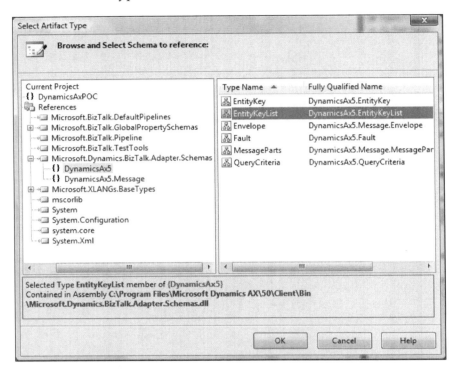

Next, depending on your organization, typically you may want to either populate the noon exchange rates or closing rates. For our example, we will use the closing USD/CAD exchange rates from the Bank of Canada. This is published at 16:30 EST on the website (http://www.bankofcanada.ca/rss/fx/close/fx-close.xml).

Since this source is already in XML, download and save a sample. We then generate a schema from Visual Studio using the BizTalk Schema Generator (right click the solution, **Add Generated Items**, **Add Generated Schemas**, using the **Well-Formed XML (Not Loaded)** document type. This will generate the schema for the message that we need to receive by our BizTalk application daily. In the example provided, the schema is **ClosingFxRates.xsd** (the wizard will generate four other .xsd files that are referenced in ClosingFxRates.xsd).

A simple way to schedule the download of this XML data file is to use the Schedule Task Adapter (`http://biztalkscheduledtask.codeplex.com/`), which can be downloaded and installed at no cost (the source code is also available). Download and install the adapter (requires Microsoft .NET Framework Version 1.1 Redistributable Package), then add using the BizTalk Server Administration Console with the name **Schedule**. We will use this adapter in our receive location to retrieve the XML via http. There are also RSS adapters available to be purchased from, for example, /nsoftware (`http://www.nsoftware.com/`). However, for this example, the scheduled task adapter will suffice.

Now, since the source of our exchange rates is a third-party schema, and your specific requirements for the source will most likely differ, we'll create a canonical schema **ExchangeRates.xsd**. As you can see in the schema below, we are only interested in a few pieces of information: **Base Currency** (USD or CAD in our example), **Target Currency** (again USD or CAD), **Rate**, and finally, **Date**. Creating a canonical schema will also simplify the rest of our solution.

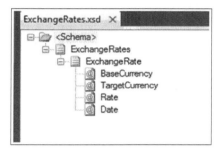

Now that we have all the schemas defined for our message types defined or referenced, we can add the messages that we require to the orchestration.

We'll begin by adding the message **msgClosingFxRates**. That will be our raw input data from the Bank of Canada with the message type from the generated schema **ClosingFxRates.RDF**.

For each exchange rate, we'll need to first query Dynamics AX to see if it exists, thus we'll need a request message and a response message. Add a message **msgAXQueryExchangeRatesRequest**, which will be a multi-part message type **ExchangeRatesService_find_Request**, and **msgAXQueryExchangeRatesResponse** that will be a multi-part message type **ExchangeRatesService_find_Response**.

Next, we'll create the messages for the XML that we'll send and receive from Dynamics AX to create an exchange rate. Add a message **msgAXCreateExchnageRatesRequest**, which will be a multi-part message type of **ExchangeRatesService_create_Request**, and **msgAXCreateExchnageRatesResponse** that will be a multi-part message type **ExchangeRatesService_create_Response**.

Finally, we'll need to create two messages, **msgExchangeRatesUSDCAD** and **msgExchangeRatesCADUSD**, which will have the message type of the canonical schema **ExchangeRates**. These messages will contain the exchange rates for USD to CAD and for CAD to USD respectively. We'll create these two messages just to simplify our orchestration for this example. In practice, if you're going to deal with several exchange rates, you will need to add logic to the orchestration to loop through the list rates that you're interested in and have only one message of type **ExchangeRates** resent several times.

As we talked about earlier in the chapter, we'll need to know the Dynamics AX company name in order to populate the metadata in our message sent to AX with the correct source and destination endpoint. For this example, we'll hard code these two company names with **daxCADCompany** and **daxUSDCompany** variables of type System.String. We'll add a variable, **needToLoadFxRateUSD**, of type System.Boolean that we'll use in our orchestration. Also, we'll hard code the variable **serviceAccountName** with the Active Directory service account that our BizTalk host instance is running under. Finally, we need a variable named **xpathQueryCADResultsExpression** of type System.String that we'll use to determine our query response message. The following is an orchestration view on the messages and variables:

Now, we'll need to add a logical receive port and two logical send ports in our orchestration.

Create a new logical receive port for the XML closing exchange rates from the Bank of Canada with the following settings:

Port Name	ReceiveClosingFxRates_Port
Port Type Name	ReceiveClosingFxRates_PortType
Communication Pattern	One-Way
Port direction of communication	I'll always be receiving messages on this port
Port Binding	Specify Later

Create a new send-receive logical port to Query Dynamics AX with the following settings:

Port Name	QueryAXExchangeRates_Port
Port Type Name	QueryAXExchangeRates_PortType
Communication Pattern	Request-Response
Port direction of communication	I'll be sending a request and receiving a response
Port Binding	Specify Later

Create a new second send-receive logical port to send the exchange rates create message with the following settings:

Port Name	CreateAXExchangeRates_Port
Port Type Name	CreateAXExchangeRates_PortType
Communication Pattern	Request-Response
Port direction of communication	I'll be sending a request andreceiving a response
Port Binding	Specify Later

Next, we'll need to create two maps to transform the Bank of Canada XML message to our canonical exchange rates messages. See the details for these two maps in the code example provided.

- ClosingFxRates_To_ExchangeRatesCADUSD.btm
    - CAD Base Currency — USD Target Currency

- ClosingFxRates_To_ExchangeRatesUSDCAD.btm
    - USD Base Currency — CAD Target Currency

Again, to limit the complexity of this example, we are somewhat hard-coding these two maps for our specific needs. If we needed to create many messages with different base/target currency combinations, then we would add logic to our orchestration and create a more complex map.

Now, we'll need to create two more maps to transform from our canonical ExchangeRates schema to (1) Query Dynamics AX for the particular rate and (2) ExchangeRatesService_ExchangeRates AIF schema generated by the BizTalk Dynamics AX adapter.

Dynamics AX query message

TheDynamicsAx5.QueryCriteria schema is shown in our map **ExchangeRates_To_ AXQueryExchangeRatesRequest.btm**. Each company in Dynamics AX will have a base currency, thus all exchange rates will be relative to that base. For each date, there can only exist one rate for a specific target currency, thus we'll construct a query and filter specifically for the date. Our query will return all exchange rates for a specific date with many target currencies, so we'll write an XPath expression to find the one we're interested in (shown later in this walkthrough).

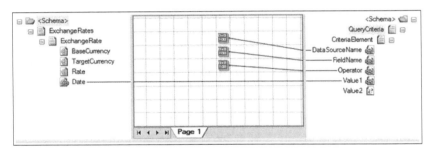

In the map above, we'll use String Concatenate functoids to store constants that we need to populate the **DataSoureName**, **FieldName**, and **Operator** elements of the **QueryCritera** schema. The **DataSouce** is the Dynamics AX 2009 table name, ExchRates. The **FieldName** is the column, the table, FromDate. Finally, the **Operator** we'll set to Equal.

Dynamics AX create message

As shown in the map **ExchangeRates_To_AXCreateExchangeRatesRequest.btm**, the transform is relatively simple. Dynamics AX exchange rates are based on a scale relative to 100 rather than 1, thus we'll need to multiply the value from our **ExchangeRates** schema by 100 using the Multiplication functoid as shown below. Notice that we can use this transform for any Base/Target currency combination.

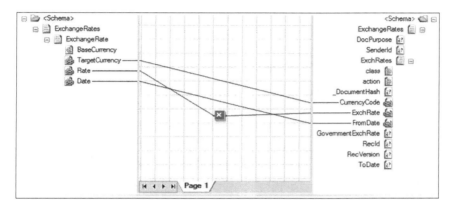

Also, notice that there are no dimensions in the **ExchangeRates** Dynamics AX schema. Typically, in most business-orientated messages, such as Sales Order, the schema would contain a single element for the dimensions. In this case, we would recommend first adding the exact number of String Concatenate functoids as dimension in your map and add links to the **element** field under the **Dimension** record in order from top to bottom in your Dynamics AX schema as shown below:

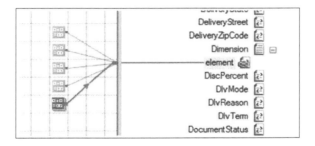

In each String Concatinate functoid as shown above, add zero length string input, and then add in the appropriate mapping logic for each dimension as an input to the relative concatenate functoid. This will ensure your output message will have the correct number of dimension elements and in the correct order, each time you add/delete/change a link in your map. To keep your maps readable, as a standard practice, you may choose to create a new page for mapping dimensions.

Continuing to build our orchestration, we'll add a **Receive** shape at the top to receive the **msgClosingFxRtes** message from the Bank of Canada and set the **Activate** property to True. Next, we'll add two **Construct** shapes to construct canonical messages **msgExchangeRatesUSDCAD** and **msgExchangeRatesCADUSD** each containing a transform shape using **ClosingFxRates_To_ExchangeRatesCADUSD. btm** and **ClosingFxRates_To_ExchangeRatesCADUSD.btm** respectively.

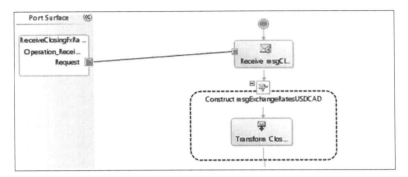

Orchestration setup

Now, we'll add one more **Construct** shape to construct our first **msgAXQueryExchangeRatesRequest** message (this will be to query our USD-based Dynamics AX company). We'll add a **Transform** shape for **ExchangeRates_To_ AXQueryExchangeRatesRequest.btm** and use the **msgExchangeRatesUSDCAD** as an input to the transform. After the transform shape, we'll need to add in Message Assignment shape to add out AIF metadata. The contents of the Message Assignment Shape are:

```
msgAXQueryExchangeRatesRequest(DynamicsAx5.MessageId) = System.String.
Format("{0:B}",System.Guid.NewGuid());
msgAXQueryExchangeRatesRequest(DynamicsAx5.Action) = "http://schemas.
microsoft.com/dynamics/2008/01/services/ExchangeRatesService/find";
msgAXQueryExchangeRatesRequest(DynamicsAx5.DestinationEndpoint) =
daxUSDCompany + "LocalEndpoint";
msgAXQueryExchangeRatesRequest(DynamicsAx5.SourceEndpoint) =
daxUSDCompany + "Endpoint";
msgAXQueryExchangeRatesRequest(DynamicsAx5.SourceEndpointUser) =
serviceAccountName;
```

This step is where we can see that our naming conversion in the AIF setup is very important. The AIF metadata in our message determines which **SourceEndpoint** and **DestinationEndpoint** (**Endpoint** and **Localendpoint** tables in the AIF setup respectively) this message is intended for. It also determines which AIF **Action** the message is executed against. The **SourceEndpointUser** must also explicitly set in the metadata for each message.

Now, we'll add in a send shape followed by a **Receive** shape to
Send the **msgAXQueryExchangeRatesRequest** and receive the
msgAXQueryExchangeRatesResponse messages. Now, connect the send and receive shapes to the **QueryAXExchangeRates_Port** port as shown in the falling image:

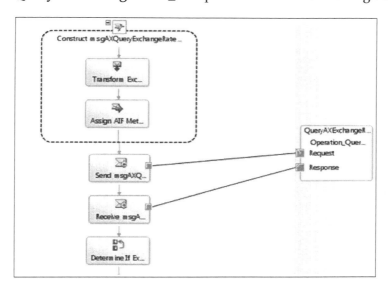

Next, we'll add in an expression shape. Since we'll receive ALL the exchange rates corresponding to a **FromDate** that we specified in our query message, we need to determine whether the USD-based company is a corresponding entry for the CAD currency. The contents of the expression shape to do this are:

```
xpathQueryCADResultsExpression = System.String.Format("/*[local-
name()='ExchangeRates']/*[local-name()='ExchRates']/*[local-
name()='CurrencyCode' and text()='{0}']", "CAD");

// If we find a result, then don't need to load
if(xpath(msgAXQueryExchangeRatesResponse.ReturnValue,
xpathQueryCADResultsExpression) != null)
{
needToLoadFxRate = false;
}
```

Since the query returns a list of exchange rates, we'll use XPath to quickly determine whether the rate for our base currency exists for the date. You'll probably notice that we've hard coded the **CAD** currency code in our **xpathQueryCADResultsExpression**. In a more complicated scenario with multiple target currencies, you'll need to add logic to find the corresponding currency code you're interested in. Also, since it's very possible that each day we won't have a rate for each currency (due to statutory holidays for example); you will need to include this logic for each currency/date combination.

Now, we'll add in a **Decide** shape based on the **needToLoadFxRate** Boolean variable we set in the expression shape. If we've found a rate for that date we'll do nothing, otherwise we'll construct the **msgAXCreateExchangeRatesRequest** message and send it to Dynamics AX.

In the branch of the decide shape where the rate was not found, we'll add in a Construct Message shape containing a transform followed by a Message Assignment shape. The map we'll use is **ExchangeRates_To_AXCreateExchangeRatesRequest. btm** with the **msgExchangeRatesUSDCAD** message as an input.

In the expression shape, we'll need again to add the AIF metadata. The contents are:

```
msgAXCreateExchangeRatesRequest(DynamicsAx5.MessageId) = System.
String.Format("{0:B}",System.Guid.NewGuid());
msgAXCreateExchangeRatesRequest(DynamicsAx5.Action) = "http://schemas.
microsoft.com/dynamics/2008/01/services/ExchangeRatesService/create";
msgAXCreateExchangeRatesRequest(DynamicsAx5.DestinationEndpoint) =
daxUSDCompany + "LocalEndpoint";
msgAXCreateExchangeRatesRequest(DynamicsAx5.SourceEndpoint) =
daxUSDCompany + "Endpoint";
msgAXCreateExchangeRatesRequest(DynamicsAx5.SourceEndpointUser) =
serviceAccountName;
```

Notice that only the **DynamicsAX5.Action** is different from the previous query message sent to AX. Also note the use of the **daxUSDCompany** variable here.

Now, add in a **Send** shape followed by a **Receive** shape to send the **msgAXCreateExchangeRatesRequest** and receive the **msgAXCreateExchangeRatesResponse** messages. Now, connect the send and receive shapes to the **CreateAXExchangeRates_Port**.

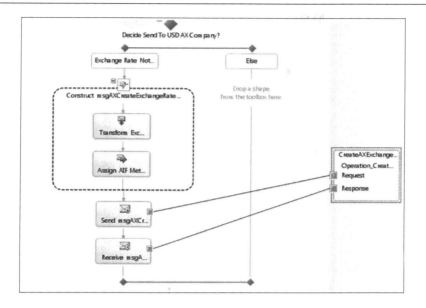

This completes the steps for sending a USD – CAD exchange rate to our USD-based Dynamics AX Company. To complete our example, we'll now add in the logic for the USD – CAD exchange rate to our CAD-based Dynamics AX Company. So, we'll repeat the above from the Orchestration Setup step using the **msgExchangeRatesCADUSD** and the **daxCADCompany** in place of **msgExchangeRatesUSDCAD** and **daxUSDCompany**. See the complete code example.

In the example source code provided, there's no error handling built into the orchestration. If there's an error an in sending a message to Dynamics AX, the port will throw an exception. Quite often, especially in versions of Dynamics AX prior to AX 2009, the error message can be quite generic or cryptic at times. Connectivity errors will have some meaningful error message; however, logical errors will not. This is because the AIF module is an external facing interface, so the detailed error message most helpful is found in the **Exceptions** (**Basic | Periodic | Application Integration Framework | Exceptions**) form in the AIF module.

Now that we can build and deploy the solution, the next step will be to set up our Port configuration in the BizTalk Server Administration Console.

Port configuration

We'll begin by creating a **Static Solicit-Response Send Port** and type in a **Name** of **AXExchangeRates_SendReceivePort**.

1. We'll set the **Type** to **Microsoft Dynamics AX 2009**, and set the **Send pipeline** and **Receive pipeline** to **XML Transmit** and **XML Receive** respectively.

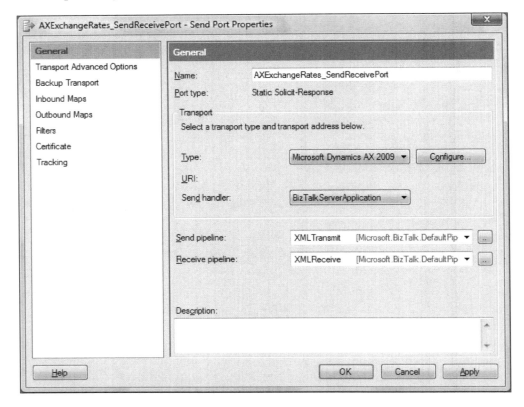

2. Click **Configure** to bring up the **Microsoft Dynamics AX 2009 Transport Properties** window.

3. Here, we'll select an **Authentication Type** to **Host User** from the drop-down list and set the **Gateway User** to our Active Directory service account that our BizTalk Host instance is running under. We'll set the **AOS Port** to **2712** and **AOS Server** to our Dynamics AX 2009 server name **AX 2009-SHARED**. We can leave the default Synchronous Timeout to 20 minutes.

4. Click **Ok** to save this configuration.

5. Next, we'll continue with the port configuration by creating a **One-way Receive Port**, named **ReceiveClosingFxRates_ReceivePort**, with a receive location named **ReceiveClosingFxRates_ReceiveLocation**. We'll use a **Type** of **Schedule** and set the **Receive pipeline** to **XML Receive**.

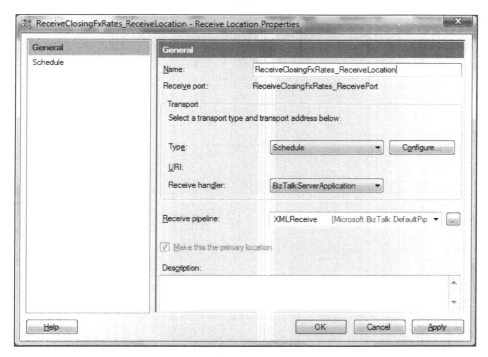

6. Next, click **Configure** to bring up the Schedule Transport Properties window. Here, we'll type in a **Name** of **Bank of Canada**, and set the configuration **Schedule** to **Daily Schedule** with a **Start Time** of **5:00 pm** (assume our server time is EST). Note we'll configure it to run daily, regardless of weekends or bank holidays (when no new rates are available), as our orchestration does the query to AX before attempting to create a new exchange rate.

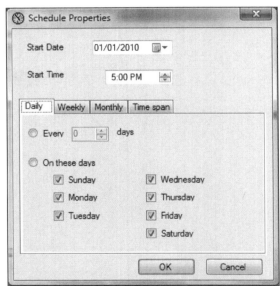

7. Now, click on the **Task properties** field form the **Schedule Transport Properties** window to bring up the **Task Properties** window.

8. Here, click **Find Task,** which brings up the **Assembly Qualified Type Name** window. Click on the **Browse** button, select the **ScheduledTask. TaskComponents.dll** assembly and click open. Now, double click **HttpDownload** and click **Select**. Click **Ok**. Finally, in the **Task Properties**window, type in the URL http://www.bankofcanada.ca/rss/ fx/close/fx-close.xml, leave the user name blank as no authentication is required. Click **OK** twice and save.

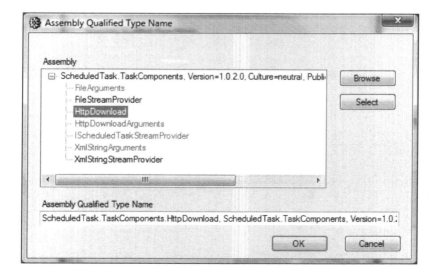

9. On the Orchestration Properties, we'll assign the logical receive port to the physical port we just created and set both Outbound Logical Ports to the physical send port to connect to Dynamics AX 2009.

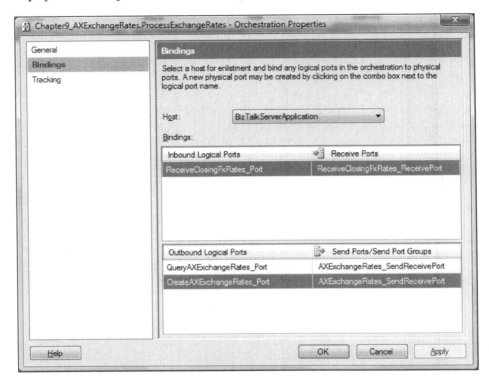

10. After we start our application, it's now time to test it. We can either wait until 5:00 pm, or simply change the **Start Time** in the **Schedule Properties** window to a couple minutes past the current time. You'll see a log message in the Windows event log indicating the configuration has changed for the schedule task.

11. After the scheduled task adapter has fired, and the orchestration has successfully completed, navigate to the **Document history** form (**Basic | Periodic | Application Integration Framework | Document History**) in Dynamics AX 2009. Here, you'll see a log for all four messages that were sent and received from our BizTalk application. You can also view the XML message by highlighting one of the Document history log entries, clicking **Document logs** to bring up the **Document log** form, and finally clicking **View XML**.

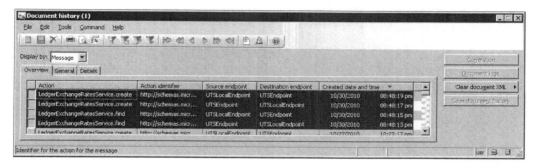

12. Verify that the exchange rate has been created in the table (**General Ledger | Setup | Exchange Rates**).

13. Note that the **Document history** form is company specific and will log all transactions both successful and those that went to error. However, the **Exceptions** form log is not company specific. Thus, attempting to link an exception to the document history entry can prove to be difficult.

Asynchronous walkthrough example— Dynamics AX message outflow

Now that the setup for sending data using AIF XML documents to AX is complete, we can also use the BizTalk adapter to retrieve data from Dynamics AX via this AIF module. This is done using the AIF **Queue manager**. Throughout Dynamics AX, there are **Send electronically** buttons that can allow you to push data into the AIF Queue with an **Outbound** direction. Similarly, asynchronous incoming messages have an **Inbound** direction parameter.

We found that rather than repeating code in several BizTalk solutions when you need to retrieve data from the AIF Queue, it's relatively simple to create a general solution to accomplish this. This solution will retrieve all data via the BizTalk Dynamics AX adapter by polling the Queue at a set interval of time. The minimum polling interval is 1 minute, thus any messages you put in the AIF Queue will not be immediately consumed by BizTalk. The complete solution (Chapter9-AXMessageOutflow) is included with the source code for this chapter.

We'll start by creating a new BizTalk project, **Chapter9-AXMessageOutflow**, in Visual Studio. Add in a new orchestration, **ProcessOutboundAXMessage.odx**, which will be the only orchestration required for this example. Also, we'll need to add reference to the **Microsoft.Dynamics.BizTalk.Adapter.Schemas** assembly and sign the project with a strong name key.

Message setup

Next, we'll add two messages to our orchestration: **msgAxOutboundMessage** and **msgAXDocument**. These will be the only two messages required in this example.

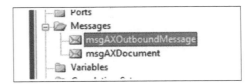

The first message, **msgAXOutboundMessage,** is of type **DynamicsAX5.Message. Envelope**. The schema is located in the referenced Microsoft.Dynamics.BizTalk. Adapter.Schemas assembly.

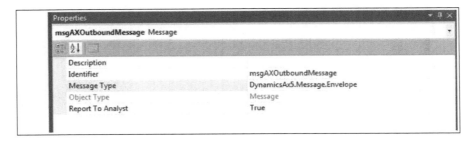

All outbound messages from the AIF Queue are of this type. As you can see from the sample screenshot below, we have some metadata in the header node but what we are really interested in is the XML contents of the Body node. The contents of the **MessageParts** node in the Body node will be of type **ExchangeRatesService_ExchangeRates.xsd** that we used in the previous example to send this same message to AX. Thus, all the schemas we require for both inbound and outbound transactions can be generated using the adapter.

For the second message, since we don't want to specify a document type, we will use **System.Xml.XmlDocument** for the **Message Type**.

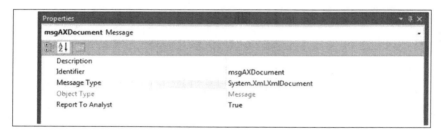

Using the **System.Xml.XmlDocument** message type allows for great flexibility in this solution. We can push any message to the AIF queue, and no changes to this BizTalk application are required. Only changes to consuming applications may need to add the AX schema of the message in order to process it.

Orchestration setup

Next, we create a new a logical port that will receive all messages from Dynamics AX via the AIF Queue with the following settings:

Port Name	ReceiveAXOutboundMessage_Port
Port Type Name	ReceiveAXOutboundMessage_PortType
Communication Pattern	One-Way
Port direction of communication	I'll always be receiving messages on this port
Port Binding	Specify Later

Also, create a new send port. For this example, we'll just send to a folder drop using the FILE adapter so that we can easily view the XML documents. In practice, other BizTalk applications will most likely process these messages, so you may choose to modify the send port to meet your requirements. Send port settings:

Port Name	SendAXDocument_Port
Port Type Name	SendAXDocument_PortType
Communication Pattern	One-Way
Port direction of communication	I'll always be sending messages on this port
Port Binding	Specify Later

Next, we will need to add the following to the orchestration:

- Receive shape (receive msgAXOutboundMessage message)
- Expression shape (determine the file name for msgAXDocument)
- Message assignment (construct msgAXDocument message)
- Send shape (send msgAXDocument message)

We'll also add two variables (**aifActionName** and **xpathExpression**) of type System. String and **xmlDoc** of type System.Xml.XmlDocument.

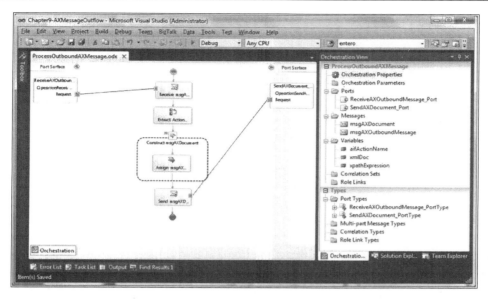

In the expression shape, we want to extract the AIF Action so that we can name the outbound XML documents in a similar fashion. This will allow us to easily identify the message type from AX.

Next, we'll put the following inside expression shape below receive to extract the AIF action name, which we'll use later in our outbound message:

```
aifActionName = msgAXOutboundMessage(DynamicsAx5.Action);
aifActionName = aifActionName.Substring(55,aifActionName.
LastIndexOf('/') - 55);
```

Now, we need to extract the contents of the body message, which is the XML document that we are interested in. Inside the message assignment shape, we will use XPath to extract the message. What we are interested in is the contents of the Body node in the DynamicsAX5.Message.Envelope message we will receive from AX via the AIF Queue. Add the following code inside the assignment shape to extract the XML, assign it to the message we are sending out, and set a common name that we can use in our send port:

```
// Extract Contents of Body node in Envelope Message
xpathExpression = "/*[local-name()='Envelope' and namespace-
uri()='http://schemas.microsoft.com/dynamics/2008/01/documents/
Message']/*[local-name()='Body'
and namespace-uri()='http://schemas.microsoft.com/dynamics/2008/01/
documents/Message']";
```

```
xmlDoc = xpath(msgAXOutboundMessage, xpathExpression);

// Extract the XML we are interested in
xmlDoc.LoadXml(xmlDoc.FirstChild.FirstChild.InnerXml);

// Set the message to the XML Document
msgAXDocument = xmlDoc;

// Assign FILE.ReceivedFileNameproperty
msgAXDocument(FILE.ReceivedFileName) = aifActionName;
```

We can now build and deploy the solution. Next, we'll go through setting up the physical ports and binding them to our orchestration.

Port configuration

Create a new receive port, **ReceiveAxOuboundMessage_ReceivePort**, and a new receive location, **ReceiveAxOuboundMessage_ReceiveLocation**. Set the type to Microsoft Dynamics AX 2009, and we need to select a **PassThruReceive** for the **Receive pipeline**.

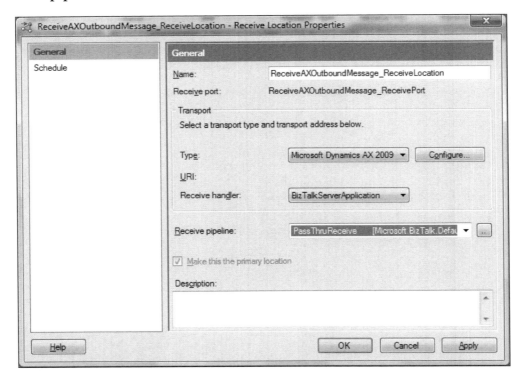

Click **Configure** to bring up the **Microsoft Dynamics AX 2009 Transport Properties** window. Here, we'll set the **Authentication Type** to **Host User**, set the **Gateway User** to the Active Directory account that our BizTalk Host Instance is running under, **AOS Port** to **2712**, and **AOS Server** to our AX server name (**AX 2009-SHARED**). Also, we set the **Polling interval** to **1** minute, and finally, we must set the **Pass Through** to **True**. This allows our solution to use the adapter without parsing the message. If we set this to `False`, the adapter will attempt to resolve the message type in the AIF queue before removing it and set it to an error status if it's unsuccessful.

Next, we'll create a **Static One-way Send Port** with **Name** set to **SendAxDocument_ SendPort** to bind to our logical send port. Set the **Type** to **File**, and **Send pipeline** to **PassThruTransmit** as we'll perhaps be sending different message types out as XML documents.

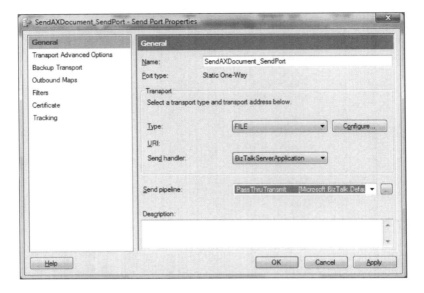

Click **Configure** to bring up the **FILE Transport Properties** window. Set the **Destination folder** to **C:\LOBIntegration\Chapter09\Chapter9- AXMessageOutflow\AXOutboundDocuments** and File name to `%SourceFileName%` `- %datetime% - %MessageID%.xml`. The `SourceFileName` for each message type will be identical as it was set in our orchestration above to the Dynamics AX action name. The `datetime` is added to the file name property because we often find it helpful in troubleshooting errors or sometimes it is required for future integration logic.

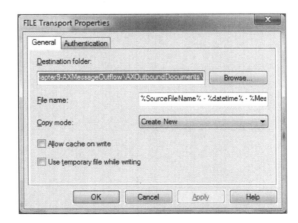

Now, we bind the two ports to the orchestration and start the BizTalk application. Since there's nothing in the AIF Queue for us to pick up, we won't see anything much on the BizTalk server side. However, if you log into Dynamics AX, go to **Online users** (**Administration | Online users**) and you can verify that your BizTalk application is indeed connected. There will be one connect, with **Session type** of **Worker** that will verify your connection. Click the refresh button continuously, and you will see the **Session type** of **Business Connector** appear every minute (our application polling interval set on the port).

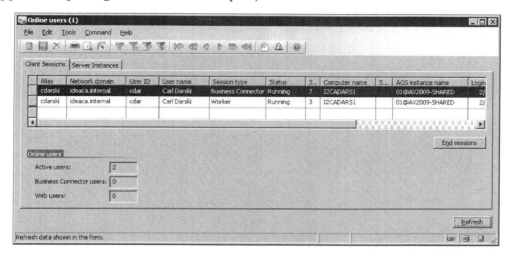

Now that we have verified that we have connectivity, we need to send a message to the AIF Queue in order to run a test. Disable the receive location for now so that we can see what's happening inside AX before it's removed from the Queue.

There are many forms in Dynamics AX (Exchange Rates for example) where you'll see a **Send Electronically** button. Click on the button from the Exchange Rates table and you'll see the **Send document electronically** window pop up. You need to select an **Endpoint ID** and can put filter criteria from the Select button if you wish. Notice that only Endpoints that have the LedgerExchangeRates AIF service actions enable will appear in the drop-down list.

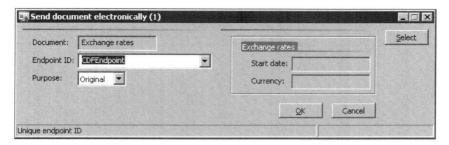

Click **Ok** to send the message to the AIF Queue. Now, try and click on **Send electronically** on the **Chart of Accounts** table (**General Ledger | Chart of Accounts**) and notice the error message as shown in the following screenshot. Since we have not activated this AIF Service, nor added the services' actions to any Endpoints, Dynamics AX does not allow us to send out this message.

Next, we'll open up the AIF **Queue manager** form (**Basic | Setup | AIF | Queue manager**) and here we can see the message we just sent from the Exchange Rates tables. Notice that the log entry is missing Channel and Source Endpoint. This is because by default, the **Send Electronically** button is an asych process that requires a batch to be run in order to specify the Channel (BizTalk in our case) based on the configuration of the **Destination endpoint**.

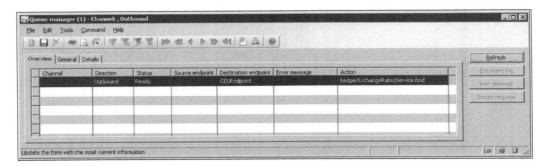

Batch setup in Dynamics AX

Now we need to set up a batch in order to send this **Outbound** message through the BizTalk channel. If we had previously sent out messages from BizTalk in an asynchronous mode, it would also have appeared here and required a batch in order to be processed. Note it is also possible to customize methods in Dynamics AX that still write messages to the AIF queue, but do not require a batch in order to be picked up by our BizTalk application.

Dynamics AX 2009 allows for batch jobs to be run on the server; however, previous versions required an active client in order to run batch jobs. As you can imagine, keeping open an active client to run a continuous batch job, or manually starting a batch job when required can be very cumbersome in a live production environment. Even with server-side batch job capability, you opt to only do synchronous integration to eliminate the need for any batch job altogether.

So, we'll need to create a batch for this example. First, we'll create a new entry in the **Batch job (Basic | Inquiries | Batch job)** table. We'll type in Job description of **AIF BATCH** and hit **Save**.

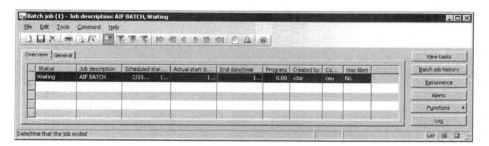

Next, click on **View Tasks** button, which will bring up the **Batch tasks** form. Here, we need to add four new entries, one for each AIF class (**AifOutboundProcesssingService**, **AifInboundProcessingService**, **AIFgatewaySendService**, **AIFGatewayReceiveService**) from the drop-down list and set the **Company accounts** for each. Since the batch tasks are company specific, you can imagine this may add significant management overhead to your integration processes.

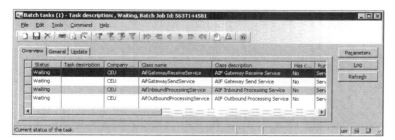

After configuring the batch tasks, save and close the window. Go back to the **Batch Job** form and click on the **Recurrence** button that will be the window below. Here, we can configure several parameters, but for our example simply set the **Recurring pattern Count** to **1** and select **Minutes**.

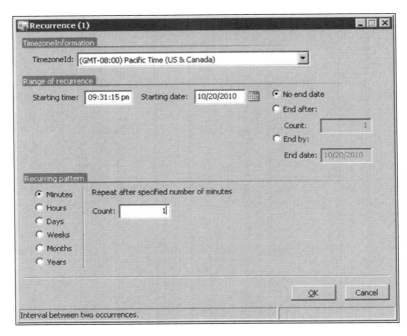

Click **Ok**. Again back on the **Batch job** form, click on the **Functions** button, which brings up the **Select new status** window.

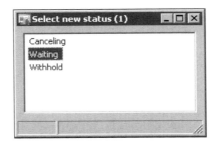

Select **Waiting** to activate the batch job. Now, we go back to the AIF **Queue manager** form. Click refresh after approximately one minute and you'll see the same **Outbound** record we previously sent. However, you'll notice the **Channel** and **Source endpoint** have now been populated. Also note that the status is still set to **Ready**.

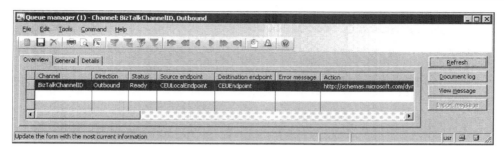

Now, we go back and enable the receive location on your BizTalk solution. You should see this record be removed from AIF Queue, and find the XML document in the folder specified on the send port.

Note that this record we just pulled from the AIF Queue will appear in the AIF **Document history** table. You can view the XML by selecting a record, clicking on **Document logs**, and then clicking on **View XML**.

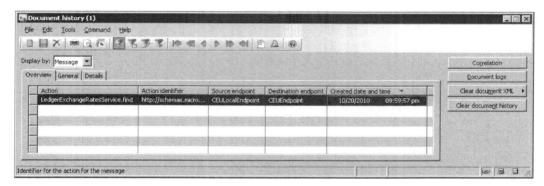

If we have any errors, a detailed message will appear in the AIF **Exceptions (Basic | Periodic | Application Integration Framework | Exceptions)** form and the status of the outbound record in the Queue manager will change to Error. It's possible to fix the error and then change the status back to Ready.

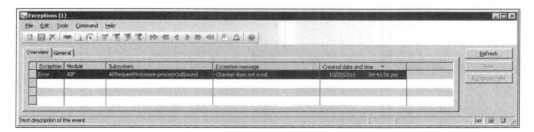

For example, if we had not specified an outbound channel in our Endpoint configuration, the error seen above would have appeared when the batch job executed. Thus, we could go back, add in the BizTalk channel to the configuration, change the status of the message in the Queue to Ready; then, the next time the batch job executed, the message would be ready to be extracted by our BizTalk application.

Using the .NET business connector

The .NET business connector allows for integration with AX without BizTalk. The BizTalk Dynamics Adapter actually leverages the .NET business connector. However, it runs independently and does not require BizTalk to be installed.

Install the business connector from the Dynamics AX setup install. You'll see it under the optional components on the AX install screen. You do not need to install the Dynamics AX client or any other Dynamics components in order for it to operate. Take caution that you install the correct version that exactly matches the version of your AX environment; otherwise at runtime you receive a generic error message in your windows event log with no clear indication as to what is wrong.

The business connector acts as a GUI-less client that can be called from a custom .NET assembly. On installation, you'll be prompted for a Dynamics environment that will be used for an initial configuration; this can be changed after installation. As shown in the example included with the source code for this chapter, the AX instance to which the business connector is configured to can be specified at runtime. The best practice is to use the configuration file that your Dynamics AX system administrator should provide (this is the same configuration file that the AX client uses in order to establish a connection to the AOS). If at runtime, you do not specify a configuration, the default configuration from the business connector setup will be used. Run the **Microsoft Dynamics AX Configuration Utility** to manage your default configuration, shown as follows:

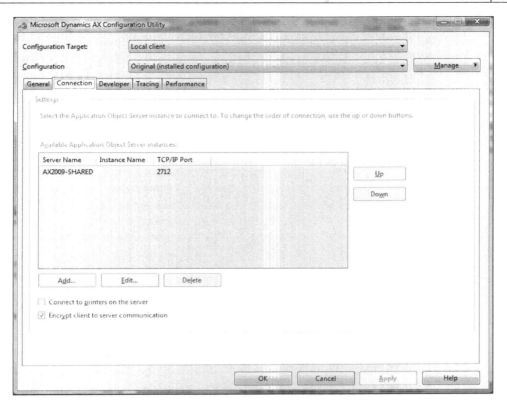

In the attached console application example (complete solution **Chapter9-AXBusinessConnector** is included with the source code for this chapter) we create a simple session object to query a table in Dynamics AX. A more practical example would be to call a static method with parameters that returns, for example, an AxaptaContainer object. See `http://msdn.microsoft.com/en-us/library/aa659581.aspx` for more details on the use of the .NET Business Connector as we could write an entire chapter on this topic alone which is not the intent of this book.

Note that it's very important to correctly dispose of each connection as the .NET business connector will not handle this on its own if an error occurs. As you can imagine, going unmonitored could have disastrous consequences that could result in requiring a restart of your AOS.

Each connection is similar to a connection using the Dynamics AX client in terms of security. Thus, be aware of possible performance issues if your AX user is a member of multiple security groups. Also, keep in mind that classes in Dynamics AX are not thread safe, so verify that your integration logic takes this into account. Use the .NET business connector with your custom code with care.

This example simply does a query on an AX table for the company name, however, it does point out a few key concepts including disposal of your connection, use of retries, and authentication. In the **Program.cs** file, simply replace the constants, build, and run.

 Note we need to reference **Microsoft.Dynamics. BusinessConnectorNet** and **System.Web** assemblies, and the code provided has a Target framework set to **.Net Framework 3.5**.

Other development and configuration notes

Development

It is very possible that your integration needs with Dynamics AX will require some sort of customization in order to take advantage of the AIF module. Many organizations are very much against over customizing third-party systems. However, Dynamics AX was built on the concept of customizations, thus a happy medium can usually be reached in custom development requirements for integration.

A custom service can be created to integrate on practically any Dynamics AX object, which will allow for find, create, read, update, and delete actions to be customized. Dynamics AX versions prior to AX 4.0 SP2 do not allow for delete actions to be performed in AIF actions. If required, you can customize the existing code functionality to perform delete action if required, for example, by setting a custom flag. However, you will still need to use existing actions that are exposed.

For development, it is recommended the user under which Visual Studio is running be a member of the Admin security group in your development instance of Dynamics AX. Your production BizTalk service account can also be a member of the Admin role, which makes it a powerful account, but eliminates the need for granular security requirements.

Configuration

Typically, your organization will have multiple AOS instances running in order to ensure high availability and acceptable online performance. You may be able to schedule all your high resource demand integration tasks during off-peak hours by running batch job processes as mentioned previously in this chapter. However, typically, business level integration is required (or preferred) in near real time. In order to minimize the impact to online users, you may want to consider creating a separate AOS for integration tasks only.

On the AIF services form, the Refresh button will scan the entire **AOT (Application Object Tree)** for AIF Services and populate all the found results. If the user logged in only has partial permission to a particular service that joins multiple objects, then the schema generated may only be partly complete. Therefore, access to this table (or even more specifically the refresh button) should be limited to system administrators if at all possible.

Maintenance

Scheduling integration tasks during off peak hours also has the disadvantage that your support staff for both BizTalk and Dynamics AX is much less available to diagnose errors. Support for AX integration is often a combination of business knowledge and BizTalk technical integration skill. We highly recommend at very minimum that your BizTalk support team has view access to the AIF **Queue manager**, **Exceptions**, and **Document history** forms and all the AIF configuration forms. View access to the **On-line user's** form can also be very helpful in confirming connectivity.

After an unscheduled outage of your Dynamics AX instance, you often need to restart the BizTalk host instance to reconnect to the AOS. Thus, we would recommend running your BizTalk application for Dynamics AX under a separate host instance from your other applications. The same holds true for any services leveraging the .NET Business Connector.

Summary

In this chapter, we discussed the advantages of using the BizTalk Dynamics AX 2009 adapter for our BizTalk integration applications. We went through the required configuration setup of the Application Integration Framework module in Dynamics AX 2009.

In our first example, we used the out-of-the-box AIF services **LedgerExchangeRatesService** to create a currency exchange rate application that demonstrated the synchronous integration mode of the BizTalk adapter. In the second example, we created a generic solution to retrieve outbound message from Dynamics which demonstrated the set requirement for asynchronous integration including batch jobs.

Finally, we touched on using the .**NET Business Connector** for integration with Dynamics AX and discussed the implications to consider when writing custom applications without leveraging the AIF module. In the next chapter, we'll discuss the integration with SalesForce CRM. A popular CRM that runs in the "cloud".

10
Integrating BizTalk Server and Salesforce.com

Software as a Service (SaaS) is a trend in enterprise software that cannot, and should not, be ignored. Legitimate SaaS offerings provide a highly scalable, reliable, and configurable environment hosted outside your organization. Unlike traditional Application Service Providers (ASP), SaaS providers leverage a multi-tenet, metadata-driven architecture that typically runs a single instance and version of the software for all users. This means that customers have no upfront infrastructure costs, see regular software updates without significant "upgrade projects", and are assured of a strong service-level agreement for application performance.

While we may adopt a SaaS product such as Salesforce.com for a particular solution, what do we do with the existing on-premises systems that house our critical information and algorithms? How do we share data between SaaS environments and on-premises sources? We will answer that question in this chapter.

In this chapter, we will cover:

- What Salesforce.com is and why we might want to connect it with BizTalk Server
- How to use BizTalk Server to pull data from Salesforce.com
- Tools and techniques for sending data and query requests from Salesforce. com to BizTalk Server

What is Salesforce.com?

Salesforce.com is a cloud computing company that sells subscriptions to enterprise software solutions. It is a viable option for the standard Customer Relationship Management (CRM) focus areas such as Sales, Marketing, and Customer Service. You will find traditional CRM features such as account management, customer tracking, opportunity management, sales history, case management, and much more. Salesforce.com also has some innovative capabilities such as Chatter, which is a Facebook-like collaboration tool for sharing information across an organization.

While Salesforce.com in itself is an excellent offering, the real excitement for technologists should be reserved for their underlying Force.com platform. Force.com is the Platform as a Service (PaaS) software on which Salesforce.com is built. What's more, Salesforce.com has made the Force.com platform available to external developers to build and extend cloud-based applications.

Force.com is targeted to (structured) data-driven applications that would benefit from a cloud-hosted set of foundational platform services. Instead of focusing time and energy on constructing a hosting infrastructure, user interface framework, web service tier, security framework and reporting tools, developers can use these built-in features of Force.com to rapidly deploy rich, dependable, and secure systems.

When we write code in a Force.com application, we use a Java/C#-like language called Apex. It is a language specific to Force.com applications, but you will find it fairly easy to pick up and understand. New web pages are built using Visualforce technology that leverages standard HTML, JavaScript, and Apex-specific tags. Each object in a Force.com application can be accessed via either SOAP or REST service interfaces. This opens up a host of scenarios for integrating Salesforce.com data with data stored elsewhere.

Why integrate Salesforce.com and BizTalk Server?

BizTalk Server is a world-class integration server that excels at connecting disparate applications, translating document structures, bridging communication protocols, and executing long-running, transactional workflows. Over ten thousand organizations rely on BizTalk Server to distribute data and coordinate interactions between systems. SaaS solutions like Salesforce.com are simply another component of an organization's enterprise architecture and may be considered both a first-class recipient and source of an enterprise's data.

Like any enterprise software, Salesforce.com is going to be a silo of certain information. However, its data may be required for other business areas to operate successfully. For instance, when a physician calls a service center to ask a question about a product, they may possess a medical specialty that an entirely different department may be interested in. This customer's record could be pulled from Salesforce.com and shared with other systems at the organization. Similarly, a company may have on-premises data aggregation services that hold information useful to Salesforce.com applications.

When we expose an organization's integration server to Salesforce.com, it means that we can help prevent new data silos from forming while still taking advantage of innovative and scalable cloud software.

Communicating from BizTalk Server to Salesforce.com

How does BizTalk Server make requests of Salesforce.com or Force.com applications? We have a couple of viable choices: third-party adapters or invoking the native web service API.

There are a number of adapters built by vendors to accelerate integration with Salesforce.com. By using an adapter, developers do not need to learn underlying APIs and can avoid building extension functions to work around API shortcomings. One such adapter is the TwoConnect BizTalk Adapter for Salesforce.com which supports both push and pull interaction patterns. One of the valuable features of an adapter such as this is that it can poll Salesforce.com in a BizTalk Server receive location. There is no way to easily and reliably poll a web service endpoint with native BizTalk adapters.

As much as adapters can quicken development and introduce useful wrapper capabilities on underlying system APIs, the increasing prevalence of available web service interfaces on enterprise systems means that direct integration has become simpler than ever. Consuming web services is a standard part of the toolbox for most developers. For the remainder of this chapter, we will focus on using the native Salesforce.com APIs when integrating with BizTalk Server.

The most straightforward way for BizTalk Server to acquire Salesforce.com data is to use a query strategy. When BizTalk needs information from Salesforce.com, a query is executed using a standard set of available service operations. Later in this chapter, we will look at an effective way to push data from Salesforce.com to BizTalk, but in many cases polling or querying, is a more desirable pattern. When one system pushes data to another, the destination system has no control over the timing or volume of data coming across. If a major data change happens in the source system, then the downstream system(s) are forced to handle mountains of unexpected load. Conversely, when we use a polling or query strategy, we can control when we request information, and in the case of Salesforce.com, dictate how many messages are returned in a single request.

As you might expect, there is a rich set of operations that BizTalk can perform on Salesforce.com data. Information can be retrieved by record ID or timestamp and queried using either the Salesforce Object Query Language (SOQL), which looks like T-SQL queries, or the Salesforce Object Search Language, which does a textual search across fields in an entity. The Salesforce.com service API also exposes a wide range of "write" operations that allow us to create records, update records, upsert records (create, or if it exists, update it), delete records, or even do bulk modifications.

In some cases, the out-of-the-box API won't exactly meet your needs. For instance, the standard API does not support multi-object transactions. There are also API limits which could be reached for particularly chatty interactions. Fortunately for us, we can define custom services that may do things such as bundle up related operations or return a particular subset of an entire entity. As with the standard Salesforce.com services, the custom services have an easily consumable WSDL definition.

The Enterprise WSDL in Salesforce.com defines all of the standard, extended, and custom objects in your particular Salesforce.com account. The WSDL is always an up-to-date look at the state of your objects, meaning that if you add a new field to the Customer object, that field is instantly available in the WSDL. If you define a custom service, then a unique WSDL is available for that particular service.

One of the most important service operations in the Salesforce.com universe is called `login`. Each call to a Salesforce.com business operation requires a session token in the HTTP header. To acquire the token, a caller sends their Salesforce.com user credentials as well as an account-specific security token to the `login` function. If the credentials are valid, then this function returns a session token and service URL. A session token has a configurable lifetime applied to it, but the timeout counter gets reset each time a service operation is called. As a best practice, you should create a Salesforce.com user account dedicated to integration interactions and use that account when acquiring session tokens for Salesforce.com service calls.

In this first demonstration of this chapter, BizTalk Server will take in a message and then append some additional data elements retrieved from Salesforce.com. In this scenario, a customer of ours is requesting a reimbursement for previously purchased goods and we want to look up that customer's contact details that happen to be stored in Salesforce.com.

Configuring the foundational BizTalk components

Our solution needs some core schemas in addition to a central orchestration containing the business process that requires access to Salesforce.com data:

1. Open the `Chapter10-SFDC.sln` solution and find four pre-built projects. The first is a WCF message inspector behavior that will get used in a later exercise. The second project is a component that holds a reference to the Salesforce.com session token. The next project is a simple test application that verifies our Salesforce.com credentials. The final is a fully functional BizTalk project that will be used in the last exercise.

2. Create a new BizTalk Server project named `Chapter10-SFDC.AccountProcessing.ReimbApproval`. Set the project's strong name key and set the Deployment Application value to **Chapter10**.

3. Add a new schema named `ReimbursementRequest_XML.xsd` and set the target namespace to **http://Chapter10-SFDC**.

4. Construct the schema as shown in the following screenshot. This schema contains details about the reimbursement request and the customer's contact information.

5. Add an orchestration named `ApprovalProcess.odx` to the project. This orchestration drives the long-running approval process for a reimbursement.

6. Define two orchestration messages that represent the initial request and Salesforce.com-enriched review message. The first message is named **ReimburseInput** and the second is **ReimburseOutput** and both are of type **Chapter10-SFDC.ReimbApproval.ReimbursementRequest_XML**.

7. Sketch out an orchestration process flow that first takes in a message, then has a **Group** placeholder for the pending interaction with Salesforce.com, sends the enriched response message for approval, and finally, distributes the result.

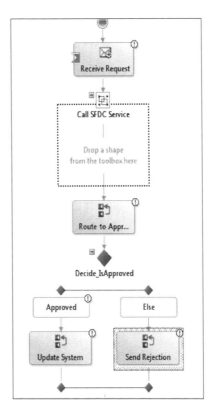

Customizing Salesforce.com data entities

Objects in Salesforce.com can be customized and we need some new fields on the Account entity.

1. Log in to your Salesforce.com account (`https://login.salesforce.com`), or create a new, free account. Note that Salesforce.com undergoes quarterly releases, so there will inevitably be subtle user interface or functionality differences from what is shown throughout this chapter.

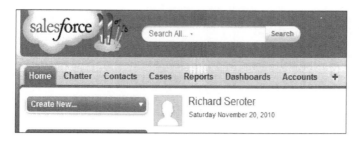

2. Much of our time will be spent configuring Salesforce.com and this requires us to access the robust Setup screens. You can access this section of the site by locating the drop-down menu below your name on the top right of the screen.

3. Under the **App Setup** section, one of the options we have is to extend the standard objects that Salesforce.com provides out of the box. In our case, we want to add a few additional fields to the Account entity. Expand the **Customize** menu and then **Accounts** to find the **Fields** option.

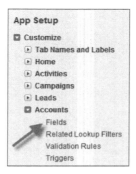

4. On the next screen, we see both the standard and customized fields for the selected entity. Our reimbursement lookup process requires a "primary contact" field and a "primary contact phone number" field on the Account entity. At the bottom of the page, there is an **Account Custom Fields and Relationships** section. Click the **New** button to start the field creation wizard.

5. Set the data type of this new field to be a **Text** value. We could have also considered doing a lookup value here and specified a specific contact record to act as the primary contact person for the account.

6. Set this new field's name to **PrimaryContactName** and define its length as 100 characters.

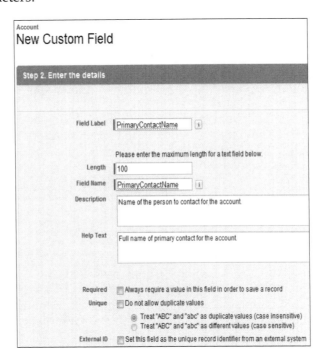

7. Keep the default security and page layout options on the subsequent two wizard pages and click **Save & New** on the final page. This creates the new field and starts the wizard over again.

8. For the data type of this new field, pick **Phone** and name the field **PrimaryContactPhone**.

9. Leave the remaining options set to the default choices and save the new field definition.

10. If everything was successful, you should see the custom fields (and their underlying API name) on the entity definition. Notice that all custom fields on a Salesforce.com have a "__c" suffix, which makes them easy to identify.

11. Recall that Salesforce.com provides an Enterprise WSDL definition that describes the operations and entities that we can interact with from our on-premises software system. Note that both custom objects as well as modified standard objects are available in the WSDL. The WSDL is dynamically generated so that it always reflects the current state of my Salesforce.com object model.

12. Navigate to the **App Setup** section, then **Develop**, and then **API** to find a link to the Enterprise WSDL.

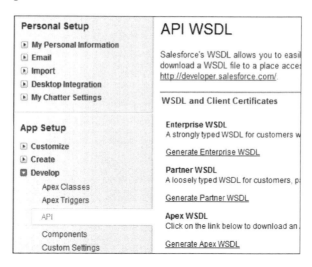

13. Click the **Generate Enterprise WSDL** link and save the resulting WSDL file with the name **SFDC_EnterpriseWSDL.wsdl** to your machine.

14. Open the WSDL file in Visual Studio 2010, find the Account object and notice that our two custom fields exist in that object's definition.

```
<element name="PartnersFrom" nillable="true" m
<element name="PartnersTo" nillable="true" min
<element name="Phone" nillable="true" minOccur
<element name="PrimaryContactName__c" nillable
<element name="PrimaryContactPhone__c" nillabl
<element name="ProcessInstances" nillable="tru
<element name="ProcessSteps" nillable="true" n
```

Consuming the Salesforce.com WSDL in BizTalk Server

The Salesforce.com Enterprise WSDL holds all the message and function definitions we need to pull in Account data. In this step, we import these definitions into BizTalk Server:

1. The WSDL file downloaded at the time of this writing was 455KB in size and contains all Salesforce.com object and operation definitions. If you only needed a single object or operation, you could choose to manually extract from the WSDL just the schemas you need and construct the BizTalk messaging endpoint by hand. For this scenario, we will reference the entire WSDL and have BizTalk generate the schemas, orchestration port, and binding file for us. If it was likely that you would reuse these Salesforce. com artifacts across multiple projects, then it makes sense to create a distinct BizTalk project to contain them. That said, we will go ahead and add a reference to the Salesforce.com WSDL in our primary BizTalk Server project.

2. Right-click our BizTalk project and choose to **Add Generated Items** and then select **Consume WCF Service**.

3. Once the wizard pops up, choose the source of service metadata to be **Metadata files** since we have a physical WSDL file to consume.

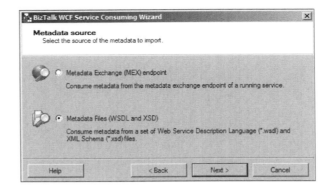

4. When prompted to add the metadata files, browse to the WSDL named `SFDC_EnterpriseWSDL.wsdl` on your machine.

5. Keep the suggested namespace and complete the wizard.

6. A series of files get created by this wizard:

   ° The `SforceService.BindingInfo.xml` file contains the details necessary to create a **WCF-BasicHttp** send port that consumes the Salesforce.com service.

   ° The `SforceService.odx` file is an orchestration that has a single **Port Type** definition named **Soap**, which holds all the operations that you can perform on the Salesforce.com WSDL. This orchestration also has multi-part message definitions for each input and output that correspond to a port type operation.

   ° The `SforceService_Custom.BindingInfo.xml` file is a **WCF-Custom** adapter binding that provides us additional opportunities to customize the call to the Salesforce.com web services.

   ° The `SforceService_enterprise_soap_sforce_com.xsd` schema describes each of the root message types (e.g. `login`, `sendEmail`, `update`, `queryAll`) used by the Salesforce.com operations. The underlying message types are in a different schema.

   ° The `SforceService_fault_enterprise_soap_sforce_com.xsd` schema defines all of the possible fault types returned by the Salesforce.com service.

   ° The `SforceService_sobject_enterprise_soap_sforce_com.xsd` schema holds all of the business entities (for example, **Account**, **Campaign**, **Case History**) available in your Salesforce.com domain.

7. Back in our original orchestration, `ApprovalProcess.odx`, create a new configured port named **CallSFDCPort** that uses the existing, generated port named **Chapter10-SFDC.AccountProcessing.ReimbApproval.Soap**. Set it to send a request and receive a response and specify the port binding later.

8. When the orchestration port configuration wizard is complete, we see every operation in that service exposed on the orchestration's port surface. We have two choices here. First, go back to wizard-generated orchestration and delete these unused operations from the port type. This is not overly practical if we were using this Salesforce.com reference in a shared assembly that other BizTalk projects plan on using. Our second, and best, option is to simply ignore the operations that we don't need and deal with the additional clutter on our orchestration surface.

9. Create the input and output messages expected by the Salesforce.com service. The first message, named **SFDC_QueryRequest,** is of multi-part type **Chapter10-SFDC.AccountProcessing.ReimbApproval.queryRequest** and the second message, named **SFDC_QueryResponse**, is of multi-part type **Chapter10-SFDC.AccountProcessing.ReimbApproval.queryReponse**.

10. Add a **Transform** shape to the existing **Group** placeholder and set the **Construct Message** shape's **Message Constructed** value to the **SFDC_QueryRequest** message. This map creates our service query message.

11. Double-click the **Transform** shape and create a new map named **ReimbRequest_To_SFDCQuery** and choose the **ReimburseInput** message as the map's **Source Transform** and the **SFDC_QueryRequest.parameters** message as the map's **Destination Transform**.

12. The destination schema's only field (`queryString`) holds the Salesforce Object Query Language (SOQL) statement necessary to retrieve the Account attributes we need. Drag a **Scripting** functoid to the map's grid surface. Drag the `AccountId` field from the source schema into the functoid.

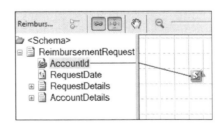

13. Double-click the functoid and switch to the **Script Functoid Configuration** tab and set the **Select script type** value to **Inline C#**.

14. Add the following code, which takes in the account ID value from the source schema and builds up a query statement, to the **Inline Script** window of the functoid:

```
public string BuildSFDCQuery(string accountId)
{
string query;

query = "SELECT Name, BillingStreet, BillingState, BillingCity,
BillingPostalCode, BillingCountry, PrimaryContactName__c,
PrimaryContactPhone__c FROM Account WHERE AccountNumber ='" +
accountId + "'";

return query;
}
```

15. Save the functoid's configuration and connect the functoid to the destination schema's `queryString` element.

16. After the **Construct** shape, add a **Send** shape (named **Send Request**) and a **Receive** (named **Receive Response**) shape. Associate the **SendRequest** shape with the **SFDC_QueryRequest** message and associate the **Receive Response** shape to the **SFDC_QueryResponse** message. Connect these shapes to the **query** operation in the orchestration port.

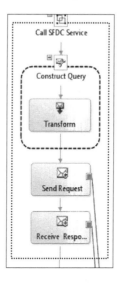

17. Below the **Receive Response** shape, drag a **Transform** shape. Set the **Construct** shape's **Message Constructed** property to **ReimburseOutput**.

18. Double-click the **Transform** shape and create a new map with **two** input messages, **ReimburseInput** and **SFDC_QueryResponse**, and **ReimburseOutput** as the single output message. This multi-part map mashes together two input values and results in a single, fully-populated, output message.

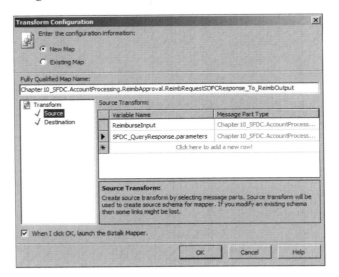

19. In the new map, expand the first message part in the source schema. Connect all of the fields, except those under `AccountDetails`, to the destination schema. Recall that our initial message doesn't have any contact details yet so there's no reason to map those fields.

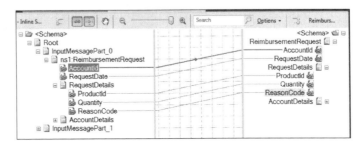

20. Next up, map the output of the Salesforce.com service query to the `AccountDetails` portion of the destination message. Because the Salesforce.com query response sends back an sObject type (which represents all known types), the type list beneath the `records` node includes all of the possible types that inherit from the sObject. Find the `Account` object and map the desired fields to the destination schema.

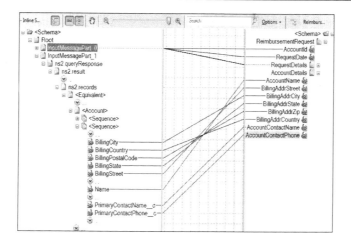

21. Save the map and return to the orchestration. Create an orchestration receive port, which absorbs the initial reimbursement request message.

22. For this example, in lieu of actually sending out the message for review and updating a backend application, we will set the **Expression** shapes to write to the system Event Log.

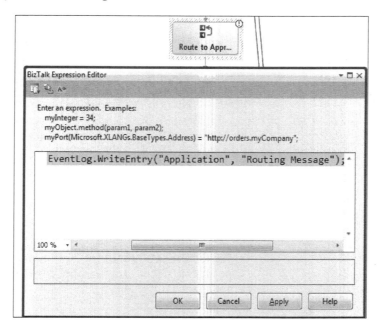

23. Add a new **Send** shape to the very bottom of the orchestration and send out the **ReimburseOutput** message out of the orchestration. This will confirm to us that we have successfully merged the Salesforce.com data with the original data.

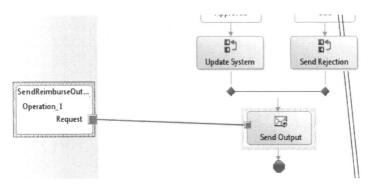

24. The development portion of the solution is nearly complete. However, recall that our call to Salesforce.com must be authenticated. Calls to Salesforce.com require an attached security token acquired by calling the `login` operation of the Salesforce.com service. Within the provided Visual Studio 2010 solution is a class library (`Chapter10-SFDC.TokenManager`) containing a singleton object that calls the Salesforce.com service upon initialization and retrieves a session token. Every hour, the singleton refreshes the token. Note that the default timeout of a Salesforce.com token is two hours. Each call to a Salesforce.com service resets the clock of this timeout. While you can acquire multiple tokens at once (in the case of a singleton being used by multiple different BizTalk hosts), note that Salesforce.com limits the number of simultaneous queries (based on the type of Salesforce.com account that you have), so you may need to introduce a throttling mechanism in your solution.

25. Edit the `TokenManager` class and include your Salesforce.com credentials (`sfdcUserName`, `sfdcPassword`, `sfdcSecurityToken`). The composite login password is a combination of account security token and account password. Build this component and then run the `Chapter10-SFDC.TokenTester.exe` application. This application connects to the Salesforce.com service and tries to perform a successful login. If the credentials are correct, we get back a `LoginResult` object that holds the unique Session ID and service URL. Copy and save the service URL that is returned as we will need this later in our BizTalk send port.

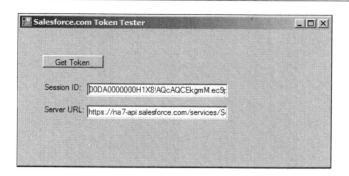

26. Add the `Chapter10-SFDC.TokenManager.dll` component to the Global Assembly Cache and then add a reference to this component in our BizTalk project.

27. The last remaining development task is to add our session token to the outbound message. This token does not go into the payload of the message, but rather, gets added to the outbound header. In our orchestration and within the **Construct** shape that builds the query, drop a **Message Assignment** shape immediately below the **Transform** shape. Add the following line of code. Do not forget to put a namespace on the `SessionHeader` node as the Salesforce.com API is strict about this and will return an invalid token message if the namespace is missing.

```
SFDC_QueryRequest(WCF.
Headers) = "<headers><SessionHeader xmlns='urn:enterprise.
soap.sforce.com'><sessionId>" + Chapter10_SFDC.TokenManager.
TokenManager.SessionId + "</sessionId></SessionHeader></headers>";
```

28. Build and deploy the BizTalk project.

29. Before you leave Visual Studio 2010, generate an XML instance of the `ReimbursementRequest_XML.xsd` and save it to your project folder.

Configuring BizTalk messaging ports to call Salesforce.com

Our development is complete and now we can add the BizTalk send and receive ports necessary to finish our solution:

1. Open the BizTalk Administration Console and confirm that you have a **Chapter10** application.

2. Create the initial receive port (**Chapter10.ReceiveReimbursementRequest**), receive location (**Chapter10.ReceiveReimbursementRequest.FILE**), and the concluding send port (**Chapter10.SendCompleteReimbursement.FILE**). All file adapters should have addresses that point to folders in the "FileDrop" section of the solution folder.

3. Remember that adding a reference to the Salesforce.com WSDL generated a pair of binding files. Right-click the BizTalk application in the BizTalk Administration Console and choose **Import** and then **Bindings**. Point to the `SforceService_Custom.BindingInfo.xml` in the BizTalk project folder. A new send port is produced by this operation.

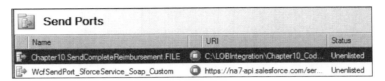

4. Open the custom send port named **WcfSendPort_SforceService_Soap_Custom**. Notice that the **Address(URI)** value points to the Salesforce.com login service. Change this address to the URL returned from the token tester application we used previously. In real life, we should pull the Salesforce.com URL from the Login operation and dynamically set the address on the outbound send port. For this example, the hard-coded value will do.

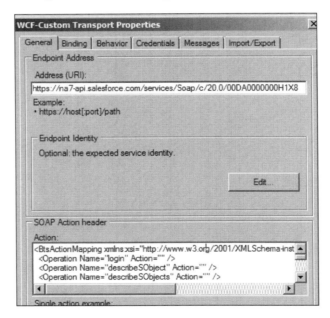

5. Finally, go the Orchestrations folder in the Console and double-click the **ApprovalProcess** orchestration. Switch to the **Bindings** tab and configure the host, initial receive port, service send port, and final send port. Start the send ports, receive location, orchestration, and host.

Testing the application

Our code is deployed and the required messaging configuration is complete. All that remains is to test that our application can successfully enrich inbound data with Salesforce.com data.

1. To test the application, go to your Salesforce.com site and either create a new account, or get the Account Number from an existing account. Put that value into the XML instance file that BizTalk will receive.

2. Send in the reimbursement request and monitor for the output message. If everything is configured correctly, you will see the data from your initial message combined with results from your Salesforce.com Account object.

```xml
<ns0:ReimbursementRequest xmlns:ns0="http://Chapter10-SFDC.Accou
    <AccountId>300</AccountId>
    <RequestDate>2011-06-01</RequestDate>
  <RequestDetails>
      <ProductId>ABC</ProductId>
      <Quantity>10</Quantity>
      <ReasonCode>Too big.</ReasonCode>
  </RequestDetails>
  <AccountDetails>
      <AccountName>Vandalay Industries</AccountName>
      <BillingAddrStreet>1445 Main Street Suite 1004</BillingAddrStreet>
      <BillingAddrCity>Los Angeles</BillingAddrCity>
      <BillingAddrZip>92130</BillingAddrZip>
      <BillingAddrZip>CA</BillingAddrZip>
      <BillingAddrCountry>USA</BillingAddrCountry>
  </AccountDetails>
</ns0:ReimbursementRequest>
```

In this exercise, we saw how to customize a Salesforce.com object and pull an Account record into a BizTalk Server orchestration. The Salesforce.com Enterprise WSDL makes it very easy to discover and consume the operations that we need.

Communicating from Salesforce.com to BizTalk Server

Integration shouldn't be a one-way-only pattern for a SaaS solution. While most mature SaaS offerings provide a set of query services, it is less common to have robust options for retrieving on-premises data from within a cloud application. As it turns out, Salesforce.com provides multiple strategies for integrating with external applications.

First and foremost, Salesforce.com has a feature called **Outbound Messaging**. Using Outbound Messaging, we can specify what changes to a given entity should result in events being sent to an external URL. This feature is directly related to Salesforce.com workflows. Sending an outbound message is one possible action for a workflow. Outbound Messaging provides queuing and reliable delivery and runs as a background process. Calls to external services aren't asynchronous and require the recipient service to return a Boolean acknowledgement. Messages may be sent more than once, so our services should be idempotent, meaning that multiple invocations with the same data will execute successfully with no side effects. If we are worried about a backlog in processing or accidentally processing older records prior to new ones, we can choose to send a session token in the outbound message and require the receiving service to do a callback to actually pull the changes to the record.

While Outbound Messaging is amazingly useful, there are some downsides. For one, you cannot do any customizations to the outbound HTTP request. This means that if you want to add HTTP headers, or transform the data into a different format, you are out of luck. Similarly, a specific WSDL is produced for each Outbound Message and the receiving service must comply with it. This could be a problem when integrating directly with legacy systems instead of through an integration server.

While we can call web services directly from Apex code by generating a proxy class through a WSDL import, there are still limitations in the customizations that you can perform. We will not be demonstrating that particular capability here, but, we will show how you can use native functions in Force.com to do low-level HTTP requests and response handling. When working with the raw Salesforce.com HTTP objects, we control the definition of the service messages, the invocation of the service, any encoding or decoding, cryptography, and security.

The next two exercises show us first how to leverage the Windows Azure AppFabric Service Bus to facilitate Outbound Messaging and second, how to perform a low-level Apex service invocation from Salesforce.com to BizTalk Server. **Why should we introduce Windows Azure AppFabric to this scenario?** In order for Salesforce.com to access a company's services, those services must be located on the public Internet. An organization may not be comfortable exposing their services publicly and the AppFabric Service Bus provides a secure, clean way to keep our services on the internal network and avoid adding Internet-facing proxies to the extranet.

Sending outbound messages from Salesforce.com to BizTalk Server

In this demonstration, we set up Salesforce.com to send an outbound message whenever the billing address changes on an Account record. Ideally, we would use the client authentication capabilities of the AppFabric Service Bus to secure our on-premises service. However, we cannot control low-level HTTP details of the Salesforce.com outbound message, and therefore cannot directly authenticate with the AppFabric Service Bus. Instead, we will apply a custom WCF behavior to the inbound BizTalk channel that looks for a unique token inserted during the outbound transmission from Salesforce.com.

Configuring a Salesforce.com workflow with Outbound Messaging

In this first part of the exercise, we extend the Account object and then craft a workflow containing an Outbound Messaging activity.

1. Log in to your Salesforce.com site (assuming you have previously signed up for a free Force.com account) and go to the **Setup** screen. Choose to **Customize** the **Accounts** object. Navigate to the **Fields** view.

2. Create a new custom field that will be populated with a token before Salesforce.com sends a message. Choose the **Text** data type. Set the name to **AzureValidationToken**.

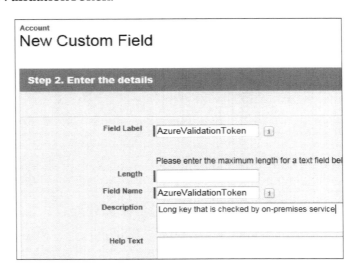

3. On step four of the wizard, when asked to add the field to a page, deselect all options because this field should not be visible on any user interface.

4. Under the **App Setup** menu, choose **Create** and then **Workflow & Approvals**. Click **Workflow Rules**.

5. Click the **New Rule** button to start the workflow wizard and then select the **Account** object as the entity that this workflow acts upon.

6. Next, name the rule **BillingStreetChanged** and set the **Evaluation Criteria** to run **Every time a record is created or edited**.

7. Set the rule to run if the formula evaluates to true and set `ISCHANGED(BillingStreet)` as the formula. This formula returns true if the field has a different value than it did before. Save this configuration and proceed.

8. Specify two workflow actions. The first action adds a unique token to the Account object and the second workflow action actually sends the outbound message to BizTalk Server through the Azure AppFabric Service Bus.

9. Set the first workflow action to **New Field Update**.

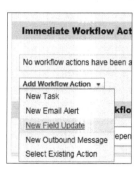

10. Set the action name to **SetAzureToken**, choose the **AzureValidationToken** field from the **Field to Update** list, and specify a GUID as the new value.

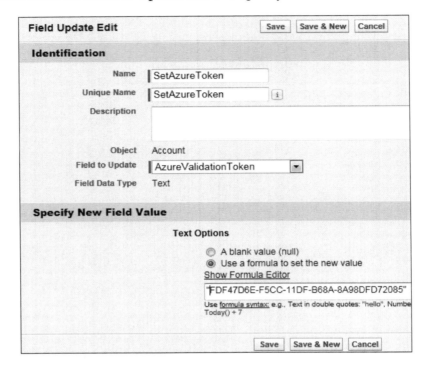

11. Choose to add another workflow action to our **BillingStreetChanged** rule. Select the **New Outbound Message** action to leverage the Outbound Messaging functionality in Salesforce.com.

12. Set the Outbound Message name to **CallBillingUpdateService** and type in a temporary **Endpoint URL** such as `http://localhost`. We do not yet have the cloud-based address for the on-premises service, so a placeholder address will do for now.

If we wanted to support a callback pattern, we could choose to send **SessionID** in the message payload. Choose to send the following fields: **AccountNumber**, **BillingStreet**, **BillingCity**, **BillingState**, **BillingPostalCode**, **BillingCountry**, **AzureValidationToken__c**, **Name**, and **LastModifiedDate**. The **LastModifiedDate** field is useful if you suspect that you could have backlog in your on-premises processing and need a way to find the most recent update.

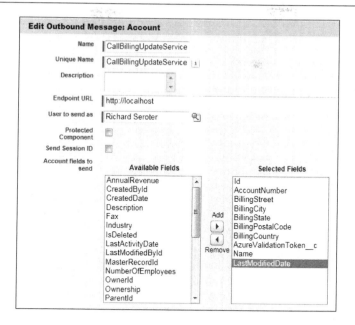

1. Save the outbound message configuration.

2. On the **App Setup** menu, under the **Create** menu and **Workflows & Approvals** menu, select the **Outbound Messages** link.

3. Click the Name of our Outbound Message to view its details. Save the Endpoint WSDL with the name `workflowOutboundMessage.wsdl` to your development machine.

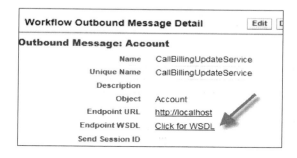

Building the BizTalk recipient of the Outbound Message

With our Outbound Message set up, we need to configure BizTalk to understand the messages, expose the receiving service, and send the expected acknowledgement:

1. In the existing Visual Studio 2010 solution, create a new empty BizTalk project named `Chapter10-SFDC.AccountProcessing.ChangeRouting`.

2. Assign a strong name key to the project and set the Deployment application to **Chapter10**.

3. We could choose to manually build the schemas and matching orchestration ports to receive and process the Salesforce.com Outbound Message, or, we can leverage one of BizTalk's development wizards to do most of the work. Right-click the BizTalk project and choose to **Add Generated Items**.

4. Select the **Consume WCF Service** option and select the **Metadata files** source. While we typically use this wizard to consume a service that BizTalk will invoke, we can also use it to generate inbound service artifacts.

5. On the Metadata files page of the wizard, browse to the Salesforce.com WSDL that you saved to your machine earlier. Complete the wizard and import the references.

6. The output of the wizard includes schemas that contain all the message definitions as well as an orchestration containing a port type that describes the interaction.

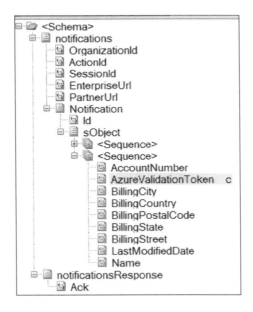

7. The Salesforce.com Outbound Messaging process requires an acknowledgement from the service. This means that we cannot just receive the message into BizTalk and route it. Rather, we need an orchestration that is capable of returning a synchronous, Boolean acknowledgement back to Salesforce.com. Add a new orchestration named `ProcessSFDCMessage.odx` to the project.

8. Create two orchestration messages. The first message, named **BillingChangeInput,** is of type **Chapter10-SFDC.AccountProcessing. ChangeRouting.notificationsRequest** while the second message, named **BillingChangeOutput,** is of type **Chapter10-SFDC.AccountProcessing. ChangeRouting.notificationsResponse**.

9. We typically use any generated orchestration ports as a way to call a service that we have referenced. However, we can also use this generated port to describe the **inbound** interaction. Drag a newly configured port to the **Port Surface** and choose the existing Port Type named **Chapter10-SFDC. AccountProcessing.ChangeRouting.NotificationPort**. Choose to receive a request and send a response and finish the port configuration wizard.

10. Arrange orchestration shapes in the following order: **Receive** shape, **Construct Message** shape that contains a **Message Assignment** shape, a **Send** shape, and another **Send** shape. This orchestration takes in the Salesforce.com outbound message, generates the acknowledgement message, returns it to Salesforce.com, and finally publishes the outbound message to the BizTalk bus for more processing.

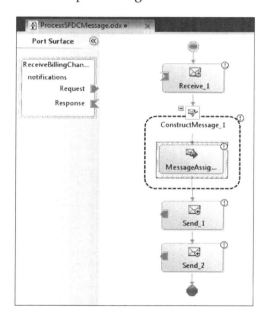

11. The top most **Receive** shape should use the **BillingChangeInput** orchestration message. The **Construct** shape should set the **Message Constructed** valueto **BillingChangeOutput**. The next **Send** shape should be associated to the **BillingChangeOutput** message, and the final send shape should be tied to the **BillingChangeInput** message.

12. Create a new orchestration variable named **tempXml** that is of type **System.Xml.XmlDocument**.

13. In the **Message Assignment** shape, instantiate the **XmlDocument** variable, load XML content indicating a "true" acknowledgement, and set the variable equal to the response message.

```
tempXml = new System.Xml.XmlDocument();
tempXml.LoadXml("<ns0:notificationsResponse xmlns:ns0='http://
soap.sforce.com/2005/09/outbound'><ns0:Ack>true</ns0:Ack></
ns0:notificationsResponse>");

BillingChangeOutput.@response = tempXml;
```

14. Finally, create a configured orchestration port to send our received billing change event out for further processing. Choose the option to specify the transport channel later on. The final orchestration should look like this:

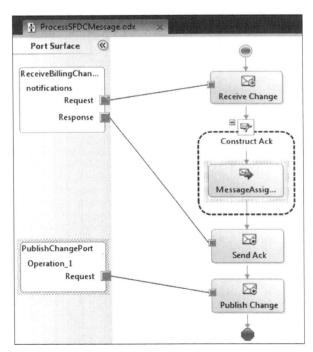

15. Build and deploy the application and switch over to the BizTalk Administration Console.

16. We have a few service hosting options to choose from. For this scenario, we will host the cloud endpoint directly within the BizTalk process vs. within the IIS web server. This does not require us to build a physical service. Begin this step by creating a new Request-Response receive port named **Chapter10. ReceiveBillingChangeNotification**.

17. Add a new Request-Response receive location named **Chapter10. ReceiveBillingChangeNotification.HttpRelay** to the port. Set the **Type** to be **WCF-Custom** and the receive pipeline to **XMLReceive**.

18. Click the **Configure** button next to the adapter type. On the **General** tab, set the **Address (URI)** to `https://<your namespace>.servicebus.windows. net/AccountProcessing/BillingChange.svc`.

19. On the **Binding** tab, set the **Binding Type** to Azure-provided **basicHttpRelayBinding**. Expand the **Security** binding configuration and ensure that the security mode is set to **Transport** and that the **relayClientAuthenticationType** is **None**. Recall that Salesforce.com Outbound Messaging transport details cannot be tweaked by a developer, so we cannot formally send additional credentials or directly authenticate to the Service Bus.

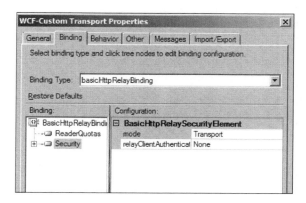

20. Navigate to the **Behavior** tab and add a new Endpoint behavior. Select the **transportClientEndpointBehavior** from the list. This behavior provides the credentials that BizTalk needs to connect to, and listen on, the Service Bus endpoint address. Pick the **SharedSecret** credential type and populate the **issuerName** and **issuerSecret** values of your AppFabric Service Bus account.

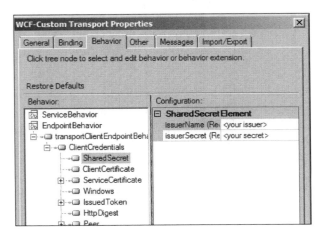

21. Save the receive location configuration.

22. Create a new one-way send port (named **Chapter10.SendBillingChange. FILE**) that our orchestration will bind to and send the billing change message to. The port should send its output to the file system.

23. Bind the **ProcessSFDCMessage** orchestration to the host, the relay receive location and finally FILE send port.

24. Start the dependent send port, orchestration, and lastly the receive location. If the receive location is configured correctly, you should now be listening on the cloud.

Triggering the outbound message from Salesforce.com

With our configuration complete, we can initiate an outbound message and confirm that BizTalk is capable of receiving it:

1. Go back to your Salesforce.com site and edit the outbound message configuration so that the Endpoint URL now points to `https://<yournamespace>.servicebus.windows.net/ AccountProcessing/BillingChange.svc`. Make sure that our workflow rule is activated.

2. Find an account in your Salesforce.com site and change the **BillingStreet** value so that our workflow is triggered and a message is sent out.

3. Switch to the **Outbound Messages** view and click the **View Message Delivery Status** button to see the status of the transmission. Confirm that you have received a message into BizTalk and see a message on the file system.

4. The final exercise is to apply a level of security to our endpoint. Right now, anyone who knows our Service Bus URL would be able to send a message into this service. To rectify this, we can utilize a custom WCF behavior to locate and verify that long security token that was added to our outbound message.

5. In the Visual Studio 2010 solution, find an existing project named `Chapter10.XmlMessageInspector`. This WCF behavior looks for a specified node and value and unless it finds it, the user gets an HTTP unauthorized error and nothing gets published to the BizTalk MessageBox. Build this project and add it to the machine's Global Assembly Cache.

6. In order for BizTalk Server to recognize this WCF behavior, we must add an entry to the `machine.config` file under the `System.ServiceModel/extensions.behaviorExtensions` node:

```
<add name="XmlInspectorBehavior" type="Chapter10_SDFC.
XmlMessageInspector.XpathInspectorBehaviorExtension,
Chapter10-SFDC.XmlMessageInspector, Version=1.0.0.0,
Culture=neutral, PublicKeyToken=<strong name key value>"/>
```

7. Open the BizTalk Administration Console and find the receive location that connects to the cloud. Double-click the receive location and click the **Configure** button next to the adapter type.

8. Switch to the **Behavior** tab and choose to add a new endpoint behavior. Find the **XmlInspectorBehavior** and select it. Set the **namespaceValue** property to **urn:sobject.enterprise.soap.sforce.com**. The behavior maps an XPath prefix called "custom" to whatever namespace is designated in the **namespaceValue** field. Therefore, the XPath statement that finds the validation token can be expressed as **//custom:AzureValidationToken__c**. Finally, set the actual value that this node must contain. In our case, it's the GUID value we set up in the Workflow rule.

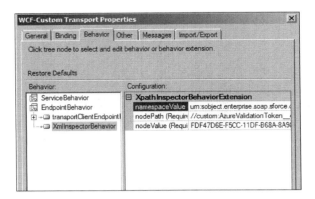

9. Save the configuration and once again trigger an outbound message from Salesforce.com. Everything should proceed as expected and a message should be emitted by the BizTalk send port. How can we confirm that our WCF behavior works as expected? Go back to Salesforce.com and navigate to **Field Updates** under the **Workflow & Approvals** menu. Change the formula value by appending a character to the end of the existing GUID. By doing this, we have created a mismatch between what Salesforce.com sends and what BizTalk Server expects.

10. Save the update and trigger the Outbound Messaging again by changing an account's billing street address. Observe in the **Outbound Messaging Delivery Status** that delivery failed with an **HTTP 401 (Unauthorized)** message.

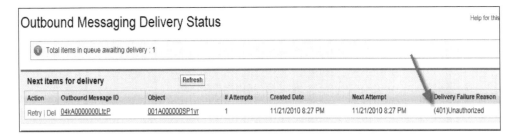

While not a fool-proof security mechanism, this last step showed us that if we sent the wrong value, or omitted the node entirely, that the service call would fail and BizTalk would never process the message. Overall, Outbound Messaging is a powerful feature that makes Salesforce.com very event-driven and reduces the need to do inefficient polling operations.

Querying BizTalk Server from Salesforce.com

Outbound Messaging is great, but there can certainly be cases where we want to send more than just after-the-fact, asynchronous requests to on-premises systems. What if we have sensitive or complex data and queries embedded in local systems but need access to them in the cloud? We could choose to replicate that data and logic, but there could be a both logistical and legal reason why that is suboptimal.

Instead, we can expose our on-premises systems to Salesforce.com through the Azure AppFabric Service Bus. To do this, we need to do low-level Apex programming that exposes access to the raw HTTP request and response payloads. In our previous exercise, we injected a long token into outbound messages and verified that token in BizTalk Server. We did this because we couldn't directly authenticate to the Service Bus. However, this isn't a problem when we do Apex programming. However, a new challenge arises: REST-based services that listen on the Service Bus expect the Access Control token in the HTTP header. This makes it easy to build and attach the token to Service Bus calls. Unfortunately, SOAP-based services that listen on the Service Bus expect a complex token in the SOAP headers and it is much more difficult to create the proper token. For this chapter's solution, we will build a REST service proxy in front of a BizTalk-generated SOAP service. This way, we can officially authenticate to the Service Bus before sending a request/reply message to BizTalk Server.

The last part of this exercise requires us to build a Visualforce page that calls the Service Bus. Our completed solution reflects an end-to-end scenario where the Salesforce.com user needs on-premises data and BizTalk Server fulfils that request.

Building the cloud-enabled REST service proxy

For this scenario, we already have a running BizTalk process that calculates discounts that we give our customers. This is proprietary knowledge that we do not want to replicate in the cloud. In this first step, we expose this BizTalk orchestration as a web service and put a cloud-ready REST web service in front of it:

1. Deploy the existing BizTalk project named `Chapter10-SFDC.AccountProcessing.ContractCalc`.

2. Initiate the BizTalk WCF Service Deployment Wizard and create a new web service (and receive location) from the LookupDiscountRate orchestration. Complete the wizard and ensure that the service was successfully deployed to the web server. Bind the new receive location the LookupDiscountRate orchestration and start both the orchestration and corresponding receive location.

3. To create the cloud-enabled REST proxy service, return to Visual Studio 2010 and add a new website to the solution. Choose the **WCF Service** type and name the site **Chapter10-SFDC.AccountProcessing.RestDiscountService**.

4. Add a service reference named **CalcServiceReference** to the WCF service that we previously generated from the BizTalk project.

5. Open the `IService.cs` file that defines the interface for the web service. Create an object type named **Discount** that represents the relevant pieces of the payload that is returned by the BizTalk service.

```
[DataContract (Namespace="http://Chapter-SFDC.AccountProcessing")
]
public class Discount
{
    [DataMember]
    public string AccountId { get; set; }
    [DataMember]
    public string DateDelivered { get; set; }
    [DataMember]
    public float DiscountPercentage { get; set; }
    [DataMember]
    public bool IsBestRate { get; set; }
}
```

6. Build the service contract for the **IDiscountService** interface that takes in an account ID and returns a **Discount** object. Note that we are decorating this operation with a REST attribute called **WebGet** that allows us to pass input values to the service through the URI.

```
[ServiceContract]
public interface IDiscountService
{
    [WebGet (UriTemplate="/{accountId}/Discount")]
    [OperationContract]
    Discount GetDiscountDetails(string accountId);
}
```

7. Open the `Service.cs` file and create a service class and inherit from the **IDiscountService** interface. Add a service reference named CalcServiceReference to the BizTalk-generated web service and insert the code needed to invoke the service.

```
public class DiscountService : IDiscountService
{
  public Discount GetDiscountDetails(string accountId)
  {
    Discount customerDiscount = new Discount();
    CalcServiceReference.Chapter10_SFDC_AccountProcessing_
ContractCalc_LookupDiscountRate_ReceiveDiscountRequestPortClient
client = new CalcServiceReference.Chapter10_SFDC_
AccountProcessing_ContractCalc_LookupDiscountRate_
ReceiveDiscountRequestPortClient();

    CalcServiceReference.DiscountRequest req =
new CalcServiceReference.DiscountRequest();
    req.AccountId = accountId;

    CalcServiceReference.Discount discount =
client.GenerateDiscount(req);

    customerDiscount.AccountId = accountId;
    customerDiscount.DateDelivered = discount.DateDelivered;
    customerDiscount.DiscountPercentage =
discount.DiscountDetails.DiscountPercentage;
    customerDiscount.IsBestRate =
discount.DiscountDetails.IsBestRate;

    client.Close();

    return customerDiscount;
  }
}
```

8. Open the `Service.svc` file and make sure to update the referenced service class and add a Factory attribute for our REST service.

```
<%@ ServiceHost Language="C#" Debug="true"
Service="DiscountService" CodeBehind="~/App_Code/Service.cs"
Factory="System.ServiceModel.Activation.WebServiceHost
Factory" %>
```

9. Next, update the `web.config` file to connect this REST service to the cloud. First, we create a binding element and specify that client-side security is required. Our previous (outbound messaging) service turned off client security and forced the service to authenticate the user. In this example, we are forcing Salesforce.com to provide a valid Service Bus authentication token before transmitting a request.

```
<bindings>
<webHttpRelayBinding>
<binding name="WebRestBinding">
```

```
<security relayClientAuthenticationType="RelayAccessToken" />
 </binding>
</webHttpRelayBinding>
</bindings>
```

10. Define a behavior that specifies the connection details for the on-premises service and the webHttp behavior that is used for RESTful services. These credentials are sent to the Service Bus when the service attempts to begin listening on the cloud address.

```
<endpointBehaviors>
        <behavior name="CloudBehavior">
          <transportClientEndpointBehavior>
            <clientCredentials>
              <sharedSecret issuerName="owner" issuerSecret=
              "<your secret" />
            </clientCredentials>
          </transportClientEndpointBehavior>
          <webHttp />
        </behavior>
      </endpointBehaviors>
```

11. Lastly, we tie it all together by defining our service and endpoint. Reference the binding and behavior that we created above.

```
<services>
<service name="DiscountService">
<endpoint
address="https://<your namespace>.servicebus.windows.net/
DiscountService"
behaviorConfiguration="CloudBehavi
or" binding="webHttpRelayBinding"
bindingConfiguration="WebRestBinding"
name="CloudRestEndpoint"
contract="IDiscountService" />
</service>
</services>
```

12. Deploy the service to the IIS web server and start the service. Ensure that you can connect successfully by browsing to your cloud service endpoint (in my case, it is `https://richardseroter.servicebus.windows.net/DiscountService/12345/Discount`) where you should get a message saying that the authorization header is missing. Our service requires client authentication and our browser isn't passing valid service bus credentials, so this message is expected.

Building a Visualforce page that consumes the cloud service

In this step, we construct a Visualforce page and Apex controller. The controller is responsible for acquiring the Access Control token and then passing that token into a Service Bus call. The Visualforce page contains the markup needed to display the Account details and Service Bus results:

1. Our on-premises and cloud-connected environment is ready for consumption. Go to Salesforce.com and get into the Setup screens.

2. In order for a call between Apex code and Azure to succeed, we have to explicitly allow outbound calls to the Service Bus endpoints. Specifically, we have to register the Azure Access Control and Service Bus URLs with our Salesforce.com account. Under **Administration Setup**, navigate to **Security Controls**, and click on **Remote Site Settings**.

3. Click the **New Remote Site** button and provide the name **AzureAC**, set the **Url** to `https://<your namespace>-sb.accesscontrol.windows.net`, and make sure that the **Active** flag is checked.

4. Add another remote site named **AzureSB** and set the **Url** to `https://<your namespace>.servicebus.windows.net` and set the site to **Active**.

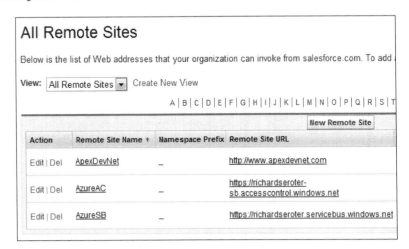

5. Our goal here is to add to the account object the discount details that we look up from BizTalk Server. Therefore, let us extend that object with the fields necessary to hold the desired values. While still on the Setup screens, navigate to **App Setup**, then **Customize,** and find **Accounts**. Click the **Fields** link. Add a new field called **DiscountPercentage** that uses the **Percent** data type, has a **Length** of sixteen and holds up to two decimal places. Next, add a field named **DiscountLastUpdated** that has a **Text** data type and a length of 50 characters. Finally, create a field named **DiscountBestPrice** that uses the **Checkbox** data type.

6. Confirm that our fields were successfully added by viewing any account in our Salesforce.com site and locating the new fields.

7. We are now ready to build a custom VisualForce page that shows account details and allows us to query our BizTalk Server service through the cloud. Salesforce.com uses a Model View Controller (MVC) pattern and our on-premises service is called from the controller. The first thing to build is the controller used by our custom page. Navigate to **App Setup**, then **Develop**, and choose **Apex Classes**. Click the **New** button to build a new Apex class. The next screen you see is the web-based Apex IDE.

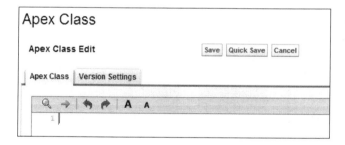

8. Within the Visual force environment, we have a choice of controller types. The **standard controllers** are associated with out-of-the-box Salesforce.com objects like Accounts. They expose operations like Save that save changes to the underlying object. A **custom controller** is one that does not use standard controllers and specifies entirely new behaviors. Finally, the **controller extension** extends either a standard or custom controller. We want to use the controller extension so that we get the existing operations and data associated with the Account controller while adding new functions to call the cloud. Begin the controller class by defining a local reference variable that points to the active account and instantiate it in the default constructor.

```
public class accountDiscountExtension{

private final Account myAcct;

public accountDiscountExtension(ApexPages.StandardController
controller) {
        this.myAcct = (Account)controller.getRecord();
    }


}
```

9. Define the operation that will call the Azure AppFabric service. Add an `Http` object variable that performs HTTP communication. Then, add HTTP request objects for both the Access Control (AC) service and the Service Bus service.

```
public void GetDiscountDetails()
    {
        Http httpProxy = new Http();
        HttpRequest acReq = new HttpRequest();
        HttpRequest sbReq = new HttpRequest();
    }
```

10. Create variables that hold the AC URL as well as the encoded password.

```
// ** Getting Security Token from STS
String acUrl =
'https://<your namespace>-sb.accesscontrol.windows.net/WRAPV0.9/';
 String encodedPW = EncodingUtil.urlEncode(<issuer password>',
'UTF-8');
```

11. Set up the HTTP request to do a POST to the AC service. Notice that we manually build up the payload with the issuer name, password, and the scope of the request. Remember from Chapter 6 that we can associate issuers with scopes at more granular levels; in reality, you would define an issuer for Salesforce.com and assign it only to the scopes it has access to. In this case, we will leverage the account owner credentials.

```
acReq.setEndpoint(acUrl);
acReq.setMethod('POST');
acReq.setBody('wrap_name=owner&wrap_password=' + encodedPW +
'&wrap_scope=http://<your namespace>.servicebus.windows.net/');
acReq.setHeader('Content-Type', 'application/x-www-form-
urlencoded');
```

12. We are now ready to call the AC service. The result of the service call is put into a string variable for post-processing.

```
HttpResponse acRes = httpProxy.send(acReq);
String acResult = acRes.getBody();
```

13. The token that we received from the AC service does not exactly match the format needed by the Service Bus. The raw response from the AC service looks like this:

```
wrap_access_token=net.windows.servicebus.action%3dListen%252cSe
nd%252cManage%26Issuer%3dhttps%253a%252f%252frichardseroter-sb.
accesscontrol.windows.net%252f%26Audience%3dhttp%253a%252f%252fr
ichardseroter.servicebus.windows.net%26ExpiresOn%3d1290807349%26
HMACSHA256%3dEcvteRJ9T1hDo9gWT5MWwfhOLOOReoeCKP9esorp7JA%253d&wr
ap_access_token_expires_in=1200
```

14. The SB doesn't want all of that, so we need to parse out a few bits. First, remove the portion after the ampersand (`wrap_access_token_expires_in`), and then pull out the beginning portion (`wrap_access_token=`) and finally do a URL decoding. Our token needs the `WRAP access_token=` prefix so that the Service Bus knows what kind of authentication has been provided.

```
// clean up result
        String suffixRemoved = acResult.split('&')[0];
        String prefixRemoved = suffixRemoved.split('=')[1];
        String decodedToken = EncodingUtil.urlDecode(prefixRemoved,
'UTF-8');
        String finalToken = 'WRAP access_token=\"' + decodedToken +
'\"';
```

15. With a Service Bus-consumable token in hand, we can call the Service Bus endpoint and invoke our on-premises BizTalk service (through the REST proxy). Because we have a REST service, there is no "body" to pass in the HTTP request as all of the details are in the URL. We build up the REST URL with the account number of the customer and add an authorization header to the HTTP request.

```
String sbUrl = 'https://<your namespace>.servicebus.windows.net/
DiscountService/' + myAcct.Account_Number + '/Discount';
sbReq.setEndpoint(sbUrl);
sbReq.setMethod('GET');
sbReq.setHeader('Content-Type', 'text/xml');
sbReq.setHeader('Authorization', finalToken);
```

16. Invoke the Service Bus by sending the request and then load the response into an XML document.

```
// invoke service bus
HttpResponse sbRes = httpProxy.send(sbReq);
Dom.Document responseDoc = sbRes.getBodyDocument();
Dom.XMLNode root = responseDoc.getRootElement();
```

17. Finally, parse the response and pull out values to set on the account fields.

```
myAcct.DiscountPercentage__c = Decimal.valueOf
        (root.getChildElement('DiscountPercentage',
        'http://Chapter10-SFDC.AccountProcessing').getText());
myAcct.DiscountLastUpdated__c = root.getChildElement
        ('DateDelivered', 'http://Chapter10-SFDC.
        AccountProcessing').getText();
myAcct.DiscountBestPrice__c = Boolean.valueOf
        (root.getChildElement('IsBestRate',
        'http://Chapter10-SFDC.AccountProcessing').getText());
```

18. We can now build our custom Visualforce page. One easy way to get an empty page to work with is to go to the browser URL and put in a (non-existent) page address, and Salesforce.com will prompt you to create the page. After the server address (in my case, `https://na7.salesforce.com/`), put `apex/DiscountLookup`.

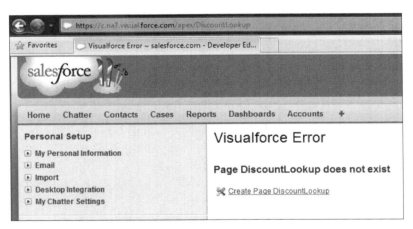

19. Click the **Create Page DiscountLookup** link and you get a new, blank Visualforce page. If you have "development mode" turned on (**Setup, Personal Setup, My Personal Information, Personal Information, Development Mode** checkbox), you will see a **Page Editor** button at the bottom that lets you view the source of the page and edit it live.

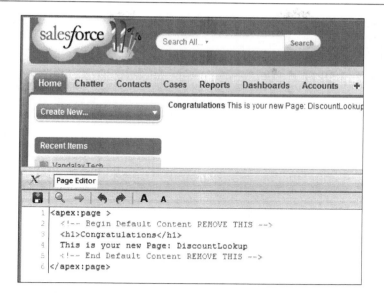

20. Recall that we built a controller extension earlier, so in the page declaration here, we want to call out both the `standardController` for the `Account` object, and the `extensions` as `accountDiscountExtension`. By choosing the Account controller, the Account tab is selected on the page and we can provide an account ID in the URL in a later step.

```
<apex:pagestandardController="Account" extensions="accountDiscount
Extension">
<!-- Begin Default Content REMOVE THIS -->
<h1>Congratulations</h1>
  This is your new Page: DiscountLookup
<!-- End Default Content REMOVE THIS -->
</apex:page>
```

21. We want to see account details on this page and a single Apex tag makes the entire object details grid visible. The `relatedList` attribute determines whether related details are pulled in or just the core account details. Add this tag right before the close of the page tag:

```
<apex:detailrelatedList="false" />
```

22. Nothing will show up on your page yet because we are not providing an account to show. The displayed account is read from a query string value. View a current account in Salesforce.com and observe the URL. In my case, the value is `https://na7.salesforce.com/001A000000SP1yr`. Pull the unique ID from the URL and go back to your page editing view and append `?id=[your account id]` to the URL and see an account visible on the page.

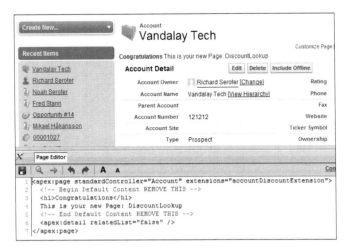

23. That is an impressive amount of page content for five lines of code! Next, replace that default placeholder text (starting with the `begin default content` comment and ending with the `end default content` comment) with an Apex page block that welcomes the user by name and shows the name of the selected account.

```
<apex:pageBlock title="Contract Discount Lookup">
    Hello {!$User.FirstName } <br />
    You are viewing the {!account.name} account.
</apex:pageBlock>
```

24. The final task is to add the form that shows the fields from the account and the buttons to invoke the web service, and then save the results back to the account. The `Save` button comes from the default Account controller, while the `Get Discount` button calls the operation in our controller extension. The `outputText` field with the `rendered=false` attribute exists because the standard controller queries the account object based on the fields referenced in the Visualforce page. Our controller extension needs the `AccountNumber` field to build the REST query string, so we have to put that (invisible) field on the form in order for this field to be accessible to the controller.

```
<br /><br />
<apex:form >
<apex:outputText value="{!account.AccountNumber}"
rendered="false"/>
<b>Customer Discount Percentage: </b>{!account.
DiscountPercentage__c}<br />
<b>Last Discount Calculation Date: </b> {!account.
DiscountLastUpdated__c} <br />
<b>Is Best Discount: </b> {!account.DiscountBestPrice__c}<br /><br
/>
<apex:CommandButton value="Get Discount" action="{!GetDiscountDeta
ils}"/><apex:CommandButton value="Save" action="{!save}"/>
</apex:form>
```

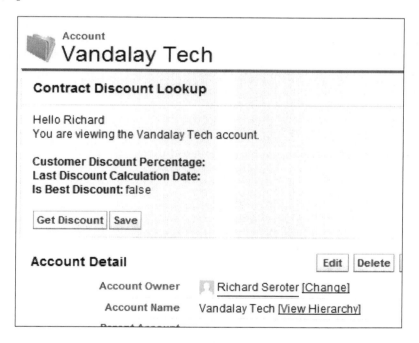

25. Ensure that the cloud endpoint is online, and if so, click the **Get Discount** button to have Salesforce.com call our on-premise service.

In this exercise, we saw that the Azure AppFabric Service Bus is for more than just WCF clients. We can securely and quickly leverage on-premises resources from a SaaS environment without unnecessarily duplicating data or changing network infrastructure.

Summary

In our first example, we saw how to consume the strongly-typed Salesforce.com WSDL within a BizTalk solution. In our second set of examples, we looked at strategies for sending requests from Salesforce.com to on-premises services. Both demonstrations leveraged Windows Azure AppFabric to relay messages from the cloud back to an internal service. The first example, which used Salesforce.com Outbound Messaging, used a message-embedded token to authenticate the caller. In the second example, we used Salesforce.com APEX code to acquire an AppFabric Access Control token and authenticate our client to the Service Bus. The request message was then relayed to a proxy service that then sent a message into BizTalk Server.

To be sure, we could have communicated between Salesforce.com and our on-premises systems through publicly exposed services or proxies. If your organization has a mature extranet strategy with reverse-proxy communication to internal services, then you do not need to leverage Microsoft cloud integration services. However, Windows Azure AppFabric gave us a powerful way to expose our internal services in a simple and secure way and without the need for additional hardware or software.

Salesforce.com is an exceptional SaaS environment and Force.com opens up new possibilities for solution development. As long as there are investments in on-premises software there will be a need for integration technologies. BizTalk Server is a strong compliment to a Salesforce.com solution because of its native web service adapters and robust messaging engine.

Index

Thank you for buying
Microsoft BizTalk 2010: Line of Business
Systems Integration

About Packt Publishing

Packt, pronounced 'packed', published its first book "Mastering phpMyAdmin for Effective MySQL Management" in April 2004 and subsequently continued to specialize in publishing highly focused books on specific technologies and solutions.

Our books and publications share the experiences of your fellow IT professionals in adapting and customizing today's systems, applications, and frameworks. Our solution based books give you the knowledge and power to customize the software and technologies you're using to get the job done. Packt books are more specific and less general than the IT books you have seen in the past. Our unique business model allows us to bring you more focused information, giving you more of what you need to know, and less of what you don't.

Packt is a modern, yet unique publishing company, which focuses on producing quality, cutting-edge books for communities of developers, administrators, and newbies alike. For more information, please visit our website: www.packtpub.com.

About Packt Enterprise

In 2010, Packt launched two new brands, Packt Enterprise and Packt Open Source, in order to continue its focus on specialization. This book is part of the Packt Enterprise brand, home to books published on enterprise software – software created by major vendors, including (but not limited to) IBM, Microsoft and Oracle, often for use in other corporations. Its titles will offer information relevant to a range of users of this software, including administrators, developers, architects, and end users.

Writing for Packt

We welcome all inquiries from people who are interested in authoring. Book proposals should be sent to author@packtpub.com. If your book idea is still at an early stage and you would like to discuss it first before writing a formal book proposal, contact us; one of our commissioning editors will get in touch with you.

We're not just looking for published authors; if you have strong technical skills but no writing experience, our experienced editors can help you develop a writing career, or simply get some additional reward for your expertise.

SOA Patterns with BizTalk Server 2009

ISBN: 978-1-847195-00-5   Paperback: 400 pages

Implement SOA strategies for Microsoft BizTalk Server solutions with this book and eBook

1. Discusses core principles of SOA and shows them applied to BizTalk solutions

2. The most thorough examination of BizTalk and WCF integration in any available book

3. Leading insight into the new WCF SQL Server Adapter, UDDI Services version 3, and ESB Guidance 2.0

Applied Architecture Patterns on the Microsoft Platform

ISBN: 978-1-849680-54-7   Paperback: 544 pages

An in-depth scenario-driven approach to architecting systems using Microsoft technologies with this book and eBook

1. Provides an architectural methodology for choosing Microsoft application platform technologies to meet the requirements of your solution

2. Considers solutions for messaging, workflow, data processing, and performance scenarios

3. Written by a distinguished team of specialists in the Microsoft space

Please check **www.PacktPub.com** for information on our titles

Printed in Great Britain
by Amazon